The Gettysburg Address

The Gettysburg Address

Perspectives on Lincoln's Greatest Speech

Edited by

SEAN CONANT

Foreword by

HAROLD HOLZER

OXFORD
UNIVERSITY PRESS

OXFORD
UNIVERSITY PRESS

Oxford University Press is a department of the University of Oxford.
It furthers the University's objective of excellence in research, scholarship,
and education by publishing worldwide.

Oxford   New York
Auckland   Cape Town   Dar es Salaam   Hong Kong   Karachi
Kuala Lumpur   Madrid   Melbourne   Mexico City   Nairobi
New Delhi   Shanghai   Taipei   Toronto

With offices in
Argentina   Austria   Brazil   Chile   Czech Republic   France   Greece
Guatemala   Hungary   Italy   Japan   Poland   Portugal   Singapore
South Korea   Switzerland   Thailand   Turkey   Ukraine   Vietnam

Oxford is a registered trade mark of Oxford University Press
in the UK and certain other countries.

Published in the United States of America by
Oxford University Press
198 Madison Avenue, New York, NY 10016

Library of Congress Cataloging-in-Publication Data
The Gettysburg Address : Perspectives on Lincoln's Greatest Speech / edited by
Sean Conant ; foreword by Harold Holzer.
p.   cm.
Includes bibliographical references and index.
ISBN 978-0-19-022745-6 (paperback) — ISBN 978-0-19-022744-9 (hardcover)
1. Lincoln, Abraham, 1809-1865. Gettysburg address. I. Conant, Sean.
E475.55.G36 2015
973.7'349—dc23
2014042814

1 3 5 7 9 8 6 4 2

Printed in the United States of America on acid-free paper

Contents

Acknowledgments

MY WORK ON this volume has enriched my understanding of the themes tackled in *The Gettysburg Address* film—a multi-year production examining the influences for and impacts of Lincoln's greatest speech. I hope this collection of essays has a similar effect on the reader. To that end, thank you to my contributors for their unique perspectives and outstanding efforts.

Thank you also to Gabor Boritt, Eric Foner, Harold Holzer, Martin P. Johnson, Jim McPherson, Jim Oakes, Mark Summers, and Doug Wilson for their efforts and encouragement along the way.

Thank you to the keepers of the five Gettysburg Address copies and to my friends and acquaintances from the institutions where they repose: Michelle Krowl of the Library of Congress, James Cornelius of the Abraham Lincoln Presidential Library and Museum, Katherine Reagan of the Carl A. Kroch Library at Cornell University, and William Allman of the White House Office of the Curator. Thanks to their support I had the privilege of intimately examining all copies of the Address for the film and this volume. The faithful transcriptions herein are but one result of those memorable experiences.

As a descendent of Oxford University Vice-Chancellor Rev. John Conant (1608–1694), it is especially meaningful to me to publish this volume with Oxford University Press, who I thank for the opportunity. At Oxford, thank you to Tim Bent and his assistants, Keely Latcham and Alyssa O'Connell, for shepherding the project through the publishing process.

Thank you to my friends and family. For years this work has consumed me, and still they remain present and supportive always.

Lastly, thank you to the soldiers, both here and gone, and to Abraham Lincoln—whose sacrifice and language, respectively, I honor and admire.

Sean Conant

Foreword

NOVEMBER 19 IS a sacred day at Gettysburg. The village welcomes what seems to be its entire population—along with hundreds of out-of-town visitors—for the annual commemoration of Abraham Lincoln's greatest speech. Each and every November 19, a solemn celebration takes place inside the town's eternally haunting Soldiers' cemetery. The great Lincoln reenactor James Getty dons frock coat and stovepipe hat to intone the Address impeccably. Prayers are invoked. A local baritone sings "The Battle Hymn of the Republic." The ceremony is as predictable and comforting as a religious service. Only the "sermon" changes. For generations, as historian Thomas Desjardin points out in his essay for this book, leading American orators have journeyed here on the anniversary of the Gettysburg Address to try providing the definitive appreciation of the most famous speech in American history by offering one of their own.

Inevitably most fall somewhat short in comparison. After all, how can anyone approach the sublime mastery of Lincoln's original? How can anyone express the full essence of the Gettysburg Address, when scholars have variously traced its origins and inspirations—as other contributors to this book will remind us—to everything from classical oratory (Nicholas Cole) to native democratic ideals (Sean Wilentz), to reigning political eloquence (Craig Symonds) to American philosophical originality (Dean Grodzins) and to the unavoidable pall of wartime death and suffering (Chandra Manning, Mark Schantz). So many roots to trace; so many inspirations to consider. It is no wonder that while scores of latter-day Gettysburg orators have tried, they have usually less than overwhelmed the vast audiences that reliably attend these yearly events in the eternal hope of hearing another immortal Gettysburg Address. Yet still they come, the crowds and the guest speakers alike. Of course, it took Abraham Lincoln three tries to get it right himself.

In his essay for this volume, historian Allen Guelzo notes that Lincoln offered "advance echoes" of his definitive Gettysburg observations only days after the battle. In an unscripted July 7, 1863, greeting from the White House to a crowd of serenaders, he introduced a halting reference to "eighty odd years" ago destined to be memorably massaged into "four score and seven years ago" a few months later.[1] Yet just days after delivering these impromptu remarks, Lincoln penned yet another preliminary comment on the Union victory at Gettysburg—this one soon completely erased from history.

Apparently, the president was now so delighted by the outcome that he sat down and composed the first poem he had attempted in more than a decade. Lincoln entitled his four-line ditty, "Gen. Lees invasion of the North written by himself." In a sense, however irreverent, it constituted yet another early draft of the Gettysburg Address:

In eighteen sixty three, with pomp, and mighty swell,
   Me and Jeff's Confederacy, went forth to sack Phil-del,
The Yankees they got arter us, and giv us particular hell,
   And we skedaddled back again, and didn't sack Phil-del.[2]

Peering behind the humorist's facade, the modern reader can still intuit the enormous sense of relief that must have inspired this piece of doggerel. Historians have long emphasized the anguished letter Lincoln drafted to Union commander George Gordon Meade just five days earlier, in which he described himself as "distressed immeasurably" by the general's failure to pursue Lee's army after it retreated from Gettysburg—predicting that as a result of this lost opportunity, "the war will be prolonged indefinitely."[3] Yet the doggerel reveals Lincoln in a radically different, almost buoyant, mood just five days later. Clearly believing in retrospect that a Lee triumph at Gettysburg might have threatened the entire Keystone State, and with it, the Union itself, Lincoln now seemed comforted enough by the victory to express a kind of triumphalist jubilation.

But he was also politically astute enough to file away his irreverent composition forever. It would not do to let the public know how close he believed Philadelphia had come to annihilation. And it would certainly not do, even for the nation's humorist-in-chief, to crack wise about the battle when so many "brave men" had died at Gettysburg that the nation might live. The poem remained hidden away in presidential secretary

John Hay's files, unknown and undiscovered, for more than a century.[4] Nor, interestingly enough, did Lincoln actually send his angry letter to the commander of the Army of the Potomac. After relieving himself of his pain merely by composing the message, the president filed it away, marking it: "To Gen. Meade, never signed, or sent."[5] Ridicule and recrimination: they had no place in the final Gettysburg Address.

Yet reconsidering the long-ignored rhyme, it is easy to understand why Lincoln's sense of relief became manifest by July 19. In retrospect, he came to recognize that however regrettable Lee's unchallenged retreat south, had the Confederate commander triumphed at Gettysburg, as Lincoln's poem suggested, rebel forces might have taken direct aim next at the nation's cradle of liberty: Philadelphia. And had Lee occupied or laid waste to the city where American independence had been consecrated in 1776, the North might have been forced to abandon the war effort altogether, with no choice but to sue for peace and allow the Confederacy to maintain a separate government unopposed.

Lincoln may have reached his rhetorical zenith in another part of the state, but there can be little doubt that his heart belonged to the city where the nation had struggled to invent itself four score and seven years earlier. So strongly did Lincoln feel about protecting Philadelphia that, on a Washington's Birthday visit to Independence Hall two years earlier, he had declared, his voice choking with emotion: "I would rather be assassinated on this spot than to surrender it."[6] As his audience that morning well understood, Lincoln was not only talking about offering his life to save a landmark building but also to preserve the ideas that had been ratified there to form the core belief system of American independence: what Lincoln in 1861 called "the spirit that animated our fathers" and later canonically redefined at Gettysburg as our "new birth of freedom."[7] No wonder Lincoln journeyed to Pennsylvania in November 1863: Gettysburg fulfilled what had been promised in Philadelphia.[8]

Today, of course, November 19 Gettysburg orators have but one chance to get it right, little chance to offer leaks, afterthoughts, jokes, or poetry, and no place to practice but before their own mirrors. Soon enough comes the fearful day of reckoning on that hallowed ground. To accommodate the ceremonies, the National Park Service years ago erected a permanent brick speakers' platform where, each fall, a glaring sun invariably and distractingly rises behind the dignitaries' backs for the annual morning ceremonies. The backlit scene casts the faces of all those gathered to speak in blurred shadow, like a tintype hastily exposed and imperfectly developed on a battlefield. Yet the audience, facing the stage, bathed in stark light, bears witness in what seems like high relief. Was the sun at his back when Lincoln rose to speak? More to the point, does this modern stage stand precisely where Lincoln once stood? No one seems to know for certain, but it is close enough to intimidate most modern speakers.

Not all of them. I was proudly on hand here when my then-boss, Governor Mario M. Cuomo of New York, gave the annual oration in 1989. After preparing carefully for weeks, writing draft after draft by hand, he made national news that day amidst speculation that he would soon run for president (he did not). What he did instead was argue that Lincoln's battle against slavery was but a prelude to the modern struggles by women, African Americans, poor people, and, yes, Italian Americans like Cuomo, to fulfill Lincoln's promise that all are indeed "created equal."[9]

I was also on hand among the two thousand attendees who could not help but squirm when one drizzly November 19 Chief Justice William Rehnquist was paralyzed into immobility, gripping the lectern in helpless silence for ten almost unendurable minutes, after his microphone short-circuited. Not knowing quite what to do when the sound system failed, Rehnquist simply stayed put, rain dripping from his eyeglasses, as technicians labored below him to reconnect his microphone. When he recovered, the chief justice simply continued where he had left off, declaring of Lincoln: "He was not just articulate; he was able to convey ideas in simple terms, and yet with force and sometimes passion"—unlike most of the speakers who have followed him here.[10]

I was also on hand for speeches by Republicans like Justice Sandra Day O'Connor and Democrats like Congressman Richard Durbin. I was there when Shelby Foote provided a good idea of how shocked the 1863 audience must have been by Lincoln's brevity by himself intoning fewer words than Lincoln did—and in less time, resuming his seat to groans of disappointment from his fans. I have witnessed speeches by politicians and scholars alike: Representative Jack Kemp, historian John Hope Franklin, politician Jesse Jackson, Jr., New York Governor George Pataki, author Doris Kearns Goodwin, producer and director Steven Spielberg, and my good friend, Rhode Island jurist Frank J. Williams. Another friend, actor Richard Dreyfuss, labored so intently on his 2009 remarks—up to and beyond the last minute—that he became the first speaker ever to miss the wreath-laying ceremony that by tradition precedes the ceremony. Undaunted (unlike his hosts), Dreyfuss offered a Mr. Holland-like call to turn back, in Lincoln's name, to the required teaching of ethics.

All these speakers did remarkably well under challenging circumstances. Of course, there remains only one Gettysburg Address, one Lincoln. And as hospitably as modern Pennsylvanians welcome twenty-first-century visitors to town every November 19, this is one tough audience to please, now as then.

One year I was invited to provide one of these orations. I have no idea why this honor came to me, unless it was because the organizers had run out of truly deserving speakers, or perhaps because I had visited Gettysburg so many times by then for research, conferences, annual Lincoln Forum symposia, book signings, parades, performances, and celebrations that the town fathers mistook me for a handily available part-time resident.

In both preparing my own words and in rising to speak on November 19, 2005, it is no exaggeration to admit that, like many before me, or so I suspect, I felt a sinking feeling, made up of equal doses of imagined presumption and reasonable dread of failure. Yet when I began to talk where Lincoln had talked, the emotional baggage somehow evaporated, replaced by an inexplicable calm that soon approached elation. Looking back, it was an almost absurd reaction to the knowledge that I was climaxing my own modest career as a Lincoln historian by orating where Abraham Lincoln had done nothing less than rededicate America to the struggle of the unfinished work of securing freedom.

What I said at Gettysburg, 142 years after Lincoln, was that "Nine score and 17 years ago—on the very same day, though an ocean apart—not one, but two babies were born, each of them destined to grow up and do nothing less than change the world. In one of the great coincidences of history, not only Abraham Lincoln, but also Charles Darwin, first saw life on the identical date: February 12, 1809." I pointed out that each would arouse love and scorn, wrote words that would "long endure," and would defy expectations, "one rejecting the pulpit to become a man of science; the other aspiring higher than the land to become a man of law and politics."

There, I argued, the similarities ended. Darwin articulated a theory about survival of the fittest—a process of natural selection that empowered the strong and eliminated the weak. Those who have turned his hard science into social science believe natural limitations preclude success. Abraham Lincoln, on the other hand, embraced, articulated, and personally symbolized the ideal of equal opportunity—encouraging today's slave to become tomorrow's freeman; today's laborer to become tomorrow's owner—through education, a level playing field, the blessings of liberty, and, as he put it, "work, work, work."

> . . . Disciples of that other February 12th baby, Charles Darwin, might argue that our destiny is preordained, our future trapped within limited expectations. But Lincoln, to his eternal credit . . . encouraged "the humblest man" to seek "an equal chance." He preached a "patient confidence in the ultimate justice of the people" in "a union of hearts and hands" where "right makes might." What he said on taking the oath of office can still be said with pride and confidence to the latest generation: "Is there any better, or equal, hope in the world?"

Admittedly, there is folly in quoting oneself—no more perhaps than daring to speak at Gettysburg on November 19—but I hope the passage, at least, suggests how Gettysburg continues to incubate diverse thought about Lincoln's long historical and oratorical shadow. Besides, I am consoled by the knowledge that there will be many more intimidated speakers at Gettysburg Dedication Day ceremonies in the years to come. Let them, too, try their best to get right with the original.

The Gettysburg Address, to put it mildly, is an extremely tough act to follow. And yet it remains a living organism, continuing to inspire analysis and explication of the highest order. That is what documentarian Sean Conant has achieved with his penetrating new film, *The Gettysburg Address*, and, as readers will discover, what the authors of this companion book's riveting essays express with such originality and conviction. Which all goes to remind us afresh of Lincoln's one misstatement at Gettysburg: the world would "little note nor long remember" what he said there.

Sometimes actions speak louder than words (not so where Lincoln was concerned, of course). I am proud to say that one of the first accomplishments of the US Abraham Lincoln Bicentennial Commission, which I chaired from 2001 through 2010, was to steam-clean the words of the Gettysburg Address that are etched on the interior wall of the Lincoln Memorial in Washington. Decades of exposure to the capital's unforgiving climate and unrelenting auto emissions had left those 272 words smudged and indistinct. Restoring clarity required only a modest appropriation and a fast-tracked work order. As a result, the words of the Gettysburg Address stand out today in the pristine perfection they were meant to convey for all time.

In its way, too, this book accomplishes a new birth of fresh analysis for those who still love those words and still yearn to better understand them. Cleaning away grime was easy. Clearing away myth and misunderstanding is far harder to accomplish—but no less easy to appreciate and treasure. This volume was inspired by a film a young man named Sean Conant made to tell the story of the Gettysburg Address; a documentary, in turn, based on a journey where Sean and his father embarked to seek out all five handwritten copies of the Address. In the process of this quest, they sought the knowledge and guidance of scholars. Through Sean's efforts, essays by those historians have been brought together in this volume, which celebrates and culminates a century of scholarship on the Gettysburg Address. And what is more, it can be enjoyed not only on November 19, but, as Lincoln might have put it, "for all time to come."[11]

Harold Holzer

Notes

1. Response to a Serenade, July 7, 1863, and Gettysburg Address, November 19, 1863, in *The Collected Works of Abraham Lincoln*, ed. Roy P. Basler, 9 vols. (New Brunswick, NJ: Rutgers University Press, 1953–55), 6:319, 7:17 (hereafter cited as *CW*).

2. Verses on Lee's Invasion of the North, July 19, 1863, in *The Collected Works of Abraham Lincoln*, Supplement 1832–65, ed. Roy P. Basler (Westport, CT: Greenwood Press, 1974), 194.

3. Lincoln to George G. Meade, July 14, 1863, *CW*, 6:327–328.

4. "Lincoln Doggerel Just Discovered," AP, *Sarasota Journal*, Oct. 6, 1969. The verse was discovered by Brown University librarian David A. Jonah in the John Hay Papers there.

5. Lincoln's manuscript, complete with this notation, is in the Abraham Lincoln Papers, Library of Congress.

6. Speech at a flag raising at Independence Hall, Feb. 22, 1861, *CW*, 4: 420.

7. Ibid., 4:421.

8. Lincoln seized an opportunity to speak in the City of Brotherly Love seven months later but utterly failed to approach the eloquence he had achieved at Gettysburg. Lincoln even declared himself as "without anything to say" during the last of his five unremarkable speeches at Philadelphia on June 16, 1864. See *CW*, 7:394, 398.

9. "Cuomo, at Gettysburg, Rails at 'New Slavery,'" *New York Times*, Nov. 20, 1989.

10. AP report, published, for example, in *Sumter Item* (South Carolina), Nov. 20, 1988.

11. From Lincoln's campaign speech to the 166th Ohio Regiment, Aug. 22, 1864, *CW*, 7:512.

The Gettysburg Address

PART I

Influences

I

Classical Democracy
and the Gettysburg Address

Nicholas P. Cole

AT THE END of the first year of the Peloponnesian War in the fifth century BCE, a leader stood to make a speech on the occasion of the burial of those killed in battle. The war in which his state was embroiled pitted against each other Greek societies that shared many elements of politics and culture but which also disagreed on fundamental principles of political organization. There are obvious parallels with the conflict nearly two and a half thousand years later that also turned on fundamental principles and disagreement about where the balance of power should lie in a society and about who should be considered citizens. The exact words delivered by Pericles are now lost, and the text that is now known as his Funeral Oration is taken from the historian Thucydides, who wrote a history of the conflict between Athens, Sparta, and their allies. According to Plutarch's biography of Pericles, unlike Lincoln, he had made a formal and careful study of oratory, and the style and power of his speeches was both mocked and admired by his contemporaries. His task as he made this famous funeral oration, however, was the same as Lincoln's at Gettysburg: to honor the sacrifices of the fallen, to pay proper respect to their memory, and to give some meaning to the sacrifice that they had made. The power with which he did so accounts for the fame of this speech both in antiquity and among modern readers of the classics. In an influential work in 1992, *Lincoln at Gettysburg: The Words that Remade America*, Garry Wills drew a close parallel between Pericles's words in the fifth century BCE and Lincoln's remarks in November 1863. The occasions, Wills argued, paralleled each other, and the speeches made on those occasions, as well as covering similar themes, both served to shape the way that the two conflicts were understood. So much light did Wills think that the Periclean speech shed on the power and importance of Lincoln's words that he printed a translation of the entire earlier speech at the end of his work.

Wills did not mean to suggest that Lincoln framed his words in light of Pericles's text or that there was any direct influence that the one work exerted on the other. His suggestions, that the power of both texts could be understood better by considering both of them and that there were striking ways in which the themes on these two occasions paralleled each other, were more subtle than that. All the same, Wills's approach has frustrated some readers. Rather than setting Lincoln's words in the context of Athenian funeral oratory, it is perhaps more natural to explain both the form of Lincoln's words and their popular reception at the time in the context of the Fourth of July orations that would have been immediately familiar to both Lincoln and his audience.[1] Lincoln was neither a student of classical history nor formally trained in oratory, although many of his contemporaries were both. A man from humble origins, Lincoln had had little formal education, something that put him at a disadvantage in a world that especially privileged knowledge of the classics and that until the late nineteenth century held that the ability to translate Latin and Greek was the mark of an educated man. Despite enduring criticism of this interest in the ancient world, formal education in America continued to emphasize familiarity with the ancient world from the founding of the Republic until the twentieth century.[2] Lincoln mocked both the obsession with the classics and the poor standards of many teachers and students, writing of education on the American frontier that "If a straggler supposed to understand Latin happened to sojourn in the neighborhood, he was looked upon as a wizard."[3] If there was any connection between the oration by Pericles and Lincoln's remarks at Gettysburg, it was a most indirect one at best. When his reading is reconstructed, it reveals little interest in classical literature or history.[4] Indeed, to attempt to find a connection where no real one exists would be to undervalue Lincoln's skill both as an orator and as a statesman, whose powers of speaking—the products predominantly of his own natural gifts—produced a speech at Gettysburg that bears comparison with the words of one of the finest orators of antiquity.

The other speaker at Gettysburg, however, *was* a product of formal education, and was not only aware of the parallels with antiquity but also choose to open his speech with them. Edward Everett was not only one of the finest orators of his day, but one who was famous in particular for ceremonial rhetoric. Most of his best speeches and orations were composed for public occasions, rather than as works of political oratory, and, as he made clear at Gettysburg, he was well aware that by making the connection in his audience's mind between the traditions of Athens and the modern situation, he was able to lend the burial of America's war dead a special solemnity and importance.

Everett opened his address with an account of the Athenian customs that had paid tribute to those who had fallen in battle, though he drew a parallel not between the current conflict and the Peloponnesian War, which had pitted the more democratic Athens against the allies of the more aristocratic Sparta, but with the earlier conflict that had seen Greece as a whole resist the invasion of the despotic Persia. The men who had fallen at Gettysburg, he suggested to his audience, bore comparison with those who had fallen at the battle of Marathon, a crucial battle that had ensured the survival of the Greek states. At that ancient battle, they too had rolled back "the tide of an invasion, not less unprovoked, not less ruthless, than that which came to plant the dark banner of Asiatic despotism and slavery on the free soil of Greece."[5] The comparison was unflattering and uncompromising in its characterization of the Confederacy—even a comparison with Sparta would have been more flattering—but the idea of comparing the events of American history, the nation's politicians, and its political institutions to those of the ancient world was one that stretched back to the founding years of the Republic, and was not only woven into the nation's systems of education and traditions of writing and political oratory, but was also recalled in the architecture of its private and public buildings, not least of which were those in Washington, DC.

The enduring American preference for building its most important public buildings in neoclassical styles can be traced directly to Thomas Jefferson, who pushed the State of Virginia in the 1780s to model its new capitol building at Richmond on the temple at Nîmes. His principal aim was to confound European criticisms of America by proving that even on the western shore of the Atlantic, buildings could still capture the aesthetic qualities of ancient architecture.

> It is very simple, but it is noble beyond expression, and would have done honour to our country as presenting to travelers a morsel of taste in our infancy promising much for our maturer age . . . But how is a taste in this beautiful art to be formed in our countrymen, unless we avail ourselves of every occasion when public buildings are to be erected, of presenting to them models for their study and

imitation? . . . You see I am an enthusiast on the subject of the arts. But it is an enthusiasm of which I am not ashamed, as its object is to improve the taste of my countrymen, to increase their reputation, to reconcile to them the respect of the world and procure them its praise.[6]

The idea that Americans might become the true heirs of the ancients was one that captivated American imaginations. Everett even alluded to it in his remarks at Gettysburg, recalling his own visit to the burial site at Marathon as a "youthful pilgrim from a world unknown to ancient Greece."[7]

Everett's willingness at Gettysburg to compare America and the Union not only with Greece but also with the Athenian democracy in particular reflected a broader trend in nineteenth-century thought to describe America as a "democracy" and to praise the politicians of Athens in a way that a previous generation would have recoiled from. Carl J. Richard identifies what he calls the "rehabilitation of the Athenian Democracy" in nineteenth-century American political discourse.[8] Richard is right to suggest that this shift was in large part caused by the pressure of mass politics. Criticisms of Athens that had been the staple of previous ages gave way to praise as American politicians embraced the idea of "democracy" and wished to avoid seeming elitist. Paradoxically, praise of Athens and Athenian politicians reflected a decline in the influence of the Greek political theory that had for so long made Western political thought suspicious of democratic government and Americans fearful for the future of their polity and its institutions.

America's first generation of politicians had been primed to think about politics in classical terms and to be suspicious of the viability of democracies. Though they were not constrained by it, American thinkers in the eighteenth and nineteenth centuries stood in a long tradition in which writers turned to ancient political theory and classical history for guidance, even while coming to radically different conclusions than those of the ancients.

Educated readers shared a familiarity with central concepts of ancient political theory. These same concepts had exerted a profound influence on modern political thought, and ancient thinkers therefore exerted their influence both directly and indirectly on the modern audience. Most fundamental to many ancient and early modern discussions of politics was the notion that all forms of government could be categorized as one of a limited number of basic species distinguished primarily by where and in how many people the sovereign authority of the state was vested. As William Blackstone, whose influential *Commentaries on the Laws of England* were published in the second half of the 1760s, summarized in his introduction:

> The political writers of antiquity will not allow more than three regular forms of government; the first, when the sovereign power is lodged in an aggregate assembly consisting of all the members of a community, which is called a democracy; the second, when it is lodged in a council, composed of select members, and then it is styled an aristocracy; the last when it is entrusted in the hands of a single person, and then it takes the name of monarchy. All other species of government, say they, are either corruptions of, or reducible to, these three.[9]

It is significant that Blackstone did not demur. Instead, he suggested that the ancient idea of a constitution that blended all three was not "visionary whim" (a view he ascribes to the Roman historian Tacitus), but rather something that the British constitution had managed to realize. Ancient and modern writers agreed that the three species of government, democracy, aristocracy, and monarchy, all had "their several perfections and imperfections." Democratic assemblies were characterized as just and patriotic in intention but prone to foolishness. Aristocracies were held to be wise, but less honest than democracies, and monarchies the most powerful form of government, deriving their power from unity of purpose and the concentration of power, yet by the same token the most potentially dangerous and oppressive.[10] Most modern writers, even through the nineteenth century, continued to perpetrate some version of this basic scheme.

One of the most striking and quotable features of Lincoln's remarks at Gettysburg is that he makes the cause of the North the cause of democratic government. The note on which he ends, that those fallen at Gettysburg had died in order to secure the future of popular government, not just in America, but for the whole world, was not a rhetorical flourish or exaggeration invented by Lincoln. Rather, it reflected a much longer tradition of American rhetoric and political thought that considered America's relationship to the ancient world. Everett himself had alluded to some of this in his remarks before Lincoln stood up to speak, but perhaps it is even more obvious in a speech that Everett gave to celebrate Independence Day in Charlestown in 1828.

On that earlier occasion, Everett had taken as his theme the history of liberty, and in particular a celebration of the ways in which American institutions had given a reality and stability to popular government and to liberty that had eluded the ancients. Commenting on the historians of ancient Greece, he wrote that "we nowhere find in them an account of a populous and extensive region, blessed with institutions securing the enjoyment and transmission of regulated liberty." The ancient Greeks, he continued, had "profound and elegant scholars" but lacked the technology for the general diffusion of knowledge, the navigational skills for a great commercial empire, and the systems of representative government necessary to secure liberty on a grand scale.[11] The remainder of his address on that occasion took his audience through the sweep of European and American history, explaining why it was in the United States of America, and there alone, that popular government and liberty had a chance to flourish. "The eyes of the world are turned for example to us," he told his audience, and so too were the "noble spirits of anquitity [sic]"—that is, men like Caesar's assassin, Brutus, who had given their lives in the cause of liberty, only to see their hopes dashed by the inadequacies of previous peoples and states. Many men had faced the rack, the scaffold, or the scimitar in the cause of freedom, he reminded them. He closed with words that seem to anticipate the speeches that he and Lincoln would give more than thirty years later:

> Let us then, as we assemble, on the birth day of the nation, as we gather on the green turf, once wet with precious blood, let us devote ourselves to the sacred cause of CONSTITUTIONAL LIBERTY. Let us abjure the interests and passions, which divide the great family of American freemen. Let the rage of party spirit sleep to-day. Let us resolve, that our children shall have cause to bless the memory of their fathers, as we have cause to bless ours.[12]

Lincoln's closing remarks at Gettysburg, therefore, were part of a much longer history of oratory that celebrated America's form of government as a sacred trust and the United States as a nation charged with a particular and special purpose: that of proving whether or not popular government could ever be successful. Even without any classical education, Lincoln would have easily absorbed this recurring theme from listening to the rhetoric of others. Everett was a particular master of summing up the detail of classical history in a speech and turning it to some particular purpose suitable to an occasion, but the general theme was pervasive. Yet aside from the general tone, it is perhaps worth noting, too, that although Everett in 1828 and 1864 praised liberty and the "constitutional liberty" of the United States, Lincoln offered a much more powerful formulation celebrating the government of the people by themselves. It was a rejection of the cautious tone adopted toward popular government by many of those with more classical educations.

At the time of the Revolution, questions and premises that were ultimately derived from ancient thinking had become so firmly embedded in many aspects of Western political thought that it is difficult or impossible to disentangle the precise web of influences.[13] In a famous book on the "Aristotelian and Machiavellian tradition" in Western thought, the historian John Pocock declared that for Americans living at the end of the eighteenth century, "there was (it would almost appear) no alternative tradition in which to be schooled."[14] It would be easy to overstate both the homogeneity of American political thought and its debt to previous traditions, and thereby not only rob the revolutionary generation of its ingenuity and distinctiveness, but also lose sight of the very real battles fought to shape contemporary and future republicanism. American writers deployed the ancient world in support of a wide range of positions, emphasizing different aspects of the classical tradition as they did so. The proper interpretation and value of the ancient world in early American political thought was itself the subject of profound disagreement and debate, and became a proxy for contemporary battles. This mode of debate continued well into Lincoln's age. It is feasible to detect in the Southern desire to produce their own classical textbooks in the mid-nineteenth century a sense that to do so would be to strengthen the Southern cause, by not only controlling the content of the textbooks but by also asserting their intellectual independence from the North and laying claim to the classical tradition.[15]

In architecture and in the arts generally, the mid-nineteenth century was the age of the Greek Revival. In his speeches, Everett frequently referred to the modern history of Greece, which had won independence during a war in the early nineteenth century. Sympathy for the plight of Greece reinforced a taste for Greek architecture. Surveys of Greek ruins, published from the mid-eighteenth century onward, led to a specifically Greek-influenced style of neoclassical architecture, popular in both private and public buildings. The interiors of buildings, too, reflected a

self-consciously classical style. Orators, such as Everett, connected the
American quest for liberty to Greece's modern struggle for freedom. In
1828, while the question of independence had still not been settled, he
expressed hope that "the prospect is fair, that the political regeneration,
which commenced in the West, is now going backward to resuscitate the
once happy and long deserted regions of the older world." The flame of liberty that ancient Greece and Rome had been unable to keep alive had in fact
been passed back to Europe by the success of the American experience.[16]

Lincoln stood partly outside this discourse. Without the classical
schooling common to so many of his peers, his speeches and writings
lack the kind of engagement with the ancient world of which they were
capable. All the same, he must have been aware, as he spoke at Gettysburg, that part of the power of his remarks was produced by the fact that
they engaged a debate about democracy that had occupied the thinkers
of the ancient world and had led the best minds of Europe to declare for
two thousand years that democracy was an impractical form of government. After all, why should anyone fear that government of the people
and by the people might vanish from the earth? Why was the success
of the United States so vital? For Lincoln and his audience, this was not
merely a flourish of rhetoric, but a question that in its important elements
predated the Republic itself.

Any study of history or of political thought in the nineteenth century
reminded students of the rarity of democracies and the remarkable nature
of the American experiment. For a long time even the word "democracy"
was suspect, and although by the mid-nineteenth century attitudes had
begun to change, neither speaker at Gettysburg used the word to describe
America. Modern readers of ancient history and political thought (that
is to say, anyone with formal schooling and a university education) were
taught to be suspicious of popular government in general and of democracy in particular. In his work *Politics*, the Greek philosopher Aristotle
had denied "democracy" from his "correct" forms of government and
sided with ancient critics of the more radical versions of Athenian democracy. He likened the likely actions of a truly democratic government to
many of the worst features of tyrannical and oligarchic government, and
defines it more precisely as a government in which the "free, who are also
poor and the majority" of citizens govern.[17] A great danger of democracy,
he suggested, is instability of the law, a criticism that would be echoed by
many modern analyses of republics.[18] Popular governments are likely to
change the law frequently and in ways that are oppressive. Indeed, where

the citizen body rules supreme, ungoverned by the law, demagogues will encourage the people to make decrees that will be every bit as oppressive as the edicts of tyrants.[19] It was this criticism that was better remembered in modern America, rather than his less empirical and more philosophical criticism that a radical democracy insisted on political equality instead of respecting differing levels of political skill and virtue.

Readers of the Greek historian Thucydides, or the various modern précis of him, were familiar with several examples that seemed to prove the unsuitability of democratic government. A famous example was the "Mytilenian debate." When a group of Mytilenian prisoners was brought to Athens after the city's defeat, in an angry mood the Athenians decided not only to put all the prisoners to death but also the whole male citizenry of Mytilene and to enslave their women and children. They sent out a ship with instructions to that effect. The following day, however, they repented this cruel and unprecedented decision, and the question was debated again. By the time the debate concluded and messengers were dispatched to announce that the city of Mytilene had won a narrow reprieve, the first ship had a head start of about twenty-four hours, and it was only by good fortune that the Athenian democracy was not further embarrassed by seeing its decree of clemency arrive too late. In a dramatic scene, Thucydides relates that the decree of clemency arrived just after the order to massacre the city had been read aloud. Thucydides uses this episode to raise the same question that often has been in the mind of those who have cited it since—whether or not a democracy is a suitable form of government. As he has Cleon, the proponent of the most severe treatment of Mytilene, say to the Athenians as they debate clemency: "Personally I have had occasion enough already to observe that a democracy is incapable of governing others, and I am all the more convinced of this when I see how you are now changing your mind." Both speakers in that debate fear that the Athenians will make a decision based on emotion (variously, misplaced compassion, anger, or fear), and the episode as a whole underlines the role of the demagogue in democratic politics.[20] Elsewhere in Thucydides, even the great democratic leader Pericles accuses the Athenians of being shortsighted in their decision making. As for Thucydides, the historian was critical of democracy as a form of government. Pericles, he says, led the Athenians well but with such overwhelming preeminence that "in what was nominally a democracy, power was really in the hands of the first citizen." His successors, on the other hand, competed with each other to secure positions of leadership, resorting to demagogy and losing control of affairs. It was, in the end, internal strife, Thucydides says, that led to the ultimate defeat of Athens.[21]

Athenian democracy was also infamous in the modern world for the execution of the philosopher Socrates, condemned to death in 399 BCE on a charge of corrupting youth. The two accounts of his trial that survive from antiquity, written by Plato and Xenophon, are both sympathetic to Socrates. The politics of the trial was more complicated than it has often seemed to later commentators, who have presented Socrates as an innocent victim. One of Socrates's pupils had been a leading member of the brutal regime that briefly governed Athens after their defeat in the Peloponnesian War. The charge against Socrates, shortly after the restoration of the democracy, was undoubtedly politically motivated, though the charges focused on religious offenses to avoid the terms of amnesty that prevented trial for prior political misconduct. The political context of the trial, however, was less remembered than the execution of a philosopher on a trumped-up charge by the most radical form of Greek democracy. *A New History of the Grecian States*, for example, which was reprinted in America in 1794, promising "an account of their most memorable sieges and battles; and the character and exploits of their most celebrated heroes, orators, and philosophers," devoted extensive space to the trial and execution of Socrates, following closely the sympathetic ancient accounts. It then used more than a page to describe the Athenians' "grief" once they realized their mistake, the punishment by execution or banishment of Socrates's accusers, and the statue that was erected to his memory. Socrates's modern reputation was so great that this history noted that "upon the account both of his belief in the Deity, and the exemplariness of his life, some have thought fit to rank him among the Christian philosophers."[22] Although there were other incidents of this type, it is almost certain that James Madison referred to the execution of Socrates when he condemned the Athenian democracy for bringing the idea of "popular liberty" into disrepute and bringing upon it the "indelible reproach of decreeing to the same citizens, the hemlock on the one day, and statues on the next."[23] Indeed, Socrates's reputation was perhaps better secured by his status as victim of democracy and warning against the evils of such a government than it was by his pupils' attempts to preserve his contributions to philosophy. Both Jefferson and John Adams were disappointed in particular by Plato, the latter declaring that he had learned only two things from reading him, perhaps the more significant of the two being that "Sneezing is a cure for Hiccups."[24]

While there is no evidence that Lincoln made a close study of ancient history, he does seem to have read Charles Rollin's survey of ancient history, as well as some of Plutarch, and would have been aware of the classical mistrust of democracy and demagogues from those authors.[25] The significance of Lincoln's insistence upon "equality" as a founding principle of the American nation, a principle with which he both starts and ends his remarks at Gettysburg, was very much at odds with a more classical understanding of politics. Everett's long oration that day had not used the word, except to describe military numbers, and in his other oratory he shied away from it too. Lincoln's words, of course, are taken from the Declaration of Independence and are addressed most immediately to the institution of slavery. They have a deeper power even than that, though, contesting the classical understanding of politics that still inflected much of American and European discourse, despite frequent challenge. Lincoln seems to have read Constantin Volney's essay on the subject of equality, written at the height of the French Revolution, which is sharply critical of the classical insistence on the inequality of man.[26]

Modern readers may easily miss the fact that Lincoln's words at Gettysburg were a repudiation of a classical understanding of politics that would have been much more familiar to many in his audience. To understand some of the power of his words and the significance of this speech as a pivotal moment, it is important to understand just how deeply woven notions of inequality had become to Western thought and the long history of debate on this subject even in postrevolutionary America. Aristotle had recommended something that is often translated as "constitutional government" (a phrase that Everett employed for several orations). In its detail, this was not a form of purely popular government at all, but a "mixed" form of government that blends elements of democratic and oligarchic government.[27] It was, Aristotle contended, the most practicable form of government. The notion that the disadvantages of the different species of government could be offset by blending different forms of government within the same state was developed further by other writers. Cited by Blackstone on the point at the start of his *Commentaries*, the dictum by Cicero that the best form of government was that which blended elements of kingly, aristocratic, and popular government was familiar to lawyers and politicians in the eighteenth century. Americans encountered this theory repeatedly in a range of classical authors popular in curricula and in more general reading.

The most influential ancient account of mixed government was found in the pages of the historian Polybius, a Greek who wrote in the second century BCE about the rise of Rome. A fear that the American Republic might not survive unless special care is taken to preserve it, an idea that is almost ubiquitous in American thought, can be traced in part to the influence of this writer. Polybius placed greater emphasis than previous writers on the historical relationship that he detected between all these forms of government. They are, he argued, interconnected in the sense that there appears to be a predictable historical cycle through which each form of government comes into being, decays, and is overthrown. In the earliest societies, he reasoned, one man would come to preeminence through his physical strength, but as societies developed notions of justice, support for the ruler became a matter of reason rather than force. Yet kingship, he argued, especially hereditary kingship, had a tendency to degenerate into a tyranny, and certain people in the state would begin plotting against the king. The men most likely to form such conspiracies would, he reasoned, be the noblest and most courageous men in the state, and this together with the gratitude of the people after the overthrow of monarchy would pave the way for government by aristocracy. Yet just as monarchy tends to tyranny, so aristocracy tends to oligarchy, and in turn provokes a popular uprising since, fearing now both kings and oligarchs, the people will attempt to rule themselves.[28] Democracy, however, is not the end of the cycle. The generations who inherit the equality and freedom of democracy will cease to value them, he suggested, and some men, most likely the rich, will begin to compete for preeminence through the seduction of the people, encouraging them to adopt measures that will, in the end, transform a democracy into a state that is corrupt and violent. In time, one man will emerge as the master and tyrant of the state. This cycle, Polybius argued, amounted to an inevitable law of nature. Rome's early history, Polybius argued, perhaps demonstrated this natural cycle better than any.[29]

Yet Polybius also saw a way in which the cycle might be averted. Rome, he argued, had developed a mixed constitution that would delay this cycle considerably. Polybius contrasted the Roman experience with that of the Greek city Sparta. The Spartan lawgiver, Lycurgus, he said, had perceived the natural cycle of constitutions and saw that all constitutions founded on a single principle—that is, all states that were simple monarchies, aristocracies, or democracies—were unstable. Lycurgus had therefore given the Spartans a constitution that incorporated elements of all types of state in equilibrium. In this way the virtues and vices of the different forms balanced and counteracted each other, and for this reason the Spartan constitution had been the longest lasting of all history to date. The Romans had evolved a similar, mixed form of government, not through the actions of a lawgiver, but through learning gradually from experience and disaster.[30] Unlike the Spartans, the Romans had no kings, but, in the Polybian analysis, kingly power was exercised in certain respects by the two annually elected consuls, aristocratic power by the Senate, and democratic power by Rome's popular assembly. The cooperation of all these powers was necessary to govern the state. Each element of the state could control to some extent the actions of the others, and could either help or hinder it. Working together, against an external threat or toward a common goal, the constitution possessed great strength; yet if any one part of the constitution became corrupted or overambitious, it would be restrained by the actions of the other two.[31] Polybius defined the virtuous constitution as the one that had the capacity to weather any chance of fortune, and the republican constitution of Rome was the most ideal.[32] It possessed the advantages of any of the basic forms of government, the flexibility to respond to changing circumstances, and the internal strength to resist the usual cycle through which states decay. Yet Polybius did not believe that the Roman state would last forever, and his reputation among modern readers was secured as much by his apparent prescience as his description of the Roman constitution. The Roman republic did, as he seemed to have predicted, degenerate as leading men struggled for preeminence, pitting the popular assemblies against the Senate, and the conclusion of a generation of internal conflict and civil war was the dictatorship of Julius Caesar and rule of the Roman emperors. The republic had been replaced by monarchy.

By the founding of the American Republic, a Polybian analysis of the constitution provided one of the most standard ways to explain and champion Britain's constitutional monarchy. The king, the House of Lords, and the House of Commons mapped easily onto the monarchy, aristocracy, and democracy of ancient political theory. These three elements, as Blackstone put it, "actuated by different springs, and attentive to different interests, composes the British Parliament . . . there can no inconvenience be attempted by one of the other two; each branch being armed with a negative power, sufficient to repel any innovation which it shall think inexpedient or dangerous."[33] Blackstone set out in some detail the advantages of this delicate balance and the "singular nature" of the British constitution, though he presented it as a uniquely British achievement. In support of his praise of the British system he cited Tacitus, who stated that all nations and cities were ruled by the people, the nobility, or one man and that a constitution formed through the mixture of these elements, though easy to recommend, was not easy to create.[34] This ancient model of government perhaps worked rather more easily in the British case, for Polybius had only been able to describe the Roman constitution in such terms by glossing many aspects of Roman institutions and law.

Twenty-first-century readers, unused to thinking in these terms, may be surprised at the extent to which such ideas lingered in American thought in the eighteenth and nineteenth centuries, and may miss the fact that at Gettysburg Lincoln took the opportunity to reject them and offer a new understanding of the American nation. In the 1780s, a distrust of democracy (at least, the direct democracy of the Athenian model) and a veneration for ancient political theory had colored the way in which the founders of the Republic defended and justified the Constitution. James Madison might have presented a perfectly coherent account of the federal Constitution, and in particular the nature of the Senate, that avoided all discussion of the ancient world and which described the nature of the compromise at the Constitutional Convention. Instead, he offered an account of the Senate that drew heavily on ancient mixed-government theory. It is worth noting that his characterization of the lower house fluctuates between a vision of it as too closely representing the people—in particular in being liable to passions and emotional impulses—and a description of it as inadequate representation, too numerous and too changing for its members to be held responsible for their actions.[35] Madison writes of the need to "blend stability with liberty," for which he employs the ancient republics as the "instructive proofs." The "liberty" of which he writes is the government of the people by themselves and in accordance with their own wishes. Popular will should, at least on some occasions, be resisted:

> I shall not scruple to add that such an institution [a senate] may sometimes be necessary as a defence to the people against their own temporary errors and delusions . . . there are particular moments in public affairs when the people, stimulated by some irregular passion, or some illicit advantage, or misled by the representations of interested men, may call for measures which they themselves will afterwards be the most ready to lament and condemn.[36]

The Senate was to be able to provide the interference "of some temperate and respectable body of citizens," until "reason, justice and truth can regain their authority over the public mind."[37] Unlike John Adams, who had written at far greater length on this subject in his *Defence of the Constitutions of Government of the United States of America,* Madison was more conscious of American sensibilities, and scrupulously avoided characterizing the Senate or its members with the term "aristocracy." Instead, he inserted a line noting that the senates of the ancient world were, in many but unspecified ways, unfit for emulation in America.

Madison argued that the need for such a body was proved by reflecting on the fate of previous republics. "It adds no small weight to these considerations to recollect that history informs us of no long-lived republic which had not a senate," and indeed, he suggests, the examples of Sparta, Rome, and Carthage are the only examples of republics worthy of consideration. The first two he knew to have appointed a senate for life, the last he thought had probably done so. The alternative to some senatorial body was the "fugitive and turbulent existence of other ancient republics."[38] The form of these ancient senates, Madison admitted, was repugnant to the "genius of America," but some institution that performed their same institutional purpose—opposing when necessary the wishes and passions of the people—was necessary, and America was not as dissimilar from the ancient world as some might argue:

> I am not unaware of the circumstances which distinguish the American from other popular governments, as well ancient and modern; and which render extreme circumspection necessary in reasoning from one case to the other. But after allowing due weight to this consideration it may still be maintained that there are many points of similitude which render these examples not unworthy of our attention. Many of the defects, as we have seen, which can only be supplied by a senatorial institution, are common to a numerous assembly frequently elected by the people, and to the people themselves.[39]

This contrast between the "democratic" House of Representatives and the more "aristocratic" Senate has never entirely vanished from the American imagination. Perhaps commentators are even tempted to exaggerate the differences between the two bodies in their descriptions of the institutions. Contrasting the Senate with the House, Alexis de Tocqueville wrote:

When you enter the House of Representatives in Washington, you
feel yourself struck by the vulgar aspect of this great assembly.
Often the eye seeks in vain for a celebrated man within it . . . In
a country where instruction is almost universally wide-spread, it
is said that the people's representatives do not always know how
to write correctly. Two steps away is the chamber of the Senate,
whose narrow precincts enclose a large portion of the celebrities of
America.[40]

Lincoln does not appear to have read Tocqueville, but there is every
reason to suppose that Tocqueville was doing little more in this passage
than reflecting a common American understanding of the contrast between the Senate and the House of Representatives, and one that lingers
in some contrasts between the two bodies to this day. Yet long before
he wrote that description, the place of classical theory and its suspicion
of democracy had been challenged by some of America's leading politicians. Thomas Jefferson had championed the translation of Destutt de
Tracy's *Commentary and Review of Montesquieu's Spirit of Laws*.[41] Jefferson received the manuscript in 1810 and assisted in its translation and
publication.[42] Of this work Jefferson wrote in 1816, "None in the world
equal the Review of Montesquieu" as "the best elementary book on the
principles of government."[43] Jefferson had become dissatisfied with Montesquieu, bemoaning the fact in 1790 that "in the science of government
Montesquieu's spirit of the laws is generally recommended," despite the
fact that "it contains indeed a great number of political truths; but also an
equal number of heresies."[44]

The central heresy that Tracy exposed and that won him acclaim
from Jefferson was Montesquieu's division of the states into different
types. Montesquieu did not follow exactly the classifications of ancient
writers, but the similarity of his scheme to that of antiquity makes
Tracy's attack on him for "classing governments according to the accidental circumstances of the number of men invested with authority"
applicable to both. He condemns Montesquieu and the ancients for as-
cribing to different types of government distinctive characteristics.[45]
He was especially suspicious of the idea that there were "moving principles of each [type of] government" and of the idea that the "moving
principle" of a republic is virtue, or that "honour" and "ambition" are
the principles of monarchy, or that "moderation" is the principle of an
"aristocratic republic." Surely, Tracy argued, these principles could be

found in many kinds of state.[46] Montesquieu's division of governments into "republican," "monarchical," and "despotic" he rejected as "defective on several counts."[47] He argued that the whole scheme was defective: that "all of these classes, containing very opposite and very different forms, the explanation of each of them must be very vague, or not applicable to all states comprised in the class."[48] Nor did he agree with Helvetius that governments were either good or bad, for it struck him that there was no form of government "which may not at some time be classed among the good or the bad." This rejection of an alternative to Montesquieu was an important insight, for it led him to search for a single form of government of which he approved.[49]

Instead, Tracy divided governments into the "national" or the "special," the difference between them being whether they recognized "social rights which are common to all" or whether they recognized "particular or unequal rights." From here, he proceeded to conclude that the precise form of government was less important than its origin. The somewhat awkward formulation that he offered is one that Lincoln surpassed at Gettysburg, but a similar force animates both:

> In whatever manner governments may be organized, I shall place in the first class all those which recognize the principle, that all rights and power originate in, reside in and belong to, the entire body of the people or nation; and that none exists, but what is derived from, and exercised for the nation.[50]

In spite of his love of classical literature, Jefferson took seriously the idea that ancient political theory, with its distrust of democracy, had to be jettisoned from American thinking. Asked by one correspondent for the recommendation of a new and more accurate translation of Aristotle, Jefferson replied that it was unnecessary to master him in detail:

> The introduction of this new principle of representative democracy has rendered useless almost everything written before on the structure of government; and in a great measure, relieves our regret if the political writings of Aristotle, or any other ancient, have been lost, or are unfaithfully rendered or explained to us.[51]

At Gettysburg Abraham Lincoln captured even better than Jefferson this more modern understanding of democracy, describing America as a government "of the people, by the people and for the people." There is no trace in this definition of any classically inspired suspicion of a political system immediately responsive to the wishes of its people. Indeed, the end of his speech seems to be a complete rejection of such an approach to politics.

There is a certain irony, therefore, in the way that Lincoln has been best memorialized. Lincoln knew no Greek and little Latin. Unlike his predecessor, John Quincy Adams, he had not been a professor of rhetoric who published a series of lectures on the subject.[52] Indeed, his style of speaking was at odds with the classically inspired rhetoric of many politicians of his day and certainly reflected no formal training. Unlike Everett, who filled his speeches with carefully chosen and richly developed historical comparisons, and whose speeches were masterfully constructed, Lincoln adopted a plainer style. To be sure, his sentences emulated and exceeded those of others in their rhythm and elegance, and the force of his intellect is obvious in the way he dissects questions to get right to the heart of the matter at hand. Yet he never consciously emulates the ancient orator either in his material or in the structure of his speech. Instead, he adopts a frank, almost conversational style. It was in death, rather than in life, that he was most strongly connected to the ancient world. Any visitor to the nation's capital can scarcely avoid a monument modeled on the Athenian Parthenon, the temple dedicated to the patron goddess of Athens that stands on the Acropolis overlooking Athens.[53] An inscription behind the seated statue of Lincoln that takes the place of the Athenian goddess even describes the monument as a temple. Over to one side, the text of the Gettysburg Address is inscribed. In this iconic memorial, dedicated in 1922, then, Lincoln is remembered by a monument that compares him not only to ancient statesmen but also to the goddess that was the patron of the most famous (and for a long time the most controversial) ancient democracy, Athens. Garry Wills is not alone in wishing to compare America's politicians in general and Lincoln in particular to the statesmen of the ancient world. His work and the Lincoln Memorial are part of a longer tradition of memorializing America's politicians and representing the state using classical iconography and vocabulary—a vocabulary that America has used for over two hundred years to celebrate its most significant achievements, to debate the workings of republican government, to announce the nation's importance in the history of the world, and to remember the achievements of its most important statesmen.

Notes

1. Linda Selzer, "Historicizing Lincoln: Garry Wills and the Canonization of the 'Gettysburg Address,'" *Rhetoric Review* 16, no. 1 (1997): 126–129.

2. Caroline Winterer, *The Culture of Classicism: Ancient Greece and Rome in American Intellectual Life 1780–1910* (Baltimore: John Hopkins University Press, 2002).

3. Carl J. Richard, *The Golden Age of the Classics in America: Greece Rome and the Antebellum United States* (Cambridge, MA: Harvard University Press, 2009), 43.

4. Robert Bray, "What Abraham Lincoln Read: An Evaluative and Annotated List," *Journal of the Abraham Lincoln Association* 28, no. 2 (2007): 28–81.

5. Garry Wills, *Lincoln at Gettysburg: The Words That Remade America* (New York: Simon and Schuster, 1992), 215.

6. Jefferson to James Madison (September 20, 1785), in Thomas Jefferson Papers, Library of Congress, Washington, DC.

7. Wills, *Lincoln at Gettysburg*, 215.

8. Richard, *Golden Age of the Classics in America*, 46–53.

9. William Blackstone, *Commentaries on the Laws of England: A Facsimile of the First Edition of 1765–1769*, vol.1 (Chicago and London: University of Chicago Press, 1979), 49.

10. Ibid., 49–52.

11. Edward Everett, "Oration Delivered Before the Citizens of Charlestown, on the 4th of July, 1828" in Everett, *Orations and Speeches on Various Occasions* (Boston: American Stationers, 1836), 143.

12. Ibid., 162.

13. The connection of American ideas of balanced government to British and older traditions of political thought has long been recognized, a point that was made by many of the essays written for an American Historical Association conference held to mark the 150 years of the Constitution: Conyers Read, ed., *The Constitution Reconsidered* (New York: Columbia University Press, 1938). For "classical" conceptions of the Constitution in England see Corinne Comstock Weston, "Beginnings of the Classical Theory of the English Constitution," *Proceedings of the American Philosophical Society* 100, no. 2 (1956): 133–144; Corinne Comstock Weston, "English Constitutional Doctrines from the Fifteenth Century to the Seventeenth: II. The Theory of Mixed Monarchy under Charles I and after," *English Historical Review* 75, no. 296 (1960): 426–443. For the British tradition using readings of history as one source of political thought Zera S. Fink, *The Classical Republicans: An Essay in the Recovery of a Pattern of Thought in Seventeenth Century England* (Evanston: Northwestern University Press, 1945).

14. J. G. A. Pocock, *The Machiavellian Moment: Florentine Political Thought and the Atlantic Republican Tradition* (Princeton, NJ: Princeton University Press, 1975), 506–507.

15. Robert I. Curtis, "Confederate Classical Textbooks: A Lost Cause?," *International Journal of the Classical Tradition* 3, no. 4 (1997): 433–457.

16. Everett, *Orations*, 159–160.

17. Aristotle, *Politics* IV.4.

18. For example, James Madison to Jefferson, Oct. 24, 1787, and Jefferson's reply on Dec. 20. Both men talk about the problem of the "instability of the laws" in America.

19. Aristotle, *Politics* IV.4.

20. *Thucydides* III.36ff. Translation from Thucydides, *History of the Peloponnesian War*, translated by Rex Warner (London: Penguin, 1972), 213.

21. *Thucydides* II.65. Translated ibid., 164.

22. R. Johnson, *A new history of the Grecian states; from their earliest period to their extinction by the Ottomans. Containing an account of their most memorable sieges and battles; and the character and exploits of their most celebrated heroes, orators, and philosophers. Embellished with copper-plate cuts. Designed for the use of young ladies and gentlemen.* (Lansingburgh, NY and Albany, NY: Silvester Tiffany, 1794), 57–59.

23. For the influence of this criticism of democracy in the modern world, see Jennifer T. Roberts, *Athens on Trial: The Antidemocratic Tradition in Western Thought* (Princeton, NJ: Princeton University Press, 1994).

24. Jefferson to John Adams, July 5, 1814; Adams to Jefferson, July 16, 1814.

25. Bray, *What Abraham Lincoln Read*, 72, 175, 70.

26. Ibid., 77.

27. Aristotle, *Politics* IV.8.

28. *Polybius* 6.8–6.9.

29. Ibid., 6.9.

30. Ibid., 6.10.

31. Ibid., 6.18.

32. Ibid., 6.2. This idea, amplified by Machiavelli, is the subject of Pocock's *The Machiavellian Moment.*

33. Blackstone, *Commentaries on the Laws of England*, 51.

34. Tacitus, *Annals* IV.33, cited in Latin in Blackstone, *Commentaries on the Laws of England*, 50.

35. For the latter, see the opening of *Federalist* 62: James Madison, Alexander Hamilton, and John Jay, *The Federalist Papers*, ed. Isaac Kramnick (London: Penguin, 1987), 369–370.

36. Ibid., 371–372.

37. Ibid., 371.

38. Ibid., 172.

39. Ibid., 372.

40. Alexis de Tocqueville, *Democracy in America*, ed. Harvey C. Mansfield and Delba Winthrop (Chicago: University of Chicago Press, 2002), 192.

41. The importance of this work for understanding Jefferson's political thought was realized by Joyce Appleby, "What Is Still American in the Political Philosophy of Thomas Jefferson?," *William and Mary Quarterly* 39, no. 2 (1982): 209–309.

42. Emmet Kennedy, *A Philosophe in the Age of Revolution: Destutt de Tracy and the Origins of "Ideology"* (Philadelphia: American Philosophical Society, 1978), 210–211. See also Jefferson's letter to Thomas Law, June, 13, 1814, at which point Jefferson has not read the whole, but has translated the commentary on Montesquieu's eleventh book, and is quite confident, from the other parts he has read, of the value of the work.

43. Jefferson to Joseph C. Cabell, Feb. 2, 1816.

44. Jefferson to Thomas Mann Randoph, May, 30, 1790.

45. Destutt de Tracy, *A Commentary and Review of Montesquieu's Spirit of Laws*, trans. Thomas Jefferson (Philadelphia: William Duane, 1811), 147.

46. Ibid., 15–17.

47. Ibid., 46, 9.

48. Ibid., 11.

49. Ibid., 12.

50. Ibid., 13.

51. Jefferson to Isaac Tiffany, Monticello, Aug. 26, 1816.

52. Donald M. Goodfellow, "The First Boylston Professor of Rhetoric and Oratory," *New England Quarterly* 19, no. 3 (1946): 372–389.

53. For an account of the design and construction of the memorial, see: Christopher A. Thomas, "The Marble of the Lincoln Memorial: 'Whitest, Prettiest, and . . . Best,' " *Washington History* 5, no. 2 (1993): 42–63.

2

"We Here Highly Resolve"

THE END OF COMPROMISE AND THE RETURN
TO REVOLUTIONARY TIME

Robert Pierce Forbes

LINCOLN'S GETTYSBURG ADDRESS is often viewed today as marking a decisive break from the nation forged by the founders, as the founding charter, with the Reconstruction Amendments, of the Second American Republic. With the Address, it is said, Lincoln surreptitiously launched a "secret constitution," a redefinition of American democracy along new egalitarian lines.[1] One admirer even described the Address as a "giant (if benign) swindle."[2] Lincoln disagreed. For him, the Civil War did not constitute a "second American Revolution," but an extension of the first one, a resumption of the nation envisioned by the founders that had been diverted from its first principles by the corrosive influence of slavery. To Lincoln, the resounding assertion of the Declaration of Independence that "all men are created equal" did not come with an asterisk; its framers meant precisely what they wrote. And so did Lincoln.

The Gettysburg Address is indeed a sharp break from the past: not from the founders' vision, but from the language of compromise that had debased American politics almost since the nation's inception. This baneful rhetoric had become so habitual that historians have understandably taken it to be the nation's natural political idiom—as did many contemporaries. But Lincoln believed that most Americans felt otherwise, and that they would embrace his call for a return to the ideals of the Revolution. Viewed against the backdrop of the era of compromise, Lincoln's words at Gettysburg can be seen not as an exercise in deception, but as a return to first principles.

* * *

The president-elect's train reached Philadelphia on his way to Washington on Thursday, February 21, 1861. Alan Pinkerton, the private detective hired by the railroad to protect him, informed Lincoln that night that his agents in Baltimore had uncovered a plot to assassinate him when he changed trains in that city. To thwart the plotters, Pinkerton urged Lincoln to leave Philadelphia immediately and make for Baltimore ahead of schedule. Lincoln refused. "I can't go tonight," he declared. "I have engaged to raise the flag on to-morrow morning over Independence hall" and to speak at the Pennsylvania state house. "After these engagements are fulfilled you are at liberty to take such course as you please."[3]

That night Lincoln addressed the crowd that gathered around the Hotel Continental from his balcony, where he mentioned his intention "to consult, or, as it were, to listen to those breathings arising within the consecrated walls where the Constitution of the United States, and, I will add, the Declaration of American Independence were originally framed and adopted." He expressed his hope

> that I shall do nothing inconsistent with the teachings of these holy and most sacred walls. I have never asked anything that does not breathe from those walls. All my political warfare has been in favor of the teachings that come forth from these sacred walls. May my right hand forget its cunning and my tongue cleave to the roof of my mouth if ever I prove false to those teachings.

At seven o'clock the next morning, Lincoln walked into the room where the Declaration of Independence had been signed and a surge of emotion swept over him as he attended to the "breathings" of the long-dead founders. It was evident that his insistence on speaking at Independence Hall did not stem merely from his unwillingness to break a commitment.[4] February 22 was Washington's Birthday, and Lincoln had been asked to perform the ceremonial raising of the new thirty-four-star flag (adding one for Kansas, which had entered the Union a month earlier) as part of a day-long commemoration. Lincoln made clear in his address—brief, but almost twice the length of the Gettysburg Address—that his journey to Independence Hall marked an indispensable component of his passage to the capital. It was a pilgrimage, a solemn dedication of his administration to the founding principles adopted there in July 1776.

"I am filled with deep emotion at finding myself standing here, in this place," Lincoln began.

> I have never had a feeling politically that did not spring from the
> sentiments embodied in the Declaration of Independence . . . I have
> often inquired of myself what great principle or idea it was that kept
> this Confederacy so long together. It was not the mere matter of the
> separation of the Colonies from the motherland; but that sentiment
> in the Declaration of Independence which gave liberty, not alone to
> the people of this country, but, I hope, to the world, for all future time.

This universal principle—that all men are created equal, that they are endowed with the rights to life, liberty, and the pursuit of happiness—this,
for Lincoln, was the bedrock of the Union, the reason for its existence.

> Now, my friends, can this country be saved upon that basis? If it
> can, I will consider myself one of the happiest men in the world if I
> can help to save it. If it can't be saved upon that principle, it will be
> truly awful. But, if this country cannot be saved without giving up
> that principle—I was about to say I would rather be assassinated on
> this spot than to surrender it.

This somewhat unsettling avowal, clearly arising from the plausi-
ble threats Lincoln had received, strayed far from his resolution to avoid
any provocative statements before his swearing in. "My friends, this is
a wholly unprepared speech," he explained. "I may, therefore, have said
something indiscreet." ("No, no," his listeners shouted in reply.) But he
would not walk it back: "I have said nothing but what I am willing to live
by, and, in the pleasure of Almighty God, die by."[5]

When Lincoln finished, the Rev. Henry Steele Clark delivered a prayer,
and the president-elect removed his coat, rolled up his sleeves, spat on his
hands, and rubbed his palms together. As he tugged on the halyard, the
enormous flag rose smoothly into the sky, unfurling in the early-morning
breeze, the crowd shouting louder as the banner ascended. While can-
nons roared, the band broke into "The Star-Spangled Banner." Lincoln
was escorted from the stage, and the crowd dispersed.

But just as at Gettysburg thirty-three months later, Lincoln's role in
the celebration was intended only as a supporting one. The main event
began at eleven o'clock with the reading of Washington's Farewell Address, followed by a workingmen's procession of "Employés of the Indus-
trial Works," wearing black-and-crimson badges and marching in their
shops and crafts behind banners inscribed with "OUR UNION—NOW
AND FOREVER," "UNITED WE STAND—DIVIDED WE FALL," and, in

one case, "We the employés of Messrs. WILSON, CHILDS & CO., go for the Crittendon [*sic*] Compromise" on the front, and "UNION AND CON-CESSION" on the back.

The grand procession, led by Bierhalter's Cornet Band and the Scott Rifles, arrived back at National Hall at three o'clock. The assembly elected officers—somewhat sweaty and winded after their strenuous parade—and listened to a second reading of the Farewell Address, cheering Washington's admonition to "indignantly frown . . . upon the first dawning of every attempt to alienate any portion of our country from the rest." After this, the gathering of Philadelphia workingmen, "with a fervent and patriotic desire to assist in preserving the Union . . . now endangered by . . . wicked and evil-designing men, North and South," unanimously resolved "that we earnestly invoke zealous and energetic action at once by Congress, either by the adoption of the Crittenden, Bigler or Guthrie amendments, or by some other full and clear recognition of the equal rights of the South in the Territories."

Since "our Government never can be sustained by bloodshed, but must live in the affections of the people," the assembled mechanics and artisans proclaimed themselves unalterably hostile to war, whatever the cost. Further, they called for "the immediate repeal of all acts of the Assembly of Pennsylvania" inconsistent "with a spirit of friendliness to our sister States"—that is to say, laws ensuring the rights of blacks. After addresses by Union-loving emissaries from Kentucky and Virginia, the meeting called for the adoption of constitutional amendments that would "tend to secure peace and amity between the different states," and enjoined the members of the "Peace Convention" then meeting in Washington not to adjourn until they had submitted "some patriotic plan that the people will promptly adopt, and thus make our Union what it deserves to be—PERPETUAL."[6]

In the events of this February morning at the birthplace of the Republic, one can see the last throes of the era of compromise, which had held sway for almost three-quarters of a century, and the beginning of the return to revolutionary time: to the furnace of destructive and creative forces that forged the American nation, and its rechartering in the words of the Gettysburg Address.

*   *   *

In the Border States and the North, the language of compromise, the stilted vernacular of antebellum American politics, reached its apogee in the weeks between Lincoln's election and Inauguration Day. As the prospect of actual war drew closer, even committed Republicans began to lose their nerve and advocated concessions to the South. Lincoln was willing to pledge the government to enforce the Fugitive Slave Law and to call for the repeal of all state laws in conflict with it; but he adamantly rejected any compromise on the extension of slavery. This was the essential issue on which he had campaigned for the presidency, and he considered his election a mandate and a pledge. "On that point hold firm, as with a chain of steel," he wrote to a supporter, one of dozens of such letters before the inauguration.[7]

In his Inaugural Address, Lincoln adopted the language of the Washington's Birthday meeting of workingmen in Philadelphia and of countless other gatherings throughout the country calling for concession and compromise, quoting from the Republican Party platform on which he had been elected: "*Resolved*, That the maintenance inviolate of the rights of the States, and especially the right of each State to order and control its own domestic institutions according to its own judgment exclusively, is essential to that balance of power on which the perfection and endurance of our political fabric depend; and we denounce the lawless invasion by armed force of the soil of any State or Territory, no matter under what pretext, as among the gravest of crimes."[8] In retrospect, this passage may be seen as the final statement of the Era of Compromise, the closing declaration of "the Union as it was."

It has become fashionable to argue, as David Herbert Donald asserted, that "Lincoln's commitment to maintaining the Union was absolute."[9] Usually this claim, backed by numerous suggestive quotations, as well as the fact that slavery is not mentioned in the Gettysburg Address, is made to undercut Lincoln's supposed hostility to slavery. But it is plainly untrue. The Union had been formed by the people, Lincoln asserted, first by revolution, then by the ratification of the Constitution; and the people could undo both those acts: "This country, with its institutions, belongs to the people who inhabit it. Whenever they shall grow weary of the existing Government, they can exercise their *constitutional* right of amending it, or their *revolutionary* right to dismember or overthrow it." What was not legitimate was the secession of a minority from the whole:

A majority, held in restraint by constitutional checks and limitations, and always changing easily with deliberate changes of popular opinions and sentiments, is the only true sovereign of a free people. Whoever rejects it, does, of necessity, fly to anarchy or to despotism. Unanimity is impossible; the rule of a minority, as a permanent arrangement, is wholly inadmissible; so that, rejecting the majority principle, anarchy or despotism in some form is all that is left.[10]

The Union, in Lincoln's view, had the providential purpose, rooted in the propositions of the Declaration of Independence, of demonstrating that self-government was possible. If and when the Union could no longer advance that purpose, it no longer deserved to endure; indeed, it was already dead. If the price of union was the surrender of the principle of the rule of the majority; if, in terms specific to the present hour, Lincoln could only preserve the Union by "breaking his pledges, and surrendering to those who tried and failed to defeat him at the polls, this government and all popular government is already at an end."[11]

Lincoln himself provided a striking insight into the nature of his relationship to the Declaration in his speech at the Philadelphia flag raising when he quoted from Psalm 137: "'May my hand lose its cunning and my tongue cleave to the roof of my mouth,' if I ever prove false to these teachings." This is the well-known song of Israel's exile:

> *By the rivers of Babylon, there we sat down,*
> *yea, we wept, when we remembered Zion.*
> *We hanged our harps upon the willows in the midst thereof.*
> *For there they that carried us away captive required*
> *of us a song; and they that wasted us required of us mirth,*
> *saying, Sing us one of the songs of Zion.*
> *How shall we sing the Lord's song in a strange land?*
> *If I forget thee, O Jerusalem, let my right hand forget her cunning.*
> *If I do not remember thee, let my tongue cleave to the roof of my mouth;*
> *if I prefer not Jerusalem above my chief joy.*

Less well known, and much more rarely quoted, are the final three verses, which are also relevant here:

> *Remember, O Lord, the children of Edom in the day of Jerusalem;*
> *who said, Rase it, rase it, even to the foundation thereof.*
> *O daughter of Babylon, who art to be destroyed; happy shall he be,*
> *that rewardeth thee as thou hast served us.*
> *Happy shall he be, that taketh and dasheth thy little ones*
> *against the stones.*

If we follow Lincoln's figure to its source, then, he is envisioning the Declaration as Zion, and himself and his countrymen as the exiled Israelites. We should take the reference seriously because of Lincoln's pattern of employing biblical phrases to convey important truths. (It was one day earlier after all, at Trenton, the scene of the Christmastime battle that saved the Revolution, that Lincoln denominated Americans as the Almighty's "almost chosen people."[12]) Furthermore, this interpretation, while dramatic, is consistent with all of his pronouncements about the nation's founding document—including the prophecy that its enemies would suffer retribution: "If God wills that [this war] continue until all the wealth piled by the bondsman's two hundred and fifty years of unrequited toil shall be sunk, and until every drop of blood drawn with the lash shall be paid by another drawn with the sword, so still it must be said, 'the judgments of the Lord are true and righteous altogether.'"[13]

This is the essential context for grasping Lincoln's conception of compromise. The meaning and purpose of the Revolution was the validation of the Declaration's principle that "all men are created free and equal." A compromise was valid only so long as it preserved this indispensable principle. Thus in his Cooper Union Address, Lincoln asserted that the nation's framers marked slavery "as an evil not to be extended, but to be tolerated and protected only because of and so far as its actual presence among us makes that toleration and protection a necessity."[14] The function of the antebellum compromises, in Lincoln's understanding, was not to strike a balance between slavery and freedom; they preserved the Union until such time as it could finally fulfill its universal purpose.

To view the Union in this way, essentially as a nation exiled from its true promise as a vehicle for universal liberation, requires a certain temper of political imagination, "the substance of things hoped for, the evidence of things unseen," not especially common among antebellum politicians—nor, for that matter, the historians who study them. More typical was the belief in an unchanging Union, or at least, a Union, unchangeable for the better. "I go for the Constitution as it is, and for the Union as it is," Daniel Webster avowed in 1830, providing the watchword for a generation of conservatives. Perceptive slaveholders recognized that change was inevitable, and that any change was dangerous to their interests; thus John C. Calhoun, in 1832, asserted flatly that "the Southern section of this Union" was "rendered by local circumstances altogether incapable of change."[15] Long before Representative

John Quincy Adams in 1842 affirmed the right of Congress to abolish slavery in a time of domestic unrest—and ceaselessly ever afterward— Southerners feared the latent power of the Constitution to dismantle slavery. "What these Southern conservatives realized," R. Kent Newmyer observed, "—what historians have missed by focusing too much on the conservative motives of the framers of the Constitution and not enough on the document they framed—was that the Constitution of 1787 was a Trojan horse of radical social and economic transformation."[16] The truth of this statement was demonstrated by the fully constitutional election of November 6, 1861. It was the South, after all, that opted out of the compact.

What was at stake in the great showdowns settled by the compromises of the antebellum period? Not the balance of congressional representation of North and South, or the rate of a national tariff, much less a debate between slavery and freedom. All the crises, from Missouri onward, hinged on whether one or more of the slaveholding states would quit the Union. The "compromises" consisted in finding a legislative formula by which they would agree to stay; and each of these formulae further eroded the principles of the Declaration.

In essence, the contradiction between the persistence and growth of chattel slavery and the nation's founding principles of liberty and equality was intrinsically insoluble. Much as Americans sought a way around the dilemma, it could not be done without making a wreck of both principles. Indeed, much of antebellum American politics can be understood as the search for a solution to an insoluble problem—the attempt, as Robert J. Loewenberg has described it, "to keep the nation half slave and half free *in fact*," which had resulted in the "dreadful consequence" of becoming "half slave and half free *in principle*."[17] Morally, philosophically, and politically, this state of things was unsustainable.

This meant that for forty years, Americans came of age in a climate of rancorous politics punctuated with episodes of mortal danger to the Republic, catastrophe averted at the last moment by high-wire acts of legislative derring-do, usually performed by Kentucky's Henry Clay. These heart-stopping retreats from the precipice came to be denominated "compromises," earning Clay the title of "Great Compromiser," and came to seem conventional, if not routine. In retrospect, it even became possible to view this lurching from showdown to showdown as normative, and the resort to arms of 1861 as a tragic departure from tradition. "It was because we failed to do the thing we really have a genius for, which is compromise," the novelist Shelby Foote asserted, explaining the cause of the Civil War. "Our whole government's founded on it. And, it failed."[18]

Although this has the ring of eloquence (particularly as delivered in Foote's sagacious, avuncular Mississippi drawl), it demonstrates a fundamental misunderstanding of the nature of antebellum politics. (It would be useful for Civil War historians to have a stronger grounding in the events of the Early Republic, just as it would be beneficial for Early Republic historians to bear in mind that their period ended in civil war.)

Compromise can be viewed as an expedient, a workaround. In his famous essay "*Nomos* and Narrative," the late Robert Cover memorably described law "as a system of tension or a bridge linking a concept of a reality to an imagined alternative."[19] Particularizing and "Lincolnizing" Cover's figure, the American government appears a bridge of law from "the Union as it is" to Lincoln's Zion, a redeemed republic that has risen up to achieve its ultimate purpose: as a later American would put it, "to live out the true meaning of its creed."[20]

In the center of the bridge is a huge breach that blocks the way and threatens the integrity of the entire structure. To preserve the bridge, craftsmen cobble together a makeshift patch; it mars the bridge and obstructs passage, but it keeps it from collapsing.

Over time, the people become so used to the patch that they forget its purpose. Some, impatient to reach the other side, view it only as an obstacle and want to rip it up. Others, who have no desire to cross the bridge, find they can get what they want by threatening to burn it down. A third group has forgotten that the bridge has a destination and worship the patch as an end in itself.[21] Only a few remember that it is a *bridge*.

While the Allegory of the Bridge is inelegant, it captures Lincoln's understanding of the function of compromise and the indispensability of law as the underpinning of the nation. There can be no doubt that Lincoln viewed the American union as a means to an end and understood the long succession of unlovely compromises as temporary, if necessary, expedients. What is more, he was absolutely certain that the founders—the men who envisioned and designed the bridge—intended the American nation, "conceived in liberty, and dedicated to the proposition that 'all men are created equal,'" to advance the cause of liberty for all mankind.

*   *   *

The website Dictionary.com offers two very different meanings for the word "compromise":

> 1. a settlement of differences by mutual concessions; an agreement reached by adjustment of conflicting or opposing claims, principles, etc., by reciprocal modification of demands

and

> 2. an endangering, especially of reputation; exposure to danger, suspicion, etc.: *a compromise of one's integrity.*

Compromise is an unlovely word; it is often difficult to distinguish between the first variety and the second. In the context of the Early Republic, it is nearly impossible. It is hard today—it was difficult at the time—to reconcile Lincoln's soaring vision of the American Republic with his support for repugnant measures such as the Fugitive Slave Law and the proposed constitutional amendment barring Congress from interfering with slavery in the states. We can, I believe, gain an insight into Lincoln's understanding of compromise by taking seriously his admiration for the "Great Compromiser," Henry Clay, his "beau ideal of a statesman."[22]

Clay is a peculiarly inaccessible figure to twenty-first-century Americans. It is hard from his speeches to derive a sense of his skill as an orator; far more than Webster or Everett, whose masterful presence and delivery contemporaries regarded as essential to their power, Clay falls flat on the printed page. And unlike them, he did not look the part of the romantic hero. (In Matthew Brady's photographs from the 1840s, Clay bears an unfortunate resemblance to a genial Lon Chaney's Phantom.) And yet his reputation as a spellbinding speaker is on a par with theirs, and the devotion, even love, he engendered among his followers—Lincoln included—is perhaps unrivaled in American politics.

"To understand Clay's ideology," notes Daniel Walker Howe, "one must realize that 'compromise' and 'principle' are not necessarily opposites. For Clay, compromise was itself a principle; that is, he believed saving the Union was a matter of continual adjustment of competing interests."[23] This is correct, but it requires two corollaries. First, Clay pursued the principle of compromise as a means of *saving the Union*, not as an intrinsically useful aspect of politics. It is true that compromise is an essential feature of republican government—indeed, of all aspects of life, as Lincoln stressed in a lecture to law students: "Persuade your neighbors to compromise whenever you can."[24] But the kind of life-or-death brinksmanship that characterized antebellum crises should never be granted the status of conventional political behavior. Second, for Clay, as for Lincoln, saving the Union was not an absolute value; it only obtained for a Union worth saving.

Clay and Lincoln shared many core values. Like Lincoln, Clay believed that democracy did not consist simply of the will of the majority; it must be exercised through the rule of law. (It was this conviction that prompted Clay's politically damaging opposition to Andrew Jackson's Florida adventures, which Clay's first biographer believed destroyed his presidential hopes; and that secured Lincoln the presidential nomination over William H. Seward and his belief in a "higher law."[25]) Both Lincoln and Clay viewed government as a practical engine for improving the lives of its citizens, and both shared the conviction that the American Republic had a providential role to play in fostering liberty throughout the world. As Lincoln put it, Clay "loved his country partly because it was his own country, but mostly because it was a free country; and he burned with a zeal for its advancement, prosperity and glory, because he saw in such, the advancement, prosperity and glory, of human liberty, human right and human nature. He desired the prosperity of his countrymen partly because they were his countrymen, but chiefly to show to the world that freemen could be prosperous."[26]

Both were quintessential self-made men (Clay was even thought to have coined the term), with an immigrant's gratitude for the opportunities for advancement the nation had provided them; in an era when monarchies were still the rule, neither took this for granted.[27] Both were tall, homely Kentuckians (though one moved in, and one moved out) whose principal allegiance was always to their nation, not their state. Each viewed politics as public service, yet both relished the practice of the craft. (In this, though, Lincoln was the master; Daniel Walker Howe justly observed that "Clay has been overrated as a politician and underrated as a statesman."[28]) Clay's sincere assertion that he "would rather be right than President" testified powerfully to his passion to be right, since few individuals in the nation's history have coveted the office more. In this as well, Clay closely resembled the man whose ambition was "a little engine that knew no rest."[29]

When Clay died in 1852, Lincoln took the lead in organizing a memorial to his life in Springfield. The opening of his eulogy parallels strikingly—in theme if not in expression—the first two paragraphs of the Gettysburg Address:

On the fourth day of July, 1776, the people of a few feeble and oppressed colonies of Great Britain, inhabiting a portion of the Atlantic coast of North America, publicly declared their national independence, and made their appeal to the justice of their cause, and to the God of battles, for the maintainance [sic] of that declaration.	Four score and seven years ago, our fathers brought forth upon this continent a new nation, conceived in liberty, and dedicated to the proposition that all men are created equal.
Within the first year of that declared independence, and while its maintainance [sic] was yet problematical—	Now we are engaged in a great civil war, testing whether that nation, or any nation so conceived and so dedicated, can long endure.
while the bloody struggle between those resolute rebels, and their haughty would-be masters, was still waging . . .	We are met on a great battlefield of that war.

In his Clay oration, Lincoln speaks of a revolution that is long since past; at Gettysburg, he speaks in the midst of a revolution: but the parallels of language show that it is the same struggle.

In Lincoln's eulogy, the birth of freedom, still at risk in 1777, is coincidental with the birth of Henry Clay: "The infant nation, and the infant child began the race of life together." Clay and America are essentially described as siblings: "For three quarters of a century they have traveled hand in hand. They have been companions ever." The two have reached maturity; Clay has died, but the nation lives: "The nation has passed its perils, and is free, prosperous, and powerful."

The key here is this: *the nation has passed its perils*. Another way to state it is that Clay's heroic efforts to save the Union—resolving the Missouri crisis of 1819–1821, the nullification crisis of 1832–1833, and the territorial crisis of 1846–1850—have borne fruit and carried the nation to safety. Clay, the Great Pacificator, is the preeminent statesman of the Era of Compromise; but that era has come to a close.

In Lincoln's portrait, Henry Clay stands as the archetypal representative of the dutiful generation of the sons of the fathers—that diffident generation depicted by George B. Forgie, Fred Somkin, Joseph Ellis, and Joyce Appleby.[30] Born too late to reap the glory of founding the Republic, the highest achievement to which they could aspire would be to maintain it. In that limited sphere of action, Clay's greatness stood unchallenged. But Lincoln himself, in his 1838 Springfield Young Men's Lyceum Address, had disparaged that calling as pedestrian and unambitious (albeit as a young man, and before the perilous epoch of the late 1840s). In the heroic era of the founding, by contrast, "all that sought celebrity and fame, and distinction, expected to find them in the success of that experiment . . . Their ambition aspired to display before an admiring world, a practical demonstration of the truth of a proposition . . . *the capability of a people to govern themselves*." They proved it so and won their glory. "But the game is caught; and . . . with the catching, end the pleasures of the chase. This field of glory is harvested, and the crop is already appropriated."

Viewed from the vantage point of the Lyceum Address, then, Clay must be seen as one among those "whose ambition would aspire to nothing beyond a . . . presidential chair," a figure *"not [of] the family of the lion, or the tribe of the eagle"*—not a "towering genius" who "thirsts and burns for distinction" and "will have it, whether at the expense of emancipating slaves, or enslaving freemen."[31]

Many students of Lincoln have seen a veiled self-portrait in these words, an interpretation that gains strength from a passage Lincoln quoted in the eulogy for Clay from a laudatory obituary in a Democratic paper. While Lincoln asserts that "the nation has passed its perils," the Democratic editor has no such confidence: "Alas, in those dark hours . . . of peril and dread which our land has experienced, and which she may be called to experience again—to whom now may her people look up for that counsel and advice, which only wisdom and experience and patriotism can give, and which only the undoubting confidence of a nation can receive?" The editor allusively answers his own question: "Perchance, in the whole circle of the great and gifted of our land, there remains but one on whose shoulders the mighty mantle of the departed statesman may fall . . . brother, friend ever, yet in political sentiment, as far apart as party could make them. Ah, it is at times like these, that the petty distinctions of mere party disappear."[32] Clearly, the author is seeking to bestow the Great Compromiser's mantle on the Democrat Stephen A. Douglas, who had salvaged Clay's bills of 1850 and shepherded them to passage.

By quoting this familiar trope of the Little Giant as the successor to Henry Clay, Lincoln was far from endorsing the choice; but he was, indeed, affirming the idea of a deliverer, a national savior, while tacitly staking his own claim to be a far more loyal and logical heir to Clay's legacy. Out of politics for three years, Lincoln was signaling his ambition to step forward in the coming "dark hour of peril and dread" when the structure of compromise collapses: a "man possessed of the loftiest genius, coupled with ambition sufficient to push it to its utmost stretch."[33]

Lincoln had known for some time that the path of compromise had failed. "Experience has demonstrated, I think, that there is no peaceful extinction of slavery in prospect for us," he wrote a slaveholding Kentucky politician in 1855. "The signal failure of Henry Clay, and other good and great men, in 1849, to effect any thing in favor of gradual emancipation in Kentucky, together with a thousand other signs, extinguishes that hope utterly."

The nation's deepening accommodation with slavery negated the promise of the Republic and made a mockery of the Revolution:

> On the question of liberty, as a principle, we are not what we have been. When we were the political slaves of King George, and wanted to be free, we called the maxim that "all men are created equal" a self evident truth; but now when we have grown fat, and have lost all dread of being slaves ourselves, we have become so greedy to be *masters* that we call the same maxim "a self-evident lie." The fourth of July has not quite dwindled away; it is still a great day—*for burning fire-crackers!!*[34]

Prefiguring David Brion Davis's discussion of "the perishability of revolutionary time,"[35] Lincoln mourned:

> That spirit which desired the peaceful extinction of slavery, has itself become extinct, with the *occasion*, and the *men* of the Revolution.

Under the impulse of that occasion, nearly half the states adopted systems of emancipation at once; and it is a significant fact, that not a single state has done the like since. So far as peaceful, voluntary emancipation is concerned, the condition of the negro slave in America, scarcely less terrible to the contemplation of a free mind, is now as fixed, and hopeless of change for the better, as that of the lost souls of the finally impenitent. The Autocrat of all the Russias will resign his crown, and proclaim his subjects free republicans sooner than will our American masters voluntarily give up their slaves.[36]

When Lincoln delivered his eulogy for Henry Clay, he could not have known that the Era of Compromise would be killed off in two years by his rival for Clay's mantle, Stephen A. Douglas. His Kansas-Nebraska Bill of 1854 opened part of the Louisiana Territory to slavery, thereby abrogating the Missouri Compromise—a measure that, in 1850, Douglas had described as "a sacred thing, which no ruthless hand would ever be reckless enough to disturb."[37] By repealing the "solemn covenant" that had governed national expansion for more than a generation, Douglas had kicked out the supports from under the entire structure of sectional compromise—in a sense, returning the nation to the stark sectional showdown of 1819. The literal truth of this statement is attested by the fact that political pamphlets from the Missouri crisis were reprinted without commentary during the Kansas-Nebraska contest.[38] But in fact, Douglas's act did more than this: as Lincoln recognized, in putting slavery on an equal footing with freedom, it had the effect of nullifying the Revolution itself and returning America to a prerevolutionary state.

After the passage of the Kansas-Nebraska Act, Lincoln returned to politics with a single-mindedness he had not shown in any enterprise before. With logic, patience, passion, and humor, he laid out for a widening range of audiences the narrative of American history and the fatal direction in which it was heading. Where modern historians regard the Civil War and the campaign against slavery as a second American Revolution, Lincoln regarded the campaign to *extend* slavery as a revolution in reverse, an antirevolution that was rolling back and repealing the Republic "dedicated to the proposition that all men are created equal" that the founders had created. The Kansas-Nebraska Act functioned for Northerners much as Parliament's Declaratory Act of 1766 had for the colonists: it made explicit their subjection within the political order.

If the Kansas-Nebraska Act was the Declaratory Act of this Anti-Revolution, the *Dred Scott* decision three years later was its Proclamation for Suppressing Rebellion and Sedition. Chief Justice Taney's opinion closed off any possible avenue of compromise, in effect declaring opposition to the extension of slavery into the territories—the raison d'être of the Republican Party—unconstitutional and out of bounds. Taney did this, as Lincoln demonstrated in his Springfield speech of June 27, 1857, by inventing a through-the-looking-glass account of the founding era in which the framers believed that Africans were "so far inferior that they had no rights which the white man was bound to respect,"[39] and then interpreting the Constitution on the basis of this spurious "original intent." To the contrary, Lincoln argued, the oppression of blacks was worse now than ever before. "In those days, our Declaration of Independence was held sacred by all, and thought to include all; but now, to aid in making the bondage of the negro universal and eternal, it is assailed and sneered at, and construed, and hawked at, and torn, till, if its framers could rise from their graves, they could not at all recognize it . . . It is grossly incorrect to say or assume, that the public estimate of the negro is more favorable now than it was at the origin of this government."[40]

In language again prefiguring the Gettysburg Address, Lincoln described Douglas's "anti-founding" of the nation: "Three years and a half ago, Judge Douglas brought forward his famous Nebraska bill," dedicated, in effect, to the proposition that the drafters of "the Declaration of Independence . . . referred to the white race alone, and not to the African, when they declared all men to have been created equal." Lincoln parsed the "mangled ruin" Douglas's interpretation made "of our once glorious Declaration":

I had thought the Declaration contemplated the progressive improvement in the condition of all men everywhere; but no, it merely "was adopted for the purpose of justifying the colonists in the eyes of the civilized world in withdrawing their allegiance from the British crown, and dissolving their connection with the mother country." Why, that object having been effected some eighty years ago, the Declaration is of no practical use now—mere rubbish—old wadding left to rot on the battle-field after the victory is won.[41]

Garry Wills described the Gettysburg Address as "the recontracting of our society on the basis of the Declaration as our fundamental charter."

To Wills, Lincoln's interpretation of the Declaration as the founding idea of "government of the people, by the people, and for the people" was "a very nice myth," a "useful falsehood."[42] Wills elaborated on this thesis in detail in *Lincoln at Gettysburg*, arguing that Lincoln's performance there constituted "one of the most daring acts of open-air sleight-of-hand ever witnessed by the unsuspecting . . . a giant (if benign) swindle."[43] Similarly, George P. Fletcher divined a "secret constitution" of the American nation, articulated by Lincoln at Gettysburg and promulgated in the Thirteenth, Fourteenth, and Fifteenth Amendments. A bemused Allen Guelzo has noted that in stressing the radicalism and innovation of Lincoln's conception of the American Republic, Lincoln's liberal interpreters have ironically adopted the reactionary outlook of twentieth-century conservative critics such as Wilmoore Kendall and M. E. Bradford[44]—although the liberals celebrate what they take to be Lincoln's ideological legerdemain instead of condemning it.[45]

But how valid is this interpretation? It is logical if one accepts Stephen A. Douglas's argument that the Declaration applied only to white British Americans, or Chief Justice Taney's assertion that the framers intended to erect "a perpetual and impassable barrier . . . between the white race and the one which they had reduced to slavery, and governed as subjects with absolute and despotic power."[46] If Douglas and Taney were right, then the Constitution is indeed Garrison's "covenant with death" and "agreement with hell," and Rufus Choate was correct that the Declaration is no more than "glittering and sounding generalities of natural right." Who is to say that the Gettysburg Address is not merely a masterful piece of equalitarian propaganda with no organic connection to the American founding?

The problem with this view—apart from its towering cynicism—is that it abstracts the Address from the political and oratorical setting in which it appeared. Lincoln's 272 words were not uttered in a vacuum. They constituted a distillation of his assertions about the meaning of the Union, honed and polished over more than a decade of thorough and comprehensive disputation with the preeminent spokesman for the opposing side—taken together, the most penetrating symposium on democracy history has afforded. The dispute between Lincoln and Douglas—the entire contest, not merely the celebrated Senate debates of 1858—is unmatched in elucidating the essential questions at stake in the American enterprise. In the early years, the two had only Springfield as spectators, then the state of Illinois, and eventually the entire nation. Lincoln's conception of America and Douglas's had a full airing, free from spin doctors and soft-money propaganda campaigns, and the American electorate—going to the polls in numbers never seen before, and in percentages never seen since—made their choice. If the electoral process and the constitutional order count for something, Lincoln's well-articulated understanding of the meaning of the American nation and its founding documents, far from being "smuggled in," received a decisive mandate from the American people—first with their votes, and then with their blood.[47]

The Gettysburg Address can be best understood in juxtaposition with the First Inaugural Address—and vice versa. In the opening salutation of his Inaugural Address, "Fellow-Citizens of the United States," echoing the Constitution's "We, the People," Lincoln signaled a decisive nationalism—unlike all his predecessors, eight of whom had addressed their audience as "Fellow-Citizens" alone, and five of whom employed no salutation.[48]

While Lincoln nowhere quoted the Declaration of Independence in the Inaugural, it courses silently just below the text. As observed above, he reassured the South by quoting the fourth plank from the Chicago Republican Platform promising noninterference with slavery:

> *Resolved,* That the maintenance inviolate of the rights of the States, and especially the right of each State to order and control its own domestic institutions according to its own judgment exclusively, is essential to that balance of power on which the perfection and endurance of our political fabric depend; and we denounce the lawless invasion by armed force of the soil of any State or Territory, no matter under what pretext, as among the gravest of crimes.

Many in his audience, however, would recall the *second* resolution of that platform:

> That the maintenance of the principles promulgated in the Declaration of Independence and embodied in the Federal Constitution, "That all men are created equal; that they are endowed by their Creator with certain inalienable rights; that among these are life, liberty, and the pursuit of happiness; that to secure these rights, governments are instituted among men, deriving their just powers

from the consent of the governed"—is essential to the preservation
of our Republican institutions.[49]

For generations, defenders of slavery and their Northern doughface supporters had taken refuge in a pro-slavery-inflected, self-described "strict"
construction of the Constitution; the first national Republican president
took office on the principle of the intrinsic connection between the Declaration and the Constitution—the "apple of gold" within the "picture of
silver."[50]

Lincoln devoted nearly a quarter of the Inaugural Address to assur-
ances to the people of the South that their constitutional rights would
be respected, and the Fugitive Slave Law enforced—albeit with "all the
safeguards of liberty known in civilized and humane jurisprudence" applied to prevent the rendition of a free person as a slave, and with the
constitutional provision that "the citizens of each State shall be entitled to
all privileges and immunities of citizens in the several States" enforced.
Here he points to the constitutional clause, in Article IV, Section 2, most
in concord with what he takes to be the essence of the Declaration. (Since
1821 and the second Missouri Compromise, this clause had been trampled on by Congress and the Southern states, particularly with regard to
blacks; but a right withheld is a right nonetheless.)

In his assertion that "the Union is much older than the Constitution,"
Lincoln again silently invokes that document as authority. "It was formed,
in fact, by the Articles of Association in 1774." This can be derived from
Article II, Section 1, which requires that any person eligible to be presi-
dent must "have been fourteen Years a Resident within the United States."
Counting back fourteen years from the first election in 1788 brings us
to 1774. (One can hardly believe that Washington was constitutionally
unqualified to serve.) Thus the Union, "matured and continued by the
Declaration of Independence in 1776," precedes the nation as well as the
Constitution.

This somewhat scholastic argument for the perpetuity of the Union is
followed by a curiously Thomistic one. One proof of the existence of God,
Aquinas asserted, stems from the fact that "that which exists actually
and mentally is greater than that which exists only mentally. Therefore,
since as soon as the word 'God' is understood it exists mentally, it also
follows that it exists actually."[51] Similarly, Lincoln argued that "one of the
declared objects for ordaining and establishing the Constitution was 'to
form a more perfect Union.' But if destruction of the Union by one or by a

part only of the States be lawfully possible, the Union is less perfect than before the Constitution, having lost the vital element of perpetuity."[52]

What Lincoln is undertaking here is an almost algebraic demonstration of the unity of the revolutionary project—from First Continental Congress through Declaration of Independence, Articles of Confederation, and Constitution. He unhesitatingly affirms the "revolutionary right" of the people to overthrow the government if circumstances warrant it: "acts of violence, within any State or States, against the authority of the United States, are insurrectionary or revolutionary, according to circumstances."[53] In the present circumstance, given the nature of the Revolution that founded the American Union, a revolt against the legitimate constitutional order was insurrection, to be suppressed by national authority, just as any nation has the right to defend its existence. In the case of the United States, however, the stakes were infinitely higher—whether a nation "dedicated to the proposition that all men are created equal" could "long endure."

Lincoln recognized that the essential question of the impending war was the same as that of the Revolution—that, indeed, they were the same struggle. But this time the outcome of the struggle was to be "a more perfect Union," not a "separate and equal station." The contrasts with the Declaration—never far beneath the surface of Lincoln's address—are telling. Echoing the Declaration's sage observation "that mankind are more disposed to suffer, while evils are sufferable, than to right themselves by abolishing the forms to which they are accustomed," Lincoln asks his dissatisfied countrymen, "Will you hazard so desperate a step while there is any possibility that any portion of the ills you fly from have no real existence? Will you, while the certain ills you fly to are greater than all the real ones you fly from, will you risk the commission of so fearful a mistake?"[54]

In his first draft, Lincoln closed his speech by posing a stark alternative to the South: "Shall it be peace, or a sword?"[55] His former rival and designee for secretary of state, William Seward, once the party's notorious antislavery "ultra" and now its most prominent advocate of compromise, suggested appending a less belligerent conclusion. Lincoln reshaped Seward's passage, fashioned of sentimental and stilted Victorian language studded with evocative and moving images, into a transcendent vision of a republic not just redeemed but sacralized:

> I am loth to close. We are not enemies, but friends. We must not be enemies. Though passion may have strained it must not break

our bonds of affection. The mystic chords of memory, stretching from every battlefield and patriot grave to every living heart and hearthstone all over this broad land, will yet swell the chorus of the Union, when again touched, as surely they will be, by the better angels of our nature.[56]

Lincoln's language looks forward from the current conflict not merely to a future of national harmony but to a moment outside time.[57] The "mystic chords of memory" that link the revolutionary dead to "every living heart and hearthstone" are both musical chords (they will "swell the chorus of the Union") and tangible ones (they can be "touched").[58] While not literally quoting any passage of scripture, the words are evocative of many: the chords and angels call to mind Jacob's ladder, with its angels ascending and descending (Genesis 28:12–16); the vision of Isaiah's seraphim, chanting "Holy, holy, holy, is the Lord of hosts" (Isaiah 6:1–4); or Ezekiel's vision of a restored spiritual temple measured with a cord of flax (Ezekiel 40:4–49). Perhaps most importantly, Lincoln has, a priori, given meaning to the sacrifice of the "honored dead" who are soon to fill new battlefields and patriot graves.

With the first shot at Fort Sumter, the Era of Compromise came to a decisive end. Indeed, as James Moorhead has shown, many of the most bloodthirsty advocates of unconditional Confederate surrender were Northern clergymen who had preached concession to the last.[59] As in the weeks after September 11, 2001, oceans of American flags engulfed the nation; even the arch-compromiser Edward Everett, at a flag-raising in Boston three weeks after Sumter, remarked on "a patriotic unity not witnessed in 1775."[60] A compulsion toward conciliation shifted seamlessly into a zeal for retribution. The language of compromise now became an emblem of Copperheadism. Rapidly, "the Union as it was" was becoming as difficult to conceptualize as a Union purged of slavery had been only weeks before.

For Lincoln, in the chronology of revolutionary time, the Battle of Gettysburg, the supreme blood sacrifice of the war, taking place on Pennsylvania soil three days before Independence Day, was not merely symbolic: it was an act of rededication and redemption.[61] Today we can review Lincoln's words in the calm serenity of hindsight as a unique historical document; in the midst of war, they would take their place in the cacophony of meaning with the myriad of soldiers' letters, newspaper headlines, casualty lists, funeral orations, and the wounded soldiers themselves—"orators," as Lincoln described them, whose "very appearance spoke louder than tongues."[62] For those who heard or read his remarks in the midst of this, Lincoln's words would not "remake America"; they would underscore and illuminate the process of remaking that was all around them.

As we have seen, Lincoln was good at dedications and appears to have enjoyed them: a useful trait for a politician. In this he differed from Henry Clay, his "beau ideal." As a rule, as Lincoln noted in his eulogy, Clay did not "do" ceremonial occasions; oratory for its own sake he left to the professionals like Webster and Everett. "He never delivered a Fourth of July oration, or an eulogy on an occasion like this." But Lincoln clearly took inspiration from Clay in composing the Address: "As a politician or statesman, no one was so habitually careful to avoid all sectional ground. Whatever he did, he did for the whole country."[63]

These thoughts must have been on Lincoln's mind when he read the formal invitation from David Wills, the cemetery's organizer. "Sir," it began, "the several States having soldiers in the Army of the Republic, who were killed at the Battle of Gettysburg . . . have procured grounds on a prominent part of the Battle Field for a Cemetery." Wills worked closely with the governors of the states with "soldier-dead on the battlefield," and it was under their auspices that the cemetery was created. This was a perfectly normal way to view the fallen, who had been recruited by state agency and had served in state units. For most purposes, the states were the operative form of government; indeed, Lincoln had been invited in their name. Yet in the Address, Lincoln employed the word "nation" five times—more than any other noun—and spoke the word "state" not once.

"These Grounds will be Consecrated and set apart to this Sacred purpose," Wills had continued, "by appropriate Ceremonies, on Thursday, the 19th instant . . . It is the desire that, after the Oration, you, as Chief Executive of the Nation, formally set apart these grounds to their sacred use by a few appropriate remarks."[64] As at the flag raising at Independence Hall in 1861, Lincoln officially was to have only a small supporting role.

As in Philadelphia, he began with an evocation of the moment of independence and its universal import:

> *Four score and seven years ago our fathers brought forth on this continent, a new nation, conceived in Liberty, and dedicated to the proposition that all men are created equal.*

Now we are engaged in a great civil war, testing whether that nation, or any nation so conceived and so dedicated, can long endure.

Lincoln seemed to have the words of David Wills's invitation in mind when he stated:

We are met on a great battlefield of that war. We have come to dedicate a portion of that field, as a final resting place for those who here gave their lives that that nation might live. It is altogether fitting and proper that we should do this.

But, in a larger sense, we can not dedicate, we can not consecrate, we can not hallow this ground. The brave men, living and dead, who struggled here, have consecrated it, far above our poor power to add or detract.

These words, stately and eloquent as they sound today, would have had a compelling emotional resonance at that time and place that we can hardly imagine.

The world will little note, nor long remember what we say here, but it can never forget what they did here.

This was not ingenuousness or false modesty. Lincoln was not referring principally to his three-minute contribution to the three-hour-long program, but to the entire ceremony, from the introductory music by Bingfield's Band and the prayer by the Rev. T. H. Stockton, D.D., to Alfred Delaney's "Dirge" and the final benediction by Pennsylvania College's president H. L. Baugher.[65] And indeed, every other part of the day's events, Edward Everett's imposing oration included, has been swept from memory.

It is for us the living, rather, to be dedicated here to the unfinished work which they who fought here have thus far so nobly advanced. It is rather for us to be here dedicated to the great task remaining before us—that from these honored dead we take increased devotion to that cause for which they gave the last full measure of devotion—

For more than seven decades, the work of patriotic Americans was holding the Union together—repairing the compromised, unlovely patch that sustained the bridge. Now the "unfinished work" was constructing the nation that had taken its place—rebuilding the unobstructed bridge, sus-pended upon "mystic chords of memory."

It is instructive that, like "state," Lincoln never uttered the word "Union" in the Gettysburg Address. That word possessed a defensive quality; in the mouths of Webster, Jackson, Clay, Benton, Houston, and so many other statesmen, it explicitly or implicitly countered *"disunion"*—as it would in the election campaign of 1864, when Republicans abandoned their party label and ran under the banner of the National Union Party, to draw a contrast with the supposedly disunionist and partisan Democrats. But here, at Gettysburg, defending the old confederacy of states was done.

One last time, Lincoln harkened back to his First Inaugural and to the decades of the regime of concession of which it marked the end. "Re-solved," he had quoted then, "That the maintenance inviolate of the rights of the States, and especially the right of each State to order and control its own domestic institutions according to its own judgment exclusively, is essential to that balance of power on which the perfection and endurance of our political fabric depend."[66]

The Era of Compromise had served its purpose. But now, the expe-dients, the ultimatums, and the obfuscations were at an end. In place of the temporizing resolution of the 1860 Republican platform, Lincoln now could substitute an uncompromising resolution that still makes its claims on us today:

That we here highly resolve that these dead shall not have died in vain— that this nation, under God, shall have a new birth of freedom—and that government of the people, by the people, for the people, shall not perish from the earth.

Notes

1. George P. Fletcher, *Our Secret Constitution: How Lincoln Redefined American Democracy* (New York: Oxford University Press, 2001).

2. Garry Wills, *Lincoln at Gettysburg: The Words That Remade America* (New York: Simon & Schuster, 1992), 38.

3. Douglas L. Wilson et al., eds., "Norman B. Judd (William H. Herndon Interview)" in *Herndon's Informants: Letters, Interviews, and Statements About Abraham Lincoln* (Urbana: University of Illinois Press, 1998), http://lincoln.lib.niu.edu/file.php?file=herndon432.html.

4. *Philadelphia Inquirer*, Feb. 23, 1861, 2.

5. *Collected Works of Abraham Lincoln*, ed. Roy P. Basler, 9 vols. (New Brunswick, NJ: Rutgers University Press, 1953–1955), 4:240–241 (hereafter cited as *CW*).

6. *Philadelphia Inquirer*, Feb. 23, 1861, 1.

7. Lincoln to Elihu B. Washburne, Dec. 13, 1860, *CW*, 4:151; Harold Holzer, *Lincoln President-Elect: Abraham Lincoln and the Great Secession Winter 1860–1861* (New York: Simon & Schuster, 2008).

8. *CW*, 4:263.

9. David Herbert Donald, *Lincoln* (New York: Touchstone, 1995), 269.

10. "First Inaugural Address—Final Text," *CW*, 4:268.

11. "First Inaugural Address—First Edition and Revisions," *CW*, 4:259.

12. Address to the New Jersey Senate at Trenton, NJ, Feb. 21, 1861, *CW*, 4:236.

13. Second Inaugural Address, *CW*, 8:333.

14. *CW*, 3:535.

15. [John C. Calhoun], "Report of the Committee, to whom was Referred the Act to Provide for the Calling of a Convention of the People of this State, &c.," in *The Statutes at Large of South Carolina*, ed. Thomas Cooper, vol. 1 (Columbia, SC, 1836), 312.

16. R. Kent Newmyer, "John Marshall and the Southern Constitutional Tradition," in *An Uncertain Tradition: Constitutionalism and the History of the South*, ed. Kermit L. Hall and James W. Ely, Jr. (Athens: University of Georgia Press, 1989), 115.

17. Robert J. Loewenberg, *Freedom's Despots: The Critique of Abolitionism* (Durham, NC: Carolina Academic Press, 1976), 10.

18. Ken Burns, *The Civil War* (PBS television series, 1990), episode 1.

19. Cover, "*Nomos* and Narrative," *Harvard Law Review* 97 (Nov. 1983): 9.

20. Martin Luther King, Jr., speech at the Lincoln Memorial, Aug. 28, 1963.

21. This group had a large following at the time and continues to generate a substantial body of influential scholarship

22. First debate with Stephen A. Douglas at Ottawa, IL, Aug. 21, 1858, *CW*, 3:29.

23. Daniel Walker Howe, *The Political Culture of the American Whigs* (Chicago: University of Chicago Press, 1984), 124–125.

24. *CW*, 2:81.

25. Calvin Colton, ed., *Works of Henry Clay, Comprising His Life, Correspondence and Speeches*, vol. 5 (New York: Henry Clay Publishing, 1897), 179.

26. "Eulogy on Henry Clay," July 6, 1852, *CW*, 2:127.

27. This point is well articulated in the history podcast *BackStory*, "Civil War 150th: II. Why They Fought," March 31, 2001, http://backstoryradio.org/shows/why-they-fought/.

28. Howe, *American Whigs*, 124.

29. William Herndon and Jesse W. Weik, *Herndon's Life of Lincoln* (New York, 1930), 304.

30. George B. Forgie, *Patricide in the House Divided: A Psychological Interpretation of Lincoln and His Age* (New York: Norton, 1979); Fred Somkin, *Unquiet Eagle: Memory and Desire in the Idea of American Freedom, 1815–1860* (Ithaca, NY: Cornell University Press, 1967); Joseph Ellis, *After the Revolution: Profiles of Early American Culture* (New York: Norton, 1979); and Joyce Oldham Appleby, *Inheriting the Revolution: The First Generation of Americans* (Cambridge: Belknap Press, 2000).

31. *CW*, 1:113–14.

32. "Eulogy on Henry Clay."

33. *CW*, 1:114.

34. *CW*, 2:318.

35. David Brion Davis, *The Problem of Slavery in the Age of Revolution* (Ithaca, NY: Cornell University Press, 1975), 306–326;

36. *CW*, 2:318.

37. Quoted in Robert Walter Johanssen, *Stephen A. Douglas* (Urbana and Chicago: University of Illinois Press, 1997), 255.

38. Robert Pierce Forbes, *The Missouri Compromise and Its Aftermath: Slavery and the Meaning of America* (Chapel Hill: University of North Carolina Press, 2007), 279.

39. *Dred Scott v. Sandford*, 407.

40. Speech at Springfield, IL, June 26, 1857, *CW*, 2:404.

41. *CW*, 2:407.

42. Garry Wills, *Inventing America: Jefferson's Declaration of Independence* (New York: Mariner, 2002 [first published 1978]), xviii, xix.

43. Wills, *Lincoln at Gettysburg*, 38.

44. Fletcher, *Our Secret Constitution* (New York: Oxford University Press, 2001), passim; Allen C. Guelzo, "Apple of Gold in a Picture of Silver: The Constitution and Liberty," in *The Lincoln Enigma: The Changing Faces of an American Icon*, ed. Gabor Boritt (New York: Oxford University Press, 2001), 86–107.

45. Not the least of the ironies implicit in this outlook is that its adherents attribute to Lincoln a kind of Straussian esoteric agenda, while the Straussian scholar Harry Jaffa has demonstrated the clarity, logic, and democratic essence of Lincoln's political philosophy. See *Crisis of the House Divided* (New York: Doubleday, 1959) and *A New Birth of Freedom* (Lanham, MD: Rowman & Littlefield, 2004).

46. Decision of Chief Justice Roger B. Taney, *Dred Scott v. Sandford*, http://www.law.cornell.edu/supremecourt/text/60/393#writing-USSC_CR_0060_0393_ZO.

47. For an excellent statement of this view, see James L. Huston, "The Lost Cause of the North: A Reflection on Lincoln's Gettysburg Address and the Second Inaugural," *Journal of the Abraham Lincoln Association* 33 (Winter 2012): 14–37. Also see Lewis E. Lehrman, *Lincoln at Peoria: The Turning Point: Getting Right with the Declaration of Independence* (Mechanicsburg, PA: Stackpole Books, 2008).

48. Washington addressed "Fellow-Citizens of the Senate and of the House of Representatives;" Jefferson "Friends and Fellow-Citizens"; Pierce "My Countrymen." Both Adamses, Madison, Harrison, and Taylor omitted any salutation.

49. *CW*, 4:262–263.

50. "Fragment on the Constitution and the Union," *CW*, 4:168–169.

51. Thomas Aquinas, *Summa Theologica*, Part 1, Question 2.

52. "First Inaugural Address—Final Text," *CW*, 4:265.

53. Ibid.

54. *CW*, 4:266–267.

55. *CW*, 4:261.

56. *CW*, 4:271.

57. See Robert Cover's discussion of the creation of a *nomos*, a "normative universe": "Yet form the mundane flow of our real commonalities, we may purport to distill some purer essence of unity, to create in our imaginations a *nomos* completely transparent—built from crystals completely pure. In this transparent *nomos*, that which must be done, the meaning of that which must be done, and the sources of the common commitment to the doing of it stand bare, in need of no explication, no interpretation—obvious at once and to all. As long as it stands revealed, this dazzling clarity of legal meaning can harbor no mere interpretation." Cover, "*Nomos* and Narrative," 14.

58. Garry Wills usefully notes that "Lincoln spelled 'chord' and 'cord' interchangeably—they are the same etymologically." Yet he is incorrect that they are "not musical *sounds*" as well. *Lincoln at Gettysburg*, 159.

59. James Moorhead, *American Apocalypse: Yankee Protestants and the Civil War 1860–1869* (New Haven: Yale University Press, 1978), 54.

60. *New York Times*, May 5, 1861.

61. Thus Harry S. Stout: "Only as casualties rose to unimaginable levels did it dawn on some people that something mystically religious was taking place, a sort of massive sacrifice on the national altar. The Civil War taught Americans that they really were a Union, and it absolutely required a baptism of blood to unveil transcendent dimensions of that union." *Upon the Altar of the Nation: A Moral History of the Civil War* (New York: Viking, 2006), xvi.

62. Gabor Boritt, *The Gettysburg Gospel: The Lincoln Speech That Nobody Knows* (New York: Simon & Schuster, 2006), 12.

63. *CW*, 2:126.

64. Harold Holzer, *Dear Mr. Lincoln: Letters to the President* (Carbondale: Southern Illinois Press, 2006), 287.

65. The order of exercises is printed in Boritt, *Gettysburg Gospel*, 234.

66. *CW*, 4:263.

3

Democracy at Gettysburg

Sean Wilentz

AT GETTYSBURG, ABRAHAM Lincoln famously proclaimed the expanded goals for which the North was fighting. With his speech's mention of "a new birth of freedom," he affirmed the nation's commitment to abolishing slavery, which had become a second war aim alongside preserving the Union. Yet the speech also changed the very meaning of America. By citing the Declaration of Independence and not the US Constitution as the nation's cornerstone—defined, he said, by "the proposition that all men are created equal"—Lincoln singlehandedly (and sneakily) recast the American creed along more egalitarian lines.[1]

The second of these claims, though, is erroneous and the first is incomplete. Whatever else Lincoln may have said at Gettysburg, the idea that the Declaration contained the nation's fundamental political principles had been a staple of antislavery politics at least since the outbreak of the Missouri crisis in 1819. The second plank of the Republican platform on which Lincoln ran in 1860 repeated the assertion. As president, Lincoln entrenched the idea as no other previous figure had or could, but he neither invented it nor smuggled it into his remarks at Gettysburg. Having borrowed it from earlier antislavery politicians, he had been expounding the idea for nearly a decade. At Gettysburg, he repeated yet again what had long since become a set piece in his speeches as well as in the politics of the Republican Party. The Gettysburg Address hardly amounted to what one historian has called "one of the most daring acts of open-air sleight-of-hand ever witnessed by the unsuspecting."[2]

As for Northern war aims, the Address is remarkably circumspect with regard to both the Union and slavery. It contains not a single explicit reference to saving the Union, although no one could doubt that this remained one of Lincoln's overriding goals. Its one allusion to slavery seems nearly as clear-cut as it was important, yet Lincoln did not use the word. This is not surprising given the continuing displeasure among many Northerners about the Emancipation Proclamation he had issued nearly eleven months earlier.

The Address's most emphatic and now iconic passage came at the very end, and it concerned neither the Union nor slavery per se: the great cause for which the Union dead had given the last full measure of devotion, Lincoln said, was to prevent government of, by, and for the people from perishing with them. A familiar word for this form of government, then and (even more) now, is democracy. And although the three were entwined, preserving the Union and abolishing slavery were not exactly the same as securing democracy. Abolishing slavery had become in itself a crucial explicit goal, but it also served as a means to vindicate democracy. And although the concepts of democracy and the Union were tightly linked, they were also distinct: Union, in the American context, was an indispensable condition for the practice and preservation of democratic government.

Much as he did with the word "slavery," Lincoln had his reasons to avoid "democracy" at Gettysburg. But whatever word or words he used, Lincoln took the occasion to proclaim that the Union was determined to preserve democracy. It was a point that he and many other Northerners had made often, even before the attack on Fort Sumter. But never, before or after, would Lincoln make the point as emphatically as he did at Gettysburg. Here, at the core of the Gettysburg Address, was something akin to a third transcendent war aim—saving democracy—that to achieve required crushing secession and freeing the slaves.[3]

* * *

The Address's avoidance of the word "democracy" is not mysterious. Since the election of Andrew Jackson in 1828, the political party that Jackson and his supporters established had been known as the Democratic Party or, more familiarly, the Democracy. Lincoln, a life-long Whig partisan until the Whig Party ceased to exist in 1854, had little good to say about Jackson's Democracy. As a Republican, he had nothing good to say about the slaveholder-dominated Democracy of the 1850s, stripped of its Northern antislavery adherents.

So thoroughly had the Democratic Party blurred the distinction, though, that a veteran party man like Lincoln found it difficult to refer to democracy as a form of government without creating confusion, at least in his own mind. Lincoln's published collected works contain 527 separate entries using the word "democracy" or "democratic." Virtually all refer to the political party and not a political system. "But great is Democracy in its resources;" he wrote to his friend and supporter Anson G. Henry as the 1860 campaign heated up, "and it may yet give its fortunes a turn."[4] As ever, Lincoln meant the Democracy, and not democracy.

Lincoln preferred terms like "self-government," "free government," or "popular government," which also frequently appeared in other political leaders' speeches and in the partisan press. "Allow ALL the governed an equal voice in the government," he said in his famous Peoria speech in 1854, "and that, and that only, is self government." The "common object" of the slaveholders and their political supporters, he wrote in some fragmentary notes, probably in 1858, "is to subvert, in the public mind, and in the practical administration, our old and only standard of free government, that 'all men are created equal.'" The Southern rebellion, he charged in his first Annual Message to Congress, "is largely, if not exclusively, a war upon the first principle of popular government—the rights of the people."[5]

One of the rare occasions when Lincoln departed from his usual practice came when he spoke as president, in his message to the special session of Congress that convened on July 4, 1861. Lincoln used the word almost off-handedly, but the example was telling. The issue of secession, Lincoln wrote, "presents to the whole family of man, the question, whether a constitutional republic, or a democracy—a government of the people, by the same people—can, or cannot, maintain its territorial integrity, against its own domestic foes."[6] By using "constitutional republic" and "democracy" as bywords, as if testing out which fit best, Lincoln affirmed the inexactness and multiplicity of the American political vocabulary in 1861. Without question, though, more than two years before the Gettysburg Address, Lincoln had begun devising his famous phrase about "government of" and "by the people"—he had only to include the ineffable "for"—in order to describe democracy.[7] He also made it clear that, from the very start of the conflict, he had perceived secession and the crisis of the Union as a crisis of democracy.

At Gettysburg, Lincoln connected democracy's preservation with "a new birth of freedom," and on one earlier occasion, Lincoln appears to have defined the word "democracy" in direct opposition to slavery. The provenance of the tantalizing document is questionable, as is the date, although the editors of his collected works conjectured that he wrote it on August 1, 1858. "As I would not be a *slave*, so I would not be a *master*," the scrap of paper reads, apparently in Lincoln's handwriting. "This expresses my idea of democracy. Whatever differs from this, to the extent of the difference, is no democracy."[8]

If Lincoln indeed wrote these words, he understood the meaning of democracy to embrace legal and social relations between humans as well as a political system: a democratic polity could never tolerate the essentially undemocratic condition of masters and slaves. By this definition, the slave South was no democracy. And by this definition, the crisis of democracy predated Southern secession. Six weeks before he purportedly wrote these words, Lincoln commenced his senatorial campaign against Stephen A. Douglas. Just as "a house divided against itself cannot stand," he declared, he believed that "this government cannot endure, permanently, half *slave* and half *free*."[9] According to the later definition of democracy, this also would have meant that the government could not endure half *democratic* and half *nondemocratic*. The growing conflict over slavery in the 1850s would inherently have been a struggle for democracy, as it would have been since the nation's founding.

Lincoln expressed this particular formulation about slavery and democracy nowhere else in his writings. Yet at Gettysburg, he concluded by extolling both the nation's "new birth of freedom" and democracy's preservation as if one followed from the other. And the idea that slavery was undemocratic—both the relation between master and slave, and the polity and legal structures built on that relation—was commonplace among antislavery Northerners before war began as well as after. The slave South was an oligarchy that oppressed negro slaves and the "great mass" of its white population, Horace Greeley's influential *New-York Daily Tribune* observed; and so the war involved a collision "between democracy on the one hand, and this foreign element and doubly aristocratical institution of negro slavery on the other."[10]

Slaveholders, while sometimes holding to less-than-democratic ideals of an organic and hierarchical social order, responded that they had built a perfect representative democracy, in which the bondage of inferior blacks enabled white equality. "There is no proposition clearer to my mind, than this—banish African Slavery from among us and you destroy Democratic liberty," a delegate to the Alabama secession convention observed in January 1861.[11] Americans, and not just Americans, could easily interpret the Gettysburg Address, in light of these clashing ideas, as the latest defense of what Lincoln considered the Northern states' true democracy in contrast to the slaveholders' sham democracy.

Quite apart from the contest between slavery and democracy, though, Lincoln had ample cause at Gettysburg to describe securing democracy as the North's great purpose, even if, as was his habit, he did not use the word. Ensuring democratic government had in fact been at the heart of the matter at least since the slaveholding states began mobilizing to secede, not simply in the context of American politics but in the eyes of the world, "the whole family of man."

* * *

The Address describes democracy not simply as the American form of government but as a universal ideal—an ideal in great danger of being extinguished. America may have provided Lincoln, as it did Alexis de Tocqueville, with what Tocqueville called "the image of democracy itself."[12] But elsewhere in the Atlantic world, in the middle of the nineteenth century, democracy was in retreat. Disorder into mayhem seemed the inevitable result of popular government. The French Revolution's degeneration into the Reign of Terror and Bonapartism, followed by the Bourbon Restoration, had tainted antimonarchialism as well as democracy. Periodic republican and democratic uprisings, culminating in the revolutions that swept Europe in 1848, had been suppressed. Even in the United States, conservative Whigs bemoaned the effects of Andrew Jackson's democratic politics and what they called, behind closed doors, "the democracy of numbers and radicalism." And in the Old World, the outbreak of a civil war in America delighted old-line Tories, aristocrats, and legitimists as proof positive that republicanism and thus democracy were doomed to failure—a failure made all the more striking in the American case because it was tied to the institution of human bondage. "We were now witnessing the bursting of the great republican bubble which had so often been held up to us as a model on which to cast our British Constitution," Sir John Ramsden, M.P., told the House of Commons in May 1861.[13]

At Gettysburg as before, Lincoln was acutely aware of these stakes: Not just American democracy was on trial, he said in the Address; democracy itself as a political proposition was on trial. (Indeed, given the blows dealt to democratic movements in the Old World, it was easy enough for Lincoln and others to see America as a singular and even providential nation: if democracy failed in America, it could never succeed anywhere else.)

Northern newspapers had repeatedly observed how cynical aristocrats, in one Illinois editor's words, "affect to read in the pregnant events of the day the complete and irredeemable failure of Democracy." An Ohio newspaper spelled out the larger hazards: "It is not only a question of whether we have a government or not, here, but we believe what is now being decided whether a free government shall again spring up in any quarter of the globe." Ordinary Northern soldiers said much the same thing in their letters home: if the Southern "traitors" destroyed the government, one private in the 27th Connecticut Regiment wrote, "all the hope and confidence in the capacity of men for self government will be lost."[14] Or, as Lincoln put it at Gettysburg, the war called into question not simply the American democratic experiment but whether any nation conceived in liberty and dedicated to equality could last for long. The testing had begun with Southern secession, the great unmentioned trigger for what the Address simply called "a great civil war."

Secession came in direct response to Lincoln's election in 1860. The election's outcome conformed to the Constitution to the letter: having obtained a commanding majority of votes in the Electoral College, Lincoln was duly chosen president. But Southern secessionists would not have it. Lincoln had won only a plurality of the national popular tally in a purely sectional vote. He had run on a party platform pledged to commence slavery's eradication, which the slaveholders charged would violate what they insisted were the Constitution's guarantees of slave property as a nationally sanctioned institution. An electoral majority was about to commence trouncing the constitutional rights of a minority, which would ruin the republic. "A mere partizan election by a majority of voters . . .," the *Richmond Semi-Weekly Examiner* contended, "will be the actual destruction of the political institutions of the United States."[15] (Had the *Examiner* recalled that Lincoln's margin of victory in the popular vote was only a plurality, it could have made its point even more forcefully.) After what the pro-secession slaveholders described as a partisan electoral coup d'état, the only course left was to dissolve the Union.

The essential clash was over slavery, but framed as a constitutional question: Did the Constitution recognize property holding in slaves as a national institution? The slaveholders asserted that it did, basing their arguments in part on federal judicial decisions that had culminated in Chief Justice Roger Taney's majority ruling in *Dred Scott v. Sandford* in 1857. Any effort to restrict slavery's expansion, they charged, was unconstitutional, as it would abrogate the slaveholders' rights to hold their human property anywhere—even, some argued, in states where slavery had been abolished.

Lincoln and his supporters denounced Taney's ruling as unconstitutional. They asserted that the Constitution regarded slaves as persons not as property, that slavery was purely a state-sanctioned and not a national institution, and that claims to slave property had no force outside those states that had not abolished slavery. Accordingly, they insisted, Congress had ample authority to restrict slavery in the territories or anywhere else that fell under its jurisdiction.[16]

Lincoln and the Republicans were determined to overturn what the party's 1860 platform called "the new dogma" and the "dangerous political heresy" contained in Taney's decision, which the platform deemed "revolutionary in its tendency, and subversive of the peace and harmony of the country." Having rejected the slaveholders' property claims under the Constitution, they dismissed any argument for "carr[ying] Slavery into all or any of the Territories of the United States."[17] Here was the crucial constitutional question over which the Southern secessionists led their states out of the Union. The legitimacy of secession, in turn, became the second pivotal constitutional issue.

The secessionists argued that they were acting as their revolutionary forebears had in 1776, freeing themselves from what had become tyranny, which they commonly described, as one leading Alabamian did, as "a consolidated, centralized General Government."[18] Some secessionists, basing their claims on the so-called compact theory of the Constitution as restated by John C. Calhoun, asserted that the separate sovereign states actually had the clear constitutional right to withdraw.

Lincoln and the Republicans, as well as Union Democrats and antisecession Southerners, repudiated both arguments. There had been, they said, no abrogation or revision of the Constitution, nor would there be; there had only been successive resolutions of the political and moral questions concerning slavery's expansion. "One section of our country believes slavery is *right* and ought to be extended, while the other believes it is *wrong* and ought not to be extended," Lincoln said in his First Inaugural Address. "This is the only substantial dispute."[19]

For seventy years, the slaveholding South had enjoyed the upper hand. The electoral success of Lincoln and the Republicans had certainly shifted the politics of the controversy by turning what had been a minority into a majority, but that legitimate change was not fixed by some illusory consolidated tyranny. What the secessionists deemed intolerable centralization basically amounted to the possibility that the *Dred Scott* decision would be overturned—a reversal that would be no more permanent than the original decision had been.

The compact theory, meanwhile, was, to Lincoln and his supporters, a constitutionally flimsy yet dangerous artifice. They upheld instead the nationalist ideas previously propounded in different ways by leaders as diverse as Daniel Webster and Andrew Jackson. By these lights, the American people, and not the states, had created the nation, as an improvement of the Union that predated the Constitution. Instituted by and for "We, the People," the nation was distinct from any association of states, with powers that the states had ceded to it. The Union, far from a contingent compact, was perpetual. Secession, one Rhode Island editor observed, did not follow "the character of the American constitution" but was instead "a departure from the obligations of that instrument," a treasonous display of "violent contempt of popular authority."[20]

With the states of the lower South having already issued their ordinances of secession, Lincoln devoted a good deal of his First Inaugural Address to refuting sharply the secessionists' rationales. "Plainly," he said, "the central idea of secession is the essence of anarchy." As in all constitutional disputes, either the majority would acquiesce to the will of the minority or vice versa. So long as the majority was subject to constitutional constraints and limitations, and so long as its predominance could be easily ended "with deliberate changes of popular opinions and sentiments," majority rule was "the only true sovereign of a free people." Permit a minority to secede and it would only be a matter of time before a minority within that minority would secede—a formula for chaos. "Rejecting the majority principle," Lincoln concluded, would mean that "anarchy or despotism in some form is all that is left."[21]

Lincoln's logic deserves amplification. The destruction of the Union, he said, was an act of rebellion, based on an untenable theory of government in general and of the US Constitution in particular. Elsewhere in his First Inaugural, Lincoln dwelled on the virtues of the Union itself, above and beyond its primacy to the American constitutional order. The speech's famous peroration, on the "mystic chords of memory" swelling "the chorus of the Union," contained the most striking images of this kind of nationalist sentiment of the entire Civil War era, as an appeal to national unity and identity. But Lincoln's dissection of secession consisted chiefly of a defense not of national unity but of government by majority rule, which is to say of democracy. Secession flouted the nation and the bonds of nationality, but even more important it repudiated democracy.

Lincoln's democratic argument was no more peculiar to him than were his views on slavery and the Declaration of Independence. Nearly three months earlier, the *Iowa State Register* of Des Moines, contemplating the impeding secession of South Carolina, stated that "if the will of the majority is no longer the governing power in this country, free government is at an end."[22] Similar declarations appeared in pro-Republican newspapers across the North during the secession crisis. Lincoln simply stated, with eloquence and presidential force, what had become the common sense of the subject among his fellow Unionists. In doing so, he completed a shift toward an increasingly pointed defense of democracy that appeared full-blown elsewhere in his First Inaugural, which he would restate, even more eloquently, at Gettysburg.

* * *

Before the Gettysburg Address, Lincoln's thoughts about democracy had evolved in response to changing political circumstances. Over the half-decade before 1860, his pronouncements on the subject turned largely on the concept of popular sovereignty. In 1847 and 1848, mainstream Northern Democrats, faced with rising opposition to extending slavery, seized upon the phrase to denote what they posited as a moderating democratic solution to the sectional controversy. Antislavery forces were demanding slavery's prohibition in the territories; proslavery forces were demanding no restrictions at all. If, instead, though, the federal government granted to territorial residents what Democratic Senator and 1848 presidential nominee Lewis Cass called the right "to regulate their concerns in their own way," then the slavery question could be settled in, allegedly, the most directly democratic manner imaginable.[23] Cass lost in 1848, but the idea of "popular sovereignty" became a primary organizing principle of the Northern Democracy in the 1850s, especially after the passage of the Kansas-Nebraska Act in 1854. Lincoln's Illinois rival, Senator Stephen A. Douglas, became popular sovereignty's greatest champion.

For Lincoln, this appropriation of a democratic principle was as much a fraud as the idea of a slaveholders' democracy. Ostensibly democratic, the "popular sovereignty" proclaimed by Cass, Douglas, and their supporters imagined democracy as a kind of micropolitics, in which local assemblies of citizens made decisions on the basis of majority rule. But the micropolitics of popular sovereignty slighted the macropolitics of the democratic nation. Specifically, it conferred rights to self-government to settlers in territories where, under the Constitution, those rights were severely constrained. Article IV, Section 2, after all, expressly granted to Congress, and not to territorial settlers, the power "to dispose of and make all needful Rules and Regulations respecting the Territory or other Property belonging to the United States."

In plain violation of that provision, "popular sovereignty" would, on Lincoln's view, permit slaveholders to rush into new territories and give slavery the foothold it needed to become intractable. Democratic verbiage would cloak the spread of slavery by acknowledging, he wrote to one supporter, "that slavery has equal rights with liberty." And when put to the test, as it was in "Bleeding" Kansas after the passage of the Kansas-Nebraska Bill in 1854, "popular sovereignty" deteriorated into territorial civil war. Far from democratic, the idea, Lincoln charged during his debates with Douglas in 1858, was *nothing but a living, creeping lie from the time of its introduction, till to-day.*"[24]

Lincoln propounded what he called "genuine popular sovereignty," which involved the norms of the larger national democracy. "A general government," he explained in 1859, "shall do all those things which pertain to it, and all the local governments shall do precisely as they please in respect to those matters which exclusively concern them."[25] In accord with his insistence that the federal government enjoyed, under the Constitution, certain exclusive powers over slavery, this rendering of popular sovereignty upheld the divided sovereignty that was a hallmark of the American democratic republic. But Lincoln's divided and divisive election to the presidency, which sparked off Southern secession, in time forced him to think more directly about democracy and majority rule.

During the weeks before the election of 1860, as Lincoln's victory appeared increasingly certain, Southern disunionists made it clear that were he elected, secession would quickly follow. Pro-Republican newspapers responded forcefully. Would it be shown, a Connecticut editor wrote, "that the will of a peaceful voting majority can no longer govern the nation; that any minority wicked enough and desperate enough can govern us on the great principle of a pirate in a powder magazine, who will blow the ship to atoms if his orders are not complied with?" The election, according to the *Daily Pittsburgh Gazette*, was "no longer a mere contest between four men, but a struggle for the maintenance of the great majority principle in this Government. Shall the people rule?" Nearly two months after the election, and four days after South Carolina issued the first ordinance of secession, a West Virginia newspaper commented on Lincoln's disunionist Southern Democratic foes with mock surprise: "They were beaten—fairly, honorably, constitutionally, overwhelmingly beaten.—What is the sequel? They submit, of course. No; they do not."[26]

Lincoln maintained a strategic silence between Election Day and his inauguration, although he made it clear that he now considered himself, as he wrote New York's Governor Edwin D. Morgan, "the representative for the time being of the majority of the nation."[27] Preparing what would become his Inaugural Address's democratic refutation of secession, though, he fixed on the legitimacy of his election as a clear expression of the majority's constitutional as well as democratic will. A number of voices had urged him, in the face of the crisis, to support some sort of compromise that would stave off secession by forcing him to relent on his (and his party's) opposition to slavery's extension. Such surrender, he wrote in a draft of the address, would mark the ruin not just of a man or a party but also "the ruin of the government itself." If a president-elect felt duty-bound suddenly to abandon the most essential principles and promises on which he had run, what was the use of holding a democratic election in the first place? As for his selection as president being an unalterable coup d'état, Lincoln allowed that people could err in any election, including his own, but he would also remind the public that under a popular government, "the true cure is in the next election; and not in the treachery of the party elected."[28]

In the Inaugural Address's final text, Lincoln, defending his presidency's legitimacy, delivered the most stirring defense of democratic politics and government offered by any American president since Thomas Jefferson. "Why should there not be a patient confidence in the ultimate justice of the people?" he asked:

> Is there any better or equal hope in the world? In our present differences, is either party without faith of being in the right? If the Almighty Ruler of Nations, with His eternal truth and justice, be on your side of the North, or yours of the South, that truth and that justice will surely prevail by the judgment of this great tribunal of the American people.

In 1801, Jefferson had called the national government, founded on the will of the majority, "the world's best hope." Silently citing Jefferson and then updating him, Lincoln spoke in even loftier terms about the democratic citizenry—"this great tribunal of the American people"—while he reemphasized how the destiny of all mankind hung in the balance of American democracy's success. He would make both points again at Gettysburg, after more than two-and-a-half years of carnage, and with an even sharper sense of the threats that the slaveholders and the war posed to democracy.[29]

* * *

At Gettysburg, Lincoln did not envisage democracy's possible death simply in terms of the collapse of the government created by the American Revolution. He also perceived his Confederate foes as an embodiment of antidemocratic principles in the very structure of the government they were trying to establish—the first republic in world history created in order to uphold racial slavery. Undemocratic slavery, he thought, fostered undemocratic political institutions that preserved, protected, and defended the power of a slaveholding oligarchy.

Secession, a crisis for American democracy, rattled democratic institutions inside the insurgent South. Designing new national and state governments posed a dilemma to the slaveholders: How were the proudly sovereign states of the new Confederacy to handle the tensions between the states' existing liberal democratic institutions and the hierarchy and order of a slaveholders' republic? For some secessionists, the issue came down to preserving the existing democracy by explicitly excluding all but adult white males from active citizenship. The seceding states did exactly that, replicating, in the most conspicuous ways, the pre-war institutional status quo. But difficult questions remained.

Throughout the South, secession had been hotly disputed, especially in areas dominated by Democratic, slaveless, small farmers' households. Accordingly, would the state secession conventions run the risk of permitting the citizenry at large to approve or disapprove of their work? Although adult white male suffrage was the norm, some slaveholding state governments, above all South Carolina, were far less democratic than others. (South Carolina demanded high property qualifications to serve as governor, gave the power to elect governors and presidential electors to the state legislature, and apportioned representation unequally in enormous favor of affluent slaveholders' districts.) Would the revised state constitutions, without changing prominent institutions like suffrage, look to the less democratic models and adopt subtler restrictions?

Even before secession, spokesmen in areas controlled by large plantation slaveholders, most of them one-time Whigs, had expressed concern about what they considered the ignorant and possibly fractious democratic yeomanry. The unease intensified as secession created a temporary yet possibly turbulent period of transition from one political order to another. Would the latent suspicions of democracy lead the new state governments to restrict popular government?

As the Southern state conventions turned to reforming their state constitutions as well as writing and approving ordinances of secession, antidemocratic voices found an opening to shout at the top of their lungs. "Some of the wisest and best citizens propose a hereditary monarchy," one Georgia editor exclaimed; less monarchical sages, he said, favored what he called "additional safeguards," including "an *Executive for life, a vastly restricted suffrage,*" and senators elected for life. (As if responding to these outbursts, a county public meeting in November 1860 declared its adamant opposition "to the overthrow of our present republican form of Government and the establishment in lieu thereof of a 'Constitutional Monarchy' in these Southern States."[30])

The convening of the Georgia secession convention inspired one newspaper reader to bid the delegates to "check the radical tendencies of the age," chiefly by giving all high court appointments to the governor, subject to approval by two-thirds of the state senate. Without those reforms, he wrote, "the transitive state through which we are now passing" might lead to anarchy and mob rule. Still other commentators desired modifications that would rid the legislatures of "mere wrangling demagogues" and "county politicians," in favor of "better legislators" who were truly "representative of the honor and the interests of the State." Some of the more temperate delegates grew worried about what one Mississippian called "crude opinions" concerning the conventions' authority to redesign state governments, fostering an "absolutism" inside the conventions that "changed the form of our government from a representative democracy to an oligarchy."[31]

The temperate voices prevailed at the state conventions, and the shifts in the new constitutions toward a less democratic system were fairly minor. "Property does not have the proper constitutional influence," the antidemocratic South Carolina planter David Gavin complained about his state's revised constitution.[32] Still, the antidemocratic strain in

Southern politics was unmistakable. Only three of the seceding states, for example—Virginia, Tennessee, and Texas—held public referenda on their respective ordinances of secession. And the Constitution of the Confederate States of America, adopted on March 11, 1861, enshrined the fear of possibly divisive democracy in other ways, particularly with respect to party politics.

Since the nation's founding, a strong animus against parties and party conflict had shaped American politics, especially conservative politics. Lincoln and his fellow liberal, New School Whigs wholly rejected such thinking; Lincoln climbed up the ladder in Illinois as a masterful party pol; the Republican Party's great achievement was to combine Jacksonian democratic ideas and Whig ideas about economic development together with antislavery politics. But the antiparty animus and its elitist tone remained strong in much of the country, above all in the slaveholding South with its vaunted ideals of honor, harmony, and disinterested virtue.[33]

In 1850, a typical article in the *Southern Quarterly Review*, while contrasting the South and the North, had lambasted "the systematic immoralities of political parties, and the utter shamelessness with which they grasp at power, in the teeth of principle." In February 1861, a writer for the New Orleans *Daily Picayune* told the delegates to the Louisiana state convention to beware "the horns and hoofs of that devil that vexes us— party spirit." The Confederate Constitutional Convention, which gathered in Montgomery that same month, crafted provisions designed to limit electioneering and the dispensing of party patronage, including a one-term, six-year presidency. Curbing the machinations of parties and party politicians, the prominent Alabamian Robert H. Smith declared, would help prevent the Confederacy from degenerating into something "much worse than . . . a pure democracy . . . a mere oligarchy, and that not of intelligence and virtue but of low ambition."[34]

The reactionary effusions and antiparty principles of the seceding South affirmed Northern arguments about the basically undemocratic character of the slaveholding states—and Abraham Lincoln took special notice. "It continues to develop that the insurrection is largely, if not exclusively, a war upon the first principle of popular government—the rights of the people," he remarked in his first Annual Message to Congress, delivered on December 3, 1861. Pointing to "grave and maturely considered public documents" along with "the general tone of the insurgents," Lincoln charged that Southerners were now propounding abridgment of the existing rights of suffrage and selection of public officers, and advancing "labored arguments to prove that large control of people in government, is the source of all political evil." The Southerners' antidemocratic zeal knew no bounds: "Monarchy itself," Lincoln observed, "is sometimes hinted at as a possible refuge from the power of the people." What had begun as an attempt to repudiate a democratic national election had evolved into a "returning despotism," against which, as president, Lincoln said he had no choice but to raise his voice in warning.[35]

Lincoln exaggerated: the Southern antidemocratic upsurge was not nearly as fierce as his rhetoric suggested. Unquestionably, though, fear and loathing of democracy was a political force inside the slaveholders' ranks, and Lincoln described it as an emblem of all that the Union was up against. "This is, essentially, a People's contest," Lincoln had told a special session of Congress five months earlier, with the Union struggling to maintain "that form, and substance of government, whose leading object is, to elevate the condition of men." In the First Annual Message, he described that form and substance as "the popular principle applied to government." A year later, in his Second Annual Message, having announced the preliminary Emancipation Proclamation, Lincoln turned his earlier emendation of "the world's best hope"—Jefferson's phrase about democratic government—into "the last best hope of earth."[36] At Gettysburg, with astonishing concision, he would complete the evolution of his democratic thinking.

* * *

The Gettysburg Address builds to a mighty crescendo. It begins calmly, in a scriptural cadence, relating that "four score and seven years ago"— that is, in 1776, not 1787—the founding generation created a new nation "conceived in liberty" and dedicated to equality. Here, compressed into a single sentence, is the crux of the political argument that Lincoln and the Republicans had been making since 1854, that the egalitarian liberty proclaimed in the Declaration is the taproot of American politics and government. Implied in those thirty words is the entire justification for the national government ensuring that slavery would remain, as Lincoln had phrased it in his "House Divided" speech, "in the course of ultimate extinction."[37]

The next four sentences describe the consequences of Southern resistance and disunion: "a great civil war," which would decide the fate of egalitarian government. Having specified the bitter fruits of secession, the

Address then pauses to honor all those, living and dead, who had fought to resist disunion and vindicate the Declaration. Suddenly, though, the speech enlarges its scope and heightens the emotional tension, focusing now entirely on the honored dead, and placing upon Lincoln's listeners and the entire Union the burden of completing the work that the slain had advanced.

Then the tension peaks. A question instantly flashes to mind: What, exactly, is the unfinished work demanding rededication that Lincoln is talking about; what are the tasks that remain? A listener or reader might expect the speech to return to where it began, to the tasks of safeguarding liberty and equality. But instead, in sonorous litany and conclusion, the speech reaches a still more exalted level: what remains are two momentous goals as yet unmentioned, the destruction of slavery in nothing less than "a new birth of freedom," and beyond that—beyond everything else, encompassing all—the defense and validation of democracy, the last best hope of earth.

Between the Revolution and the Civil War, American politics at bottom involved struggles over democracy—over how democratic the nation should be, and over what sort of democracy was best. Abraham Lincoln had played a leading role in those struggles beginning in 1854, and he had helped mightily in shaping the outcomes. The seemingly democratic idea of "popular sovereignty," invented and touted by partisans of what was still called the Democracy, were not democratic at all, he charged, but a shill, an evasion of the Constitution intended not to secure the people's will but instead to spread slavery. The idea of a proslavery democracy was an oxymoron; secession, while claiming to be resistance to tyranny, was in fact an anarchic repudiation of democracy. No political question, no matter how divisive, could fail to be settled justly by the tribunal of the American people. Any doubts about the despotic character of the self-declared republic of slavery had only to listen hard to some of its adherents propound every conceivable curtailment of popular government, up to and including hereditary monarchy.

The exigencies of secession and Civil War had deepened the crisis of American democracy, which was a crisis for democracy the world over. In that deepening, the separate strands of Lincoln's thinking about liberty, equality, and democracy had pulled together, ever tighter, and reached full circle. Undemocratic secession had severed the Union; reclaiming that Union would require crushing an ever more despotic threat; repulsing that threat would come to require, in time, military emancipation of the slaves, whose status as human property had been the fundamental reason behind undemocratic secession. By the autumn of 1863, the war for the Union had become a radicalized war of liberation, and from that Union and that liberation would come the salvation of democracy. This was the point of Lincoln's Gettysburg Address.

Notes

1. All citations to the Gettysburg Address are to the final text published in *The Collected Works of Abraham Lincoln*, ed. Roy P. Basler, 9 vols. (New Brunswick, NJ: Rutgers University Press, 1953–1955), 7:23 (hereafter cited as *CW*). On the Declaration, the Constitution, and the Gettysburg Address, see above all Garry Wills, *Lincoln at Gettysburg: The Words That Remade America* (New York: Simon and Schuster, 1992). The argument about the Address and the redefinition of Union war aims appears more widely; for an excellent formulation, see David Herbert Donald, *Lincoln* (New York: Simon and Schuster, 1995), 460–466.

2. Wills, *Lincoln at Gettysburg*, 38. On antislavery politics and the Declaration in the Missouri crisis, see Robert Pierce Forbes, *The Missouri Compromise and Its Aftermath: Slavery and the Meaning of America* (Chapel Hill: University of North Carolina Press, 2007), esp. 38–39. For Lincoln's earlier pronouncements on the theme, see, for example, his famous Peoria speech in 1854 as well as various remarks during his senatorial campaign against Stephen A. Douglas four years later, in *CW*, 2:248, 255, 266, 271, 275–276, 500; 3:16, 29, 90. Wills's book ignores the line of antislavery politics that ran from the Missouri debates through the Liberty and Free Soil Parties to the Republican Party. In particular, it ignores the crucial writings, in the 1840s, of Salmon P. Chase, who, one historian writes, "made the argument that Lincoln and others adopted, linking the antislavery natural rights philosophy as expressed in the Declaration of Independence to the Constitution," John Niven, "Lincoln and Chase, a Reappraisal," *Journal of the Abraham Lincoln Association*, 12 (1991): 1–15. On Chase and antislavery ideas, see above all Eric Foner, *Free Soil, Free Labor, Free Men: The Ideology of the Republican Party Before the Civil War* (New York: Oxford University Press, 1970), 73–102. See also Linda Selzer, "Historicizing Lincoln: Garry Wills and the Canonization of the 'Gettysburg Address,'" *Rhetoric Review* 16 (1997): 120–137. Selzer takes Wills's book to task for turning the Address into a pseudo-origin myth, but like Wills, she also ignores the political antislavery writers and movements from whom Lincoln actually borrowed his thinking about the Declaration, the Constitution, and slavery.

3. I do not mean to imply that historians have been blind to the centrality of democracy in the Gettysburg Address. See, for typical examples, the historians' essays in Mario M. Cuomo and Harold Holzer, eds., *Lincoln on Democracy* (1990; New York: HarperCollins, 1991), including Hans Trefousse's remark (p. 302) on how the Address affirmed that "the war was a struggle for democracy, for if a popular decision by ballots could be challenged by bullets, democratic government was at an end." The trouble, I think, is that historians too often elide democracy with the Union and antislavery in Lincoln's thought and in pro-Union political thinking more generally. We have thus neglected how, at Gettysburg, Lincoln built on longstanding disputes over what, in fact, democracy was

and ought to be. The Gettysburg Address declared the war a struggle for democracy but also declared what had become Lincoln's conception of democracy. For a recent interesting treatment of democracy and the Gettysburg Address, see Allen Guelzo's essay, "Lincoln's Sound Bite: Have Faith in Democracy," *New York Times*, Nov. 17, 2013.

4. Lincoln to Henry, July 4, 1860, in *CW*, 4:82.

5. Speech at Peoria, IL, Oct. 16, 1854; "Fragments: Notes for Speeches"; "Annual Message to Congress," Dec. 3, 1861, *CW*, 2:266; 3:205; 5:51.

6. Message to Congress in Special Session, July 4, 1861, *CW*, 4:426.

7. The earliest semblance of the phrase in Lincoln's writings appeared in a speech he delivered in Cincinnati on September 17, 1859: "In the first place we know that in a Government like this, in a Government of the people, where the voice of all the men of the country, substantially enter into the execution,—or administration rather—of the Government—in such a Government, what lies at the bottom of all of it, is public opinion," "Speech in Cincinnati, Ohio," *CW*, 3:438. According to his law partner William H. Herndon, Lincoln first encountered the phrase in a sermon by Theodore Parker, which appeared in a volume of Parker's writings that Herndon had given to him early in 1858. Herndon and Jesse William Weik, *Herndon's Lincoln: The True Story of a Great Life*, 3 vols. (1889; Springfield, IL: Herndon's Lincoln Publishing Co., 1921), 2:396.

8. ["Definition of Democracy"], *CW*, 2:532. The document, unsigned, was given to Lincoln's widow by a married couple who had succeeded in getting her released from confinement in a private insane asylum in 1875. It is, the editors of Lincoln's collected works wrote, "associated with no speech" of Lincoln's of which they were aware. Despite its dubious origins, though, the editors deemed it fit for inclusion.

9. "A House Divided: Speech at Springfield, IL, June 16, 1858," *CW*, 2:461.

10. *New-York Daily Tribune*, Nov. 27, 1860. On the sectional crisis as a clash between Northern and Southern conceptions of democracy, see Wilentz, *Rise*, 521–768, passim.

11. William Russell Smith, *The History and Debates of the Convention of the People of Alabama, Begun and Held in the City of Montgomery, on the Seventh Day of January, 1861* (Montgomery, AL: White, Pfister & Co., 1861), 224.

12. De Tocqueville, *Democracy in America*, trans. Henry Reeve (New York: G. Adlard, 1839), 12.

13. James Kent quoted in Wilentz, *Rise*, 4; Ramsden quoted in Amanda Foreman, *A World on Fire: Britain's Crucial Role in the American Civil War* (New York: Random House, 2010), 98–99.

14. *Daily Whig and Republican* (Quincy, IL), May 3, 1861; *Gazette* (Columbus, OH), June 21, 1861; quotation in James M. McPherson, *For Cause and Comrades: Why Men Fought in the Civil War* (New York: Oxford University Press, 1997), 113.

15. *Richmond Semi-Weekly Examiner*, Nov. 27, 1860.

16. Although antislavery writers, notably Salmon Chase, had been making this basic point for many years, they never nailed down the history of how the framers, in 1787, defeated attempts by Southern delegates to have the Constitution explicitly recognize slaves as property, even in connection with the fugitive slave clause. The effect was to weaken their arguments regarding constitutional antislavery precedent. See Sean Wilentz, "Antislavery, Slavery, and the Federal Constitution" (paper delivered at the conference on the Antislavery Bulwark, City University of New York Graduate Center, Oct. 17–18, 2014).

17. "Republican Party Platform of 1860, May 17, 1860," Gerhard Peters and John T. Woolley, *The American Presidency Project*, http://www.presidency.ucsb.edu/ws/?pid=29620.

18. David Clopton in Russell, *History and Debates*, 441.

19. "First Inaugural Address—Final Text," *CW*, 4:268–269.

20. *Newport Mercury*, May 25, 1861.

21. "First Inaugural Address—Final Text," *CW*, 4:268.

22. *Iowa State Register* (Des Moines), Dec. 12, 1860.

23. Cass to A. O. P. Nicholson, in *Union* (Washington, DC), Dec. 30, 1847. Cass is sometimes wrongly described as the inventor of this version of popular sovereignty; for a corrective, see Willard Karl Klunder, *Lewis Cass and the Politics of Moderation* (Kent, OH: Kent State University Press, 1996), 168.

24. Seventh and Last Debate with Stephen A. Douglas at Alton, IL; Lincoln to John D. Defrees, Dec. 18, 1860, *CW*, 3:306; 4:155.

25. "Speech at Columbus, Ohio", CW, III, 405.

26. *Evening Press* (Hartford, CT), Oct. 26, 1860; *Daily Pittsburgh Gazette*, Nov. 2, 1860; *Daily Intelligencer* (Wheeling, VA), Dec. 24, 1860.

27. Lincoln to Morgan, Feb. 18, 1860, *CW*, 4:225.

28. "First Inaugural Address—First Edition and Revisions," *CW*, 4:259.

29. "First Inaugural Address—Final Text," *CW*, 4:270; Barbara Oberg et al., *The Papers of Thomas Jefferson*, 41 vols. (Princeton, NJ: Princeton University Press, 1950–), 33:148–152.

30. *Chronicle and Sentinel* (Augusta, GA), Dec. 8, 12, 1860, quoted in Michael P. Johnson, *Toward a Patriarchal Republic: The Secession of Georgia* (Baton Rouge: Louisiana State University Press, 1977), 100–101; "Resolutions from the County of Upson, Presented by Mr. Horsley," in *The Confederate Records of the State of Georgia*, ed. Allen D. Candler, 6 vols. (Atlanta, GA: Chas. P. Byrd, 1909), 1:65. Johnson's is the best study to date of this Southern antidemocratic reaction during the secession crisis, but see also Stephanie McCurry, *Confederate Reckoning: Power and Politics in the Civil War South* (Cambridge, MA: Harvard University Press, 2010).

31. "Georgia" to Editor, *Telegraph* (Macon, GA), Jan. 24, 1861; "Clyde" to Editor, *Chronicle and Sentinel* (Augusta, GA), Mar. 1, 1861; "Troup" to Editor, *Morning News* (Savannah, GA), Mar. 21, 1861, quoted in Johnson, *Patriarchal Republic*,

143, 170–171; J. L. Power, *Proceedings of the Mississippi State Convention, Held January 7th to 26th, A. D. 1861* (Jackson, MI, 1861).

32. Gavin quoted in McCurry, *Confederate Reckoning*, 81.

33. On the history of antipartisan and, more recently, "postpartisan" currents in American politics, see Sean Wilentz, "The Mirage," *New Republic*, Oct. 26, 2011, http://www.newrepublic.com/article/books/magazine/96706/post-partisan-obama-progressives-washington.

34. "The Southern Convention," *Southern Quarterly Review* [new series] 2 (1850): 198; *Daily Picayune* (New Orleans, LA), Feb. 5, 1861; Robert H. Smith, *An Address to the Citizens of Alabama, on the Constitution and Laws of the Confederate States of America* (Mobile, 1861), 14.

35. "Annual Message to Congress," Dec. 3, 1861, *CW*, 5:51

36. "Message to Congress in Special Session," July 4, 1861; "Annual Message to Congress," Dec. 3, 1861; "Annual Message to Congress," Dec. 1, 1862, *CW*, 4:438; 5:53, 537.

37. "A House Divided," *CW*, 2:461.

4

Daniel Webster, Abraham Lincoln, and the Gettysburg Address

Craig L. Symonds

IN DECEMBER 1856, Illinois Republicans organized a dinner in Chicago to celebrate the election of their candidate for governor, William Henry Bissell. As usual, the event was lubricated by a number of toasts. At one point, the master of ceremonies called upon Abraham Lincoln, the once and future Republican Senate candidate, to respond to the toast: "The UNION—The North will maintain it—the South will not depart therefrom." In his extemporaneous remarks, Lincoln offered a line that nearly everyone in the room recognized as coming from a speech that Daniel Webster had made back in January 1830: "Not Union without liberty, not liberty without Union, but Union and Liberty, now and forever, one and inseparable." According to the transcript printed in the *Illinois State Journal*, Lincoln's rendition of that sentence brought "Loud Cheers" from the enthusiastic audience. Lincoln then concluded his remarks with a jab at the newly elected Democratic candidate for president, James Buchanan, who, in an effort to quiet sectional antagonism, had recently declared that all states should be equal—implying that Northern states must be willing to meet the valid concerns of Southern states about slavery. Challenging that view, Lincoln remarked that it was time to demonstrate not that all *states* were equal, but that "all *men* are created equal." That, too, elicited loud cheers from the audience.[1]

The members of the audience needed no concordance to recognize both of Lincoln's references: not only his concluding quotation from the Declaration of Independence, but also his earlier reference to the quarter-century-old speech that Webster had presented on the floor of the US Senate in response to remarks by Senator Robert Y. Hayne of

South Carolina. To Lincoln's generation, the peroration from Webster's "Reply to Hayne" was nearly as famous as the Declaration itself. Moreover, Webster's presentation—not merely its galvanic conclusion, but the whole of his argument—was a touchstone for American nationalists like Lincoln and was an important contribution to his evolving philosophy of government. Indeed, an echo of Webster's famous remarks is evident in a number of Lincoln's speeches as president, including the poetic Gettysburg Address.

* * *

The origins of Webster's famous phrase emerged, curiously enough, out of a proposal to sell government land to citizens. What gave it such significance was the context in which it occurred. Two years before, during a debate over the passage of a tariff bill in 1828, Southern congressmen had tried to kill the bill by loading it up with poison pill amendments. That gambit proved a disastrous failure when the bill passed anyway by a vote of 105–94. Southerners, who had voted 64–4 against it, labeled it the "Tariff of Abominations" and insisted that it could not be enforced in any state that had opposed its passage. That assertion triggered a constitutional crisis concerning the powers of government and the rights of states.[2]

In December 1828, the sitting Vice President, John C. Calhoun, anonymously penned a manifesto entitled "South Carolina Exposition and Protest" that in many ways was the springboard for a decades-long national dispute over the powers of the national government and the rights of the individual states. Calhoun had been a nationalist for most of his political career and, in fact, remained one as long as he thought it possible that he might succeed Andrew Jackson as president. Once he saw that this prize was beyond his reach, however, he became the champion of his state, and by extension of all the individual states. In doing so, he tapped into a view of government with deep roots, including the anti-Federalists who had opposed ratification of the Constitution in 1787–1789, and the authors of the 1798 Virginia and Kentucky resolutions.

In his "Exposition," Calhoun argued that the tariff of 1828 was unconstitutional because while the Constitution did authorize Congress to impose tariffs for the purpose of raising revenue, it did not sanction such laws for the purpose of protecting domestic industry. "The violation," Calhoun wrote, "consists in using a power granted for one object to advance another." The importance of Calhoun's argument was less his specific opposition to the tariff, however, than it was his philosophical argument about the powers of government generally, for he articulated an interpretation of government authority, and of democracy generally, that was very nearly the opposite of the nationalist vision that was espoused by Webster in his debate with Hayne, and subsequently by Lincoln at Gettysburg.[3]

Calhoun began by observing that all political authority was "delegated by the people." On that, at least, almost all the participants in the debate agreed. He insisted, however, that the Constitution delegated that authority to *two* institutions, not only to what he called the "General government" but also to each of the several states. It was an awkward argument, for it created a kind of dual sovereignty, which is very nearly a contradiction in terms. Sovereignty, after all, denotes an agency that is "the supreme authority" in a society. Calhoun struggled, sometimes awkwardly, to square this circle. In composing his essay, he wrote that there were "two distinct and independent sovereignties" in the United States. Then, as if recognizing the absurdity of such a statement, he crossed out "sovereignties" and wrote in the word "governments." Later, however, he insisted that "the division of sovereign power" was the principle upon which "the whole system of our government rests." Calhoun argued that a kind of dual sovereignty was essential to the survival of the kind of republic he envisioned, not only to protect the rights of individual citizens, but also— and more particularly—to protect the interests of the different sections. Without state sovereignty, the general government could enact policies and programs that imposed an undue burden on one section of the country in order to benefit another, precisely as the Tariff of Abominations proposed to do.[4]

From the moment it appeared, it was evident that Calhoun's "Exposition and Protest" targeted more than the Tariff of Abominations. At its core it was a vehicle designed to protect South Carolina in particular, and the slaveholding South in general, from all sorts of undesirable or oppressive national laws. To Calhoun, and those who agreed with him, self-government did not mean rule by a national majority but rather rule by separate majorities within each of the individual states. A truly national government—a democracy as opposed to a republic—would, from his perspective, constitute simply a different form of tyranny. "The relation of equality between the parts of the community, established by the Constitution, would be destroyed," Calhoun wrote, "and in its place there would be substituted the relation of sovereign and subject, between the stronger and weaker interests, in its most odious and oppressive form."[5]

Significantly, Calhoun's "Exposition" appeared at a time when the South was becoming increasingly defensive about the institution of slavery, and the crisis morphed very quickly into a broader discussion of government authority as it applied to slavery and its future. The issues were intertwined, and indeed inextricable, for only a national government endowed with broad powers could be strong enough to impose either external tariffs or to interfere with a state's "domestic institutions"—the contemporary euphemism for slavery. The Southern appreciation of this reality was at the root of most of the theoretical arguments about the ultimate source of government authority. To Southerners like Calhoun, a powerful central government—a truly national government—was a threat to liberty of all kinds, but expressly and especially to the liberty to hold slaves in bondage. That spurred a new and more assertive defense of the doctrine that has come to be known as states' rights, including the assertion that essential sovereignty rested equally in the states as well as in the national government.

* * *

It was in the context of this public conversation that Robert Hayne of South Carolina rose on the Senate floor in January 1830 to speak against a bill that would authorize the federal government to sell public lands to individual citizens. A handsome thirty-nine-year-old lawyer and planter from South Carolina, Hayne was in his second term as a US Senator. He did not oppose the idea that the public lands should be distributed to citizens. What he objected to was that the government should charge anything for that land; he preferred that the government simply give it away. In addition to the self-evident benefit of making land more easily available to more citizens, Hayne favored the free distribution of public land because selling it would bring additional revenue into the public treasury, and that would effectively strengthen the national government. To him, any activity that empowered the central government was a threat to American liberty. That led him into an assault on Henry Clay's "so-called American System," a neo-Hamiltonian national economic program the end goal of which was the establishment of a nationwide network of roads, canals, and eventually railroads. To fund these programs (both then and now labeled as "internal improvements"), Clay called for high tariffs, which would also encourage manufacturing, and a national bank. To Hayne this plan was "a rude, disjointed, and misshapen mass." Far from binding the Union together, Hayne insisted, this kind of centralization of power would only weaken the bonds that kept the states in the Union at all.[6]

Hayne's objection to the expansion of government power was not rooted solely, or even principally, in questions about land sales or road systems. Significantly, he soon shifted into an explanation and defense of slavery as a labor system. At this time, the South had not yet adopted the assertive, even pugnacious, defense of slavery that would characterize Southern discourse in the 1850s—including the insistence that slavery was "a positive good." In 1830, Hayne was willing to acknowledge that many men considered slavery "an evil." Even if that were true, however, Hayne insisted that his generation was innocent of any responsibility for it because the institution had come down to them from their ancestors. Their stewardship of this labor system was a duty, perhaps even a burden, for which they should not be penalized by an unsympathetic government. "We did not sit down to speculate on abstract questions of theoretical liberty," he explained. "We met it as a practical question of obligation and duty." That duty was inescapable. It was clear that the slaves could not be returned to Africa, and it was equally evident to him that they could not be set free. He asserted that those few who had been freed for one reason or another and who had found their way into the Northern states suffered horribly. "Sir, there does not exist on the face of the whole earth, a population so poor, so wretched, so vile, so loathsome, so utterly destitute of all the comforts, conveniences, and decencies of life, as the unfortunate blacks of Philadelphia, and New York, and Boston." Therefore, he continued, the earnest and responsible slaveholders of the South must continue to bear the burden imposed on them and manage their slaves humanely.

If Hayne was unwilling to "speculate on abstract questions of theoretical liberty" as they pertained to slaves, he was positively eager to do so in regard to the guarantees of liberty for American citizens. That liberty, he insisted, was best ensured by protecting the state governments from "being drawn into the vortex, and swallowed up by one great consolidated Government." To Hayne, the great issue of the day was the schism between "the lovers of freedom," by which he meant the defenders of state autonomy, and "the devoted advocates of power," by which he meant the champions of more centralized authority whether it was manifested by selling public land, raising tariffs, or interfering with a state's domestic institutions. The true friends of liberty, he insisted, were those who would "make this a federal and not a national Union."

Hayne's two-and-a-half hour disquisition provoked a three-hour reply from Webster. Nine years older than Hayne, Webster in 1830 was in his first term as a senator from Massachusetts, but he had built a national reputation as a constitutional authority due to his several powerful, and successful, presentations before the Supreme Court. In a series of famous cases, including *McCulloch v. Maryland* (1819) and *Gibbons v. Ogden* (1824), Webster had argued that states should not be allowed to inhibit the programs and policies of the national government. Given that, it was evident that he would oppose Hayne's views at almost every point.

The exchange between Hayne and Webster lasted four days and filled 291 pages in Niles's *Register of Congress.* It ranks with the Lincoln–Douglas debates as an explication of the dominant political issues of the nineteenth century. The ostensible topic of their exchange may have concerned land sales, but both Hayne and Webster fully understood that the principle at stake was much larger. In effect, both men addressed the question Lincoln asked at Gettysburg thirty-three years later: Could a national government strong enough to defend itself from its own internal foes continue to protect the liberties of the people?

In his initial reply to Hayne, Webster cited the Northwest Ordinance of 1787 as an example of the power that the national government had over public lands. That touched a nerve, because that same ordinance also forbade slavery in the Western territories. Consequently, it provoked what Webster called "a labored defense of slavery" from Hayne. From that point on, the issue of the central government's powers over a state's "domestic institutions" swallowed up the question of public land sales, or tariffs, and generated a full-blown debate about slavery and the nature of the American government. On January 27, Webster rose again in the Senate to deliver a second lengthy "Reply to Hayne" that became a coda for nationalists of his generation and for generations to come.[7]

As if to demonstrate that nationalism did not mean an absence of affection for one's home state, Webster began with a paean to Massachusetts that was so moving it drew tears from several members of the Senate as well as observers in the gallery. After that, however, Webster set out to explain and defend what he declared to be "the true principles of the Constitution." Was the US government the agent of the states or the agent of the people? he asked. "If the government of the United States be the agent of the State governments, then they may control it, provided they can agree in the manner of controlling it." But if, on the other hand, "it be the agent of the people, then the people alone can control it, restrain it, modify, or reform it."

Webster left no doubt about his views. Labeling it "an absurdity" that the Founding Fathers had intended the national government to act only when a particular issue found favor with majorities in all the states, he insisted that because the government's authority derived from the people—*all* the people, collectively, from *all* the states—it was a national government. "It is, Sir, the people's Constitution," he lectured Hayne, "the people's government, made *for the people*, made *by the people*, and answerable *to the people*" [italics added]. Here were ringing phrases that Lincoln would memorialize three decades later.

Webster was willing to stipulate that the states were "sovereign" over many things (something that Lincoln himself refused to acknowledge), but Webster insisted that neither the states nor any other agency was, or could be, sovereign over the people, for "we are all agents of the same supreme power, the people." Moreover, Webster noted that whatever sovereignty the states possessed was strictly limited. After all, the Constitution specifically prohibited the states from declaring war, making treaties, or printing money. If they were "sovereign," it was a very strange kind of sovereignty.

Webster insisted that Hayne's whole argument was based on "a total misapprehension . . . of the origin of this government, and the foundation on which it stands." The nation was not an assemblage of states, he insisted, but "a popular government, erected by the people." He fully acknowledged "the right of *the people* to reform their government," but he denied that "*the States* have a constitutional right to interfere, and annul the law of Congress." He recalled that popular unhappiness with the Articles of Confederation had led to the drafting of the Constitution in the first place. "Sir, the very chief end, the main design, for which the whole Constitution was framed and adopted, was to establish a government that should not be obligated to act through State agency, or depend on State opinion and State discretion. The people had quite enough of that kind of government under the Confederation."[8]

To underscore his argument, Webster cited what is often called the supremacy clause from Article VI: "This Constitution, and the laws of the United States which shall be made in Pursuance thereof; and all Treaties made or which shall be made, under the authority of the United States shall be the supreme Law of the Land; and the judges in every State shall be bound thereby, any Thing in the Constitution or Laws of any State to the contrary notwithstanding." Webster took a few liberties in quoting the passage, omitting the reference to treaties, for example, and trimming it down to its essentials. Nonetheless, it was clear to him that, as he put it, "No State law is valid which comes in conflict with the Constitution."

To this point, Lincoln embraced the whole of Webster's thesis: government authority came from the people; the national government represented all the people; and the states were subordinate to both. Here, however, Webster added one more plank to his argument that subsequently caused Lincoln some difficulty. This was Webster's assertion that the final arbiter of all constitutional issues was the Supreme Court. To Webster, the fact that the Supreme Court could overturn state law, a legal doctrine that he had done much to establish in his own pleadings before the Court, must have seemed decisive, and Webster proclaimed that the Supreme Court was "the keystone of the arch" that made the United States a nation and not a confederation. However, as Mark E. Neely, Jr. demonstrated in his superb book *Lincoln and the Triumph of the Nation* (2011), the Supreme Court constituted an unreliable "keystone" for Lincoln because the Court of Lincoln's day was headed by Roger B. Taney, whose *Dred Scott* decision remained infamous to Lincoln and to all Republicans. Writing for a divided majority, Taney had asserted in 1857 not only that the blessings of citizenship were reserved to "white men only" but also that the national government had no authority to restrict slavery from the federal territories. Clearly, the court, even (or maybe especially) the Supreme Court, could be fallible.[9]

For Lincoln, however, that did not refute the broader truth of Webster's thesis, for in the end, the Supreme Court, too, was subject to the popular will. Musing about this in his First Inaugural Address in March 1861, Lincoln noted that "if the policy of the government" was to be "fixed by decisions of the Supreme Court," then "the people will have ceased to be their own rulers." Thankfully, Lincoln noted, the Court was also subject to the ultimate authority of the people. Bad decisions by the Court could be overturned when new elections produced new leaders who appointed different judges. Thus the ultimate source of government authority remained the same. To Lincoln, the "keystone" was, as always, the authority of the people.[10]

Webster concluded his remarks in 1830 with the subsequently famous peroration that Lincoln quoted at the 1856 dinner in Chicago. Denying Hayne's contention that true freedom could be had only by relying on the states to limit the power of the national government, Webster insisted that it was not a matter of choosing between liberty or union, but rather embracing them both: "Liberty *and* Union, now and forever, one and inseparable."[11]

* * *

The Webster–Hayne debate about the character of the American government marked an important milestone in the evolving definition of government powers and in the schism between North and South. It also marked an important moment in the evolution of Lincoln's political philosophy. The speeches of both men were printed and reprinted in newspapers across the country and elicited much editorial comment. While Lincoln did not join in the public dialogue at the time, it is certain that he read the speeches, that he read them carefully (as he did most things), and that he read Webster's speeches with approval. Lincoln had long considered Henry Clay (whose American System he greatly admired) his ideological pole star. In the 1840s, he began to add Webster's name to Clay's as a second reference point in his political speeches. During both of his campaigns for the Senate, in 1854 and 1858, he referred to his admiration of Clay and Webster as a kind of shorthand to signal that he supported both Clay's national economic program and Webster's vision of the character of the nation. In 1858, he found it both annoying and patently dishonest whenever Stephen Douglas tried to co-opt either Clay or Webster as his own ideological predecessors. Douglas frequently noted that both Clay and Webster had been willing to compromise, and he asserted that because he, too, was an advocate of compromise (by which he meant accommodating the South), that made him—Douglas—their ideological successor. Lincoln responded to these claims by noting that Douglas's notorious Kansas-Nebraska Act had specifically repealed Clay's 1821 Missouri Compromise, and in Lincoln's view that alone was enough to discredit Douglas as the heir to Clay's mantle.

Lincoln understood that the debate between Webster and Hayne in 1830, and ultimately the split between North and South in 1860, were only superficially about either the tariff or states' rights—or even the meaning of the Constitution. At its most fundamental level it was about slavery. In 1828 when Calhoun wrote his "Exposition and Protest," and in January 1830 when Hayne and Webster marked out their competing views about the powers of government, the national argument about slavery had not yet become the dominant issue it would be twenty years hence, though even then the question of slavery's future cast a perceptible shadow over the debate. Calhoun's tortured doctrine of coequal sovereignty had been devised from the outset as a defensive fortification in the South's determined effort to protect and defend slavery from government interference. Even in 1830, Southerners peered into the future and envisioned a Northern majority that might attempt to interfere with their "domestic institutions."

In his groundbreaking book *Prelude to Civil War* (1965), William W. Freehling demonstrated that despite heated arguments about unfair tariffs and the tortuous effort to construct a viable states' rights doctrine, the understood subtext of the debate was the South's determination to defend and protect slavery. Even the father of the doctrine, John C. Calhoun, admitted that "I consider the Tariff, but as the occasion, rather than the real cause" of the national crisis. The real cause, he acknowledged, was the need to secure protection from "the majority of the Union" that might be tempted to interfere with "the peculiar domestic institutions of the Southern States." Another Southerner, William Harper, confessed that "in contending against the Tariff, I have always felt that we were battling the symptom rather than the disease," which was the potential for an unsympathetic national government that might upset the South's labor system.[12]

Events would demonstrate that the dispute between the champions of national government and the defenders of states' rights was less a debate about the distribution of authority in the Republic than it was about what a strong national government might *do* with the power it possessed. In fact, the professed champions of states' rights enthusiastically espoused national supremacy whenever it was used to protect slavery, as they did, for example, in their support of a national Fugitive Slave Law. In crafting the Compromise of 1850, Clay and Douglas had added a strong federal Fugitive Slave Law to the package of bills in order to entice Southerners to vote for it. That legislation was as obnoxious to many Northern states in the 1850s as the Tariff of Abominations had been to South Carolina in 1828. When Wisconsin and other states subsequently passed state legislation that would nullify the Fugitive Slave Law—laws known collectively as "Personal Liberty Laws,"—Southerners were loud in their insistence that federal law must be supreme over the laws of Wisconsin and of every other state. In this case, it was not the principle of states' rights that mattered, but Northern respect for Southern institutions.

Defenders of slavery feared that absent such respect, their labor system was doomed.

Lincoln agreed with Southern critics that a respect for national laws must trump state action, even when those national laws were (as Calhoun or Hayne might have said) "odious and despicable." As Lincoln told an audience in Peoria in 1854, "We are under legal obligations to catch and return their runaway slaves to them." He acknowledged it was a "dirty, disagreeable job," but it had been mandated by lawful authority, and he would hold his nose and obey it. Southerners, it seemed to him, wanted it both ways: a dominant federal law when it was needed to protect slavery, and a passive, submissive federal government when the Southern states sought to make their own rules. While a Southern commitment to states' rights was no doubt genuine, it was strengthened by fears that a powerful federal government might create the circumstances where slavery could no longer thrive, or even survive. The Southern commitment to states' rights, then, was more situational than Lincoln's commitment to nationalism.

Lincoln did not espouse a strong national central government because he saw that such an instrument would be useful in stopping the spread of slavery into the territories. Nor did he become an opponent of slavery because it would empower the national government. Instead, he was both a nationalist *and* a foe of slavery, and he remained faithful to both of those convictions even when they conflicted, as they did in the enforcement of the Fugitive Slave Law.[13]

* * *

The philosophical links between Webster's "Reply to Hayne" in 1830 and Lincoln's public remarks about government are nowhere more evident than in the first address the new president sent to Congress on July 4, 1861, two weeks before the Battle of Bull Run, and two years before the Battle of Gettysburg. In those written remarks, he explained in his carefully argued, almost professorial way what he understood to be the relationship between the national government and the states. His primary objective was to discredit secession as a legitimate response to losing a national election. After all, if the losing party in an election could overturn the outcome simply by removing itself from the body politic, the whole concept of a democracy was fatally flawed. In such circumstances, the nation—if it *was* a nation—would eventually become so fragmented it would dissolve into scores of disparate units until North America came to resemble the walled cities of medieval Europe.

To make this point, Lincoln, like Webster, declared that the states making up the Union were not "sovereign" at all, insisting that they had never been sovereign in any meaningful way. Indeed, Lincoln went beyond Webster by denying that something called a "state" even existed, or ever had existed, separate from its membership in the whole Union. "The Union," Lincoln noted, "is older than any of the States, and, in fact, it created them as States." Whatever legal status the states possessed, he told Congress, was a product of their being part of the Union, "and they have no other legal status." Before the American Revolution, they had been colonies of Britain, and afterward, they were component parts of a free national government. Except for Texas—which had briefly been a republic—they had never been sovereign. To assert such a status now, he insisted, was merely a lawyer's trick to make rebellion appear respectable. He subsequently labeled secession as "an ingenious sophism" invented to disguise what was in fact simple rebellion from lawful authority. The Southern insurrection was not the action of states, he told Congress, but of "a disloyal portion of the American people."[14]

In these remarks, Lincoln noted that the word "sovereign" did not appear in the constitution of any state, nor, for that matter, in the Constitution of the United States. The leaders of the Southern rebellion soon fixed that. The constitution they adopted to guide their nascent nation was nearly identical to the original, largely because they insisted that despite a perverse pride in being called "rebels," theirs was not a rebellion at all, but a kind of counterrevolution. It was Lincoln and the "black Republicans," they insisted, who had departed from the original meaning of the great founding document. They were simply restoring the kind of government the Founding Fathers had intended.

Nevertheless, in crafting their new version of the hallowed document, the leaders of the Confederate movement did feel obliged to correct what they saw as a few errors or oversights by the founders. Regarding the decades-old dispute over the future of slavery in the territories, the Confederate constitution specifically stipulated that "the institution of negro slavery, as it now exists in the Confederate States, shall be recognized and protected by Congress and by the Territorial government." On a more theoretical level, the Confederate founders also modified the preamble. In place of "We the People," the Southern version ascribed the origins of government to "We the deputies of the sovereign and independent States."

Here was the fundamental and decisive difference between Webster and Lincoln on the one hand, and "states' rights" Confederates on the other. Webster and Lincoln held that the United States was a single national government divided for administrative convenience into subordinate sections; to the Confederates, it was a voluntary association of sovereign and independent preexisting states that had banded together for mutual support.[15]

Lincoln knew that the challenges he confronted as president in 1861 could not be met at all unless the government he led was strong enough to meet them. To some extent, then, Lincoln's nationalism as president was undergirded by necessity. His willingness, even eagerness, to expand the powers of the national government, and particularly the executive, was a pragmatic reaction to the crisis he faced. Not only did a nationalist interpretation discredit secession, but it also justified the executive powers he would soon employ to conscript an army, blockade the southern coast, and suspend habeas corpus.

For all his pragmatism, however, Lincoln was a nationalist not simply out of convenience. For most of his adult life, he had thought deeply about the character of government in general and the American experiment in democracy in particular. He greatly revered both the Declaration of Independence and the Constitution and saw the great crisis of the 1860s as a test of whether a democracy based on the ideals they articulated could survive an internal challenge such as the one posed by the Southern rebellion. In responding to that crisis, he reached back not only to the founding documents but also to Henry Clay and Daniel Webster.

* * *

In 1861 it was still an open question whether the American experiment in democracy and self-government would work at all. Eighteenth-century European critics had frequently asserted that a democratic republic was too weak and too fragile to serve as a structure of government for so callous and volatile a species as humankind. It was a Hobbesian view that Lincoln disputed. He was no Pollyanna who believed that mankind was entirely trustworthy. That, after all, was why the founders had built checks and balances into the Constitution. But neither did he believe, as some argued, that a government must be either too powerful to tolerate individual freedom or too weak to maintain itself. In that context, the Civil War was democracy's trial by fire. As Lincoln put it in his July 4,

1861, address to Congress: "This issue . . . presents to the whole family of man, the question, whether a constitutional republic, or a democracy—a government of the people, by the same people—can or cannot maintain their territorial integrity, against its own domestic foes." In crafting those phrases, he almost certainly recalled Webster's similar phrasing in the "Second Reply to Hayne." Two-and-a-half years later he would transform them into poetry.[16]

Lincoln's nationalism, then, was both a pragmatic embrace of the kind of authority he would need as president to save the country and a philosophical commitment to the idea of how democracy worked—indeed, how it *had* to work if democracy was to survive. In 1787, as Benjamin Franklin was leaving the Constitutional Convention, a woman asked him, "Well, doctor, what have we got, a Republic or a Monarchy?" Franklin is reputed to have replied, "A Republic, madam, if you can keep it." Franklin knew that the keeping of it, as much as the making of it, would be a severe test of the national will. At Gettysburg, Lincoln reminded his generation, and future generations as well, that the great challenge was "whether that nation, or any nation" dedicated to the ideals of the founders could "long endure."[17]

There are several reasons why Lincoln's remarks at Gettysburg have survived for half a dozen generations as part of America's collective national memory. One, surely, is the lyric poetry of his language. Another, very likely, is the brevity of the speech—a mere 272 words. In a Twitter-driven world, such a compact explication of our national values at least stands a chance of being read from beginning to end. In addition, however, Lincoln's Gettysburg Address continues to resonate because he defined the war as a test of the great American experiment in democracy and self-government, reminding Americans that sustaining a nation based on the ideals of liberty and equality was a responsibility, a duty of citizenship that sometimes requires sacrifice—even "the last full measure of devotion"—to ensure that "this nation might live."

The nation for which the men at Gettysburg fought and died had been dedicated from its first moments to "the proposition that all men are created equal." For Lincoln, that alone made it worth the fight. In addition, however, the United States stood alone, throughout the world, as a practical experiment in erecting and maintaining a people's government. As Webster had lectured Hayne thirty-three years earlier: it was "the people's Constitution, the people's government, made for the people, made by the people, and answerable to the people." Should that government fail of its own weaknesses, of its inability to survive a hotly contested election—or fail to defend itself from rebellion—the critics of self-government would conclude that "any nation so conceived and so dedicated" was doomed. To save freedom and liberty, Lincoln had to be a nationalist.

Lincoln's views on the nature of government and human liberty continued to evolve to the very end. So, too, did the climate in which he articulated those views. War was—and is—a powerful agent of historical change. The country that went to war in 1861 was a very different thing two years later when Lincoln presented his remarks at Gettysburg. Today, more than a century and a half after the fact, it has become common to observe that before 1861 it was not unusual to employ a plural verb when referring to the United States (the United States *are*), whereas after 1865, it became nearly universal to use the singular (the United States *is*). It was the Civil War that made the United States a nation. In that respect, it is noteworthy that in his First Inaugural Address in March 1861, Lincoln did not use the word "nation" at all (though "national" appears twice), preferring to use the word "Union," which appears no less than seventeen times. At Gettysburg, two-and-a-half years later, he told his audience that what "our Fathers brought forth on this continent" was "a new *nation*." And in a speech of only 272 words, he used the word "nation" five times. In many ways the Civil War did that. But in many other ways, Lincoln himself had done it.

Notes

1. Speech at a Republican Banquet, Dec. 10, 1856, in *The Collected Works of Abraham Lincoln*, ed. Roy P. Basler, 9 vols. (New Brunswick, NJ: Rutgers University Press, 1953–1955), 2:383 (hereafter cited as *CW*).

2. F. W. Taussig, *The Tariff History of the United States* (New York: G. P. Putnam's Sons, 1910), 1:44–47.

3. Calhoun's "Exposition and Protest," in its several iterations, is printed in Clyde N. Wilson and Shirley B. Cook, *The Papers of John C. Calhoun* (Columbia: University of South Carolina, 1976), 10:444–539. The passage quoted here is from p. 446.

4. The definition of sovereignty is from the *Oxford English Dictionary*. The passages in the "Exposition" are in *The Papers of John C. Calhoun*, 10:495–496.

5. "Exposition and Protest," ibid.

6. Haynes's speech is in Niles's *Register of Congress* (21st Cong., 1st Sess.), 6:43–58. Quotations in this and the next two paragraphs are all from this speech.

7. Webster's "Reply to Hayne" is in Niles's *Register of Debates in Congress* (21st Cong., 1st Sess.), 6:58–80. Quotations in this and subsequent paragraphs are all from this speech.

8. Ibid., 6:73. Italics added.

9. Mark E. Neeley, *Lincoln and the Triumph of the Nation: Constitutional Conflict in the American Civil War* (Chapel Hill: University of North Carolina Press, 2011), 45–46.

10. Inaugural Address, Mar. 4, 1861, *CW*, 4:268.

11. Niles's *Register of Debates in Congress* (21st Cong., 1st sess.), 6:80.

12. Both Calhoun and Harper are quoted by William W. Freehling in *Prelude to Civil War: The Nullification Controversy in South Carolina, 1816–1836* (New York: Harper and Row, 1965), 250–256.

13. Speech at Peoria, Oct. 16, 1854, *CW*, 2:268.

14. Message to Congress, July 4, 1861, *CW*, 4:421–441. Quotations are from pp. 433, 434. One hundred twenty years later, another Republican president directly contradicted Lincoln's explication of the origins of government authority. Whereas Lincoln declared, "The Union is older than any of the States, and, in fact, it created them as States," Ronald Reagan in his 1981 Inaugural Address asserted that "the federal government did not create the States . . . the states created the Federal government." Reagan embraced this view of history because his goal was to diminish the power and authority of the national government, whereas Lincoln's goal, on the cusp of the Civil War, was not only to discredit secession but also to confirm the powers of government in order to win the war for national unity.

15. The Confederate founders also added an appeal to "Almighty God" to the preamble, thus eschewing the rigid secularity of the original document.

16. Presentation to Congress, July 4, 1861, *CW*, 4:426.

17. Franklin's quip is from notes taken at the convention by James McHenry and is quoted in "Papers of Dr. James McHenry on the Federal Constitution of 1787," *American Historical Review*, 11 (Apr. 1906): 618.

5

"Of all, by all, for all"

THEODORE PARKER, TRANSCENDENTALISM, AND THE GETTYSBURG ADDRESS

Dean Grodzins

IN THE GETTYSBURG Address, Abraham Lincoln declared that Union soldiers fought to preserve "government of the people, by the people, for the people."[1, 2] The poet Walt Whitman soon pronounced these words "a formula whose verbal shape is homely wit, but whose scope includes both the totality and all minutiæ" of the "political section" of democracy.[3] Whitman's judgment became the global consensus. In 1949, when an international group of scholars conducted the first survey of what people around the world meant by the term "democracy," they did not hesitate to use Lincoln's phrase as a "point of departure for clarification of the essential criteria" of the democratic concept.[4] Yet nowhere in the Address itself did Lincoln actually utter the word "democracy." We can be confident that Lincoln meant his words to refer to "democracy," however, because we know he adapted them from a profoundly moral concept of democracy articulated by a New England Transcendentalist, Theodore Parker.

Parker, a minister from Boston, was what we today would call a "public intellectual."[5] He could read more than twenty languages and seemed able to discourse learnedly on any topic, from theology to geology, law to literature, history to agriculture. At the same time, his many books and pamphlets were best-sellers on both sides of the Atlantic; his preaching attracted nearly 2 percent of the Boston population to his congregation; and his lectures packed halls from Maine to Illinois. In the mid-1840s, he began to describe America as, at least potentially, an ideal democracy, which he defined as a "government of all, by all, for all."[6] He later used this definition, or some variant of it, in many sermons and speeches, including some that Lincoln is known to have read.[7]

Lincoln respected Parker and found his definition of democracy compelling. Yet he also disagreed with Parker's thinking about the US Constitution and the rule of law. At Gettysburg, Lincoln reworked Parker's definition for his own purposes.

* * *

Lincoln never met or corresponded with Parker, but they had a personal connection through "Billy" Herndon, who worked with Lincoln for sixteen years as his junior law partner and political sidekick and later became his biographer. Herndon bought Parker's books, corresponded with him for five years, and met him twice: in 1856, when the intense, deep-voiced Parker gave a lecture in Springfield (Lincoln seems to have been out of town that day), and again in 1858.[8]

Herndon admired Parker as a religious thinker—"about the only man living," he once explained, "who can hold me steady."[9] Parker was the leading theologian of the New England Transcendentalist movement, which had taken shape in the 1830s and flourished through the middle decades of the nineteenth century. It is remembered today principally for its impact on American literature. Among the well-known writers affiliated with it were Ralph Waldo Emerson, Henry David Thoreau, Margaret Fuller, and Louisa May Alcott.[10] Yet while Transcendentalism had an important literary dimension, its fundamental concerns were religious. The Transcendentalists rejected the claim that the Bible had special, miraculous authority and developed a new theory of divine revelation.

Traditional Christian theology had distinguished between "natural" and "revealed" religion. Revealed religion was the supposedly miraculous, infallible, and authoritative revelation of God's word given to a few historical figures, such as St. Paul and above all Jesus, and recorded in scripture; natural religion, presumably exemplified in the ancient pagan philosophies and religions, was what fallible human reason, using only observation and logic, could figure out about God, morality, and immortality. Transcendentalists did away with this distinction, declaring that God in fact revealed truth to all people at all times in the same natural way. For the Transcendentalists, there was no essential difference between a poet and a prophet, in the sense that both were divinely inspired, nor any essential difference between different forms of religion, such as Christianity and Hinduism, in the sense that all were products of natural, divine revelation.[11] The Transcendentali believed people could intuitively know religious and moral truths that "transcended" observation; it is from this claim that the movement got its name.[12]

Parker preached Transcendentalism. Everyone, he insisted, received divine inspiration constantly and naturally from God, although no one could take in more inspiration than their minds and souls could comprehend, and none saw the whole truth, which he referred to as the Absolute Religion. Parker argued that the biblical writers were, like us, divinely inspired but limited and fallible. He honored their sincerity and heroism, but held that their views were sometimes warped by the ignorance and barbarism of the times in which they lived. Civilization had, he believed, through divine providence, grown more enlightened and moral since they wrote, so in some things, we were more divinely inspired than they had been. For example, we now knew, as many of them apparently did not, that slavery was morally wrong. Parker had no interest in the debate, raging in his day among Protestant evangelicals, over whether the Bible was against slavery. As he once remarked, if St. Paul had condoned slavery (as some held that he had, in the Letter to Philemon), "then so much the worse for Paul."[13]

Parker's Transcendentalist theology appealed to people like Herndon, who had a skeptical view of scripture and traditional theology but a powerful need for faith, a strong commitment to social reform, especially antislavery, and an intellectual bent. Years after both Parker and Lincoln had died, Herndon, as well as another old Lincoln friend, Jesse Fell, author of Lincoln's presidential campaign biography in 1860, would claim that Lincoln "generally much admired and approved" Parker's religious writings; in Fell's words, "If . . . I was called upon to designate an author whose views most nearly represented Mr. Lincoln's on . . . [religion], I would say that author was Theodore Parker."[14] Yet based on the sparing remarks Lincoln made regarding his own faith—he was generally reticent on the subject—these claims that Lincoln was somehow a Transcendentalist appear exaggerated.

Lincoln, like Herndon, is known to have had skeptical tendencies, both toward traditional Christian theology and toward scripture.[15] He ling the Bible, but had no desire to take everything ese matters, Lincoln would have found in Parker he seems to have had respect for Transcendental- ovement, at least insofar as it was represented by erson, who by the 1850s was generally recognized as the leading American man of letters. During the Civil War, Emerson was introduced to Lincoln at the White House, and the president greeted him cheerfully: "O Mr. Emerson, I once heard you say in a lecture, that a Kentuckian seems to say by his air & manners, *'Here am I; if you don't like me, the worse for you.'*" Emerson had in fact uttered these words from a podium in Springfield nine years earlier, while delivering a series of lectures there; Lincoln had been interested enough in Emerson to have gone to hear him and, as a native Kentuckian, had been struck forcefully enough by this remark to recall it (very accurately, in fact), long afterward.[16]

Lincoln never gave any hint, however, that he shared the Transcendentalists' view of divine inspiration, and his view of God differed from Parker's. The Transcendentalists, at least in their more mystical moments, believed people could be so infused with divine inspiration as to know God's will and nature; Parker was confident that God was infinitely loving and benevolent. By contrast, Lincoln seems to have feared that any unqualified claim to know God's will would lead to fanaticism, and late in the Civil War, as the brutal conflict dragged on, contrary to the fervent hopes and prayers of both sides, he concluded that the "Almighty has his own purposes"–to punish both North and South for having condoned slavery for so long—a very un-Parkerian idea that Lincoln expressed in his Second Inaugural Address.[17]

Nonetheless, Lincoln seems to have found compelling Parker's thinking about democracy, which was shaped by Parker's Transcendentalist outlook. Parker was among the first important American thinkers to claim both that America was and ought to be a democracy, and that democracy and slavery were fundamentally incompatible and could not coexist.

Parker's position on democracy can be distinguished from that of the American founders. The founding generation tended to associate the concept of "democracy" with the people legislating directly in open-air assemblies, as in ancient Athens, a system they believed inevitably degenerated into mob rule. They therefore preferred to describe the government they were creating as a "republic," in which the people had ultimate authority but little direct control over governmental affairs, operating instead through representatives and with the power of the people checked by law.

Many Americans during antebellum era still stood proudly within this tradition, including the lawyer and statesman Daniel Webster, who along with Parker probably helped inspire Lincoln's "government of the people" phrase in the Gettysburg Address. In Webster's most famous speech, delivered in a US Senate debate with Robert Hayne of South Carolina in 1830, he had denied Hayne's argument that the Constitution was a compact among sovereign states, each of which had the authority to nullify federal laws it believed violated that compact. Is the Constitution, Webster asked, "the creature of the State legislatures, or the creature of the people?" He answered his own question emphatically, drawing language from the preamble of the Constitution ("We the People"): it is "the people's Constitution, the people's government, made for the people, made by the people, and answerable to the people."[18]

Lincoln considered this speech, known as the "Second Reply to Hayne," to be "the grandest specimen of American oratory" and is said to have committed much of it to memory.[19] He agreed with Webster's nationalist interpretation of the Constitution, and, in his First Inaugural Address and elsewhere, adapted the arguments Webster had made against nullification to refute Southern claims that secession was constitutional. No doubt, therefore, Webster's reference to the "people's Constitution" was on Lincoln's mind at Gettysburg, because the Constitution was on his mind there. Yet, democracy was also on Lincoln's mind, and he would have gleaned nothing about America as a democracy from the "Second Reply." In fact, Webster never, in any writing, referred to the United States as a democracy. He considered it, as had the founders he so admired, a constitutional republic. In Webster's last major address, he distinguished between the government of America and the "pure democracy" of ancient Athens, which had lacked both "the principle of representation" and, more importantly, "a fixed, settled, definite, fundamental law, or constitution, imposing limitations and restraints equally on governors and governed."[20]

Webster, twenty-seven years older than Lincoln, spoke for his generation, among whom suspicion of democracy was still commonplace. By the 1830s, however, when both Lincoln and Parker (born eighteen months apart) launched their careers, near-universal white male suffrage had been achieved; members of their generation took for granted that America was a democracy, and that this was a good thing.[21]

Lincoln himself, in an early speech, referred to "the sacred name of Democracy."[22] By democracy, most Americans meant a popular majority actually running the government according to its will, although they continued to hold that the power of the majority should be constrained by the Constitution. As Lincoln himself explained in his First Inaugural Address, "A majority, held in restraint by constitutional checks, and limitations, and always changing easily, with deliberate changes of popular opinions and sentiments, is the only true sovereign of a free people."[23]

Parker, however, considered the concept of democracy as simply lawful majority rule to be amoral and therefore inadequate. He was particularly disgusted with the many American politicians who championed democracy for whites only, while defending slavery. In Parker's view, their idea of democracy was "Satanic." "Celestial" democracy, he believed, would look quite different.[24]

American democracy, according to Parker, had developed from what he saw as the fundamental American sentiment, love of freedom. This sentiment had been articulated as an idea, which he called "the American Idea," in the Declaration of Independence: that all persons had inalienable rights, that in respect to these rights they were equal, and that governments were established to protect these rights. The great American project, he believed, was to turn this transcendental idea, which we knew intuitively to be true even though it contradicted most historical experience, into a historical fact. Put another way, as Parker did in a lecture from 1844, America needed *"to organize the Rights of man*—not the privileges of a class." Americans must therefore recognize that *"there is no permanent & real welfare for any one portion in Society except in connection with the welfare of all the rest of society."*[25] Parker came to describe the form of government that America was destined to create as a "government of all, by all, for all." In *this* vision of democracy, slavery, which by its very nature involved the exploitation of one portion of society by another, could have no place.

The best-known story of how Parker's Transcendentalist definition of democracy first impressed Lincoln comes from Herndon. In his biography of his friend, he described taking a trip in 1858 to meet eastern Republican Party leaders and gauge their support for Lincoln's upcoming Senate campaign against Stephen Douglas. Among other places, Herndon stopped in Boston, where he heard Parker preach, called on him at home, and picked up copies of his recent publications. One of these, Herndon recalled, was a pamphlet sermon, *The Effect of Slavery on the American People*, which he brought back to Illinois and lent to Lincoln. Lincoln eventually gave it back to him with the following sentence marked in pencil: "Democracy is direct self-government, over all the people, for all the people, by all the people."[26] Herndon's story has been accepted by many authorities, but it cannot be accurate: Herndon's visit to Boston took place in March 1858, while Parker did not preach and publish the sermon until July. Still, Lincoln may well have read and marked it as Herndon said.[27]

Yet Lincoln probably already knew of Parker's phrase by 1858, having most likely noticed it in 1854. That May, Congress passed the Kansas-Nebraska Act, allowing every Western territory to decide for itself whether to permit slavery. Lincoln strongly opposed the law and helped organize what became the Republican Party, which made a congressional ban on slavery in the territories its central demand. Until this point, Lincoln, however much he privately hated slavery, had been decidedly moderate in his public opposition to it. Now his criticism of slavery grew more forceful and pointed. He had started down an antislavery path that would eventually lead him to issue the Emancipation Proclamation and to write the Gettysburg Address.

In this same pivotal year, Parker delivered a series of high-profile sermons and speeches on the mounting sectional crisis, and Herndon began a regular correspondence with him. In Herndon's first letters to Parker, written in May and June, he claimed that he owned all of Parker's published works and specifically praised Parker's recent political pronouncements for their *"Eloquent & Enthusiastic* power."[28] Among most important of these pronouncements was a long sermon on the "Nebraska Question," which Parker had preached in February and published a few weeks later, as the Kansas-Nebraska legislation was being debated in Congress. Parker here denounced the proposed law as an "Assault upon Freedom in America." Lincoln almost certainly read this discourse, which was on a subject of burning interest to him. If he did so, he would have encountered Parker's definition of democracy two times, each conspicuous.

Parker always liked to place current events in broad historical context. He here described the fight over the Kansas-Nebraska Bill as an episode in a struggle that had been going on for centuries, ever since the "Anglo-Saxons" first settled in North America, between two instincts, one "stationary, if not retrogressive," the other "progressive." According to Parker, the former instinct condoned or promoted, while the latter aimed to destroy, a "fourfold despotism": "Theocracy," which he defined as the subordination of the needs of the human soul to arbitrary theological claims about the authority of the Bible and church; Monarchy, "the subordination of the mass of men to a single man"; Aristocracy, "the subordination of the many to the few, of the weak to the strong"; and "Despotocracy," the "subordination of the slave who toils to the master that enjoys."[29] Parker argued that the progressive program had for its ultimate aim to establish "a Democracy, which . . . is the government of all, for all, by all."[30]

Parker portrayed America as having succeeded in uprooting monarchy, aristocracy, and much of theocracy, but despotocracy, in the form of Southern slavery, remained. Owing to the cupidity and cowardice of the North, slavery had won repeated victories over the course of US history, starting with the compromises of the Constitution and continuing through the Fugitive Slave Act. The Kansas-Nebraska Bill was its latest attack on democracy but would hardly be its last, unless the North found the courage to stand up to Southern aggression. In the final paragraph of the sermon, where Lincoln could not have missed it, Parker predicted that if "we put slavery under our feet," then the "blessing of Almighty God will come down upon the noblest people the world ever saw—who have triumphed over Theocracy, Monarchy, Aristocracy, Despotocracy and have got a Democracy—a government of all, for all, and by all—a Church without a Bishop, a State without a King, a Community without a Lord, and a Family without a Slave."[31]

Lincoln may have quietly appreciated Parker's attack on "Theocracy." But the concept of a "family without a slave" would have struck him forcefully. He had remarked in an early speech, "I used to be a slave"—a reference to his father forcing him to stay home from school and toil without pay. Lincoln remained bitter enough about this treatment that he later refused to visit his father when the old man lay dying or to help pay for his headstone.[32] Insofar as "government of all, by all, for all" meant "a family without a *slave*," then Lincoln would have been for it. "As I would not be a slave, so I would not be a *master*," Lincoln wrote in the late 1850s. "This expresses my idea of democracy. Whatever differs from this, to the extent of the difference, is no democracy."[33]

Lincoln seems to have found appealing Parker's moral vision of democracy grounded on human rights, and Parker's writings appear to have influenced a number of Lincoln's pronouncements in the late 1850s. For example, in a speech Lincoln delivered in late 1856, he sounded a great deal like Parker when, according to a news report, he "showed the tendency and aim of the Sham Democracy to degrade labor to subvert the true ends of Government and build up Aristocracy, Despotism and Slavery."[34] Again, Lincoln's "House Divided" speech (1858) se[...] enced by a sermon Parker preached in July 1854, [...] Threaten the Rights of Man in America." Here, Pa[...] as without a "national Unity of Idea," using St. [...] a "'house divided against itself'; of course it canr[...] Parker argued, two hostile ideas, "mutually inv[...]

were in competition. One was freedom, which must eventually produce a democracy—that is a "government of all, by all, for all"; the other, slavery, which must produce despotism—that is, "a government of all, by a part, for the sake of a part." Lincoln's speech, meanwhile, famously took its central metaphor from the same biblical passage and also argued that America could not remain half slave and half free, but must someday become wholly one or the other. Parker, when he read the speech (Herndon had sent him a copy), was understandably pleased and wrote to Herndon that Lincoln's statements were "*noble*."[35]

Despite the apparent appeal of Parker's ideas to Lincoln, he felt compelled, at Gettysburg, to modify Parker's definition of democracy, transforming Parker's "government of all" to "government of the people." No doubt, Lincoln made this change partly because Parker's phrase referred to an ideal form of government, one that Parker admitted had never existed, fully developed, in human history, while Lincoln wanted to refer to the actual government of the United States, and so used the language of the preamble of the Constitution (and of Webster in the "Second Reply to Hayne"). Yet Lincoln also seems to have made this change of wording because he disagreed with Parker's thinking about the Constitution and the rule of law.[36]

Their differences can be seen in their divergent responses to the Fugitive Slave Law of 1850. Many thousands of slaves had fled the South over the decades, seeking refuge in the free states, and slaveholders had long accused state officials and laws in the North of obstructing their efforts to reclaim their human property. The new federal law responded to these complaints by establishing a national slave-catching bureaucracy, composed of hundreds of federal court commissioners across the North. These commissioners could authorize the arrest, and the removal south, of any alleged runaway on the complaint of a slave catcher. The complaint was to be assumed valid unless proven otherwise at a summary hearing; at this brief hearing, the alleged slave was not required to have a lawyer and was explicitly forbidden to offer testimony on his or her own behalf. Anyone convicted of helping a fugitive escape, meanwhile, would be subjected to steep fines and prison.

The Fugitive Slave Law appalled Parker, who believed it grossly violated the human rights of all blacks, free as well as fugitive, and imposed "slave law" on Massachusetts. His view was shared by the other Transcendentalists, who all firmly believed that when human law contradicted the law of God, as it was revealed to us by divine inspiration to our conscience, we should obey the higher law. Henry Thoreau, for example, had argued in his seminal essay "Civil Disobedience" (1849) that individuals must never acknowledge the authority of an unjust government, even if such refusal meant going to jail.[37] He did not hesitate to serve as a "conductor" on the Underground Railroad, helping fugitive slaves escape capture. Parker responded to the Fugitive Slave Law by calling on the people of Boston to flout it and by founding and leading the Boston Vigilance Committee, which sought by organized, collective action to render the law inoperative in Massachusetts.[38]

In the course of Parker's fight against the Fugitive Slave Law, he came to reevaluate the speech Lincoln admired so much, the "Second Reply to Hayne." "It is customary at the North," Parker noted, in what was probably his best-selling sermon, occasioned by the death of Daniel Webster in 1852,

> to think Mr. Webster wholly in the right, and South Carolina wholly in the wrong, on the question of nullification; but it should be remembered, that some of the ablest men whom the South ever sent to Washington thought otherwise. There was a good deal of truth in the speech of Mr. Hayne: he was alarmed at the increase of the central power, which seemed to invade the rights of the States.[39]

Lincoln never admitted the right of any state, Northern or Southern, to nullify a federal law. Regarding the Fugitive Slave Law specifically, while admitting that he personally would not want to catch a runaway, and that the law was objectionable, he maintained that the North was constitutionally obligated to return fugitive slaves, and that the Fugitive Slave Law should be obeyed as the law of the land, and as way of reconciling slaveholders to the Union.[40] During the Civil War, his administration endorsed a policy of refusing to return fugitive slaves who had fled from rebel-controlled areas, declaring them "contraband of war," yet it was slow to act against the constitutional guarantees that still applied to slaveholders in the loyal Border States. Lincoln never requested that Congress repeal the Fugitive Slave Law, and it only did so in 1864, by which point the Thirteenth Amendment to the Constitution, abolishing slavery altogether and thus rendering the issue moot, was pending.

Underlying Lincoln's difference with Parker over the Fugitive Slave Law was a very different understanding of the authority of the Constitution. Parker viewed it in the same Transcendental way as he viewed the authority of the Bible. Just as we should obey scriptural injunctions only insofar as they were consonant with the Absolute Religion, so we should regard constitutional clauses as binding only insofar as they were consonant with the American Idea, expressed in the Declaration of Independence. Lincoln, by contrast, always recognized as binding the authority of all constitutional provisions. He did, however, begin to insist, as in his 1858 Senate campaign debates with Stephen Douglas, that these provisions had to be interpreted in light of the Declaration.

The deepest difference between Parker and Lincoln concerned Parker's growing support, during the 1850s, for extralegal violence. This position grew from his belief that our duty to obey the law of God far superseded any obligation to honor human law or custom, and his understanding of the processes of human moral progress, which he believed had often been furthered by violence, as in the American and French Revolutions.[41]

In Parker's first sermon in response to enactment of the Fugitive Slave Law, he argued that "the fugitive has the same natural right to defend himself against the slave catcher, or his constitutional tool, that he has against a murderer or wolf. The man who attacks me to reduce me to slavery, in that moment of attack alienates his right to life, and if I were the fugitive, and could escape no other way, I would kill him with as little compunction as I would drive a mosquito from my face."[42] Four years later, when the fugitive slave Anthony Burns was arrested in Boston, Parker spoke to a mass protest meeting urging Bostonians to act according to what he called "the Law of the People, when they are sure they are right and determined to go ahead." Those at least were the words he uttered from the podium, according to a reporter; but in the manuscript notes from which he spoke, he called it, without euphemism, *"Lynch Law."*[43] As he delivered this speech, a group of armed abolitionists did try to rescue Burns; the attempt failed, and a guard was killed. The next Sunday, in a pulpit address, Parker proclaimed the assault a righteous act and asserted that although Bostonians always obeyed laws "made by the people, for the people" that "respect justice," the Fugitive Slave Law, made by "our Southern masters," was "not worth keeping."[44]

In all this, Lincoln could not go with Parker. He could never endorse lynch law, which he had always decried as a "danger to our political institutions." Although he conceded (as in his First Inaugural Address) that the Fugitive Slave Law could never be perfectly enforced where "the moral sense of the people imperfectly supports" it, he never tried to excuse or defend violent resistance to the law.[45]

Finally, in 1858, Parker became a member of the secret committee that financed and armed John Brown's bloody, quixotic attempt to start a slave uprising in Virginia. The following year, as the captured, unrepentant Brown awaited hanging, Parker wrote a public letter defending Brown's actions. Parker declared (the emphasis was his), "A MAN HELD AGAINST HIS WILL AS A SLAVE HAS A NATURAL RIGHT TO KILL EVERY ONE WHO SEEKS TO PREVENT HIS ENJOYMENT OF LIBERTY"; and "IT MAY BE A NATURAL DUTY OF THE SLAVE TO DEVELOP THIS RIGHT IN A PRACTICAL MANNER, AND ACTU-ALLY KILL ALL THOSE WHO SEEK TO PREVENT HIS ENJOYMENT OF LIBERTY"; and, finally, "IT MAY BE A NATURAL DUTY FOR THE FREEMAN TO HELP THE SLAVES TO THE ENJOYMENT OF THEIR LIBERTY, AND AS A MEANS TO THAT END, TO AID THEM IN KILL-ING ALL SUCH AS OPPOSE THEIR NATURAL FREEDOM."[46] This letter turned out to be Parker's last major public statement. Soon after it was published, he died of tuberculosis.

If Lincoln read Parker's final pronouncement, he would no doubt have agreed with one statement: "we must give up DEMOCRACY if we keep SLAVERY, or SLAVERY if we keep DEMOCRACY." He reacted quite differently than Parker, however, to Brown's attack in Virginia.[47] In a speech delivered around the time Parker wrote, Lincoln admitted that Brown had shown "great courage" and "rare unselfishness," but insisted that what Brown had done was "a violation of law and it was, as all such attacks must be, futile as far any effect it might have on the extinction of a great evil."[48]

* * *

Lincoln won the presidency in November 1860 on a platform of barring slavery from the West; before his inaugural, in March 1861, seven Southern states responded to his victory by declaring that they had seceded from the Union. From the beginning of the crisis, Lincoln was clear that he thought secession unconstitutional. He was also sure that it was undemocratic, but he needed time to articulate exactly how. In the process, he seems to have turned to Parker's Transcendentalist definition of democracy, although he came to rework it in light of his commitments to the Constitution and the rule of law.

In Lincoln's First Inaugural Address, he claimed that the South was rejecting majority rule, with disastrous consequences: "Unanimity is impossible; the rule of a minority, as a permanent arrangement, is wholly inadmissable; so that, rejecting the majority principle, anarchy, or despotism in some form, is all that is left."⁴⁹ The problem with applying this argument to the secession crisis, however, was that although he had been *constitutionally* elected in 1860, winning a majority of the *electoral* votes, he had actually received less than 40 percent of the total *popular* vote. His own administration could therefore plausibly be seen as constituting "the rule of a minority."

Lincoln recognized this difficulty by the time he wrote his first message to Congress, in July 1861, when he argued that the fundamental issue posed by the Southern rebellion (extended now to eleven states) was "whether discontented individuals, too few in numbers to control administration, *according to organic law, in any case,* can always . . . break up their Government, and thus practically put an end to free government upon the earth" (emphasis added).⁵⁰ The key modifying phrase here was "according to organic law," meaning the Constitution. In other words, Lincoln now argued that secession did not threaten majority rule as such but democratic constitutional government.

While writing and revising this paragraph, Lincoln seems to have clarified for himself how he could adapt and use Parker's concept of an ideal "government of all." In the first draft, Lincoln simply replaced Parker's aspirational "all" with the constitutional term, "the people"; Lincoln described the Southern rebellion as having presented to the world the question of "whether a democracy—a government of the people, by the same people" could survive. In the final version, Lincoln worded the question differently reinforcing change he was making in Parker's idea: "whether *a constitutional republic, or* a democracy—a government of the people, by the same people" could survive (emphasis added).⁵¹

Lincoln's thinking about democracy and the Constitution seems to have only intensified in 1862 as he considered the problem of emancipation. Lincoln always, both before the Civil War and during it, adhered to the mainstream view that Congress had no authority under the Constitution to abolish slavery in the states. He nonetheless held that because the Constitution made him, as president, the commander in chief of the army, he was obliged to consider all militarily necessary measures to suppress the rebellion, and the Emancipation Proclamation was such a measure.

Lincoln's critics, however, rejected this constitutional reasoning, and their arguments could not be easily dismissed. One of the most distinguished of them, the former Supreme Court Justice Benjamin Robbins Curtis, argued in a best-selling pamphlet that although the Constitution unquestionably gave the federal government authority to suppress a rebellion in a state, it gave it none whatsoever to change the laws and institutions of a state, which was exclusively the prerogative of the loyal citizens of that state. In other words, the rebellion had not changed the constitutional fact that only the Southern states themselves could abolish slavery.[52] Moreover, the power of the commander in chief derived from the Constitution and so remained subject to its restrictions, and the Proclamation violated those restrictions. It took property (slaves) from citizens (slaveholders, even loyal ones, if they happened to reside in a rebellious state) without due process—a course of action that American courts had never permitted any American military officer to pursue, much less the commander in chief.[53]

Curtis's basic point concerned preservation of the rule of law, and it resonates even today. He acknowledged that the exigencies of a crisis "may imperatively demand instant and vigorous . . . action [by the president], passing beyond the limits of the laws." Yet Curtis insisted that no such acts could have any validity once the emergency had passed and must be recognized for what they were, "a legal wrong." The president who perpetrated them must eventually be held liable for them in the courts. They might there be ruled justifiable, considering the circumstances, yet their illegality must always be acknowledged by all parties or a dangerous precedent will have been established.[54] From Curtis's point of view, the Emancipation Proclamation failed the tests of a justifiable emergency measure because it permanently abrogated a large body of existing state law (regarding slavery) and overturned the authority of the states, which Lincoln conceded they had under the Constitution, to regulate their own affairs (regarding slavery).

Lincoln never responded directly to Curtis, and in fact a strong reply to Curtis's argument was difficult to make, assuming a strict understanding of American government as a limited, constitutional republic. In an 1864 letter, Lincoln declared that he "never had a theory that secession could absolve States or people from their [constitutional] obligations": "It was because of my belief in the continuation of these *obligations*, that I was puzzled, for a time, as to denying the legal *rights* of those citizens who remained individually innocent of treason or rebellion" (emphasis original).[55] He solved this puzzle by taking up a version of Parker's view of the American government as fundamentally a democracy, and of the Constitution, although the "organic law," as nonetheless only an expression of American democracy. It could not survive unless American democracy survived, and American democracy could only survive if he vastly and permanently expanded the human rights of millions of Americans, by freeing them from bondage.

Ten months after Lincoln issued the Emancipation Proclamation, he wrote the Gettysburg Address, in which he immortalized Parker's Transcendentalist definition of democracy, in modified form. Parker's "government of all, by all, for all" referred to an ideal form of democracy, based on human rights, which Americans should aspire to build; Lincoln's adaptation referred to the existing, admittedly flawed, American government, based on rule of law, and seen in the Constitution, which he was leading a war to defend. Yet the aspirational quality of Parker's phrase inhered in Lincoln's version. By the time Lincoln spoke at Gettysburg, American slavery was everywhere crumbling. Only with this "new birth of freedom," Lincoln now believed, could the American constitutional republic be infused with democracy, rule of law be reconciled with human rights, and both the Constitution and democracy not perish from the earth.

Notes

1. A few sentences of this essay are taken from Dean Grodzins, "The Abolitionist Behind the Gettysburg Address," The Root, www.TheRoot.com, Nov. 2, 2013. Used by permission.

2. Gettysburg Address, *Collected Works of Abraham Lincoln*, ed. Roy P. Basler, 9 vols. (New Brunswick, NJ: Rutgers University Press, 1951–1953), 7:23 (hereafter cited as *CW*).

3. Walt Whitman, "Democratic Vistas," in *Walt Whitman: Complete Poetry and Selected Prose*, ed. Justin Kaplan (The Library of America, 1982), 943.

4. "ON THE MEANINGS OF 'DEMOCRACY': THE UNESCO INQUIRY," *Journal of General Education* 4, no. 1 (Oct. 1949): 57.

5. Biographies of Parker include Grodzins, *American Heretic: Theodore Parker and Transcendentalism* (Chapel Hill: University of North Carolina, 2002), and Paul Teed, *A Revolutionary Conscience: Theodore Parker and Antebellum America* (Lanham, MD: University Press of America, 2010).

6. Grodzins, *American Heretic*, 405–407, 498.

7. Robert Bray, "What Abraham Lincoln Read: An Evaluative and Annotated List," *Journal of the Abraham Lincoln Association* 28, no. 2 (2007): 69, indicates that Lincoln almost certainly read the two volumes of Parker's *Additional Speeches, Addresses, and Occasional Sermons* (Boston: Little, Brown, 1855), and *The Effect of Slavery on the American People* (1858), which is reprinted in Parker, *Saint Barnard and Other Papers, Collected Works of Theodore Parker: Centennial Edition* (Boston: American Unitarian Association, 1912).

8. David Herbert Donald, *Lincoln's Herndon: A Biography* ([1948]; New York: Da Capo, 1989), 54–56; William Herndon to Theodore Parker, Nov. 12, 1856, and Parker to Herndon, Nov. 17, 1856, Herndon-Parker Correspondence, Abraham Lincoln Presidential Library (hereafter cited as ALP); Notebook, Theodore Parker Papers, vol. 16, Massachusetts Historical Society.

9. Herndon to Lydia C. Parker, Mar. 30, 1857, Herndon-Parker Correspondence, ALP.

10. For histories of the movement, see Grodzins, *American Heretic*; Barbara Packer, *The Transcendentalists* (Athens, GA: University of Georgia Press, 2007); Philip F. Gura, *American Transcendentalism: A History* (New York: Hill and Wang, 2007).

11. On the centrality of the concept of natural, universal, divine inspiration to Transcendentalism, see Grodzins, "Unitarianism," in *The Oxford Handbook of Transcendentalism*, ed. Joel Myerson, Sandy Petrulionis, and Laura Walls (New York: Oxford, 2010), 52–61.

12. Specifically, the New Englanders appropriated the term "transcendentalism" from the German idealist philosopher Immanuel Kant (1724–1804), who, however, had meant something different by it. He had argued in *The Critique of Pure*

Reason and other works that the human mind structured all sensory input according to "transcendental" categories, which could not be learned from experience, such as time, space, and cause and effect.

13. Parker, "The Slave Power in America," *Speeches, Addresses and Occasional Sermons* (Boston: Crosby and Nichols, 1852), 2:203.

14. William H. Herndon and Jesse Weik, *Herndon's Life of Lincoln* ([1888]; Cleveland, OH: World Publishing; 1943), 359.

15. An excellent discussion of Lincoln's religious development is Allen Guelzo, *Abraham Lincoln: Redeemer President* (Grand Rapids, MI: William B. Eerdman's, 1999).

16. Stephen Cushman, "When Lincoln Met Emerson," *Journal of the Civil War Era* 3, no. 2 (2013): 163–183. The quotation comes from Emerson's manuscript account of this incident; in the original, he left out the standard quotation marks, which I have supplied. Bray, "What Lincoln Read," 48, indicates that Lincoln may have read *Emerson's Essays: First Series* and *Representative Men*.

17. Second Inaugural Address, *CW*, 8:332–333. See also John Burt, *Lincoln's Tragic Pragmatism: Lincoln, Douglas, and Moral Conflict* (Cambridge, MA: Harvard University Press, 2013), 670–707.

18. Daniel Webster, "Second Reply to Hayne," The *Papers of Daniel Webster: Speeches and Formal Writings*, ed. Charles M. Wiltse (Hanover, NH: Dartmouth University Press, 1975), 1:330.

19. Garry Wills, *Lincoln at Gettysburg: The Words That Remade America* (New York: Simon and Schuster, 1992), 34.

20. Webster, "The Dignity and Importance of History," *Papers of Daniel Webster*, 2:636–637.

21. For a subtle examination of the many dimensions of this shift, see Robert H. Weibe, *Self-Rule: A Cultural History of American Democracy* (Chicago: University of Chicago Press, 1995), 13–40.

22. "Speech on the Sub-Treasury," *CW*, 1:162.

23. First Inaugural Address, *CW*, 4:268.

24. Parker, "Thoughts on America," *Additional Speeches*, 2:33; "New Crime Against Humanity," *Additional Speeches*, 2:93.

25. Parker, "Lessons taught us by the example, history & fate of other nations," mss. Lecture, 1844, Andover-Harvard Theological Library.

26. See Herndon, *Herndon's Life of Lincoln*, 323; Parker, "Effect of Slavery," *Saint Bernard and Other Papers*, 322.

27. *Bartlett's Familiar Quotations: 16th Edition* (Boston: Little, Brown, 1992), 461 n.5, accepts Herndon's version of events; but see Carl F. Wiek, *Lincoln's Quest for Equality: The Road to Gettysburg* (Dekalb: Northern Illinois University Press, 2002), 48–49.

28. Herndon to Parker, June 11, 1854, Herndon-Parker correspondence, ALP; emphasis in original. Herndon mentions having written Parker one letter some years

(evidently) before 1854, without receiving a reply; see Herndon to Parker, May 13, 1854, Herndon-Parker correspondence, ALP.

29. Parker, "The Nebraska Question" *Additional Speeches*, 1:339, 309–317, 326.

30. Ibid., 1:327.

31. Ibid., 1:380.

32. Guelzo, *Abraham Lincoln*, 121, 159–160.

33. "Definition of Democracy," *CW*, 2:532; emphasis in original.

34. "Speech at Belleville, Illinois," *CW*, 2:379.

35. Parker to Herndon, Aug. 28. 1858, Parker-Herndon correspondence, ALP; emphasis in original.

36. Parker, "The Dangers which Threaten the Rights of Man in America," *Additional Speeches*, 2:250, 256, 252, 254 see especially Wiek, *Lincoln's Quest for Equality*, 91–123.

37. Henry David Thoreau, "Civil Disobedience," in *Henry David Thoreau: Collected Essays and Poems*, ed. Elizabeth Hall Witherell (Library of America, 2001), 203–224.

38. See Grodzins, "'Constitution or No Constitution, Law or No Law': The Boston Vigilance Committees, 1841–1861," in *Massachusetts and the Civil War: The Commonwealth and National Disunion*, ed. Conrad E. Wright, Matthew Mason, and Katheryn P. Viens (Amherst: University of Massachusetts Press, 2015).

39. Parker, "Daniel Webster," *Additional Speeches*, 1:200.

40. On Lincoln's attitude toward the Fugitive Slave Law, see for example, Burt, *Lincoln's Tragic Pragmatism*, 230–235.

41. See Grodzins, "Why Theodore Parker Backed John Brown: The Political and Social Roots of Support for Abolitionist Violence," in *Terrible Swift Sword: The Legacy of John Brown*, ed. Paul Finkleman and Peggy Russo (Athens, OH: Ohio University Press, 2005), 3–22.

42. Parker, "The Function of Conscience," *Speeches, Addresses*, 1:258.

43. Grodzins, "'Slave Law' versus 'Lynch Law' in Boston: Benjamin Robbins Curtis, Theodore Parker, and the Fugitive Slave Crisis, 1850–1855," *Massachusetts Historical Review* 12 (2010), 15.

44. Parker, "Lesson for the Day," *Additional Speeches*, 2:80.

45. "Address before the Young Men's Lyceum of Springfield, Illinois," *CW*, 1:109–113; First Inaugural Address, *CW*, 4:269.

46. Parker, *John Brown's Expedition Reviewed* (Boston: The Fraternity, 1860), 4, 5.

47. Ibid., 4.

48. "Speech at Elwood, Kansas," *CW*, 3:496.

49. First Inaugural Address, *CW*, 4:268

50. "Message to Congress in Special Session," *CW*, 4:426.

51. Ibid., 4:426, 426n.

52. B. R. Curtis, "Executive Power," in *A Memoir of Benjamin Robbins Curtis*, G. T. Curtis (Boston: Little, Brown, 1879), 2:312, 318–319, 329–332.

53. Ibid., 2:321–323, 321–322n.

54. Ibid., 2:313–314. See also Stuart Streichler, *Justice Curtis in the Civil War Era: at the Crossroads of American Constitutionalism* (Charlottesville: University of Virginia Press, 2005), 159–164.

55. Lincoln to William Crosby and Henry P. Nichols, Jan. 14, 1864, *CW*, 7:132; emphasis in original.

6

Death and the Gettysburg Address

Mark S. Schantz

LINCOLN'S GETTYSBURG ADDRESS transformed America's engagement
with death during the Civil War. In dedicating the new Soldiers' cemetery at Gettysburg, Lincoln tethered himself to earlier American traditions regarding the memorialization of the dead—and the rural cemetery
movement, particularly—while simultaneously staking out new terrain.
It is impossible to read the Gettysburg Address apart from "the nineteenth century's fascination with death in general and with cemeteries
in particular."[1] At the same time, Lincoln's dedicatory remarks at Gettysburg, and the very ground on which he stood, dramatically shifted
America's culture of remembrance and reframed the meaning of death
in wartime. Rather than offering his listeners a treatise for melancholy
speculation on the meaning of mortality for one's family members or for
one's self—the hallmark of the rural cemetery's ethos—Lincoln's speech
called his listeners to be dedicated anew to the cause of the "nation," a
word he used five times within the speech.[2] Lincoln's language and the
design of the Gettysburg cemetery, created by landscape architect William Saunders, spoke to the fact that the dead now belonged primarily
to the nation. Individual reflection on the nature of mortality gave way
at Gettysburg to a new, more uniform, more nationalistic, and more
egalitarian understanding of remembrance. While Lincoln's speech and
the order of ceremonies at the dedication of the cemetery at Gettysburg
might be seen as reflective of America's culture of death in the 1840s and
1850s, what is even more striking is the change that Lincoln's address
ushered forward. The dead at Gettysburg belonged fully to the American
nation, not to their families, not to their friends, and not even, in the end,
to themselves.

Abraham Lincoln's past made him an unlikely revolutionary in the process of changing America's traditions of remembrance. He embodied much of the nineteenth century's culture of death and knew well its pathways and traditions. As had his fellow Americans, he had felt the sting of early death within his own family. Lincoln's mother died when he was a boy of nine years old, and the experience marked him for the rest of his life. Biographer Michael Burlingame writes that as a result of this loss, Lincoln "feared being abandoned and was inclined to attack those who forsook their party or their principles."[3] As adults, Abraham and Mary Todd Lincoln also experienced firsthand the common reality of the death of young children. On February 1, 1850, the Lincolns lost their second son, Edward Baker (Eddie), to pulmonary tuberculosis before he was four years old. Tuberculosis, or "consumption" as nineteenth-century Americans construed the disease, was the nation's leading killer of adults and children alike and was encased in heroic rhetoric—think of the death of "Little Eva" in *Uncle Tom's Cabin*—that belied its devastating physical impact.[4] Thus, the Lincolns loss put them in lockstep with thousands of other American families who had felt firsthand the ravages of this disease. But the Lincolns pressed forward. According to historian David Donald, the couple intended "to replace the lost boy," and within weeks Mary Lincoln was expecting again.[5] William (Willie) Wallace Lincoln came into the world, in part, to salve the wounds created by Eddie's death and emerged quickly as "the most intelligent and the best-looking of all the Lincoln children, and from the day he was born his father doted on him."[6] Lincoln's fondness for his son intensified over time, only to be shattered by Willie's death on February 20, 1862. Coupled with the military and political crises facing the Union in the winter of 1862, the death of young Willie unhinged Lincoln almost entirely. Not a religious man by nineteenth-century lights, Lincoln nevertheless spoke at length with Reverend Phineas D. Gurley, a Presbyterian minister, who "comforted him with the assurance that Willie was not dead but still lived in heaven. Lincoln may not have believed him, but he wished to believe him."[7] In such ways did Abraham Lincoln understand what others in his time comprehended—that the natural order of the world often brought death to the young before it came to the old.[8]

The creation of the Oak Ridge Cemetery in Springfield, Illinois, formed another sinew connecting Abraham Lincoln to America's prewar culture of death. Dedicated on May 24, 1860, Oak Ridge stood proudly in the tradition of other rural cemeteries, dating back to the creation of Mount Auburn Cemetery in Massachusetts in 1831.[9] Its location was perfect. "Situated about two miles north of the Capitol, with undulating surface and pleasing blending of hill and dale," recorded an 1879 history, "interspersed with a natural growth of deciduous trees, the location was peculiarly fitted for the purposes of sepulture."[10] The avatars of the rural cemetery movement sought to sequester the dead far away from the busy paths of commerce and the concerns of the world, tucked away in landscapes that included serpentine paths, shady trees, ponds, and other features that would encourage what Supreme Court Justice Joseph Story called "melancholy pleasure."[11] Within the confines of the rural cemetery, the dead would teach the living. Here was a "didactic landscape" that instructed its visitors that all flesh was mortal and that invited them to reflect upon the nature and quality of their lives.[12] In constructing these landscapes, rural cemetery advocates drew inspiration from a variety of cultural traditions, including the ancient Greeks, the Egyptians, and elements of Christianity. Without blinking an eye at their apparent contradictions, rural cemetery designers set the symbols of these diverse traditions side by side. Thus did Greek urns, Egyptian obelisks, and Christian angels all perform the cultural work of encouraging individual visitors to reflect with profit upon the dead.

In offering his remarks at the dedication of Oak Ridge Cemetery, James C. Conkling, the former mayor of Springfield and a close acquaintance of the Lincoln family (both Mary Todd and Abraham), sounded the themes that would have warmed the hearts of rural cemetery advocates across the nation. "Here we lay the foundation of no commercial emporium," he intoned, "through which are to roll with unceasing energy the rushing streams of life, and around which are to cluster unbounded visions of speculative wealth."[13] Rather, Conkling insisted, the cemetery gave concrete expression to a great spiritual truth: "The grave is the common inheritance of all mankind."[14] As was appropriate and traditional for such occasions, Conkling linked the work done at Oak Ridge with the human instinct to preserve the memory of the dead and cited familiar examples from the classical and contemporary world—the Egyptians, the Phoenicians, and "the grottoes and catacombs of Asia Minor, of Italy, and of Paris" all standing in a historical continuum that tied Oak Ridge to the past.[15] This was heady stuff, for civic leaders in America could conceive of their work as standing in a direct line stretching back to the ancients. Conkling concluded by reminding his audience that there was authentic value in the contemplation of death. Not only was it the inevitable

portion of mankind, but it also offered to the Christian the joyous prospect of eternal bliss. "If there be an immortality beyond the grave," he
reasoned in his concluding paragraphs, "if the tomb is merely the thresh-
old of eternity, what folly, what madness, to forget our destiny and banish
from our minds the thoughts of death."[16] In his finale, Conkling drew his
listeners upward, beckoning them to consider the glories of heaven even
as they looked squarely in the face of their own mortality.

Abraham Lincoln's connection to Oak Ridge Cemetery ran deep.
Scholars expect that he was on hand for the dedication ceremony and attended to the words offered by James Conkling. He and Mary Todd moved
their son Eddie to be buried there. And, of course, after his assassination
in 1865, Lincoln himself was buried there—his monument then and now
the object of thousands of visitors, which makes Oak Ridge Cemetery
second only to Arlington's cemetery as the country's most frequently visited cemetery.[17] Much of Lincoln's rhetoric at Gettysburg resonated with
the themes and images of rural cemetery advocates—the celebration of
nature, the idea of the cemetery as a liminal terrain between life and
death, the fertility language evident in the phrase "new birth of freedom,"
and his references to the "fathers" as the familial founders of the nation.[18]
He did this and more. Lincoln's words at Gettysburg echoed yet another
tradition celebrated by those who championed the rural cemetery—a veneration for the heroes of the American Revolution who were passing in
the 1830s and 1840s from the national scene. Champions of the rural
cemetery endowed their work with a civic component, casting the cemeteries they made as repositories in which to celebrate local history and
the achievements of great men who made it.[19] As Lincoln made his way to
Gettysburg, he was keenly aware of both the purposes and the rhetoric of
the rural cemetery.

* * *

Although Abraham Lincoln had begun to draft his remarks for the Gettysburg dedication before he departed from Washington, he envisioned his
"few appropriate remarks" on the ground where he would be speaking.
That ground proved decisive. Before leaving for Gettysburg to deliver his
remarks, Lincoln spent a good part of the evening of November 17, 1863,
in conversation with William Saunders, the designer of the new cemetery he would dedicate.[20] Saunders, a horticulturalist and superintendent
of the "experimental gardens with the newly created US Department of

Agriculture," played a key role in designing Oak Ridge Cemetery in the 1860s and later in designing a place for Lincoln's monument in the landscape. What Lincoln and Saunders talked about that evening, however, was not a plan for adapting the design of the rural cemetery to the purposes of a national soldier's memorial. Had Saunders or Lincoln wanted to do that, a solution stood immediately at hand—the Evergreen Cemetery at Gettysburg would have fit that use perfectly. Located now adjacent to the cemetery at Gettysburg, Evergreen Cemetery had been dedicated in 1854 and its main gate hovered over some of the fiercest fighting of the battle.[21] Appearing in Alexander Gardner's *Photographic Sketchbook of the Civil War* (1866), "the original cemetery was a very handsome enclosure and contained many elegant monuments, very few of which were injured, notwithstanding the terrible nature of the conflict."[22] Indeed, Cemetery Hill and Cemetery Ridge—iconic features of the Gettysburg battlefield—were so named before a single musket was fired, linked to the earlier Evergreen Cemetery, not to the new cemetery Saunders would design.

It is critically important to see that the model of Evergreen Cemetery—already laid out on the Gettysburg landscape—gained no traction with either William Saunders or with Abraham Lincoln or with David Wills, the Gettysburg attorney who served as Pennsylvania Governor Andrew Curtin's agent for the establishment of the cemetery. The notion of simply grafting the new cemetery onto the grounds of the Evergreen Cemetery received only fleeting attention early in the process of deciding where to situate the soldier graves. David Wills recalled that "a persistent effort was made by persons here, to have the soldiers buried in grounds controlled by the local cemetery association of this place."[23] But these efforts failed. Backed by Governor Curtin, David Wills and his supporters "all were of the decided opinion that the Soldiers' Cemetery should be entirely distinct and disconnected from the local cemetery, that to ensure success in obtaining concert of action among all the States it must be made an independent cemetery."[24] The real issue here was one of national perspective. "The grounds were subsequently laid out," Wills reported in 1864, "and the burials made in view of the national character of the project."[25] The cemetery at Gettysburg would thus belong not only to the town but also to the State of Pennsylvania and to the United States of America as a whole. In this discrete decision we can detect a seismic shift in the process of memorializing the dead: the traditions of the rural cemetery were giving way under the exigencies of war and the mass death that it created. Old models would no longer work. Indeed, to this day, the National Park Service's website uses the Evergreen Cemetery as an example of what the new, cemetery is not: "The evenness and equality of the gravestones, where men of differing rank reside side-by-side, contrasts sharply with the jumbling diversity visible in the Evergreen Cemetery."[26] Lost in the past, it is difficult now to remember that the model presented by the Evergreen Cemetery at Gettysburg had been the reigning paradigm for the cemeteries embraced by antebellum Americans. That was about to change.

What William Saunders carried with him to his November 17 meeting with the president was a "revolution in battlefield cemeteries."[27] Laid out in the design he spread before Abraham Lincoln was encoded a strikingly new way of burying the dead. The key elements in that transformation may be found in the "Remarks" that Saunders offered in 1864 as part of a larger report on the cemetery for the Pennsylvania legislature.[28] In almost every way, Saunders put distance between his design and the traditions of the rural cemetery. As David Wills had noted, this was to be a national project and key among Saunders's goals was the arrangement of the burial ground to minimize rivalry and competition among the various Union states. Most obviously, the 3,512 soldier graves would be carefully arrayed in sections demarcated by state boundaries, but all oriented in arching ranks that faced a common center. In the Saunders design, the dead were thus turned to the purposes of state building. In the rural cemeteries of the day—both North and South—the dead were buried in family plots, owned in turn by their kinsmen, who in turn were responsible for the upkeep of the graves within the plot, the maintenance of its monuments, and its plantings and trees. For all of its anticommercial rhetoric, the rural cemetery was a domain for those with the capital to ensure their remembrance. At Gettysburg, it was the national state that incurred the cost of reinterring the battlefield dead (at the cost of $1.59 per body) and the state that ultimately held their remains.[29] In the Soldiers' cemetery, the dead belonged, literally, to their states and not to their families.

William Saunders maintained as well that "the prevailing expression of the cemetery should be that of *simple grandeur.* Simplicity is that element of beauty in a scene that leads gradually from one object to another, in easy harmony, avoiding abrupt contrasts and unexpected features."[30] Here was the antithesis of the philosophy behind the rural cemetery. With the aim of cultivating a spirit of quiet reflection on mortality, the rural cemetery—with its winding routes and hidden spaces—was designed to be interesting, not simple. Given the variety of its monuments and the cultural traditions from which it drew, the rural cemetery championed the wishes of individual families and their members. It was intentionally complex and secluded and offered its visitors surprising vistas and scenes around every corner. It upheld contrasts and conflicting traditions—Greek, Egyptian, and Christian—and embraced the idiosyncratic tendencies of the families who owned its plots. While lot holders were responsible for following the rules and conventions expressed by their cemetery associations, they had wide latitude to bury their family members as they wished. The aesthetic of the rural cemetery was "the picturesque"—a harmonious blending of the civilized and the natural to create an atmosphere for contemplation.[31] All of this cut against the grain of Saunders's plan. He remonstrated against any additional plants and trees that would, he said, "destroy the massive effect of the groupings, and in time would render the whole confused and intricate."[32] The Saunders plan was clean, crisp, and organized—designed to compel something approaching public awe rather than to cultivate private contemplation.

In place of the meandering paths and walkways that marked the rural cemetery, William Saunders oriented the soldier graves "toward a common centre." At the center of the semicircle would stand a single monument that would serve to focus the cemetery. There would be little mystery about the design plan or even the entrance to the cemetery. "The gateway and gatehouse," Saunders wrote, "should also be designed in the same spirit, massive, solid, substantial, and tasteful." These were words that mattered. In maintaining the cemetery in future years, Saunders wrote passionately about his desire to preserve the elemental simplicity of his design: "With regard to the future keeping of the ground, the walks should be smooth, hard, clean, the grass kept short, and maintained as clean and neat as the best pleasure ground in the country."[33] Massive, simple, smooth, clean, hard, and substantial—this was the lexicon of the Saunders aesthetic, and it could not have been more distant from the vocabulary of the rural cemetery.

The new Soldiers' cemetery would also be relentlessly egalitarian. It was essential for William Saunders to array the graves with precise uniformity, arranging the dead by state rather than rank or station or family connection. "In order to secure regularity," he wrote, "the headstones are precisely alike throughout the entire area."[34] There would be no discrimination in Saunders's cemetery or distinctions made among individuals. Families of wealth and taste would be powerless to adorn

individual graves or to embellish them with tombs or crypts or more extensive monuments. By insisting on the regularity and the uniformity of
the graves, Saunders's design simultaneously sent a strong message of
national unity. "The cemetery at Gettysburg," writes Drew Gilpin Faust,
"was arranged so that every grave was of equal importance; William
Saunders' design, like Lincoln's speech, affirmed that every dead soldier
mattered equally regardless of rank or station."[35]

After reviewing his plan with Abraham Lincoln, William Saunders
remembered that the president recognized the originality of his work and
that he applauded it. While there may be some self-congratulatory postur-
ing in the Saunders account, he observed that the Lincoln was "much
pleased" with the design and understood that "it differed from the ordinary cemetery."[36] Indeed, Lincoln's meeting with Saunders and the trajectory of his thoughts leading up to the dedicatory speech turned him again
and again to the issue of terrain. "As the Saunders conversation so clearly
shows," writes Martin P. Johnson, "even before leaving Washington,
Lincoln had become familiar with Gettysburg, not only as a battlefield,
but also as a ceremonial and patriotic site, created by men of vision and
planned with care to inspire sentiments of sublime solemnity and reverential patriotism."[37] As Abraham Lincoln worked out the details of his
own remarks, we know that he carried with him to Gettysburg not only
the residue of antebellum America's culture of death but also new ideas
regarding the meaning of death in wartime. In remarkable ways, William
Saunders's design and Abraham Lincoln's Gettysburg Address worked
hand-in-glove to deliver a transformation in American understandings of
death and the memorialization of the dead.

Abraham Lincoln began the Gettysburg Address with a history lesson
unlike anything that would have been deployed in a traditional rural cemetery address. His focus in time was extraordinarily circumscribed, recalling his audience only to "four score and seven years ago" rather than
delving into the rich history of antiquity. There was no rehearsal of the
ancients here, no lengthy description of the human impulse toward remembrance and the veneration of the dead. There was no rendition of the
fundamental fact that all humanity was mortal. Instead, Lincoln moved
decisively to the central political point of the day: his insistence that the
nation's identity was grounded in the Declaration of Independence of 1776
rather than the Constitution of 1787 was a cardinal principle, thus rendering his opening "the most important line in the speech."[38] Rather than
waging war against a sovereign power, Lincoln insisted that the states of

the Confederacy had never really left the Union and could not have regardless of the rhetoric its leaders deployed. Although it was the bloodiest conflict in all of American history, Abraham Lincoln never considered the "Civil War" (a term he used in the speech) as a struggle against another sovereign power. The critical point here is that from the beginning, Lincoln grounded the Gettysburg Address in the particulars of the nation's founding rather than in any exploration of the wider human need to remember the dead. What is all the more remarkable is that at Gettysburg, Lincoln carried on his person the visible emblem of that mortality, for "his stovepipe hat bore a black band, to indicate that he was still mourning the death of his son Willie."[39] His son Tad, too, was gravely ill that day, and Lincoln had been receiving telegraph updates from Washington regarding his condition. If anyone could have spoken to the pains of the loss of children or of grief more broadly construed, it would have been Abraham Lincoln. But he refused the particulars of his own situation or any long, backward glance into the past. On November 19, 1863, his purposes were those of the nation.

* * *

Some glimpse of the boldness of Abraham Lincoln's rhetorical opening may be gained by comparing it to where Edward Everett began the major oration that preceded his own. Former president of Harvard College (and a great classicist) and former US Senator, Everett did exactly what Lincoln did not. He bracketed his speech masterfully with reference to the ancient Greeks. Everett opened with a nod to the funeral rites of ancient Athens and made the Union heroes who had fallen at Gettysburg brothers in arms with the Athenians of Marathon, who had died beating back the Persian invasion of the Greek city-states. It was a brilliant move. Were they not alike, he asked, who had "rolled back the tide of an invasion, not less provoked, not less ruthless, than that which came to plant the dark banner of Asiatic despotism and slavery on the free soil of Greece?"[40] By the conclusion of the speech, though, Everett had subtly changed rhetorical gears, and now cast the Confederacy's forces not as slave-mongering Persians, but as the Spartans of the Peloponnesian War. He thus recalled Pericles's funeral oration for the Athenian dead in his final paragraphs— again linking the purposes of the cemetery dedication with the noblest traditions of the Greeks. In bracketing his speech with references to antiquity, Edward Everett had aligned himself firmly with the traditions of the

rural cemetery movement. Abraham Lincoln knew by heart these rituals and the rhetorical moves that would perpetuate them, but he made
a different choice. His interests were those of the American nation, not
in validating the heroic actions of the Union troops by analogy with the
ancient Greeks.

What Abraham Lincoln called forth from his audience was a plea for
dedication to the nation. He used the word "dedicate" or "dedicated" five
times in the Gettysburg Address. As historian Martin P. Johnson has
argued, "For Lincoln, 'dedicated' was an unusual word."[41] What Lincoln
was after at Gettysburg was something far more than internal reflection,
soul-searching, and the cultivating of an interior posture of melancholy
pleasure. Those were the dispositions to be properly nurtured in the rural
cemetery, and Abraham Lincoln would have none of it. Rather than asking
his hearers simply "to stand here" and remember (words from an earlier
draft of the Address), Lincoln wanted to move them to action, to renewed
dedication "to the great task remaining before us." In deploying the language of dedication, Abraham Lincoln called forth from his audience far
more than simple remembrance or recollection. He wanted action; action
to bring forth the "new birth of freedom" he had envisioned and a salvific role for the state. Action on behalf of the nation in the future would
answer the heroic actions of the soldiers who had fallen, conferring upon
them proper honor for "what they did here."

Exactly what "they" did here—that is, the Union troops at Gettysburg—
Abraham Lincoln did not say. As scholars have observed, the Gettysburg
Address is abstract and aphoristic. It avoids particulars about the battle. It
avoids the subject of slavery. It avoids any gestures toward the specifics of
Lincoln's Reconstruction policies, which were very much on his mind in
November 1863. The Gettysburg Address is at once directly tied to its time
and place—especially the design of the William Saunders cemetery—and
yet also seems to float above and outside the history in which it was created.
Finally, what Lincoln did say was that the dead at Gettysburg had fallen
while giving "the last full measure of devotion" to the preservation and
endurance of American democracy. Once again, Lincoln lifted his rhetoric above the particular and located it firmly within the wider compass of
national mission. It remained for the living—here, now, and on earth—to
confer immortality upon Gettysburg's "honored dead" by taking up the
work for which they had given their lives. Interestingly, given his tour of
the battlefield on the morning of the Gettysburg Address, Lincoln would
have been primed to include details about the fight in his last-minute

revisions. He had seen the place where Union General John Reynolds—a martyred figure if ever there were one—had been killed on the first day of the fighting. Edward Everett had recognized the decisive role that Reynolds played in the fight early on in his speech and celebrated that Reynolds had died while leading his troops into the fray "at the head of his advance."[42] But again, Lincoln refused individual remembrance and moved to different terrain. Rather than idiosyncratic reflection, Lincoln conjured a nation out of the remains of the dead bodies that surrounded him. It would be within the construct of the American nation that the dead and the living would meet, forever conjoined to the same purposes, the devotion of the dead thus inspiring the dedication of the living.

Even if he had wanted to, Abraham Lincoln could not have named all the Union dead who had perished at Gettysburg. The cemetery itself contained two large sections containing the remains of the "unknown"—according to Samuel Weaver, the superintendent for exhuming the Union bodies, 979 of the 3,512 Union corpses buried at Gettysburg were buried without any identifying features.[43] According to his report, Weaver made heroic efforts to identify the dead and to make correct determinations regarding identity. "I saw every body taken out of its temporary resting place, and the pockets carefully searched; and where the grave was not marked, I examined all the clothing and everything about the body to find the name."[44] The 1864 report to the Pennsylvania legislature contains a heart-rending account of the ways in which Weaver and his team worked—it includes a "List of Articles" that had been used in identifying bodies—combs, pocket knives, testaments, letters, diaries, pins, and so forth. Even with these detailed efforts, large numbers of corpses remained anonymous. Weaver made it clear, however, that under no circumstances did he take the chance of including a dead Confederate in the Union cemetery. "In no instance was a body allowed to be removed which had any portion of rebel clothing on it," Weaver reported. "I firmly believe that there has not been a single mistake made in the removal of the soldiers to the cemetery by taking the body of a rebel for a Union soldier."[45] It was thus critical for Weaver to make the new cemetery the unalloyed ground of the Union dead.

Interestingly, in two ways, Lincoln's speech did not approach this level of specificity. First, he noted in his remarks "the brave men, living and dead, who struggled here" and that the actions of those men had already hallowed the ground at Gettysburg more than any future speaker could. But unlike typical cemetery addresses, Lincoln found a place for "the living" in his speech—it honored not only the dead but also those who continued the struggle. Furthermore, while Lincoln cut a clear distinction between the living and the dead, the past and the future, the individual and the nation, he did not dwell on the differences between the North and the South—other than to say that the great issue of the war was the question of whether a democracy dedicated to equality could endure. Unlike the oration delivered by Edward Everett, Lincoln spent no time in the Gettysburg Address parsing out Union and Confederate troops or assigning blame to the South for the carnage of the war. In clear contrast, Everett devoted nearly a third of his speech in taking up the question of "which of the two parties to the war is responsible for all this suffering."[46] While Lincoln was careful to lay out what was at stake in the Civil War—the momentous question of the endurance of a democratic republic—he stayed away from recrimination with respect to the secessionists. In its capacious reach—embracing the living and the dead, and in not vilifying the South or even the evils of secession in detail, the Gettysburg Address adumbrates the posture Lincoln would strike in the Second Inaugural Address in which he laid out the phrase "with malice toward none; with charity for all" as a guiding principle for the postwar nation. At Gettysburg, Lincoln opened the possibility for any American—in the North or in the South—to be dedicated to the broader mission of American democracy.

The abstract nature of Abraham Lincoln's remarks at Gettysburg matched the new reality of death on the battlefield, in which individual identities were so easily lost. No traditional rural cemetery could have contained unidentified graves. By its own rules, as mentioned, the rural cemetery was owned by its lot owners and associated corporation. The identity of the deceased was, literally, a requirement for taking in a body for burial. As such, the rural cemetery was entirely unsuited for the purposes of the Civil War, where some 40 percent of Union forces and a greater number of Confederate dead were simply "unknown."[47] The new, cemetery made room for the unknown in ways that the rural cemetery—by its very definition—could not. By comprehending all the dead (and the living) within his compass, Lincoln also made room for a more comprehensive definition of nationhood.

It would have been typical within the scope of the traditional rural cemetery oration for its pronouncer to make specific reference to heaven, and to the Christian afterlife in particular. As we have observed, this was true of James Conkling's remarks dedicating the Oak Ridge Cemetery in Springfield, Illinois. It is also true that Abraham Lincoln's debt to America's religious culture percolates throughout the Gettysburg Address. "The cadences and language—hallow, consecrate, a new birth—were more overtly biblical than in past speeches," observes historian Eric Foner.[48] As a careful student of the Bible and a masterful politician, Lincoln knew what he was doing on this score. Simultaneously, though, the "new birth of freedom" to which Abraham Lincoln referred was not a goal to be pursued in the next world, but a political program to be realized in contemporary America. The "new birth of freedom"—language probably crafted during the morning hours of November 19—would be a democracy resurrected by the bodies of the dead soldiers over which Lincoln spoke.[49] In dying for the cause of the nation, the Union dead would live on in the very fabric of the country. The dead at Gettysburg would serve as salvific for American democracy, their memory ensured by the dedication and actions of their countrymen. For Lincoln at Gettysburg, any thoughts of a glorious and heavenly afterlife were irrelevant to the purposes of the day.

In such ways did Abraham Lincoln's Gettysburg Address reframe the meaning of death in the American Civil War. He folded the dead fully into America's new, national purpose and made room in that vision for both the known and the unknown. He called for active, political dedication to America's central democratic proposition rather than for reflective remembrance on human mortality. He cut loose from the traditional tropes of the rural cemetery movement—the examples of the ancient Greeks, Egyptians, and even Christianity—to produce a state-centered oration, in which the battlefield dead would live on, not in heaven but in a renewed dedication to the American state. In a few brief minutes, Abraham Lincoln turned American remembrance of the wartime dead in a new direction.

* * *

Given Abraham Lincoln's heritage—one steeped in the rural cemetery movement and in the nation's culture of death more broadly—the nature of his break with that tradition at Gettysburg is striking and perhaps surprising. Two factors positioned Lincoln to make this dramatic move. The first was the unprecedented carnage and loss of life brought by the Civil War, which in absolute terms remains to this day America's most deadly conflict. By the time Lincoln spoke at Gettysburg on November 19, 1863, major battlefield engagements such as Shiloh, Second Bull Run,

Antietam, Fredericksburg, and Chancellorsville were routinely producing casualties that rivaled those at Waterloo. And yet the nation was woefully unprepared to deal with the slaughter it produced. The sheer scale of Civil War death demanded new approaches, particularly new ways of tending to and recognizing the dead. The movement for a national soldiers' cemetery at Gettysburg marked a decisive change in reshaping how Americans handled wartime death. Second, we know that Abraham Lincoln was a political creature who could move with the times, changing his mind and developing new approaches to issues and problems. We understand, for example, that Lincoln's position on emancipation was constantly fluid and developing, moving from one that posited colonization as a prime solution as late as 1862, to one that next envisioned free black men fighting in the Union Army, and finally to one that championed those men as potential voters in the reconstructed nation. Former Whig and now Republican president, Lincoln demonstrated time and again his willingness to make new departures and to transform his understanding in light of new evidence. The fearsome death toll of the war and Lincoln's ability to act in fresh ways facilitated the transformation he brought with him to Gettysburg.

The Southern dead at Gettysburg rested outside the culture of death that Abraham Lincoln and William Saunders crafted. Refused a place in the cemetery, they remained in the ground at Gettysburg until the early 1870s, when the women of Richmond, Virginia's Hollywood Memorial Association took up the cause. Champions of the Hollywood Cemetery, they helped spur the Virginia legislature, and other Southern lawmakers, to appropriate funds to move the Confederate dead to soil of the South. The work of reinterring the Confederate dead from Gettysburg at the Hollywood Cemetery—2,935 in all—was completed by October 1873, almost a full decade after the dedication at Gettysburg.[50] Lincoln's speech may have made room for all Americans, but, as Samuel Weaver averred, there was not a body buried at Gettysburg that had touched the fabric of a Confederate uniform. The burial of the Civil War dead thus communicated in no uncertain terms that some Americans lived, and died, outside the scope of Abraham Lincoln's elastic remarks at Gettysburg.

In remarkable ways, the burial of the Confederate dead from Gettysburg described the limits of the changes Abraham Lincoln set in motion. Most obviously, the Confederate dead were interred in a "Soldier's section" carved from an existing rural cemetery. Dedicated in 1849, the Hollywood Cemetery in Richmond was one of the nation's great rural cemeteries, designed by John Notman, who had designed Philadelphia's Laurel Hill Cemetery. In stark contrast to the clear separation between the Evergreen Cemetery and the new Soldiers' cemetery at Gettysburg, the Hollywood Cemetery had served as a site for the burial of the Confederate dead during the war. By the time the war had ended, "more than eleven thousand soldiers" had been buried there.[51] So it seemed natural for the Confederate dead from Gettysburg to find a permanent home in Hollywood. Moreover, memorials to the Confederate war dead at Hollywood included all manner of designs and, in keeping with the traditions of the rural cemetery, featured family burial sites. So, for example, General James Longstreet's three children are clustered together—victims of a scarlet fever outbreak in 1862. Indeed, the idiosyncratic ethos of the rural cemetery movement lived on most clearly at Hollywood in the variety of monuments created immediately after the war, including the famous "Confederate pyramid" and the angels surrounding the "Davis Family Circle" (which includes Jefferson Davis). Here were vestiges of Egyptian and Christian burial images laid out within the same cemetery. Individual monuments to famous Confederate generals—J. E. B. Stuart's obelisk comes to mind—are also much in evidence at Hollywood.[52] In striking ways, the burial of the Confederate dead from Gettysburg at Hollywood Cemetery marked a return to the traditions of remembrance from the early nineteenth century, laying the groundwork for the South's cult of the Lost Cause and the veneration of its pantheon of Civil War heroes.

Nevertheless, the changes that Abraham Lincoln and William Saunders set in motion at Gettysburg prevailed in America, as the rural cemetery movement receded into the past. Consider, for example, the ranks of soldiers evident in the Confederate cemetery at Vicksburg, Mississippi—laid out in neat and orderly rows that mimic the "simple grandeur" of Gettysburg. It took time, but in the end what Lincoln and Saunders launched has endured. Indeed, "the establishment of national and Confederate cemeteries created the Civil War Dead as a category, as a collective that represented something more and something different from the many thousands of individual deaths that it comprised."[53] The chief category that Lincoln introduced at Gettysburg was quite specific and exacting—that of the nation-state.

We live still with the revolution Abraham Lincoln wrought at Gettysburg.[54] As noble as were his purposes—to ensure the preservation of a democratic nation in time of war—something was also lost at Gettysburg, beyond the defeat of Robert E. Lee's Army of Northern Virginia.

Remembrance of the war dead became, and has become, increasingly the project of the American nation. This is both meet and salutary. At the same time, the antebellum emphasis on the connection of the dead to their families, to their communities, and to their particular religious congregations was giving way to a more fundamentally nationalistic rendering of the self. As Benedict Anderson once wrote, all constructions of nationhood are in large measure "imagined communities"—based on cultural artifacts that help us imagine shared identities with people whom we have never met.[55] The cemetery at Gettysburg, and the dedicatory remarks that Abraham Lincoln made there, helped Americans imagine themselves in a different way: as members of a nation-state in which death, dedication, and devotion conferred enduring citizenship.

Notes

1. Garry Wills, *Lincoln at Gettysburg: The Words that Remade America* (New York: Simon and Schuster, 1992), 71 and 63–89 more generally.

2. David Herbert Donald, *Lincoln* (New York: Simon and Schuster, 1995), 462, and Eric Foner, *The Fiery Trial: Abraham Lincoln and American Slavery* (New York: W. W. Norton, 2010), 268.

3. Michael Burlingame, *Abraham Lincoln, A Life* (Baltimore: Johns Hopkins University Press, 2008), I: 27.

4. On consumption in the nineteenth-century more broadly see Sheila M. Rothman, *Tuberculosis and the Social Experience of Illness in American History* (Baltimore: Johns Hopkins University Press, 1994).

5. Donald, *Lincoln*, 154.

6. Ibid.

7. Ibid., 337.

8. See Mark S. Schantz, *Awaiting the Heavenly Country: The Civil War and America's Culture of Death* (Ithaca, NY: Cornell University Press, 2008), 6–37.

9. The classic text on the Mount Auburn Cemetery is Blanche Linden-Ward, *Silent City on a Hill: Landscapes of Memory and Boston's Mount Auburn Cemetery* (Columbus: Ohio State University Press, 1989), see especially the cemetery design on 201; see also David Charles Sloane, *The Last Great Necessity: Cemeteries in American History* (Baltimore: Johns Hopkins University Press, 1991), 44–95; and Schantz, *Awaiting the Heavenly Country*, 70–96.

10. *Oak Ridge Cemetery: Its History and Improvements, Rules and Regulations. National Lincoln Monument, and other Monuments, Charters and Ordinances. List of Lot Owners* (Springfield, IL: H. W. Rokker, Printer and Binder, 1879), 7.

11. See Schantz, *Awaiting the Heavenly Country*, 70–73.

12. Sloane, *The Last Great Necessity*, 65.

13. *Oak Ridge Cemetery*, 11.

14. Ibid., 12.

15. Ibid., 14.

16. Ibid., 16.

17. See Edward J. Russo and Curtis R. Mann, introduction by Mayor Tom Davlin, *Images of America: Oak Ridge Cemetery* (Charleston, SC: Arcadia, 2009), 9. See also the 1872 map of the cemetery on p. 8, which William Saunders designed in the 1860s.

18. See Wills, *Lincoln at Gettysburg*, 77–89.

19. See Sloane, *The Last Great Necessity*, 80.

20. Lincoln's conversation with William Saunders is recounted, and emphasized, in Martin P. Johnson, *Writing the Gettysburg Address* (Lawrence: University of Kansas Press, 2013), 48–53 especially.

21. On the 1854 dedication address for the Evergreen Cemetery see Schantz, *Awaiting the Heavenly Country*, 93.

22. Alexander Gardner, *Gardner's Photographic Sketchbook of the Civil War* (New York: Dover, 1959), plate 39 and accompanying text.

23. The David Wills report and others cited in this essay come from an excellent collection of documents titled *Report of the Select Committee Relative to the National Cemetery Together with the Accompanying Documents, as Reported to the House of Representatives of the Commonwealth of Pennsylvania, March 31, 1864* (Harrisburg: Singerly and Myers, State Printers, 1864), 6 (hereafter cited as *Report of the Select Committee*).

24. Ibid.

25. Ibid.

26. National Cemetery Walking Tour, Four Score and Seven Years Ago . . . Abraham Lincoln, Nov. 19, 1863. stop 4, the Cemetery, PDF.

27. J. Jim Kaplan, "William Saunders: A Monumental Figure in USDA," *Agricultural Research* Sept. 2013, 12.

28. All quotes from William Saunders are from "Remarks on the Design for the Soldiers' National Cemetery, Gettysburg, Pennsylvania," *Report of the Select Committee*, 37–38.

29. *Report of the Select Committee*, 7–9.

30. Ibid., 38.

31. See Sloane, *The Last Great Necessity*, 49.

32. *Report of the Select Committee*, 38.

33. Ibid.

34. Ibid., 37.

35. Drew Gilpin Faust, *This Republic of Suffering: Death and the American Civil War* (New York: Alfred A. Knopf, 2008), 100.

36. Quoted in Johnson, *Writing the Gettysburg Address*, 51.

37. Ibid., 62.

38. Mark E. Neely, Jr., *The Last Best Hope of Earth: Abraham Lincoln and the Promise of America* (Cambridge, MA: Harvard University Press, 1995), 154.

39. Donald, *Lincoln*, 464.

40. Edward Everett Address, *Report of the Select Committee*, 82.

41. Johnson, *Writing the Gettysburg Address*, 162.

42. Edward Everett Address, *Report of the Select Committee*, 90.

43. Report of Samuel Weaver, *Report of the Select Committee*, 39.

44. Ibid.

45. *Report of the Select Committee*, 41.

46. Everett Address, *Report of the Select Committee*, 97–108.

47. Faust, *This Republic of Suffering*, 102.

48. Foner, *The Fiery Trial*, 267.

49. See Johnson, *Writing the Gettysburg Address*, 158–165.

50. Mary H. Mitchell, *Hollywood Cemetery: The History of a Southern Shrine* (Richmond: Virginia State Library, 1985), 91 and 83–92 more generally for a concise treatment of the "The Gettysburg Dead" at Hollywood.

51. Mitchell, *Hollywood Cemetery*, 60.

52. For images of these memorials in the order in which they appear in this paragraph see John O. Peters, text and photography, and Edward L. Ayers, foreword to *Richmond's Hollywood Cemetery* (Richmond: Valentine Richmond History Center, 2010), 49, 61, 115–118, 62. See also Cynthia Mills and Pamela H. Simpson, eds., *Monuments to the Lost Cause: Women, Art, and the Landscapes of Southern Memory* (Knoxville: University of Tennessee Press, 2003).

53. Faust, *This Republic of Suffering*, 249.

54. See generally on this point Jared Peatman, *The Long Shadow of Lincoln's Gettysburg Address* (Carbondale: Southern Illinois Press, 2013).

55. Benedict Anderson, *Imagined Communities: Reflections on the Origin and Spread of Nationalism*, rev. ed. (New York: Verso, 1991).

7

Shared Suffering and the Way to Gettysburg

Chandra Manning

IN THE SUMMER of 1863, nobody knew yet what would happen. Not Abraham Lincoln. Not the four million black men, women, and children held in bondage when the Civil War began. Not the soldiers who would trudge from Virginia to Pennsylvania and back or who languished on the banks of the Mississippi River or who marched and camped and fought over thousands of miles of contested ground. They did know, every last one of them, that the war they anticipated in the spring of 1861 bore precious little resemblance to the one they faced a little more than two years later. Lincoln had time to contemplate the distance between the war as expected and the war as it unfolded each day as he traveled from his family's summer cottage on the grounds of the Soldiers' Home on Washington, DC's outskirts to the White House. That daily journey took him past a refugee camp for slaves who had fled their masters and staked everything on the bet that the war would bring freedom. It also led him past eight thousand soldiers' graves. Lincoln could neither leave his home nor return to it without passing right by and through extremes of anguish, hope-beyond-hope, and death: the very extremes that characterized the war as soldiers and former slaves knew it; the very extremes that drew him and them together through the shared experience of war; and the very extremes that Lincoln would capture in a short address delivered at another cemetery in the waning days of autumn, in which he arrived at a renewed vision of the Declaration of Independence achieved and achievable specifically through shared suffering and loss.

Shrewd though Abraham Lincoln was about many things, his shrewdness failed him when it came to predicting how the war would unfold. As the election of 1860 approached, he reasoned that ordinary white South-erners shared his own Kentucky-born sensibilities and would resist what he mistakenly thought was a small number of hot-headed leaders spout-ing secessionist extremism. "The people of the South have too much of good sense, and good temper, to attempt the ruin of the government," Lincoln assured one supporter. Even after Fort Sumter suggested that at least some were willing to attempt that ruin after all, Lincoln supposed that the reasonable majority would come to its senses with minimal actual bloodshed. By the summer of 1863, he knew how wrong he was.[1]

The paucity of written records makes it harder to know for sure what four million enslaved men and women expected at war's outbreak, but certainly some of them looked for speedy liberation. By the time Lincoln won the election of 1860, John and Jesse, two slaves on the Hoggatt planta-tion in middle Tennessee, had heard their owner and all his friends fume so vehemently about Lincoln, they considered it "a settled question" that "there would be a civil war in the country, that he was against slavery and would use every means in his power to crush it."[2] As states left the Union, slaves' anticipation mounted. In March 1861, before shots had been fired, four slaves made a dash for Fort Pickens, a federal fort still held by the US Army in Pensacola, Florida. When Lieutenant A. J. Slemmer, command-ing officer of the First Artillery (US), asked them what they were doing there, they told him that they "came to the fort entertaining the idea that [soldiers] were placed here to protect them and grant them their freedom." Slemmer delivered them to the city marshal, who handed them back to their owners.[3]

The young men who joined the Union Army expected a short and painless adventure. Instead, they found themselves whipsawed between soul-crushing tedium and the nearly unspeakable terror of what Private Cyrus Boyd called the "*hell* of battle," so disorientingly violent that it "bru-talizes men and crushes out all human feeling."[4] It did not take long for the gap between expectation and experience to lead soldiers to ask serious questions about what the point of the war actually was, and how or even whether the purpose could justify the vast slaughter. Born in the state of Maine in the 1840s, Leigh Webber had led a peripatetic existence, work-ing as a farmhand in Iowa and Kansas. That same sense of adventure, activated by Lincoln's inauguration and ominous threats from Southern states, prompted Webber to set aside his pacifist "war scruples" and de-clare "I believe I would enlist" if only the Northern states would start to muster volunteers.[5] War lost little time in curing him of his romanticism;

by 1862 he reflected, "If all this untold expense of blood and treasure, of toil and suffering, of want and sacrifice, of grief and mourning is . . . to result in no greater good than the restoration of the Union as it was," then the war would "result in no real and lasting good." So what was its point?[6]

One year later, Lincoln could hardly escape Webber's question. Union Army successes at Forts Henry, Donelson, Corinth, Nashville, Memphis, and New Orleans had been counteracted by losses in the East and the Army of the Potomac's frustrating inability to capture the Confederate capital of Richmond, the embarrassing debacle at Fredericksburg, and the humiliating rout at Chancellorsville just as the summer of 1863 was getting under way. And still, the rebellion raged, and the goal of snuffing it out seemed as far off as ever. Day after day, the telegraph transmitted unrelenting lists of lives cut short: 34,000 in the Peninsula Campaign, 35,984 at the Seven Days Battles, 25,251 at Second Bull Run, 18,000 at Fredericksburg, and 24,000 at Chancellorsville.[7] Lincoln was still grieving for the loss of his own young son, Willie, who had died of pneumonia and typhoid fever in February 1862. How could endless lists of other people's dead sons not affect him?

By eight in the morning in Washington summers, the dew is largely gone from the grass unless the swampy air is simply too humid for even sweltering heat to evaporate it. So it was each summer morning in 1863, as Lincoln, never an accomplished horseman, somewhat awkwardly mounted a "good-sized, easy-going gray horse" to bounce three miles or so to the White House at a "slow trot" that left the president "somewhat rusty and dusty" even before his workday officially began. If the weather was poor, he might ride instead in a plain, unassuming four-wheeled carriage known as a barouche, but he still favored a particular route, down the Seventh Street Turnpike and into the center of the city.[8] His journey would begin in the shady hills surrounding the cottage, just opposite a cemetery dedicated in haste in 1861 after First Bull Run disabused everyone of the notion that one battle would finish the war off, which was filled with eight thousand graves, many of them fresh, by the summer of 1863.[9] Always impatient with fuss and bother, Lincoln tried to make the trip to work alone, but since 1862, when both Union Army brass and (more formidably) the president's wife insisted on at least *some* security precautions, Union soldiers accompanied him. Sometimes soldiers made small talk with the president; other times they answered his occasionally puzzling questions; and sometimes they left him to the quiet of his thoughts.

Those soldiers, and their compatriots serving in all the war's theaters, had traveled some journey of their own since the war began, often paralleling and sometimes even anticipating Lincoln's. From the very beginning, soldiers like the Union men stationed in Martinsburg, Virginia, in July 1861 explained that the Union must be preserved in order to certify the success of "the experiment of our popular government."[10] That success mattered for all people, not just for Americans, as Indiana private W. D. Wildman put it, because "the Union is not only the citadel of our liberty, but the depostory [sic] of the hopes of the human race."[11] Lincoln shared these soldiers' views on the worldwide significance of the Union. His first Message to Congress insisted that the war "embraces more than the fate of these United States. It presents to the whole family of man, the question, whether a constitutional republic, or a democracy—a government of the people, by the same people—can, or cannot, maintain its territorial integrity, against its own domestic foes." Further, the Message continued, not just power and territory, but also ideas were at stake: "Our adversaries have adopted some Declarations of Independence; in which, unlike the good old one, penned by Jefferson, they omit the words 'all men are created equal.'" In contrast, the Union stood for "maintaining in the world, that form, and substance of government, whose leading object is, to elevate the condition of men—to lift artificial weights from all shoulders."[12]

Neither soldiers nor Lincoln relinquished that vision of why the war mattered, but as the war progressed, soldiers' views evolved on how slavery and emancipation related to saving the Union whose birth the Declaration of Independence had announced in 1776. Although black Americans had advocated the destruction of slavery before the war began, most white soldiers, like Lincoln, entered the war with the belief that the Constitution forbade federal interference with slavery, and some opposed emancipation on racist grounds. Yet their wartime experiences called early views into question. With Midwestern frankness, members of the 13th Wisconsin Infantry observed, "The fact that slavery is the sole undeniable cause of this infamous rebellion, that it is a war of, by, and for Slavery, is as plain as the noon-day sun." A member of the same state's Third Infantry just as frankly stated, "You have no idea of the changes that have taken place in the minds of the soldiers in the last two months; indeed, men of all parties seem unanimous in the belief that to permanently establish the Union, is to first wipe [out] the institution" of slavery. In short, "the rebellion is abolitionizing the whole army."[13] In some cases, nobody was more surprised by the growing link between saving the Union and ending slavery than the very soldiers who now insisted on that link. "When I came into the service myself and many others did not believe in interfering with slavery but we have changed our opinions," Amos Hostetter wrote his sister and brother-in-law. "Any country that allows the curse of Slavery and Amalgamation as this has done, should be cursed and I believe in my soul that God allowed this war for the very purpose of clearing out the evil and punishing us as a nation for allowing it."[14]

Such musings were at least as much about creating a new Union as preserving the old one. By 1863, many ordinary Union soldiers, men in no way distinguishable before the war from the other ordinary men buried in the cemetery that Lincoln passed each day, or from the ordinary soldiers escorting him as he passed it, reasoned from their understanding of slavery's connection to the war that not merely a preserved Union but a reborn one was necessary. When Leigh Webber had asked the previous summer what point could possibly justify the mess that the war had become, he had answered his own question with the assertion that only "the rights of human nature and universal human freedom" could justify the sacrifice.[15] As 1863 got off to a bleak start, fittingly captured in the title "Mud March," soldiers throughout the ranks pondered similar questions. One Vermont corporal, straining his eyes for any shaft of light penetrating the gloom, focused on the "great proclamation of President Lincoln Jan. 1st," as reason to hope not that things would stay the same, but rather "that human liberty is to be planted on a firmer basis than ever before."[16]

If Lincoln could not hear these pointed commentaries in person, he could hardly have escaped the urgency of them as he continued along the route to the White House each morning in the summer of 1863. After passing through a tollgate and turning onto Rhode Island Avenue, he veered onto Vermont Avenue, and from that thoroughfare passed right by Camp Barker, one of the two contraband camps in the District of Columbia sheltering black men, women, and children who had fled slavery.[17] Contraband camps sprang up everywhere the Union Army went, throughout the entire occupied South as well as the capital region, as hundreds of thousands of slaves fled their masters and made a break for the army that they determined would destroy slavery. Falling to the army's administration by default, in a world that lacked a Red Cross or any sort of wartime humanitarian aid organizations, the camps featured conditions about as inviting as those in refugee camps anywhere. Camps in Washington lacked a clean water supply, so it did not take long for sanitary conditions to deteriorate, despite all kinds of time and energy army officials spent trying to figure out where a well might be dug, and whether three-inch pipe or four-inch pipe would do a better job of transporting waste. Those conditions, coupled with chronic food, shelter, and clothing shortages, and the starving and weakened condition in which former slaves reached the District after weeks or even longer on the run from their owners, contributed to towering mortality rates and vast human suffering far beyond the capacity of the army to relieve.[18]

Yet men, women, and children still came, reaching for freedom and willing to contribute to the Union victory they hoped for. In the fall of 1862, rumors of a Confederate raid on Washington, DC sent waves of panic through the District. As fears for the security of the US capital mounted, government officials quickly assigned fugitive slaves across the Potomac River in Alexandria, Virginia, to labor gangs that built fortifications ringing Washington. Meanwhile, army personnel organized some of the men in the District's contraband camps into a temporary armed guard to fill in spots vacated by redeployed companies of Union soldiers. As one Union Army officer explained, news of the armed guard of black men defending Washington traveled "through the rebel states like electricity" and "excite[d slaves] to renewed efforts for freedom."[19] The immediate threat to the nation's capital passed, but US reliance on contributions from former slaves remained constant. Throughout the Washington, DC region, slave refugees maintained the railroad that sent supplies to the front and unloaded and loaded cars full of supplies. Their labor on the docks kept ports at Alexandria and Georgetown in action. Washington, DC was full of army hospitals reliant on black women nursing, scrubbing, and laundering in them.[20] And when their long workdays were done, they returned, many of them to Camp Barker, where Lincoln passed each day. In fact, Mary Dines, the cook hired to work at the Lincoln family's summer residence on the grounds of the Soldiers' Home, had passed through that very camp on her journey from slavery to freedom.[21] Mary Lincoln's dressmaker, Elizabeth Keckley, worked for an aid organization known as the Contraband Relief Association in Washington. Keckley convinced Mary Lincoln to lobby the president to channel some war relief funds toward blankets and other supplies for former slaves taking refuge in Washington.[22] Simply put, former slaves gave Lincoln little choice but to take them seriously and to treat slavery not as an abstraction, but as a concrete reality that needed addressing immediately.

In late 1861 and 1862, Union war policy on slavery had begun to change. Congress passed Confiscation Acts that allowed Union Army officers to liberate slaves being used by the Confederacy to further the Confederate war effort. Lincoln signed acts abolishing slavery in Washington, DC and in federal territories. Most famously, Lincoln issued the preliminary Emancipation Proclamation in September 1862 and followed up with the final version on January 1, 1863. None of these actions destroyed the old and powerful institution of slavery in a single blow, but each one represented an important step in the long and difficult process of ending slavery and remaking the nation.

Much, in other words, had changed by the summer of 1863, and yet the war stretched on. Each day Lincoln made the journey from the cottage on the Soldiers' Home grounds, beginning and ending his commute just opposite the neat rows of soldiers' graves, and in the interim passing by the hope and desperation of Camp Barker. The intermingling of courage and longing with misery, mud, and mortality flashed by Lincoln's eyes morning and night, day after day, as he traveled his usual route and wondered if the war would ever, ever end.

Then, on the Fourth of July, General Robert E. Lee's Army of Northern Virginia began its retreat after the Battle of Gettysburg, a Union victory that turned back a Confederate invasion of Pennsylvania and, just as important, proved that Lee's seemingly unstoppable army was not invincible after all. From the War Department on the Fourth, Lincoln sent a telegram—what we would probably call a press release today—that read:

The President announces to the country that news from the Army of the Potomac, up to 10 P.M. of the 3rd. is such as to cover that Army with the highest honor, to promise a great success to the cause of the Union, and to claim the condolence of all for the many gallant fallen. And that for this, he especially desires that on this day, He whose will, not ours, should ever be done, be everywhere remembered and reverenced with profoundest gratitude.[23]

On that very same day, Vicksburg, Mississippi, fell to Union forces after a long siege, finally securing the Mississippi River in Union hands.[24] Nobody doubted the significance of the twin victories or their timing, and not just militarily. In short remarks delivered on July 7, Lincoln referred three times to the Fourth of July eighty-seven years earlier, contrasting the peril in which the ideals of the Declaration were to be found on the previous two Independence Days with the more encouraging outlook this time around.[25] Newspapers throughout the North rang with the news. In an article entitled "The Victory Undoubtedly Ours," the *New York Herald* observed, "our national anniversary, we think, may be celebrated in anticipation to-day as in honor of the nation's greatest deliverance," while the *Boston Herald* of July 4 devoted fifteen lines of type to the *headline* about Gettysburg before the text of the article reporting the news began.[26] A Union soldier serving in New Orleans hoped that the news meant "the light of Liberty is soon to shine."[27] So did former slaves who had run to Union lines at Beaufort, North Carolina, and who greeted news of Gettysburg by gathering in church to share "hymns of praise to God [and] mingled prayers for the success of the union armies" engaged in what black men and women saw as "a grand crusade against African slavery."[28]

As strategically significant as the Gettysburg and Vicksburg victories were, Union response (after the immediate euphoria) consisted more of soul-searching and less of jubilation than might be expected. Part of the reason was that the awful butchery, especially at Gettysburg, dampened the urge toward jubilation. The Battle of Gettysburg cost more human life than any other single event in US history. Its three days of murderous, unrelenting fighting left behind so much destruction and so many casualties that one historian called the battle "the greatest man-made disaster of American history."[29] Living through the battle left young Henry Matrau literally unable to put the experience into words. The long silence of the soldier from Wisconsin had his parents so convinced that their son had been killed that they wrote to the captain of his company begging for particulars about his death or capture. The officer ordered the boy, pointblank, to write home, but even under direct orders, Henry could barely find language to convey an idea of what he had endured in the "one vast slaughter pen" that was Gettysburg. The best he could eventually manage was to tell his mother and father about a dead companion who nearly fell on top of him, and then attribute his own survival to dumb luck.[30] Words also failed Cornelia Hancock, a nurse who tended the wounded at Gettysburg. There was simply nothing "in the English language to express the sufferings" of soldiers, which "robbed the battlefield of its glory," she wrote her sister.[31]

Much as Lincoln, black Americans, and Northerners generally wanted Gettysburg and Vicksburg to serve as the final victories that signaled the war's triumphant end, those battles actually heralded the onset of another long and difficult period, leading many to believe, as a Union soldier from Iowa put it, that "the chastisements of the Almighty are not yet ended."[32]

The summer of 1863 turned out to be a prelude to more interminable and indeterminate fighting of the kind that prodded soldiers to ask the deepest questions about the most fundamental matters. What else could the war be, Sergeant James Jessee wondered, except "a curse . . . upon the country for the toleration of that inhuman practice, Human Slavery.'" And if that were the case, then "not till the last slave is freed need we expect Peace," for "as sure as God is God and right is right, so sure may we look for the war to end . . . in the . . . liberation of this oppressed and down trodden race."[33] Another private saw God at work in similar ways. "Where our nation has failed to act in putting the abomination away from them God has allowed war and carnage to operate," he mused. [34] Still another echoed, "the Almighty has taken up the cause of the oppressed and . . . will deny us peace until we 'break every yoke' and sweep every vestige of the cursed institution [i.e., slavery] from our land."[35]

Black Union soldiers believed they knew a thing or two about breaking yokes and were more likely to view the war in the latter half of 1863 as "a medium through which God is helping us."[36] Even before the war, both free Northern blacks and many Southern slaves had long used the biblical story of Exodus to make sense of the experiences of slavery and racial oppression, so the war as God's way of freeing slaves fit naturally into that narrative.[37] For example, one member of the 54th Massachusetts likened President Lincoln's decision to issue the Emancipation Proclamation and to enlist black soldiers to Moses "rais[ing] up his hand" to lead the Israelites out of bondage.[38] Gettysburg and Vicksburg made the parallels with Exodus seem even stronger, because they reminded black soldiers of the plagues falling fast and furiously upon the Egyptians who refused to let the Israelites go. But just as important, as black men saw it, the war gave the Union a choice between joining the liberation or acting the part of pharaoh. The Almighty "cannot take sides with the oppressor," one black soldier admonished in the summer of 1863, so if the Union wanted to win, then it had better remake itself into a new and purer version, free from the evil of slavery.[39]

For slaves seeking to travel the path out of bondage and into freedom, the latter half of 1863 must have seemed more like the desert in which the Israelites wandered for forty years than the promised land. Near Natchez, Mississippi, to take just one of many examples, thousands of women and children rushed into a hastily assembled camp in a few short weeks that summer, overwhelming available food, clothing, and shelter to such an extent that they found "destitution, despair, and death staring them in the face."[40] In the very month that the Battle of Gettysburg took place, James N. Gloucester, a black minister and officer of the American Freedmen's Friend Society of Brooklyn, New York, filed a none-too-flattering report on conditions in the Washington camps that Lincoln passed daily, noting rickety buildings; corruption among contractors who were supposed to supply basic necessities; a scandalous clothing shortage; and "rapid mortality" among the black men, women, and children who came in search of freedom but too often lost their lives or their loved ones.[41]

For Lincoln, too, the days, weeks, and months following the victory at Gettysburg continued to be characterized chiefly by loss. After the Battle of Gettysburg, Lincoln badly wanted Union General George Meade to pursue and crush the Army of Northern Virginia. Meade's failure to do so left Lincoln so "oppressed," "distressed immeasurably," and "dissatisfied" that he poured out his disappointment with the victorious general in a letter so howling with frustration that he thought better of sending it and stuffed it in a desk drawer to fester in dark silence—much like the president's own spirits.[42] That same month, rioters protested the draft and terrorized African Americans in New York and elsewhere, signaling pockets of deep opposition to the military prosecution of the war and to emancipation. To top it all off, Lincoln's wife was injured in a carriage accident that summer and suffered a close enough call that eldest son Robert was called home. When Robert arrived at the White House, he found his father with his head down on his desk, crying.[43] The paralyzing defeat of Union forces at Chickamauga did little to cheer Lincoln up.

Small wonder that Walt Whitman, a poet-turned-army nurse who saw the president coming and going to the White House nearly every day that summer and fall, reflected that never had he seen Lincoln looking so "careworn."[44] It was a careworn Lincoln who wandered through the cemetery on the Soldiers' Home grounds, reciting,

> *How sleep the brave, who sink to rest*
> *By all their country's wishes blest*

as he somberly brooded over "numberless graves—some without a spear of grass to hide their newness."[45] It was a careworn Lincoln who hosted Andrew Curtin, governor of Pennsylvania, for visits in August and October to discuss, among other things, the dedication of a cemetery as the final resting place for soldiers who died at Gettysburg.[46] It was a careworn

Lincoln who received a letter from members of the Western Sanitary Commission in St. Louis, a benevolent organization hitherto focused on distributing supplies to sick and wounded soldiers, requesting "permission and authority to extend our labors to the suffering freed people" gathered in contraband camps throughout the Mississippi Valley, not only as "a work of philanthropy, but equally of patriotism."[47] It was a careworn Lincoln who, at almost precisely the same time he received that letter from the Western Sanitary Commission, received an official invitation from David Wills, prominent local leader in Gettysburg and Governor Curtin's agent in the actual, logistical creation of the cemetery. Wills invited the president to exercise philanthropy and patriotism in a different way, by offering "appropriate remarks" at the Gettysburg dedication ceremony to "set apart these grounds to their Sacred use."[48] It was, in sum, a careworn Lincoln who, in the autumn of 1863, pondered exactly how to consecrate the ground where soldiers had fallen on the anniversary of the Declaration of Independence.

Viewing soldiers' deaths and the Union's birth through lenses ground by loss, discouragement, and suffering, Lincoln began to compose his speech about the Declaration of Independence as key not merely to the preservation of the Union, but to its salvation, which is to say, its redemption and transformation. From opening to closing, echoes of the context in which the remarks were written can be heard, echoes composed of the shared experiences through which Lincoln, soldiers, and slaves passed in the war's first two years, and especially in the second half of 1863. If the Gettysburg Address "remade America," as one historian has famously written, it did so not behind the backs or to the surprise of soldiers or former slaves, but rather as the logical culmination of the journey they shared with the president, a journey characterized chiefly by suffering and loss, but suffering and loss that neither he nor they were willing to allow to descend into meaningless nihilism.[49] They were all plunged together into the valley of the shadow of darkness. They had not detoured around it; neither did they stop in its horrifying middle and refuse to take another step. In 1863, they continued to walk through the despair, even though they could not yet see an end to the darkness. Echoes of that shared journey rang through the Gettysburg Address then, and still do, even now.

As Lincoln stood before the crowd on November 19, 1863, to consecrate the ground where soldiers had fallen the previous July, he began just as he had in his immediate response to the battle, by invoking the memory of the Fourth of July "four score and seven years ago," in 1776. On that Fourth of July, the signers of the Declaration of Independence had attended the birth of a "nation conceived in liberty and dedicated to the proposition that all men are created equal." Now that such a nation was under threat, Union soldiers fought to see it through its hour of danger and demonstrate to the world "whether that nation, or any nation so conceived, and so dedicated, can long endure." The Declaration's architects and signers had pledged their lives to that nation, but the men who fell at Gettysburg had actually *given* theirs "that that nation might live." The men mourned and honored today, he told his listeners, were directly connected to the men who had signed the Declaration. Union soldiers certainly agreed, for they had been saying the same thing since the war began. The president himself could hardly have made the point better than Private John Inskeep of the 17th Ohio Infantry, who had marked the Fourth of July, 1862, in his encampment in Tennessee by reflecting, "Eighty six years ago to day the Declaration of Independence was signed at Philadelphia. The illustrious signers of that honored instrument pledged for the maintenance of this declaration their lives, their fortunes and their sacred honor. To day six hundred thousand of their posterity are in arms for the defense and preservation of those institutions secured to us by this great Charter of our Liberties."[50]

Lincoln concluded the Address by circling back to and amplifying the same theme. In the final paragraph, he emphasized that securing the Declaration's legacy required the descendants of the founders not simply to continue residing on the North American land mass but specifically to uphold the form of government "of the people, by the people, and for the people" that the founders had established. Attention to the importance of the government itself had been and remained a prominent theme among Union soldiers from the moment of their enlistment, through war's tedium and its horror. As discouraging as things might have looked in Virginia in 1862, Corporal Elijah Penny, for example, insisted that the Union must withstand any attempt to break it up, thus "proving to the whole world that Americans can and *will* govern themselves."[51]

Perhaps less expected, and therefore even more striking, was the attention paid to the theme of government by black Americans who had derived no benefit from a government that refused "to bring us into recognition as citizens" as it guaranteed others "the full enjoyment of every civil and religious emolument," as prominent black Philadelphian Alfred Green put the point in a speech urging black men to help defend "the great Republic" before the Union Army admitted black recruits.[52] Once enlistment of African Americans began, Joseph Williams urged fellow black men to enlist "in defence of the Republic which is our redemption," and Corporal Henry Harmon of the Third United States Colored Troops explained just two weeks before the Gettysburg Address that he fought "to battle for our country's rights, our rights, our people's rights, and to help the Government to preserve that glorious Union which our fore fathers had preserved for us."[53] As Reverend John Gloucester noted in his July 1863 report on conditions in Washington, DC contraband camps, he was particularly struck during his visit by former slaves' acute attention to affairs of government. Even amidst the suffering, they emphasized "sincere, honest affection" for President Lincoln, and they identified the fate of the "American republick" [sic] as "a question of such immense importance."[54] Even black men and women who had fled American slavery and settled in Canada revisited their ideas about government during and because of the war. One such man was Alfred Butler, who ran a store and circulating library in Toronto, which had been his home since 1855; prior to the war, he and his black neighbors considered themselves loyal to the British Empire, under whose mantle they had personally found freedom. But as the war progressed, Butler noticed "there are a great many who do not feel satisfied with the course that has been pursued by the British Government." Instead, "they look with more interest to the United States of late, especially since the President's [Emancipation] Proclamation has come out." The war itself, and the actions of Lincoln, whom they regarded as "an honest man, willing to do the right thing, and trying to do it," led migrants like Butler to discover "a feeling, after all, for the old mother land" and its government, which now, they had reason to hope, would soon extend "the opportunity of enjoying freedom in the States."[55]

Moreover, the conclusion of the Gettysburg Address articulated quite clearly exactly how the government founded by the Declaration could be, indeed had to be, saved, and its remedy matched the prescription issued by Lincoln's fellow travelers on the path through war. It would take a "new birth of freedom," Lincoln attested, affirming Alfred Butler's expectations and echoing Union soldiers' insights.[56] "The Union under the old construction" would never do, Private Thomas Covert had observed in the first days of 1863; he clearly saw the need for "a new one, that knows nothing about slavery."[57] In the summer of 1863, when the battles at Gettysburg and Vicksburg raised hopes for impending victory, and then more long months of war delayed those very hopes, Private Ransom Bedell had vowed, "we are not for the Union as it *was* But as it will Be."[58] The actions of the thousands of black men, women, and children who ran from slavery and built, dug, hauled, laundered, transported, and cooked for, as well as nursed, the Union Army, along with the actions of the black men who fought in its ranks, made the same vow even more loudly.

Despite the brevity of the Gettysburg Address, neither listeners then nor readers now could get from the opening lines about the Declaration to the culminating lines about "a new birth of freedom" without passing through a middle section—the longest of the Address—about struggle, the smallness of human effort, death, suffering, and sorrow. With the exception of "the world will little note, nor long remember, what we say here," which we like to reel off ironically from time to time, the middle section of the speech is the least likely section to be quoted, most difficult to memorize, and most likely to cause trip-ups whenever we recite the Gettysburg Address by heart. It is not, suffice it to say, the part of the speech that anyone likes the best. Yet we can't get to the resonant conclusion without going through it, any more than Lincoln or the inhabitants of the nation that he led could get through the war, or the summer and fall of 1863 that provided the context in which the Gettysburg Address was crafted, without also passing through sorrow, suffering, death, and evidence of the insignificance and even the absurdity of human effort so resounding to make it all seem perilously close to meaningless. The Address skipped none of that darkness, but neither did it end there.

Response to the Address in the weeks and months following its delivery at Gettysburg was muted. Union soldiers continued to echo the speech's themes, as for example, when Charles Henthorn wondered "where are the oppressed and down-trodden millions of the earth to look for hope" if the Union's "experiment of self-government by the people shall fail." Constant Hanks wrote of the "mighty revolution through which the nation is travailing" to secure "equal rights to all men." And the actions of former slaves in contraband camps continued to attest to their hopes that a Union victory would bring a new birth of freedom.[59] But neither soldiers nor former slaves left much written records of direct reaction to the speech, a state of affairs lamented by Gabor Boritt in *The Gettysburg Gospel*.[60] Some had low expectations of the speech to begin with; when Private William Hamilton heard that his brother would attend the ceremonies at Gettysburg, Hamilton grumbled to his mother, "there will be plenty of speeches and any amount talk, but none of that sort of stuff will terminate this war."[61] Yet the most pertinent reasons for the silence were quite simple. One had to do with timing: the absolutely crucial Battle of Lookout Mountain and the capture of Chattanooga occurred just days after the Address and quickly dominated newspaper coverage as well as private correspondence. More important, the Gettysburg Address might herald a welcome recognition of what soldiers and former slaves already knew, but it did not tell them anything new. It needed little comment at that moment because it repeated shared rather than novel insights, important ones to be sure, but ones that war's participants had already figured out for themselves. They, like Lincoln, were denied the luxury of glorifying war and also of surrendering to despair in the middle of it. Instead, they, like Lincoln, had to travel straight through the ugliest marrow of it.

In the opening week of July 1863, Northerners had given thanks for two victories, one at Vicksburg on the mighty father of waters, the Mississippi River, and another in the rolling hills of Pennsylvania. What followed was not exaltation, but the stench of decay. Not ascension, but death. Not victory, but more strife, with no end in sight. Not a lessening of violence, but a worsening of it. For Lincoln and for all, what followed was more loss. That summer, Lincoln did not allow himself easy celebration, which did not come naturally to him anyway, but neither did he permit himself the indulgence toward which he *was* inclined, melancholy or despair. Neither did most of the men in the ranks of the Union Army. Still less could the men, women, and children who had fled slavery afford to do so. Just as Lincoln's twice-daily carriage ride could neither bypass nor halt in the middle of deep suffering and human loss but must journey straight through them, so too must he and the nation he led hold both triumph and tragedy in impossible but necessary tension with each another. In the fall of 1863, Lincoln wrote that tension into the Gettysburg Address; its success in capturing that tension allows the Gettysburg Address to continue to speak. The Gettysburg Address and the new birth of freedom heralded at its climax were products of loss as much as victory, of being plunged into death and ugliness with no luxury of skipping over them or easy remedy of sinking into them, but only the necessity of trudging through them. The Gettysburg Address itself, and the context within which it was composed, disabuse us of the notion that we can choose either triumph or tragedy as the way we remember the Civil War and force us to confront the inextricable dependence of the two on each other.

Notes

1. Lincoln to John B. Fry, Aug. 15, 1860, Springfield, IL, in *The Collected Works of Abraham Lincoln*, ed. Roy B. Basler, 9 vols. (New Brunswick, NJ: Rutgers University Press, 1953–1955), 4:95 (hereafter cited as *CW*).

2. Jan Furman, ed., *Slavery in the Clover Bottoms: John McCline's Narrative of His Life During Slavery and the Civil War* (Knoxville: University of Tennessee Press, 1998), 30, 44.

3. Lt. A. J. Slemmer, First Artillery, Fort Pickens, FL, March 18, 1861, to Lt. Col. L. Thomas, Assistant Adjutant-General, US Army, *The War of the Rebellion: A Compilation of the Official Records of the Union and Confederate Armies*, series 2 vol. 1, p. 750. Accessed via http://ebooks.library.cornell.edu/cgi/t/text/pageviewer-idx?c=moawar;cc=moawar;idno=waroo114;node=waroo114%3A3;view=image;se q=764;size=100;page=root.

4. Sgt. Cyrus Boyd, 15th Iowa, diary, shortly after April 6, 1862, Pittsburg Landing, TN; and diary May 24, 1862, Corinth, MS, in *The Civil War Diary of Cyrus F. Boyd, Fifteenth Iowa Infantry, 1861–1863*, ed. Mildred Throne (Millwood, NY: Kraus, reprint, 1977), 27–39, 52.

5. Leigh Webber to friend Charly Brown and Charly's father John, Jan. 13, 1861, Page Co., IA, John S. Brown Letters, reel 2, Topeka, KS, Kansas State Historical Society.

6. Pvt. Leigh Webber, 1st Kansas Infantry, to Brown Family, July 24, 1862, Gibson Co., TN, John S. Brown Letters, reel 2, Kansas State Historical Society.

7. Civil War Casualties by Battle, University of Houston Digital History, http://www.digitalhistory.uh.edu/disp_textbook.cfm?smtID=11&psid=4468; and David S. Heidler and Jeanne T. Heidler, eds., *Encyclopedia of the American Civil War* (New York: Norton, 2002). Casualties are total Union and Confederate, which were the numbers that mattered to Lincoln, who never stopped considering the United States to be one country. Union totals for the same battles were 15,000 for the Peninsula Campaign, 15,849 for Seven Days, and 16,054 for Second Bull Run, 12,700 at Fredericksburg, and 14,000 at Chancellorsville.

8. Walt Whitman, "Abraham Lincoln," no. 45, Aug. 12, 1863, *Specimen Days*, in *Prose Works* (Philadelphia, 1892), 59–61.

9. Matthew Pinsker, *Lincoln's Sanctuary: Abraham Lincoln and the Soldiers' Home* (New York: Oxford University Press, 2003), 94.

10. "The Results of This War," *The American Union*, July 5, 1861, Martinsburg, VA, American Antiquarian Society.

11. Pvt. W. D. Wildman, 12th Indiana Infantry, to teacher, Miss Susan Griggs, Nov. 2, 1861, near Sharpsburg, MD, Virginia Southwood Collection, Western Historical Manuscript Collection, University of Missouri, Columbia.

12. "Message to Congress in Special Session," July 4, 1861, *CW*, 4:426, 438.

13. *The Wisconsin Volunteer,* Feb. 6, 1862, Leavenworth, KS, 3, Kansas State Historical Society. *The Wisconsin Volunteer* was the paper of the 13th Wisconsin Infantry; "Enlisted soldier," 3rd Wisconsin Infantry, to *Wisconsin State Journal,* Oct.
1861, near Harper's Ferry, VA, E. B. Quiner Correspondence of the Wisconsin
Volunteers, State Historical Society of Wisconsin, reel 1, vol. 1, 176.

14. Capt. Amos Hostetter, 34th Illinois, to sister and brother-in-law, Jan. 29, 1863,
Murfreesboro, TN, Illinois State Historical Library.

15. Pvt. Leigh Webber, 1st Kansas Infantry, to Brown Family, July 24, 1862.

16. Cpl. N. Newton Glazier, 11th Vermont (a.k.a. 1st Vermont Heavy Artillery) to
folks at home, Feb. 8, 1863, Fort Slocum, DC, Nelson Newton Glazier Letters,
Vermont Historical Society.

17. How contraband camps got their name: In May 1861, three slaves ran to Union-
held Fort Monroe in Virginia, commanded by Union Army General Benjamin
Butler. The Confederate colonel who owned the slaves and planned to put them
to work building Confederate fortifications demanded their return on the
grounds that the Fugitive Slave Law required the federal government to protect
his rights as a property owner. Butler pointed out that the colonel was bearing
arms against the US government and claimed that the rules of war gave the
Union the authority to confiscate enemy assets, known in the laws of war as
"contraband." The term "contraband" stuck, and as slaves flocked to army en-
campments, they became known as "contrabands," and the ad hoc refugee
camps to accommodate them came to be known as contraband camps. The
other Washington, DC contraband camp (besides Camp Barker) was at Duff
Green Row on Capitol Hill, roughly where the Jefferson Building of the Library
of Congress now stands.

18. RG 92, the Consolidated Correspondence File of the Records of the Quartermaster, National Archives and Records Administration, Washington, DC (hereafter cited as NARA); file I District of Columbia, Records of the American
Freedmen's Inquiry Commission, RG 94 Letters Received by the Office of the
Adjutant General (Main Series), (hereafter cited as AFIC Records), M619 reel
200, NARA.

19. For numbers in Washington, DC contraband camps (4,200 in October 1862),
see Testimony of Superintendent D. B. Nichols, 1863 (by that time the number
in the camps was 4,939), p. 1, and for testimony about black men guarding DC
in anticipation of the Stonewall Jackson raid, see Nichols's testimony p. 16 in
AFIC Records, file I District of Columbia, pp. 1–16, M619 reel 200, frame 106
and 120–121, NARA. For the Union officer who reported that news of the camp
spread "through the rebel states like electricity," see Lt. M. G. Raymond Testimony in AFIC Records, file I District of Columbia, p. 28, M619 reel 200, frame
133, NARA. Even more were in Alexandria. For verification of the slave work
parties who built fortifications, see *Alexandria Gazette,* Sept. 9, 1862.

20. For railroads and laundering see for example, *Alexandria Gazette*, August 26, 1862, which reported government wages of forty cents per day. Elsewhere, an aid worker in the Mississippi Valley noticed the "large numbers of negroes employed as teamsters, cooks, servants and laborers" on which Union forces relied for basic day-to-day functioning See William Butler, US Christian Commission, to W. G. Eliot, Sept. 1, 1863, St. Louis, MO (but writing about a trip taken the previous summer), William D. Butler Papers, Missouri Historical Society. For more on the particulars of former slaves' labor for the Union Army in contraband camps, see every file of the AFIC records, as well as Ira Berlin et al., eds. *Freedom: A Documentary History of Emancipation* (New York: Cambridge University Press, 1982–2010).

21. For the Washington, DC contraband camp, see RG 92, the Consolidated Correspondence File of the Records of the Quartermaster, NARA. For the map of Lincoln's routes between the Soldiers' Home Cottage and the White House, see Pinsker, *Lincoln's Sanctuary*, Map 1, p. 6. For Mary Dines, see Pinsker, pp. 16, 66–68.

22. Mary Lincoln to "My Dear Husband," New York, Nov. 3, 1862, in *Dear Mr. Lincoln: Letters to the President*, ed. Harold Holzer (Carbondale: Southern Illinois University Press, 2006), 313.

23. Announcement of News from Gettysburg, July 4, 1863, Washington, DC, *CW*, 5; 6:314.

24. Actually, a small Confederate garrison at Port Hudson, Louisiana, still held, but only barely, and everyone knew that as Vicksburg went, so would Port Hudson. It did just days later on July 9, and then the "Father of Waters" truly did flow "unvexed to the sea," as Lincoln would note in a public letter to Democratic detractors.

25. "Response to a Serenade," July 7, 1863, Washington, DC, *CW*, 6:319–320.

26. "The Victory Undoubtedly Ours," *New York Herald*, July 4, 1863, 4; "THE STRUGGLE IN PENNSYLVANIA: THE CRISIS OF THE REBELLION BOTH ARMIES RESOLVED TO WIN OR PERISH! ANNIHILATION OR VICTORY! TERRIFIC FIGHTING THURSDAY AND FRIDAY! UNION SUCCESS ON THURSDAY! THE ENEMY REPULSED AT ALL POINTS LARGE NUMBERS OF PRISONERS CAPTURED Generals Paul and Zook Killed Generals Sickles, Barlow, Graham and Warren Wounded THE BATTLE CONTINUED YESTERDAY NO IMPRESSION MADE ON THE FEDERAL POSITION The Whole of Lee's Army Engaged Rebel Generals Longstreet and Barksdale Killed CAPTURE OF A BEBEL MAIL," *Boston Herald*, July 4, 1863, 2. The news of Vicksburg and Gettysburg moved to front pages in the ensuing days, as more details became known.

27. Corporal Rufus Kinsley, 8th Vermont Infantry, diary, July 19, 1863, New Orleans, Rufus Kinsley Diary, Vermont Historical Society.

28. James Rumley Diary, Aug. 6, 1863, Beaufort, NC, Levi Woodbury Piggott Collection, North Carolina Department of Archives and History.

29. For Gettysburg's unenviable claim to casualty fame (23,000 Union casualties and 28,000 Confederate casualties), see Gabor Boritt, *The Gettysburg Gospel: The Lincoln Speech That Nobody Knows* (New York: Simon and Schuster, 2006), 9.

30. Pvt. Henry Matrau, 6th Wisconsin Infantry, to parents, July 29, 1863, and Aug. 16, 1863, Rappahannock Station, VA, in *Letters Home: Henry Matrau of the Iron Brigade*, ed. Marcia Reid-Green (Lincoln: University of Nebraska Press, 1993), 59–62.

31. Cornelia Hancock to sister, July 14, 1863, Gettysburg, PA, and Hancock, undated essay, in *South After Gettysburg; Letters of Cornelia Hancock from the Army of the Potomac, 1863–1865*, ed. Henrietta Stratton Jaquette (New York: Thomas Y. Crowell, 1956), 10 and 7.

32. Lt. J. Q. A. Campbell, 5th Iowa Infantry, diary, July 4, 1863, near Vicksburg, MS, in *The Union Must Stand*, ed. Mark Grimsley and Todd D. Miller (Knoxville: University of Tennessee Press, 2000), 110.

33. Sgt. James Jessee, 8th Illinois Infantry, diary, Dec. 31, 1863, Helena, AR, James W. Jessee Diaries, Kansas University.

34. Pvt. Ransom Bedell, 39th Illinois Infantry, "American Slavery," an original essay written for his cousin, Summer 1863, Ransom Bedell Papers, Illinois State Historical Library.

35. Lt. J. Q. A. Campbell, 5th Iowa Infantry, diary, July 4, 1863, near Vicksburg, MS, in Grimsley and Miller, *The Union Must Stand*, 110.

36. Orderly Sgt. Isaiah Welch, 55th Massachusetts Infantry, to Editor, Dec. 2, 1863, Folly Island, SC, *Christian Recorder*, Dec. 19, 1863, 2.

37. See Eddie S. Glaude, Jr., *Exodus! Religion, Race, and Nation in Early Nineteenth Century Black America* (Chicago: University of Chicago Press, 2000) for discussion of the Exodus theme among both antebellum Northern black thinkers and Southern slaves.

38. "Barquet," 54th Massachusetts Infantry, to Editor, Mar. 24, 1864, near Jacksonville, FL, *Anglo-African*, Apr. 16, 1864, 1.

39. G. E. S., 54th Massachusetts Infantry, to Editor, Aug. 7, 1863, Morris Island, SC, *Anglo-African*, Aug. 24, 1863, 1.

40. Brigadier General James R. Slack to wife Ann, Aug. 4 and 8, 1863, Natchez, MS, James R. Slack Papers, folder 6, Indiana State Library.

41. James N. Gloucester, "Report on Condition of Freemen and Camps About Washington," July 1863, Papers of the United States American Freedmen's Inquiry Commission, box 1, folder 41, Houghton Library, Harvard University.

42. Lincoln to General George G. Meade, written on July 14, 1863, but never sent, Washington, DC, *CW*, 6:237–229.

43. Pinsker, *Lincoln's Sanctuary*, 106.

44. In both June and August 1863, Walt Whitman, who observed the president heading to the White House almost every day, noted that Lincoln "looks even more careworn than usual" and seemed "very sad." See Roy P. Basler, ed., *Walt Whitman's Memoranda During the War & Death of Abraham Lincoln* (Bloomington: Indiana University Press, 1962), 6–7; and Whitman, *Specimen Days*, in *Prose Works*.

45. Francis B. Carpenter, *Six Months at the White House* (New York: Hurd and Houghton, 1866), 223–224. According to Douglas Wilson, the lines of verse come from William Collins, "Ode, Written in the Beginning of the Year 1746." See Wilson, *Lincoln's Sword: The Presidency and the Power of Words* (New York: Knopf, 2006), 321, n. 209.

46. For Curtin's visit, see Wilson, *Lincoln's Sword*, 208–209.

47. James E. Yeatman, George Partridge, John B. Johnson, Carlos Greeley, William G. Eliot, to President A. Lincoln, "Letter to the President of the United States," Rooms of the Western Sanitary Commission, St. Louis, MO, Nov. 6, 1863, William Greenleaf Eliot Papers, box 2, folder 21, Missouri Historical Society.

48. David Wills to Lincoln, Nov. 2, 1863, quoted in Wilson, *Lincoln's Sword*, 209.

49. In *Lincoln at Gettysburg: The Words That Remade America* (New York: Simon and Schuster, 1992), Garry Wills makes an eloquent case that Lincoln's Gettysburg Address revolutionized the relationship between the Declaration of Independence, the Constitution, and the American nation. By writing that each of the Address's listeners "was having his or her intellectual pocket picked," (p. 38), Wills argues that Lincoln was well ahead of the rest of the public in his new understanding, but former slaves and Union soldiers had actually been anticipating Lincoln's vision of the Union transformed for over a year.

50. Pvt. John Inskeep, 17th Ohio Infantry, diary, July 4, 1862, camp in Tennessee, John Inskeep Diary, Ohio Historical Society.

51. Cpl. Elijah Penny, 4th New York Artillery, to wife, May 11, 1862, Arlington Heights, VA, Penny Family Papers, New York State Library.

52. Alfred M. Green, *Letters and Discussions on the Formation of Colored Regiments* (Philadelphia, 1862), Schomburg Institute, New York.

53. Joseph Williams, 1st North Carolina Colored Volunteers (Wild's Brigade), to *Christian Recorder*, June 17, 1863, Camp Wild, NC, June 27, 1863, 1; Corporal Henry Harmon, Third United States Colored Troops to *Christian Recorder*, Oct. 23, 1863, Morris Island, SC, *Christian Recorder* Nov. 7, 1863, p.1.

54. James N. Gloucester, "Report on Condition of Freemen and Camps About Washington," July 1863, Papers of the United States American Freedmen's Inquiry Commission, box 1, folder 41, Houghton Library, Harvard University.

55. Testimony of Alfred Butler to the AFIC, 1863, Toronto, Canada, file 10, AFIC Records, M619 reel 201, frames 311–312, NARA.

56. Gettysburg Address, Nov. 19, 1863, *CW*, 7:23.

57. Pvt. Thomas Covert, 6th Ohio Cavalry, to wife, Jan. 11, 1863, Stafford Co., VA, Thomas Covert Papers, Western Reserve Historical Society.

58. Pvt. Ransom Bedell, 39th Illinois, to cousin Theoda, summer 1863, Morris Island, SC, Ransom Bedell Papers, Illinois State Historical Library.

59. Pvt. Charles Henthorn, 77th Illinois, to sister, March 7, 1864, recuperating in hospital in Quincy, IL, Charles Henthorn Letters, Schoff Civil War Collection, Clements Library, University of Michigan; Pvt. Constant Hanks, 20th NY Militia, to mother, Jan. 4, 1864, near Brandy Station, VA, Constant Hanks Papers, Duke University.

60. Boritt, *Gettysburg Gospel*, 136–138 and note p. 336.

61. Pvt. William Hamilton, 2nd Pennsylvania Reserves, to mother, Nov. 19, 1863, near Paoli Mills, VA, *People at War*, reel 42, collection 102, William Hamilton Papers, Library of Congress.

8

Little Note, Long Remember

LINCOLN AND THE MURK OF MYTH AT GETTYSBURG

Allen C. Guelzo

THE SHORT STORY of the Gettysburg Address is that it was a surprisingly short speech—all of 272 words—delivered by Abraham Lincoln as part of the dedication ceremonies for the Soldiers' cemetery at Gettysburg, on November 19, 1863, four-and-a-half months after the climactic battle of the American Civil War there. But the long story is that no single American utterance has had the staying power, or commanded the respect and reverence, accorded the Gettysburg Address. It has been engraved (on the south wall of the Lincoln Memorial), translated (in a book devoted to nothing but translations of the Gettysburg Address), and analyzed in at least nine full-dress critical studies over the last century.[1] On the first anniversary of the 9/11 attacks on the World Trade Center, a commemoration ceremony at Ground Zero featured New York Governor George Pataki, reading the Gettysburg Address. In 1963, Martin Luther King, Jr., told a black journalist that his "I Have a Dream" speech was designed to be a "sort of a Gettysburg Address," and he opened it with words directly modeled on the Gettysburg Address: "Five score years ago, a great American, in whose symbolic shadow we stand today, signed the Emancipation Proclamation."[2] Article 2 of the French constitution declares the guiding "principle of the Republic shall be" a phrase from the Gettysburg Address: *gouvernement du peuple, par le peuple et pour le peuple* (government of the people, by the people and for the people.)[3] In the 1935 movie *Ruggles of Red Gap*, an English butler (played by Charles Laughton), set loose on the American frontier, establishes his right to a piece of the American dream by reciting, in front of a saloon full of incredulous cowboys, the Gettysburg Address.[4]

Still, its creation and delivery have become the stuff of American myth and legend, many of which obscure the actual process by which the Address was created. The myths are many, and they range from the story invented in the 1880s that Lincoln wrote the Address as an afterthought on the back of an envelope while on the train bringing him to Gettysburg, to the equally dubious story that no one in the audience of ten to fifteen thousand people who heard Lincoln read it initially thought it was any good; from the notion that Lincoln had no strategy but only untutored eloquence to bring to play, to the furious contest over which version of the Address in Lincoln's hand is *the* Address.

Looming largest in this closet of tales is the widespread assumption that Lincoln composed the Address at virtually the last moment. In truth, Lincoln had been working on his remarks for days before leaving Washington for the dedication ceremonies—in some sense (as we shall see shortly) he was actually working on them only days after the end of the battle. He mentioned in passing to the journalist Noah Brooks, five days before the Address was delivered, that "My speech isn't long," and though "it is not finished," it "is short, short, short."[5] On the other hand, what is true was that there had been some question in the first place whether he would actually attend the ceremonies for the creation of the Soldiers' cemetery at Gettysburg, which were, after all, the event for which the Address was being composed.

The creation of the Soldiers' cemetery project at Gettysburg had begun as early as "a few days after the terrific battle," on July 10, 1863, when Pennsylvania Governor Andrew Gregg Curtin visited the battlefield and found "the feelings were shocked and the heart sickened at the sights that presented themselves at every step."

> The remains of our brave soldiers, from the necessary haste with which they were interred, in many instances were but partially covered with earth, and, indeed, in some instances were left wholly unburied . . . over the fields of arable land for miles around . . . Humanity shuddered at the sight, and called aloud for a remedy.

The "remedy" was close at hand—in fact, at Curtin's elbow, in the person of his guide to the battlefield, Gettysburg lawyer David Wills. Although Wills was only a thirty-two-year-old lawyer in practice in Gettysburg, he had sterling political connections: an Adams County native, he had graduated from Pennsylvania College in 1851, read law under Thaddeus Stevens in Lancaster, and married into the extended political clan of Alexander K. McClure, the great Pennsylvania Republican powerbroker. Curtin had been one of McClure's proteges; he and McClure helped steer the Pennsylvania delegation to the Republican National Convention in 1860 away from Simon Cameron and toward Lincoln, and the following year, he backed Curtin's successful bid for the Pennsylvania governorship. If there was anyone in Gettysburg Curtin was likely to deputize as his agent, it was David Wills.[6]

Wills had a proposal ready for Curtin in two weeks. Together with endorsements from the New York state agents, Wills eloquently described to Curtin how "our dead are lying on the field unburied. In many instances arms and legs and sometimes heads protrude and my attention has been directed to several places where the hogs were actually rooting out the bodies and devouring them . . . humanity calls on us to take measures to remedy this." As the solution, Wills "suggested . . . the propriety and actual necessity of the purchase of a common burial ground for the dead, now only partially buried over miles of country around Gettysburg," and, in fact, he already had the perfect location in mind: on Cemetery Hill, between the Taneytown road and the Baltimore pike, on the western boundary of the Evergreen Cemetery. Curtin, who saw nothing in the plan but roses for his gubernatorial re-election campaign that fall, responded by bestowing on Wills "full power to act upon the suggestions in his letter, and to correspond with the governors of all the States that had been represented by troops in the battle."[7]

This was not as easy as it sounded, and the reasons ran all the way back to the formation of the Republican Party itself. The Republicans ran their first presidential candidate only in 1856, and, even then, they were more of an antislavery coalition than a coherent, organized, single-minded political machine. Old Whigs like Alexander McClure mixed with former Democrats like Simon Cameron, linked only by their common loathing of the Slave Power. On every other issue, however, the old animosities were kept under lids with difficulty, and Pennsylvania Republicanism, like the national party itself, quickly showed itself to be of two minds. The more radical of those minds belonged, in Pennsylvania, to McClure, Stevens, Wills, and Curtin; and by 1863, Radical Republicanism had been notoriously restive under what seemed to them the unseemly caution of Abraham Lincoln. This came to a point over the cemetery proposal, because alongside Wills's proposal sprang up a rival cemetery proposal from another Republican lawyer in Gettysburg, David McConaughy, whose sentiments stood apart from Wills's and behind Lincoln. McConaughy had solid political credentials of his own, since he, like McClure, had been a delegate to the 1860 Republican National Convention, and in 1864 would serve as a presidential elector for Lincoln from Pennsylvania. There were rumors in the wind that Curtin was contemplating a reach for the Republican presidential nomination in 1864, as part of a groundswell of dump-Lincoln sentiment, and Simon Cameron warned Lincoln in October that "it is understood that [Curtin] now aspires to have your place, in the White House." So the rival cemetery proposals quickly assumed the look of a political proxy-fight among Adams County Republicans.[8]

On July 15, McConaughy made his own appeal to Andrew Curtin, arguing that whatever cemetery was created at Gettysburg should be reserved first and foremost for "the sons of Pennsylvania and not by those of other states." His solution was to set aside part of the already existing Evergreen Cemetery on Cemetery Hill "for the burial of our own dead," and then, in separate sections, he would propose burying the dead of "all the loyal states, whose sons fell in the glorious strife, on this the great Battlefield of Pennsylvania," and topping it all off with a "National Monument in memory of the battle and the dead." Wills, however, at once went into high gear and found that McConaughy was already talking about acquiring land adjacent to the Evergreen Cemetery from the cemetery's neighbor, sixty-seven-year-old farmer Peter Raffensperger. Wills "went to R[affensperger] & his wife and endeavored to induce them to break their contract," McConaughy said, "stating to them, that I had bought not for a public but for a private purpose & for speculation."[9]

Connections and wiliness paid off, and the McConaughy proposal was quietly shunted aside. (McConaughy would soon turn his energies instead to the preservation of the battlefield, founding the Gettysburg Battlefield Memorial Association and creating what would eventually become the Gettysburg National Military Park.) After that, it took Wills less than a month to obtain assents from the eighteen Northern states whose troops had fought at Gettysburg to agree to fund the purchase of seventeen acres on Cemetery Hill, bordering the western boundary of the Evergreen Cemetery. (New York's share of the expenses would amount to an economical $6,250.) By mid-August Wills had purchased the ground for the modest sum of $2,475.87 and signed agreements with a noted landscape gardener, William Saunders, for the layout of the new

cemetery; and with a local contractor, Franklin W. Biesecker, for the ex-
humation, identification, and reburial of over 3,300 bodies. The reburial
work did not actually begin until October 27 (and would not be finished
until the following March). But by then, Wills already had his plans for
a grand dedication ceremony well in hand. He recruited, as the marshal
for the ceremonies, Ward Hill Lamon, the marshal of the District of Columbia, and extended invitations to governors (especially Andrew Curtin,
and New York Governor Horatio Seymour), members of the presidential
cabinet, Henry Wadsworth Longfellow, and the diplomatic corps. Above
all, in September, he invited Edward Everett, the former Massachusetts
governor and congressman, president of Harvard, and secretary of state,
to give the formal oration. Everett wrote back, with regrets, that the date
Wills had set—October 23—was simply not enough time to prepare an
address equal to the occasion. Wills, however, was determined to recruit
Everett, and at Everett's prompting, Wills rescheduled the entire affair for
November 19.

It was not until November 2, just seventeen days before the ceremony
was scheduled to take place, that Wills formalized the idea that, "after the
oration," Abraham Lincoln should, "as Chief Executive of the nation," perform the actual dedication of "these grounds to their sacred use by a few
appropriate remarks."[10]

Lincoln was unusually reluctant to travel far from Washington and the
war-zone in northern Virginia; that fall, he had turned down an invitation from James Cook Conkling to address a statewide "mass meeting"
of Republicans in his old hometown of Springfield. And not until as late
as November 16 did Lincoln make the final, irrevocable commitment to
speak at the Gettysburg ceremonies. But by November 18, it is clear that
he had a full, finished version of his "remarks" in hand, written in ink on
two faces of Executive Mansion stationery, and had it with him when he
boarded the train "decorated with flags and streamers" that would take
him that day, first to Baltimore, then through Hanover Junction and Hanover, Pennsylvania, to Gettysburg.[11]

Lincoln did make one other speech in Gettysburg. He arrived at the
Gettysburg train station at about 6:30 p.m. on November 18, descending
from a "director's car" at the rear of the train to the station platform. On
hand to greet him was David Wills and an unusually swollen crowd of
the curious. "There was so many people that there was no comfort, to be
taken," marveled a Gettysburg resident, Susan H. White, "there was 20
thousand people in Town."[12]

Lincoln added a few more. He was accompanied by his secretaries, John Hay and John G. Nicolay; by the US Marine Corps Band; by a guard detachment from the Invalid Corps; and by three members of the diplomatic corps, William MacDougall (one of the fathers of the Canadian Federation, who was in Washington to discuss a reciprocity treaty), Henri Mercier and Joseph Bertinetti of (respectively) France and Italy and their staffs; together with three of Lincoln's cabinet secretaries (William Henry Seward, Montgomery Blair, and John P. Usher). There was only one African-American face in this entourage, and it belonged to William Johnson, Lincoln's valet.

Valet was a term of convenience. William Henry Johnson was a native of Springfield who, over the years, had been employed by the Lincoln family in a variety of odd jobs, including acting as butler on occasions when Mary Lincoln was formally entertaining. Lincoln proposed bringing Johnson with him to Washington in 1861, but he soon found that a color line existed even within the African-American staff at the Executive Mansion. Darker-skinned than the other African-American servants, "the difference of color between him and the other servants" soon generated so much ill will understairs in the servants' hall that Lincoln instead had to find him a job next door to the Mansion in the Treasury Department as a messenger. That at least kept him reasonably close on call; and from time to time, Lincoln would "borrow" Johnson's time and services, paying him out of his own pocket and, in at least one instance, endorsing a $150 loan. Johnson was "honest, faithful, sober, industrious, and handy," and, in November 1863, he brought Johnson with him to Gettysburg.[13]

The entire train trip from Washington through Baltimore to Gettysburg took approximately six hours, delayed only once at Hanover Junction by the failure of another train bearing Andrew Curtin to rendezvous there with Lincoln's. Once at the Gettysburg station (which had been pressed into service during the battle as a temporary hospital), Lincoln was whisked up the block to David Wills's house on the town "diamond" and treated to a sumptuous dinner. Wills was playing host in his spacious three-floor brick home to thirty-eight people that night, and the dinner was a lengthy one. But as Lincoln and the dignitaries (including Edward Everett) finished, "one dense mass of people" had gathered out in the "diamond," and when the dinner had concluded, a concerted shout went up for Lincoln. Students from Pennsylvania College, which had been turned into an impromptu shambles as a hospital during and after the battle, had been given an early dismissal from classes, and stood and hurrahed for Lincoln to come out and speak. They were joined by the band of the 5th New York Artillery (whose post at Gettysburg was on the same ground David Wills had bought for the new cemetery). "The college students determined to give the President a serenade, and then vociferously shouted for him to appear, and make a brief speech"—and he did, though not quite the kind they were expecting. "I appear before you, fellow-citizens, merely to thank you for this compliment," Lincoln said, but otherwise, "I have no speech to make," and since "in my position it is somewhat important that I should not say any foolish things," he would take the safe route and "say nothing at all . . . I must beg of you to excuse me from addressing you further."[14]

Lincoln, however, was not going to bed. Once he had withdrawn to the bedroom Wills had set aside for him (and Lincoln was the only one of Wills's guests to have a room to himself that night), Lincoln "wished to consider further the few words he was expected to say the next day." As a chronically fussy and unsatisfied editor of his own words, he began writing, in pencil, a new ending on a page of blue-gray lined foolscap (David Wills, who had been called up to the room to clarify some details about "tomorrow's exercises," noticed Lincoln reading from that same paper the next day at the cemetery.) Lincoln interrupted this rewriting to pay a visit to William Henry Seward, who was staying next door in the home of Republican newspaper editor Robert Harper. (It would not have been the first time Lincoln had taken something he had written to Seward for comment or criticism). The president returned to the Wills's house, spent more time on his rewrite, and then, around midnight, turned in.[15]

In the morning, as minute-guns on Cemetery Hill began booming in the morning light, Lincoln was treated to an early-hour tour of the north end of the battlefield, around the Lutheran Seminary, where the fighting had begun on July 1 and where "our gallant and brave Friend" Major General John Fulton Reynolds had been killed. It is not clear who arranged this tour, although Lincoln's curiosity for visiting battlefields was certainly well known (he had paid an extensive visit to Antietam the year before, again in the company of Ward Hill Lamon), or even how many participants there were. Ohio Governor David Tod went looking for William Henry Seward that morning and, not finding him, asked him later in the day where he had been: "I visited the ground around the Seminary this morning," Seward replied, "and Mr. Lincoln joined me"—which suggests that the jaunt may have been Seward's idea. On the other hand, Lincoln's original itinerary for the Gettysburg visit had included "two hours to view the ground before the dedication ceremonies commence," and the Canadian William McDougall told the *Washington Daily Chronicle* that Lincoln had briefed him the evening before that "we will drive to the battlefield in the morning." However it was planned, after breakfast "the party mounted buckboards and were driven to the battlefield." It must have been a sobering sight. "The ground in these vicinities is yet strewn with remains and relics of the fearful struggle—ragged and muddy knapsacks, canteens, cups, haversacks, bayonet sheaths, and here and there fragments of gray and blue jackets," not to mention the "hides and skeletons of horses."[16]

It was sobering enough to give rise to a story that surfaced first in 1865, that the experience of seeing the scarred battlefield wrought a deep religious change in Lincoln. "When I left home to take this chair of state," Lincoln supposedly told an unnamed Illinois clergyman (who in turn told a Baptist minister in Wisconsin, who published the account in the *Oshkosh Northwestern* on April 21, 1865), "I requested my countrymen to pray for me. I was not then a Christian. . . . But, when I went to Gettysburg and looked upon the graves of our dead heroes who had fallen in defense of their country, I then and there consecrated myself to Christ. Yes, I do love Jesus." Given that Lincoln never made any such profession publicly to anyone else, the account itself is dubious. Yet, Mary Lincoln, in an interview given in September 1866, to William Henry Herndon, noted, almost in passing, that although her husband "was a religious man" in a vague sense, "he felt religious More than Ever about the time he went to Gettysburg." And he made no secret of how deeply the weight of all the war's deaths was weighing on him, as though he was, like Harry the King, personally responsible for them. "If we had reached the end of such sacrifices, and had nothing left for us to do but to place garlands on the graves of those who have already fallen, we could give thanks even amidst our tears," Lincoln remarked to an officer of the escort on board the train, "but when I think of the sacrifices of life yet to be offered and the hearts and homes yet to be made desolate because of this dreadful war . . . my heart is like lead within me, and I feel, at time, like hiding in deep darkness."[17]

There was enough time afterward to spend some last minutes at the Wills house in making his final few emendations to the text of his "remarks." But there was nothing in this process that involved Lincoln writing on an envelope, on a train, or composing the Address spontaneously at almost the last minute. "There is neither record, evidence, nor well-founded tradition that Mr. Lincoln did any writing or made any notes on the train between Washington and Gettysburg," John G. Nicolay affirmed. "Composition or writing would have been extremely troublesome amid all the movement, the noise, the conversation, the greetings, and the questionings which ordinary courtesy required him to undergo in these surroundings; but still worse would have been the rockings and joltings of the train, rendering writing virtually impossible."[18]

* * *

There is even less reason to believe the canard manufactured principally by Lincoln's friend and bodyguard, Ward Hill Lamon, that the Address fell as flat as a wall on its hearers at Gettysburg. "After its delivery on the day of commemoration," Lamon wrote years later, Lincoln "expressed deep regret that he had not prepared it with greater care. He said to me on the stand, immediately after concluding the speech: 'Lamon, that speech won't scour! It is a flat failure, and the people are disappointed.'"[19] Lincoln might have been a self-consciously critical observer of his own words, but a self-condemnation that bizarre passes credibility. However, what might have seemed genuinely odd that day was Lincoln's form in the parade that marched from the "diamond," through the town on the up-and-down of Baltimore Street, to Cemetery Hill and the entrance to the Soldiers' cemetery. Henry Clay Cochrane of the Marine Band thought that Lincoln, "mounted upon a young and beautiful chestnut bay horse" and sporting "a high silk hat," towered gigantically over everyone else and "made the rest of us look small." But at the back of the procession, where a delegation of Pennsylvania College students were positioned, Henry Eyster Jacobs thought Lincoln actually looked a little silly. "In the long procession . . . as we saw it descending one hill and then ascending another on Baltimore street, near the approach to the cemetery, President Lincoln presented a rather comical appearance, with his tall form and long limbs astride a small horse, which in some unaccountable way had been assigned to him. If there had been an accident, he certainly would not have had far to fall."[20]

The parade had been scheduled to start at ten; it was twenty minutes late getting into motion, and the milling crowds took the opportunity to press close to Lincoln, "anxious for the pleasure of taking him by the hand, while he sat pleasantly enjoying the hearty welcome thus spontaneously accorded, until the marshals, having mercy on his oft-wrung arm and weary exertions, caused the crowd to desist and allow the President to sit in peace upon his horse." The parade itself was a crowd, having to accommodate numerous military bands, units of soldiers, and civic organizations—some 10,000 marchers in all—before the students, at the tail end, even got to move. The three divisions of the parade—military, presidential, and civic—had been organized by Wills and Lamon with the Marine Band at the head and detachments of the 20th Pennsylvania Cavalry and Battery A, 5th US Artillery, commanded by Major General Darius Couch (since Couch was the commandant of the Military District of the Susquehanna), followed by Lamon, Lincoln, the three Cabinet secretaries, and Everett, the state governors (including Curtin), and the chaplain and members of Congress. Bringing up a very large rear were Wills, "committees of different Religious Bodies," the Masons, the Knights Templar, 250 members of the Gettysburg Odd Fellows lodge, press correspondents, fire companies, "Other Benevolent Associations," and "citizens." The one advantage the college students gained from this arrangement was to find themselves brought to halt at the cemetery directly in front of the speakers' platform, a 12-foot-by-20-foot stand with three rows of chairs. "What a piece of luck this was, but oh, what a jam it was too," remembered one student. "I have never been so wedged in a crowd in my life as I was then, but I was determined to see it through."[21]

It was worth the discomfort, because whatever awkwardness Lincoln manifested as an equestrian disappeared when he rose to speak. "There was a tremendous outburst of applause" when Lincoln stood up, wrote Junius Remensnyder. A Union officer, standing inside the hollow square formed by the military escort around the platform, watched as Lincoln "stepped slowly to the front of the platform, with his hands clasped before him, his natural sadness of expression deepened, his head bent forward, and his eyes cast to the ground." He held what Remensnyder took for "a single large sheet of paper," and "read without the slightest attempt at declamation." Henry Eyster Jacobs, who did not notice any "paper" at first, recalled that "the first few lines of the address were spoken without notes." But then, "gradually drawing them from his pocket, he held in both hands the sheet on which they were written, making emphatic gestures, not with his hands, which were preoccupied, but by bowing from side to side with his body." To another onlooker, Lincoln seemed "like a prophet of old . . . overmastered by some unseen spirit of the scene," so that "the great assembly listened almost awe-struck as to a voice from a divine oracle." And when he was done, there was an "instant of profound silence," and then "a great and universal outburst of hearty and continued approval." Wayne MacVeagh, a Pennsylvania Republican organizer and future attorney general, was struck by how, "as each word was spoken, it appeared to me so clearly fraught with a message not only for us of his day, but for the untold generations of men," and MacVeagh "found myself possessed by a reverential awe for its complete justification of the great war he was conducting, as if conducted, as in truth it was, in the interest of mankind." Ohio Governor William Dennison remembered that even "before the first sentence was completed, a thrill of feeling, like an electric shock, pervaded the crowd." Samuel Bushman, a local farmer who attended the ceremonies, "was within thirty feet of him when he spoke," and although he could not help noticing that "one of his trouser's legs hitched up on his boot" as he spoke, Bushman remembered that "his words made a tremendous impression, and that immortal speech goes far to compensate for the horrors of the battle." Josiah Benner, whose farm was just north of town, turned to his daughters and warned them: "Children, I want all of you to stop right now and listen to me—that speech which the President made today will go down in history—it will be well for all of you to remember what he said."[22]

Rather than failing to "scour," the response of the American public was at once a mixture of astonishment and admiration over the Address. The crowd in the cemetery listened (according to a witness whose letter was published eleven days after the ceremonies) "as he slowly, clearly" read the Address, and "you could not mistake the feeling and sentiment of the vast multitude before him." The same impression was made at a distance by those who read the text of the Address in the newspapers. "This morning's paper," Henry Wadsworth Longfellow wrote to his publisher the day after the dedication ceremonies, "brings the report of Lincoln's brief speech at Gettysburg, which seems to me admirable." Ralph Waldo Emerson echoed Longfellow: Lincoln's "brief speech at Gettysburg will not easily be surpassed by words on any recorded occasion." Charles Sumner believed that Lincoln could not have been more "mistaken" when he suggested that the world would little note nor long remember any of what was said by anyone at the dedication ceremonies; "the world noted at once what he said, and will never cease to remember it. The battle itself was less important than the speech . . . Since Simonides wrote the epitaph for those who fell at Thermopylae, nothing equal to them has breathed over the fallen dead."[23] Within twenty months of its delivery, the Address was already being anthologized in elocution primers for memorization and school use.[24] But looked at from a distance, even the myths are backhanded tributes to the Address: only a document of near-divine inspiration could have been written on a train, and a speech of world-historical moment would certainly arch so far above the heads of its first hearers as to leave them baffled.[25]

* * *

However, one of the most lingering questions about the Gettysburg Address is not really whether people in 1863 understood the Address to have been a mountaintop piece of political rhetoric, but *why* it struck so many people as being such from the start. Partly, this was because of its language. It obeys the Churchillian dictum: *Short words are best and the old words when short are best of all.* Much has been written—and will be written—about the simple grandeur of the Address: its reliance on short, pungent colloquial vocabulary over against the hyperinflected Latinate lexicon beloved of so many school textbooks. In this Address of 272 words, 190 of them are single syllables; only four are four syllables. Rarely has so much been compressed into such simple and uncomplicated elements.

But the simplicity of Lincoln's vocabulary doesn't explain very much on its own; short words are not necessarily interesting words, or even clear ones; and certainly not every word in the Address is short. It is not just a simplified vocabulary that makes the Gettysburg Address remarkable, but an overall pattern of conscious simplicity that Lincoln adopted. Public speaking in Lincoln's day was actually a four-way struggle between several different patterns of speech—vernacular (or folk), technical (as in instruction manuals), middle, and classical (or academic) speech.[26] What Lincoln had always adopted as his style of speech was the pattern of "middling" speech—the speech of the lawyers, popular preachers, and newspapers. Middling speech was a mark above the slangy bluntness of folk speech but without overreaching for the inflated, euphemistic, self-conscious speech of the literati—the same middle ground occupied, culturally and politically, by Lincoln's own Republican Party, which aspired to represent the American middle class. Like the middle-class entrepreneurs, commercial farmers, and manufacturers whom Lincoln praised and defended (as over against the slave-owning plantation class), middling speech could verge on the plainness of slang (as Lincoln's sometimes did, to the discomfort of the prissy), but it was also rational enough to sustain argument; it could have both an inelegant plainness *and* occasional peaks of refined professionalism. The "middling style" was what

George Ticknor Curtis called "a talking style," with "a little more of elegant dishabille; a free, bold, Anglo-Saxon hittingness."[27]

Just how consciously "middling" Lincoln wanted the Gettysburg Address to be can be seen from how he constructed the famous opening line, *Four score and seven years ago*. On July 7, 1863, speaking to an exultant crowd that had gathered in the White House driveway to cheer Lincoln for the newly announced victories at Vicksburg and Gettysburg, Lincoln offered what should be considered as the first draft of the Gettysburg Address. This was not a planned-for occasion; Lincoln was speaking off-the-cuff, and it showed:

> How long ago is it? eighty odd years—since on the Fourth of July for the first time in the history of the world a nation by its representatives, assembled and declared as a self-evident truth that "all men are created equal." That was the birthday of the United States of America . . . Now, on this last Fourth of July just passed, when we have a gigantic Rebellion, at the bottom of which is an effort to overthrow the principle that all men were created equal, we have the surrender of a most powerful position and army on that very day, and not only so, but in a succession of battles in Pennsylvania, near to us, through three days, so rapidly fought that they might be called one great battle on the 1st, 2d and 3d of the month of July; and on the 4th the cohorts of those who opposed the declaration that all men are created equal, "turned tail" and run.[28]

We can hear the advance echoes of what will become the Gettysburg Address in these words. But they appear in the pattern of vernacular speech, unscripted and un-self-conscious—*How long ago is it? eighty odd years*—and strung along in a single awkwardly run-together sentence that piles up rebellion, Vicksburg, and Gettysburg in a disjointed stack. Four-and-a-half months later, however, these words will become the memorable *Four score and seven years ago*, and the ungainly allusion to rebellion and battle will become a swift, neat progression from a great civil war to a great battlefield of that war.

Four score and seven years ago is thus a stretch toward middle-class refinement; but notice that Lincoln does *not* stretch it all the way to becoming classical, to Simonides and Thermopylae. The model from which Lincoln developed the new vocabulary of "Four score and seven years," comes not from classical Athens, but from a contemporary political speech, a highly

touted thank you given in July 1861 by Pennsylvania Congressman Galusha Grow after his election as speaker of the House of Representatives:

> Fourscore years ago, fifty-six bold merchants, farmers, lawyers,
> and mechanics, the representatives of a few feeble colonists, scat-
> tered along the Atlantic seaboard, met in convention to found a new
> empire, based on the inalienable rights of man.[29]

There is no way of telling what it was about Grow's speech that stuck in
Lincoln's mind for two years, but it definitely cancels out any notion that
Lincoln was reaching for a classical style. If anything, the unprecedented
popularity that attached itself at once to the Gettysburg Address actually
marks the end of the prestige and dominance of classical speech in American rhetoric, and its sad consignment to oddity. The Address signals "the
end of the culture of eloquence," burying it alongside the soldiers in the
cemetery.[30]

The Gettysburg Address was not an effort by Lincoln to confine himself to a collection of monosyllabic grunts; he was showing how a great
idea could be captured without resorting to the stilted formality of classical speech. In that respect, it could not have contrasted more greatly with
the formal oration delivered by Edward Everett. The nineteen-year-old
Henry Eyster Jacobs, standing with the student delegation, admitted that
Everett "was a model of classical oratory, meeting fully a high academic
standard"; the problem was that Everett's 13,500-word doozy of an oration,
replete with classical allusions to Marathon, Pericles, and the Peloponnesian War, was too much of a model. "Every sentence was thoroughly
elaborated; the emphasis and even the gestures seemed to have been pre-
determined." Sarah Jane Hoffman, listening to Everett, was less charitable: "I thought Edward Everett's speech would never end."[31]

Lincoln's long suit, on the other hand, was his capacity to capture an
idea in the fewest and clearest words possible. John Todd Stuart, who
had been his first mentor in reading law and who knew Lincoln for over
thirty years, thought that Lincoln was, simply by temperament, "logical—
mathematical . . . He had nothing Rhetorical in his Nature." He had, after
all, been a trial lawyer in a state where juries were still pulled into the
jury box from bystanders, and he would either make his point clearly and
swiftly or he would not be practicing law for very long.

He did not rate professional orators like Everett very highly, and to
Noah Brooks, he singled out Everett as a particularly grinding example of

sound and fury signifying nothing. "Now, do you know, I think Edward Everett was very much overrated," Lincoln said. "There was one speech in which, addressing a statue of John Adams and a picture of Washington, in Faneuil Hall, Boston, he apostrophized them and said, 'Teach us the love of liberty protected by law!'" That, Lincoln admitted, "was very fine," but "it was only a good idea, introduced by noble language."[32]

Yet, for all of its compactness, the Gettysburg Address is not quite so compact as it seems. It may be only 272 words long, but those 272 words are strung out into ten complicated sentences—all of which are much more cumbersome to parse on the page than they are to hear in the open. And Lincoln does not mind throwing compactness to the wind when he wants to make a lilting impression on the ear. The well-known repetitive triplets—*we cannot dedicate, we cannot consecrate, we cannot hallow this ground* and *government of the people, by the people, for the people*—are the exact opposite of compactness, and actually constitute a puzzling luxury if we consider the Address only as a terse alternative to Everett, inclining to still more terseness. But Lincoln was not offering a treatise to be read, but an exhortation to be heard. Like middling speech, the Address is an effort to persuade rather than to ornament or decorate. And each stroke of those triplets is a powerful pull on the convictions of Lincoln's listeners, hauling them upward toward climaxes that overcome the attentive mind with emotion even as they persuade it with logic.

* * *

But nothing in the Address hit home quite so effectively as the single aspect of the Address that we are least likely to recognize at once, and that was the survival of democracy. We take democracy for granted as the default position of human societies, as the natural template of modern politics, as the end of history, and so it is difficult for us to be moved by an Address that is, at bottom, a set of reasons why democracy should not be abandoned. Like Thomas Jefferson in 1826, *we* are confident that "the light of science has already laid open to every view the palpable truth, that the mass of mankind has not been born with saddles on their backs, nor a favored few booted and spurred, ready to ride them."[33]

But in truth, even as Jefferson wrote those words, the confidence of the founders that "the disorders, oppressions, and incertitude" of Europe "will terminate very much in favor of the Rights of man" was evaporating. The French Revolution, which promised to be the American Revolution's beachhead in Europe, swiftly circled downward in the Reign of Terror and then the tyranny of Bonaparte; democratic uprisings in Spain in 1820, in Russia in 1825, in France in 1830, and across Europe in 1848 were crushed or subverted by newly renascent monarchies and Romantic philosophers, glorying in regimes built upon blood, soil, and nationality rather than the rights of man. At every point, democracy—government by the consent of the governed—lay discredited and disgraced, and a cynical Prussian nobleman—Otto von Bismarck—could advise his French counterpart that, although he "said that, in early life, his tendencies were all toward republicanism," he had discovered, "When you have governed men for several years, you, a Liberal, will be transformed from a Republican" to "a Monarchist. Believe me, one cannot lead or bring to prosperity a great nation without the principle of authority—that is, the Monarchy."[34]

The outbreak of the American Civil War only gave the monarchs further reason to rejoice, because the success of the American democracy was the one thing that unsettled their captive peoples and threw their theories about the superiority of autocracy into a shade. That this same troublesome democracy would, in 1861, obligingly proceed to blow its own political brains out—and do it in defense of the virtues of human slavery—gave the monarchs no end of delight. The success of the slave-holding secessionists in America would, breathed the king of the Belgians, Leopold I, with a sigh of relief, "raise a barrier against the United States and provide a support for the monarchical-aristocratic principle in the Southern states." "The Union is in agony," wrote the Spanish minister from Washington to his queen, "and our mission is not to delay its death for a moment."[35]

Lincoln also saw the fundamental issue of the Civil War as the question of democracy's death, only from precisely the opposite perspective as Bismarck and Leopold. This nation, Lincoln said, had been dedicated to the democratic proposition that all men are created equal; the Civil War was the test of whether democratic regimes—*whether this nation or any nation so conceived and so dedicated*—can long endure. It had survived two severe tests of such a government—"the successful establishing, and the successful administering of it." But there remained one final test, "its successful maintenance against a formidable [internal] attempt to overthrow it," and that test was now upon them. "The central idea pervading this struggle," he told his secretary, John Hay, back at the beginning of the war, "is the necessity . . . of proving that popular government is not an absurdity," for "if we fail it will go far to prove the incapability of the people to govern themselves." If democracies were too unstable to prevent self-disintegration, and too feckless to stop self-disintegration when it started, then the folly and instability of democracy would lie open and exposed for all time. As Massachusetts Congressman George Boutwell pleaded, Americans must see the Civil War as "a rebellion of tyrants against the hopes of the whole human race in the capacity of the people to govern themselves." If that rebellion succeeded, the collapse of what Lincoln called "the last, best hope of earth" could be considered as proof positive of the need for a Bismarck or a Leopold to run the show.[36]

The Battle of Gettysburg, with its astounding and seemingly bottomless list of dead and maimed, offered Lincoln the first substantial glimmer during the war that the test would indeed be passed. Gettysburg was not only a victory, but also a victory won with the Union Army's back to the wall, and its news came with symbolic appropriateness on the anniversary of American Independence. Above all, the victory was the product of enormous self-sacrifice—a third again more than all the British and allied casualties at Waterloo. And these casualties were not professional soldiers, the Duke of Wellington's "scum of the earth" who

> *Followed their mercenary calling,*
> *And took their wages, and are dead,*

nor were they dispirited peasants, driven into battle by the whips of their betters, but precisely those ordinary bourgeois citizens whom democracy's cultured despisers had laughingly doubted could ever be made to do anything but calculate profits and losses.

These people—the middle-class bourgeoisie with their middle-class manners, middle-class tastes, and middle-class speech—whom the German poet Heinrich Heine dismissed in 1834 as "boors" living in "that big pig-pen of freedom," whom Charles Dickens sneered at as "the ebb of honest men's contempt"—these had risen up and offered everything they had, present and future, that *that nation might live*.[37] The soldiers who fought at Gettysburg had astonished the world, wrote one New Jersey veteran in 1888 of the fighting; they "exhibited to the world the sublime spectacle of a nation of freemen determined that everyone within its borders should have that liberty which the Declaration of Independence had proclaimed to be the inalienable right of all men."[38] Looking out over the semicircular rows of graves in the Gettysburg cemetery, Lincoln saw in those lives a transcendence that few people, then or now, have been willing to concede to liberal democracy. And in that transcendence, he saw something all Americans could borrow, a renewed dedication to *that cause for which they gave the last full measure of devotion*, to popular self-government, *of the people, by the people, for the people*.

The genius of the Address thus lay not in its language or in its brevity (virtues though these were), much less in its being conjured up on the back of an envelope on the train, but in its triumphant repudiation of the criticisms of democracy, and in the new birth it gave to those who had become discouraged and wearied by democracy's follies.[39]

* * *

It is worth remembering how central a position the Address gives to *those who fought here*, because there is one other reason for the high esteem in which we hold the Gettysburg Address, and that is that the Union won the Civil War. The Gettysburg Address is a remarkably optimistic document, and, not surprisingly, much of its optimism was drawn from the euphoria following the battle and the fall of Vicksburg, which together gave Lincoln and the Union the happiest season they had enjoyed in the war since the early spring of 1862. The successes of the summer of 1863 continued, too, as Port Hudson surrendered after Vicksburg and opened Mississippi to almost-complete control by Union forces, followed by the nearly blood-less capture of the rebel railhead at Chattanooga. John Hay rejoiced in August that "nothing shows more clearly that the rebellion is nearing its close than the utter disorganization of its votaries North and South . . . They have been stunned by the heavy victories of Gettysburg, Vicksburg, and Port Hudson." A month later, Washington official Benjamin Brown French was sure that "everything relating to the war betokens a speedy and patriotic issue ere long, and the re-election of Lincoln, which seems, now, to be a foregone conclusion, will result in a glorious victory over the prime movers in the wicked rebellion."[40] And there were political victories, as well: against every prediction that summer, antiwar Copperhead candi-dates for governor in Ohio and Pennsylvania were resoundingly defeated in the fall elections. "The signs look better. The Father of Waters again goes unvexed to the sea . . . Peace does not appear so distant as it did," Lincoln wrote at the end of August 1863, and with it would come proof that democracies are not doomed to self-destruction, and that "among free men, there can be no successful appeal from the ballot to the bullet."[41]

But that optimism turned out to be cruelly premature. There was much bloody work ahead in 1864 and 1865, and if it had not gone well—if Grant had not taken Richmond or Sherman not taken Atlanta or Farragut not closed off Mobile Bay, and especially if Lincoln had not been reelected— then the war would have turned to a very different conclusion, with an independent Southern Confederacy hugging the Gulf and south Atlantic coastlines, strangling the Mississippi River Valley and spreading its im- perialistic proslavery tentacles into the Caribbean and Central America, while the Northern Union shrank into a Scandinavian irrelevance. In that case, the Gettysburg Address would not, and could not, have been hailed as acknowledging some great and stirring truth but would instead stand as a piece of political huff-and-puff on behalf of a sinking cause. We see great- ness in the Address only because untold numbers of soldiers died to ensure that we could, and because they kept on astonishing the world. Without that vindication in arms, the Gettysburg Address would have become little noted and not very long remembered, and the multitudes buried in the cemetery would literally have died in vain, and all of that middling terse- ness and meaning built into the Address would have counted for nothing.

* * *

The Gettysburg Address is, when reduced to its minimum, only the re- marks of an American president spoken at the dedication of a cemetery. Unlike the Emancipation Proclamation, it cannot be taken into a court of law to prove anything, and it certainly did not, as the Proclamation did, set three million slaves legally and "forever free." On that scale, it can some- times seem that the Address is simply an example of something being well known for being well known, and it may be to avoid the phenomenon of empty celebrity that we fix on the circumstances of its composition or its delivery as explanations for its high and enduring standing. It is really the *meaning* of the Address that struck observers in 1863, and that this has become dimmed in our celebrations of the Address is partly due to its own success. We see the Civil War today as an issue in racial justice or as a critical moment in constitutional history, which is what leads us to wonder why slavery and the Constitution do not appear in the Address. But the truth is that the Address speaks to an issue that flew far above slavery or jurisprudence—the issue on which the resolution of our racial injustices and constitutional shortcomings all actually depended—and that was the survival of democracy itself.[42] For what we intended to do about race or slavery or the Constitution would never come to pass at all if, as Bismarck hoped, democracy itself went down for the ten count in 1863.

Lincoln was not under any illusions that he could save democracy merely through his rhetorical power. He was more right than we think when he said that the world would *little note nor long remember what we say here*, because all that was said that November day, by himself and by Everett, rested entirely on never forgetting *what they did here*. It was from them, not from his words, that the new birth of freedom would emerge. Perhaps, in the end, the greatness we have not suspected in the Address lies not in its essential humility, but rather in its reminder that the question of democracy's survival rested ultimately not in the hands of czars but in those citizens who saw something in democracy worth dying for— something that kings could never understand. What we needed, and got so memorably, from Lincoln was precisely that reminder. We could use it again today.

Notes

1. See Roy P. Basler, *Lincoln's Gettysburg Address in Translation* (1972). The list of freestanding monographs on the Address includes Henry Sweetser Burrage, *Gettysburg and Lincoln* (1906), William E. Barton, *Lincoln at Gettysburg: What He Intended to Say; What He Said; What He was Reported to Have Said; What He Wished He Had Said* (1930), Louis A. Warren, *Lincoln's Gettysburg Declaration: "A New Birth of Freedom"* (1964), Philip H. Kunhardt, *A New Birth of Freedom: Lincoln at Gettysburg* (1983), Garry Wills, *Lincoln at Gettysburg: The Words That Remade America* (1991), Gabor S. Boritt, *The Gettysburg Gospel: The Lincoln Speech That Nobody Knows* (2006), and Martin P. Johnson, *Writing the Gettysburg Address* (2013).

2. David J. Garrow, *Bearing the Cross: Martin Luther King, Jr., and the Southern Christian Leadership* (New York: Vintage Books, 1986).

3. Diana Schaub, "Lincoln at Gettysburg," *National Affairs* 19 (Spring 2014): 115; Jared Peatman, *The Long Shadow of Lincoln's Gettysburg Address* (Carbondale: Southern Illinois University Press, 2013), 195.

4. Amy Davidson, "Ruggles of Gettysburg," *The New Yorker*, Nov. 12, 2012.

5. Brooks, "Personal Reminiscences of Lincoln," *Scribner's Monthly* 15 (Feb. 1878): 565, and in *Recollected Words of Abraham Lincoln*, ed. Don and Virginia Fehrenbacher (Stanford, CA: Stanford University Press, 1996), 46.

6. "The National Cemetery," in *Report of the Select Committee Relative to the Soldiers' National Cemetery* (Harrisburg, PA: Singerly and Myers, 1864), 62; Gabor S. Boritt, *The Gettysburg Gospel: The Lincoln Speech That Nobody Knows* (New York: Simon and Schuster, 2006), 36–37.

7. *History of Cumberland and Adams Counties, Pennsylvania* (Chicago: Warner, Beers, 1886), 172–173; Frassanito, *Early Photography at Gettysburg* (Gettysburg: Thomas, 1994), 341.

8. *History of Cumberland and Adams Counties*, 362–363; Cameron to Lincoln, Oct. 10, 1863, Abraham Lincoln Papers, Library of Congress, Washington DC (hereafter cited as ALP).

9. Kathleen R. Georg, "This Grand National Enterprise: The Origins of Gettysburg's Soldiers' National Cemetery & Gettysburg Battlefield Memorial Association," May 1982, Gettysburg National Military Park Archives, 4–5; Jim Weeks, *Gettysburg: Memory, Market, and an American Shrine* (Princeton, NJ: Princeton University Press, 2003), 12, 19.

10. "Report of David Wills" and "Report of Samuel Weaver," March 19, 1864, in *Report of the Select Committee*, 6–7 and 39–41; Margaret S. Creighton, *The Colors of Courage: Gettysburg's Forgotten History: Immigrants, Women, and African Americans in the Civil War's Defining Battle* (New York: Basic Books, 2006), 154–155; James M. Paradis, *African Americans and the Gettysburg Campaign* (Lanham, MD: Scarecrow Press, 2005), 57; Mark H. Dunkelman, *Gettysburg's Unknown Soldier: The Life, Death, and Celebrity of Amos Humiston* (Westport,

CT: Praeger, 1999), 155; Wills to Lincoln, Nov. 2, 1863, ALP; Louis A. Warren, *Lincoln's Gettysburg Declaration: A New Birth of Freedom* (Ft. Wayne, IN: Lincoln National Life Foundation, 1964), 39–47.

11. Henry Clay Cochrane, "With Lincoln to Gettysburg, 1863," *Gettysburg Star & Sentinel*, May 22, 1907.

12. Henry Eyster Jacobs, *Lincoln's Gettysburg World-Message* (Philadelphia: United Lutheran, 1919), 60; Susan Holabaugh White to Lavinia Bollinger, Nov. 20, 1863, in Susan H. White accounts, Adams County Historical Society, Gettysburg, PA.

13. Kenneth J. Winkle, *Lincoln's Citadel: The Civil War in Washington, D.C.* (New York: W.W. Norton, 2013), 138–141; Lincoln, "To Whom It May Concern," Mar. 7, 1861, in *Collected Works of Abraham Lincoln*, ed. Roy P. Basler, 9 vols. (New Brunswick, NJ: Rutgers University Press, 1951–1953), 4:102 (hereafter cited as *CW*). It is often assumed that because Johnson died in January 1864 from smallpox, he caught the virus, ironically, from Lincoln, since Lincoln came down with a milder form of smallpox known as varioloid almost as soon as he returned to Washington from Gettysburg on the evening of November 19. Lincoln was quarantined for almost three weeks, but it is not clear that Johnson caught it from Lincoln, if only because more virulent forms of smallpox were circulating in Washington. Lincoln, who insisted that "he did not catch it from me," paid for Johnson's funeral out of his own pocket and "had to help his family." There is a William H. Johnson buried in Arlington National Cemetery (plot 3346, Section 47) whose headstone carries the simple notation CITIZEN, but it is not clear that this is the same Johnson. Nor is the notation CITIZEN necessarily an effort by Lincoln to override the *Dred Scott* decision's declaration that blacks were incapable of US citizenship, since the term was often used interchangeably with "civilian." See Winkle, *Lincoln's Citadel*, 377, and Philip Magness and Sebastian Page, "Mr. Lincoln and Mr. Johnson," *New York Times*, Feb. 1, 2012.

14. Junius B. Remensnyder, "Lincoln at Gettysburg: An Intimate Story of the Martyr-President's Immortal Address," *McClure's* 54 (March 1922): 41; J. Howard Wert, "Lincoln at Gettysburg," *Harrisburg Patriot*, Feb. 12, 1909; Michael A. Colver, "Reminiscences of the Battle of Gettysburg," *The Spectrum* [Gettysburg College yearbook] 1902, Musselman Library Special Collections, Gettysburg College; Lincoln, "Remarks to Citizens of Gettysburg, Pennsylvania," Nov. 18, 1863, *CW*, 7:16–17.

15. Wayne MacVeagh, "Lincoln at Gettysburg," *Century* 79 (November 1909): 22; Frank L. Klement, *The Gettysburg Soldiers' Cemetery and Lincoln's Address* (Shippensburg, PA: White Mane Press, 1993), 11, 16, 141, 144; Martin P. Johnson, *Writing the Gettysburg Address* (Lawrence: University Press of Kansas, 2013), 91–92, 101, 103, 104, 111, 137; Charles McCurdy, *Gettysburg: A Memoir* (Pittsburgh: Reed and Witting, 1929), 33–35; John B. Horner, *Sgt. Hugh Paxton Bigham: Lincoln's Guard at Gettysburg* (Gettysburg: Horner Enterprises, 1994),

3–4; Douglas L. Wilson, *Lincoln's Sword: The Presidency and the Power of Words* (New York: Knopf, 2006), 212–213.

16. Warren, *Lincoln's Gettysburg Declaration*, 71–72; Jared Peatman, *The Long Shadow of Lincoln's Gettysburg Address*, 19.

17. William E. Barton, *The Soul of Abraham Lincoln* (New York: George H. Doran, 1920), 208; Mary Todd Lincoln, in *Herndon's Informants: Letters, Interviews & Statements About Abraham Lincoln*, ed. R. O. Davis and Douglas L. Wilson (Urbana: University of Illinois Press, 1998), 360; Edward W. Andrews, in *Reminiscences of Abraham Lincoln by Distinguished Men of His Time*, ed. Allen Thorndike Rice (New York: North American, 1886), 11.

18. Nicolay, "Lincoln's Gettysburg Address," *Century* 47 (Feb. 1894): 601.

19. Lamon, *Recollections of Abraham Lincoln, 1847–1865*, ed. D.L. Teillard (Cambridge, MA: Harvard University Press, 1911), 173.

20. Henry Eyster Jacobs, "Gettysburg Fifty Years Ago," August 7, 1913, typescript, Adams County Historical Society, Gettysburg, PA.

21. Philip Bikle, in Frassanito, *Early Photography at Gettysburg*, 382; *Washington Daily Morning Chronicle*, Nov. 21, 1863, in Klement, *The Gettysburg Soldiers' Cemetery*, 26, 42, 213; "Order of Procession," in *Address of Hon. Edward Everett at the Consecration of the National Cemetery at Gettysburg, 19th November, 1863, with the Dedicatory Speech of President Lincoln and the Other Exercises of the Occasion* (Boston: Little, Brown, 1864), 22–23; Warren, *Lincoln's Gettysburg Declaration*, 77–80.

22. Remensnyder, "Lincoln at Gettysburg," 42; Jacobs, *Lincoln's Gettysburg World-Message*, 74; Andrews, in *Reminiscences*, 516; Glenn LaFantasie, *Gettysburg Heroes: Perfect Soldiers, Hallowed Ground* (Bloomington: Indiana University Press, 2008), 168; MacVeagh, "Lincoln at Gettysburg," 22; Bushman, in *Battleground Adventures: The Stories of Dwellers on the Scenes of Conflict in Some of the Most Notable Battles of the Civil War*, ed. Clifton Johnson (Boston: Houghton Mifflin, 1915), 196; Josiah Benner account, Civilian Accounts, ACHS.

23. Richard Miller, in William Lambert, "The Gettysburg Address: When Written, How Received, Its True Form," *Pennsylvania Magazine of History and Biography* 33 (Oct. 1909): 393–394; Longfellow to Henry Ticknor Fields, Nov. 20, 1863, in Samuel Longfellow, *Life of Henry Wadsworth Longfellow* (Boston: Houghton, Mifflin, 1891), 3:23–24; Emerson, "Abraham Lincoln," *The Living Age* 35 (May 13, 1865): 283; Sumner, *The Promises of the Declaration of Independence: Eulogy on Abraham Lincoln* (Boston: J.E. Farwell, 1865), 40–41.

24. Allen A. Griffith, *Lessons in Elocution; with Numerous Selections, Analyzed for Practice. A Text Book, in Reading and Speaking, for Schools, Seminaries and Private Learners* (Chicago: Adams, Blackmer and Lyon, 1865), 213.

25. The reverence attached to the composition and reception of the Address has often spilled over into a preoccupation with determining an "authoritative" version—an *urtext* if you will—of the Address. Martin Johnson's exhaustive

review of the five copies of the Address in Lincoln's hand (in *Writing the Gettysburg Address*) identifies the "reading" or "platform" version of the Address as the so-called Nicolay copy—a two-page document with the first page on Executive Mansion stationery and a second on blue-gray foolscap, and the same papers David Wills saw Lincoln working on the evening before and producing from his coat pocket on the platform. The difficulty posed by the Nicolay copy, however, is that there is an awkward and ungrammatical break between the two pages. Johnson believes that Lincoln extemporized his way over the page break, just as he extemporized a few other words in the delivery process (such as the significant phrase "under God"). Hence, the version actually delivered by Lincoln is really captured not in the four handwritten copies Lincoln made over the following year, but in the shorthand record made by the Associated Press's designated reporter on the spot, *New-York Tribune* staffer John Davenport. Two months later, as Edward Everett was preparing his oration for publication in Boston, he requested a copy of the Address from Lincoln for reprinting along with his own. Lincoln responded with what has become known as the Hay copy, although it was not the Hay copy that Lincoln actually sent, but a third version (now known as the Everett copy) that incorporated the extemporizations captured by the Associated Press. Two further copies were made by Lincoln when the historian George Bancroft asked Lincoln for a handwritten version of the Address to be copied in facsimile and bound into a ceremonial volume of *Autograph Leaves of Our Country's Authors*, and then auctioned for charitable purposes at the US Sanitary Commission's fair in Baltimore. The version Bancroft received, however, did not fit the binding requirements of the proposed volume. The editor of *Autograph Leaves*, John Pendleton Kennedy, and Alexander Bliss (Bancroft's son-in-law) had to write to Lincoln in March 1864 to request a second copy, which Lincoln made on March 7. Bancroft, however, did not return the unused copy, and it stayed in the Bancroft family until 1929; twenty years later, it was donated to Cornell University and is one of the gems of the University's collections. The copy used for *Autograph Leaves* likewise remained in Alexander Bliss's hands until his death and was finally auctioned in 1949; the purchaser was the last Cuban ambassador to the United States, Oscar Cintas, who fled the Castro regime in 1959 and bequeathed it to the American people with the reservation that it be exhibited at the White House. The Everett copy went through many hands after Everett's death in 1865 and was finally purchased by the State of Illinois in 1944; it is currently one of the treasures of the Abraham Lincoln Presidential Library and Museum in Springfield, Illinois. The Nicolay copy and the Hay copy both ended up in Hay's possession and were donated to the Library of Congress after Hay's death. The Bliss copy is usually designated as the "official" version, although, strictly speaking, the variations among the Everett, Bancroft, and Bliss versions are fairly trivial matters of punctuation and the addition (or disappearance) of a few prepositions. The Nicolay and Hay copies contain the most variations (neither of them, for instance, includes "under God"), but it is unlikely that either represents Lincoln's own final conclusions. That leaves the Associated Press version as the best representation of what Lincoln actually said. But no single determinative version of the AP's transcript has survived; and the versions that appeared in Northern newspapers over the following days contain variorums of their own introduced by the vagaries of telegraphic transmission. Martin Johnson believes the AP text that appeared in the *Philadelphia North American* on November 20 is probably the closest to what "was telegraphed from Gettysburg on the day of the speech." See Johnson, *Writing the Gettysburg Address*, 203, and also Wilson, *Lincoln's Sword*, 220–224.

26. Kenneth Cmiel, *Democratic Eloquence: The Fight for Popular Speech in Nineteenth Century America* (New York: William Morrow, 1990), 20–21.

27. "Editor's Table—Lectures and Lecturing," *Harper's Monthly* 14 (Dec. 1856): 123.

28. "Response to a Serenade," July 7, 1863, *CW*, 6:319–320.

29. "Speech of Galusha A. Grow on Taking the Chair of the House of Representatives of the United States, July 4," in *The Rebellion Record: A Diary of American Events, With Documents, Narratives, Illustrative Incidents, Poetry, etc.*, ed. Frank Moore (New York: G.P. Putnam, 1862), 2:222.

30. James Perrin Warren, *Culture of Eloquence: Oratory and Reform in Antebellum America* (University Park: Pennsylvania State University Press, 1999), 195. There is no way of telling what it was about Grow's speech that stuck in Lincoln's mind, but it certainly stuck in a lot of other people's minds, since it was promptly anthologized in 1861 in William Ross Wallace's *Patriotic and Heroic Eloquence*, and in 1863 in Erastus Beadle's *Dime Patriotic Speaker*. See Wallace, *Patriotic and Heroic Eloquence: A Book for the Patriot, Statesman, and Student* (New York: James G. Gregory, 1861), 96; Beadle's *Dime Patriotic Speaker, Being Extracts from the Splendid Oratory of Judge Holt, General Mitchell, Dr. Orestes A. Brownson, Edward Everett, the Great Union Square (N.Y.) Addresses, Thomas Francis Meagher, Stephen A. Douglas, Daniel S. Dickinson, Carl Shurz, Rev. Dr. Bellows, and Others, Together With Poems for the Hour* (New York: Beadle, 1863), 20.

31. Jacobs, *Lincoln's Gettysburg World-Message*, 67; Mary K. Dissinger, "Miss Sadie Hoffmann Remembers Gettysburg," in Sarah Jane Hoffmann account, Adams County Historical Society.

32. Stuart, interview with William H. Herndon, Dec. 20, 1866, in *Herndon's Informants: Letters, Interviews & Statements about Abraham Lincoln*, ed. Douglas L. Wilson and Rodney O. Davis (Chicago: University of Illinois Press, 1998), 519; Brooks, "Personal Reminiscences of Lincoln," *Scribner's Monthly* 15 (Mar. 1878): 678. Lincoln seems to have been referring to a speech Everett delivered at Fanueil Hall on the Marquis de Lafayette in 1834, in which Everett, "freeing himself from every conventionality of the platform . . . turned his back upon his hearers to [Gilbert] Stuart's Washington and to the bust of Lafayette which were

behind him, and cried, 'Break the long silence of that votive canvas! Speak! Speak! Marble lips, and teach us the love of liberty protected by law.'" See Everett, "Eulogy on Lafayette, Delivered in Faneuil Hall, at the Request of the Young Men of Boston, September 6, 1834," in *Orations and Speeches, in Various Occasions* (Boston: American Stationers, 1836), 488, and Edward Everett Hale, "The Orators," in *Memories of a Hundred Years* (New York: Macmillan, 1902), 2:22–23.

33. Jefferson to Roger C. Weightman, June 24, 1826, in *Thomas Jefferson: Writings*, ed. Merrill D. Peterson (New York: Library of America, 1984), 1517; Washington to Gouverneur Morris, July 28, 1791, in *George Washington: A Collection*, ed. W. B. Allen (Indianapolis: Liberty Fund, 1988), 556.

34. Charles Lowe, *Bismarck's Table-Talk* (London: H. Grevel, 1895), 203.

35. Leopold, King of the Belgians, to Ferdinand Maximilian, Oct. 25, 1861, in A. R. Tyrner-Tyrnauer, *Lincoln and the Emperors* (London: Rupert Hart-Davis, 1962), 65–67; Gabriel Garcia y Tassara, in *Lincoln in the World: The Making of a Statesman and the Dawn of American Power*, ed. Kevin Peraino (New York: Crown, 2013), 112.

36. "Message to Congress in Special Session," July 4, 1861, *CW*, 4:439; Hay, diary entry for May 7, 1862, in *Inside Lincoln's White House: The Complete Civil War Diary of John Hay*, ed. J. R. T. Ettlinger and Michael Burlingame (Carbondale: Southern Illinois University Press, 1997), 20; Boutwell, "The Conspiracy: Its Purposes and Its Power" (speech at Harvard, July 18, 1861), in *Speeches and Papers Relating to the Rebellion and the Overthrow of Slavery* (Boston: Little Brown, 1867), 97.

37. Thomas S. Baker, *Lenau and Young Germany in America* (Philadelphia: F.P. Stockhausen, 1897), 26; Dickens, *The Life and Adventures of Martin Chuzzlewit* (London: Chapman and Hall, 1901), 317.

38. Samuel Toombs, 13th New Jersey, *New Jersey Troops in the Gettysburg Campaign from June 5 to July 31, 1863* (Orange, NJ: Evening Mail, 1888), 330–331.

39. Barry Schwartz, "The New Gettysburg Address," in *Re-Discovering Abraham Lincoln*, ed. John Y. Simon and Harold Holzer (New York: Fordham University Press, 2002), 173; Waldo W. Braden, *Abraham Lincoln, Public Speaker* (Baton Rouge: Louisiana State University Press, 1988), 86–87.

40. Hay editorial, Aug. 7, 1863, in *Lincoln's Journalist: John Hay's Anonymous Writings for the Press, 1860–1864*, ed. Michael Burlingame (Carbondale: Southern Illinois University Press, 1998), 334; French, diary entry for September 25, 1864, in *Witness to the Young Republic: A Yankee's Journal, 1828–1870*, ed. D. B. Cole and J. J. McDonough (Hanover, NH: University Press of New England, 1989), 457.

41. To James C. Conkling, Aug. 26, 1863, *CW*, 6:409.

42. Don E. Fehrenbacher, *The Slaveholding Republic: An Account of the United States Government's Relations to Slavery* (New York: Oxford University Press, 2001), 312.

PART II

Impacts

9

"A New Birth of Freedom"

EMANCIPATION AND THE GETTYSBURG ADDRESS

Louis P. Masur

THE GETTYSBURG ADDRESS is not often read in the context of Lincoln's ongoing defense of emancipation, but doing so helps to provide a deeper understanding of the speech's avowal that "all men are created equal," and its call for a "new birth of freedom."[1] The issuance of the Emancipation Proclamation on January 1, 1863, marked not an end but in many ways a beginning of Lincoln's increasingly vocal defense of emancipation, his commitment to the enlistment of black troops, and his desire to see states move toward the abolition of slavery. The Gettysburg Address can profitably be viewed as a continuing expression of those beliefs.[2]

In January, Lincoln declared, "I have issued the emancipation proclamation, and I can not retract it." He did far more than not retract it. He defended it and pressed ahead on a trajectory that, by the following year, would lead to his advocacy of a constitutional amendment to abolish slavery and his eventual endorsement of limited black suffrage. Lincoln continued in 1863 to advocate for emancipation in the Border States; he continued to encourage rebel states where military governors had been appointed to adopt new state constitutions that abolished slavery; and he aggressively defended his policies on emancipation and the enlistment of black troops, perhaps never more so than in his letter to James Conkling in late August. That public letter created a sensation and provides an important context for understanding the Gettysburg Address, which came less than three months later.

Upon signing the Emancipation Proclamation on January 1, 1863, Lincoln declared, "I never in my life felt more certain I was doing right than I do in signing this paper . . . If my name goes into history, it will be for this act and my whole soul is in it." It had been nearly six months since Lincoln first informed his cabinet of his intentions to issue an emancipation proclamation, and the document itself changed between September 22, 1862, when he issued the preliminary Emancipation Proclamation, and one hundred days later, when he signed the final decree that freed those slaves in rebel areas not under Union military control.

It took time for Lincoln to develop a constitutional rationale for emancipation. Slavery was a state institution, governed by state laws. The federal government had no power over slavery where it existed, and Lincoln never acknowledged that the Confederate states had left the Union. Therefore, they were still entitled to their rights under the Constitution, whether they wanted them or not. The rationale for the decree was military necessity: if slavery as an institution was in various ways supporting the Confederate war effort, then by attacking it Lincoln hoped to weaken the enemy. Of course Lincoln also thought slavery wrong—he always had. In April 1864, he wrote, "I am naturally anti-slavery. If slavery is not wrong, nothing is wrong. I can not remember when I did not so think, and feel. And yet I have never understood that the Presidency conferred upon me an unrestricted right to act officially upon this judgment and feeling." But his power as commander in chief under the doctrine of military necessity enabled him to act. For good measure, he added to the Emancipation Proclamation his belief that the measure was "an act of justice."[3]

The Emancipation Proclamation also provided for the enlistment of black troops. The provision is not always given the emphasis it deserves. Indeed, the preliminary Emancipation Proclamation of September 22, 1862, made no mention of black troops and instead included a provision for the voluntary colonization of free blacks. The eventual service of the 179,000 black soldiers who ultimately served in the army, as well as the nearly 20,000 African Americans who enlisted in the navy, helped not only to win the war but also to make the case for equal citizenship rights. Lincoln, like most Americans, was initially opposed to the idea of black troops. On August 4, 1862, he told an Indiana delegation that had come to offer two black regiments that "he was not prepared to go the length of enlisting negroes as soldiers." He feared that "to arm the negroes would turn 50,000 bayonets from the loyal Border States against us that were for us." But on March 26, 1863, he wrote, "the colored population is the great *available* and yet *unavailed* of, force for restoring the Union. The bare sight of fifty thousand armed, and drilled black soldiers on the banks of the Mississippi, would end the rebellion at once."[4]

Lincoln changed his mind, in part, because as the war progressed, he became less apprehensive that the Border States would leave the Union. For much of the first year of war, he devoted considerable energy trying to persuade the Border States to abolish slavery. On March 6, 1862, he even asked Congress to provide money to compensate slaveholders in any state that adopted a plan of gradual emancipation. While many abolitionists bristled at the idea of compensated, gradual abolition, Frederick Douglass, for one, marveled "that I should live to see the President of the United States deliberately advocating Emancipation was more than I ever ventured to hope." By the summer of 1862, Lincoln realized that the Border States would not act upon his entreaties, and the realization that he no longer needed to conciliate them freed him to act.[5]

During the fall of 1862, as he was considering the enlistment of black troops, Senator Charles Sumner presented Lincoln with a copy of George Livermore's book, *An Historical Research Respecting the Opinions of the Founders of the Republic on Negroes as Slaves, as Citizens, and as Soldiers.* Livermore argued that "it was general practice among the Founders of the Republic to employ negroes, both slaves and freemen, as soldiers regularly enrolled in the army," and he implored the president to take "the final step in this direction."[6]

A few weeks after Lincoln was given Livermore's book, Attorney General Edward Bates issued an opinion on "whether or not *colored men* can be citizens of the United States." Treasury Secretary Salmon P. Chase asked Bates to answer this question after a federal revenue steamer stopped a schooner mastered by a black man. Under a late-eighteenth-century law, only citizens could be masters and their vessels licensed. The question of citizenship, Bates explained, was little understood, and he had "been pained by the fruitless search" for a definition. Rights enjoyed and powers exercised—such as holding office or voting—did not bear on the question of citizenship. After all, women, children, paupers, and lunatics could not vote, but they certainly were citizens. Bates argued that "the Constitution uses the word citizen only to express the political quality of the individual in his relations to the nation; to declare that he is a member of the body politic, and bound to it by the reciprocal obligation of allegiance on the one side and protection on the other." Bates concluded "every person born in the country is, at the moment of birth, *prima facie* a citizen . . . without any reference to race or color, or any other accidental circumstance."[7]

Black soldiers did not fight at Gettysburg, but in the summer of 1863, they distinguished themselves at several battles, including Port Hudson

(May 27), Milliken's Bend (June 7), and Fort Wagner (July 18). Although the consecration of Gettysburg cemetery was for those soldiers who "struggled here" (Lincoln used the word "here" six times), and although blacks would not be allowed to be buried at the Soldiers' cemetery, part of the speech's power at the time and since was its acknowledgment of those soldiers who "gave the last full measure of devotion." The "new birth of freedom" entailed not only the Emancipation Proclamation but also the efforts of black men to fight for freedom and democracy. Throughout the year leading to the Gettysburg Address, Lincoln would defend both.

On July 31, only weeks after the Battle of Gettysburg, Lincoln told one general, "I think I shall not retract or repudiate it [the Emancipation Proclamation]. Those who have tasted actual freedom I believe can never be slaves, or quasi slaves again." Less than a week later, he repeated the message in a letter to General Nathaniel P. Banks: "I think I shall not, in any event, retract the emancipation proclamation; nor, as executive, ever return to slavery any person who is free by the terms of that proclamation, or by any of the acts of Congress." Lincoln was especially eager to see new state constitutions adopted that abolished slavery. He was concerned that if the Proclamation was challenged, it might not hold up in court. That was one reason he exempted certain areas of the Confederacy from it. The justification for emancipation was military necessity. Where there was no military necessity, as in certain counties in Virginia, in designated parishes in Louisiana, and in Tennessee, the Proclamation did not apply. When, in September 1863, Treasury Secretary Chase implored Lincoln to lift the exceptions, the president sent a blistering response:

> The original proclamation has no constitutional or legal justification, except as a military measure. The exemptions were made because the military necessity did not apply to the exempted localities. Nor does that necessity apply to them now any more than it did then. If I take the step must I not do so, without the argument of military necessity, and so, without any argument, except the one that I think the measure politically expedient, and morally right? Would I not thus give up all footing upon constitution or law? Would I not thus be in the boundless field of absolutism? Could this pass unnoticed, or unresisted?[8]

One certain way to end slavery was if individual slaveholding states adopted measures abolishing the institution. Of the four Border States, neither Delaware nor Kentucky would take any action during the war, and slavery would end in those states with the ratification of the Thirteenth Amendment. In Maryland, elections in November 1863 gave political control to a group committed to emancipation, and the following year the electorate narrowly approved a constitution that abolished slavery. Lincoln told a crowd that assembled at the White House to celebrate Maryland's action, "it is no secret that I have wished, and still do wish, mankind everywhere to be free." In June 1863, a state convention in Missouri adopted a gradual emancipation plan that would not begin until 1870. At the moment, Lincoln supported gradual emancipation as "better than *immediate* for both white and black," but by the following spring, he endorsed immediate emancipation. In Missouri, the plan adopted in June would be discarded after the fall elections in 1863, and the state would ultimately abolish slavery immediately in January 1865.[9]

In addition to providing encouragement to the Border States, Lincoln involved himself during the war in efforts to restore seceded states to the Union. He had appointed several military governors and was especially hopeful that Unionists in Louisiana and Tennessee would adopt new state constitutions that abolished slavery. On August 5, 1863, he wrote to General Nathaniel Banks, head of the Department of the Gulf, "I would be glad for her [Louisiana] to make a new Constitution recognizing the emancipation proclamation and adopting emancipation in those parts of the state where the proclamation does not apply." Looking beyond political reconstruction, he then turned to the question that was only beginning to draw attention: How would emancipation alter social relations between blacks and whites? "And while she is at it," Lincoln observed, "I think it would not be objectionable for her to adopt some practical system by which the two races could gradually live themselves out of their old relation to each other, and both come out better prepared for the new. Education for young blacks should be included in the plan." Perhaps by this Lincoln meant new wage labor relationships. It certainly meant education for black children.[10]

Two weeks before his speech at Gettysburg, Lincoln had occasion to write again to Banks. He expressed concern that conservatives in Louisiana would set up a state government that repudiated the Emancipation Proclamation and reestablished slavery. Should that happen, he wrote, "I can not recognize or sustain their work." He would not object to some temporary arrangement for landless and homeless freed persons, but any actions would have to be consistent with "general freedom." "My word is out to be *for* and not *against* them on the question of their permanent freedom," he insisted.[11]

In March 1864, Lincoln took a further step when he wrote to congratulate Michael Hahn on his election as governor. Anticipating the constitutional convention in Louisiana, he raised the issue of voting eligibility under a new state constitution: "I barely suggest for your private consideration, whether some of the colored people may not be let in—as, for instance, the very intelligent, and especially those who have fought gallantly in our ranks." He added, "This is only a suggestion, not to the public but to you alone."[12]

Lincoln had good reason not to make his preference known. Most Americans viewed extending the vote to blacks as more radical than opposing slavery. In the election of 1860, for example, New York went handily for Lincoln, but a ballot measure to abolish the requirement that blacks must own at least $250 in order to vote was defeated by nearly 150,000 votes. Apart from New York, the only other states in which blacks were enfranchised (and on the same basis as whites) were the New England states, except Connecticut. Abolitionists and radical Republicans understood the importance of giving the vote to black men. In a speech at New York's Cooper Institute on May 21, 1863, Wendell Phillips proclaimed, "give the negro a vote in his hand, and there is not a politician from Abraham Lincoln down to the laziest loafer in the lowest ward in this city, who would not do him honor . . . give a man his vote, you give him tools to work and arms to protect himself. The ballot is the true standing ground of Archimedes, planted on which a man can move his world."[13]

The state constitutional convention convened in New Orleans on April 6, 1864, and a month later adopted an ordinance that abolished slavery. Hahn proudly reported the vote to Lincoln: 70–16. The new constitution did not provide for black suffrage but authorized the state legislature to give voting rights to blacks who were literate, owned property, or fought for the Union—authority the legislature was unlikely to exercise.[14]

The convention adjourned on July 25, and Banks wrote Lincoln that the constitution "is one of the best ever penned . . . composed entirely of men of the People." Banks, perhaps saying what he thought Lincoln wanted to hear, proclaimed black enfranchisement would come: "At the beginning of the session negro suffrage was scarcely mentioned—To-day it may be regarded as secure." "The work of reconstruction in this state," asserted Banks, "is all that you can desire."[15]

Lincoln replied that he was "anxious that it shall be ratified by the people." On September 5, voters approved the constitution by a vote of 6,836–1,566. Banks informed Lincoln that the constitution "was ratified by a very large majority of votes, and that intelligent able and patriotic men have been elected to Congress." Banks concluded, "History will record the fact that all the problems involved in restoration of States, and the reconstruction of government have been already solved in Louisiana."[16]

Banks's optimistic assessment would prove erroneous, but Lincoln would not abandon his efforts to see Confederate states with newly adopted constitutions that abolished slavery restored to the Union. Indeed, he would devote his final speech of April 11, 1865, to the topic.

Just as he had focused on Louisiana in the months preceding the Gettysburg Address, he also gave attention to Tennessee. On September 11, 1863, he wrote to Andrew Johnson, military governor of the state, "I see that you have declared in favor of emancipation in Tennessee, for which, may God bless you. Get Emancipation into your new State government—Constitution—and there will be no such word as fail in your case." Lincoln again pressed for elections and advised Johnson to "let the reconstruction be the work of such men only as can be trusted for the Union." Lincoln already was thinking about reelection and reminded Johnson, "It is something on the question of *time*, to remember that it can not be known who is next to occupy the position I now hold, nor what he will do." He added, "The raising of colored troops I think will greatly help every way."[17]

Tennessee did not act until January 1865, when a constitutional convention finally met in Nashville. An amendment abolishing slavery was adopted and, on February 22, ratified by the voters. After the convention acted, Johnson wrote to Lincoln: "Thank God that the tyrant's rod has been broken . . . the state will be redeemed and the foul blot of Slavery erased from her escutcheon." Lincoln's response was muted. He offered "thanks to the Convention & to you" and asked "when do you expect to be here." If Tennessee's action did not overly excite Lincoln, it was because he had waited a long time for Military Governor Johnson to restore the state, and by the time the deed was accomplished, a constitutional amendment that abolished slavery had been approved by Congress and sent to the states for ratification. (On April 7, Tennessee became the twentieth state to ratify it.[18])

It is noteworthy that in the months prior to the Gettysburg Address, Lincoln was not only defending the Emancipation Proclamation but also pressing for the abolition of slavery in the Border States and in Confederate states that had come under Union military control. He was moving away from gradual emancipation and giving thought to the meaning of freedom, to the transition from slave labor to wage labor, and to a new set of relationships between whites and blacks. He was also taking measures to restore the Union.

In his defense of emancipation, Lincoln articulated a broader principle about the meaning of the war. Workingmen's groups in England had written in January to express support for emancipation. Lincoln responded to the workingmen of Manchester that "the duty of self-preservation rests solely with the American people." The American government, he declared, "was built upon the foundation of human rights," and, ultimately, the war's end would see "the universal triumph of justice, humanity, and freedom." In language that would be echoed at Gettysburg, Lincoln told the workingmen of London that the American people were engaged in a "test whether a government, established on the principles of human freedom, can be maintained against an effort to build one upon the exclusive foundation of human bondage."[19]

While most of Lincoln's comments on slavery, emancipation, and the meaning of the war following the Emancipation Proclamation drew public attention, he no doubt was considering the right opportunity to make a broader statement. It came on August 14, 1863, when James C. Conkling invited President Lincoln to Springfield to attend a mass rally of "Unconditional union men" on September 3. Conkling was the former mayor of Springfield and member of the Illinois House of Representatives. In a letter of introduction earlier that year, the president called him "my personal friend of long standing."[20]

Lincoln responded to Conkling on August 20, "I think I will go, or send a letter—probably the latter." Much as he desired to "meet my old friends, at my own home," he rarely left Washington except to confer with generals and visit the troops. But he understood the importance of addressing the concerns of the electorate. He had done so as recently as June in a public letter to New York Democrats who denounced the arrest and trial of Clement Vallandigham, a former Democratic congressman who had condemned the war as "wicked, cruel, and unnecessary," allegedly "with the object and purpose of weakening the power of the Government in its efforts to suppress an unlawful rebellion."[21]

That was before the heady victories in early July at Gettysburg and Vicksburg, but by month's end, the war showed no signs of abating, and some Northern Democrats (unconditional Unionists derisively dubbed them Copperheads, after the poisonous snake) continued to press for peace and demonize the president's policies. Draft riots convulsed New

York and Boston. It seemed that the "fire in the rear," as Lincoln dubbed it, might become an inferno.

The situation in Illinois proved especially problematic. In the fall elections of 1862, Democrats had won nine of fourteen House seats (including Lincoln's home district) and gained control of both chambers of the state legislature. Voters had rejected a new state constitution but approved amendments that forbade black suffrage and black immigration. Early in 1863, the legislature adopted resolutions that condemned the Emancipation Proclamation, called for its withdrawal, and protested the unconstitutional prosecution of the war. Republican Governor Richard Yates was so dismayed by the peace resolutions issuing forth, he prorogued the legislature in June and governed without them for over a year.

Lincoln's letter to Conkling is dated August 26. He addressed his detractors directly: "You desire peace; and you blame me that we do not have it. But how can we attain it?" In logical, lawyerly fashion, he considered the three available options: suppress the rebellion by force of arms, which he was attempting; relinquish the Union, which he would not do; or compromise, but no such compromise that would result in preserving the Union was possible. He added an assurance that as "the servant of the people" he would certainly consider any proposals from the leaders of the rebel army, but there were none forthcoming.

Lincoln quickly moved to the topic he wanted most to address: the Emancipation Proclamation and the enlistment of black troops that the proclamation authorized. "To be plain," he wrote, "you are dissatisfied with me about the negro." "I certainly wish that all men could be free, while I suppose you do not," he asserted; even so, "I have neither adopted, nor proposed any measure, which is not consistent even with your view, provided you are for the Union."

He then launched into a robust defense of the Emancipation Proclamation: "You say it is unconstitutional—I think differently. I think the constitution invests its commander-in-chief, with the law of war in time of war." Again, Lincoln resorted to axiomatic logic. The Proclamation as law was either valid or not valid. "If it is not valid, it needs no retraction," and "if it is valid, it can not be retracted any more than the dead can be brought to life." Lincoln's analogy was a potent reminder of the untold thousands who had already died for the cause and whose deaths would be in vain should the Union not prevail.

The war, he said, had been progressing favorably since the issuance of the Emancipation Proclamation on the previous January 1, and he reported that some of his commanders had informed him that "the eman-cipation policy, and use of colored troops, constitute the heaviest blow yet dealt to the rebellion." Lincoln intensified his assault upon the logic of opposition: "You say you will not fight to free the negroes. Some of them seem willing to fight for you; but, no matter. Fight you, then, exclusively to save the Union. I issued the proclamation on purpose to aid you in saving the Union. Whenever you shall have conquered all resistance to the Union, if I shall urge you to continue fighting, it will be an apt time, then, for you to declare you will not fight to free negroes."

African-American soldiers had demonstrated their bravery and for-titude. Why do they fight, Lincoln asked. Like all men they act upon motives: "If they stake their lives for us, they must be prompted by the strongest motive—even the promise of freedom. And the promise being made, must be kept."[22]

As Lincoln moved toward the conclusion, he began with a somewhat whimsical paragraph that shifted the tone. "The signs look better," Lin-coln reported. He praised all who contributed to the opening of the Mis-sissippi ("the Father of Waters again goes unvexed to the sea") and, in a curious phrase, reminded the audience that "Uncle Sam's Web-feet" (i.e., the navy) must not be forgotten. William O. Stoddard, one of Lincoln's secretaries, later recalled that the president read the letter aloud and in-vited criticism. Stoddard found fault with the aquatic metaphor, but Lin-coln said, "I reckon the people will know what it means."[23]

The passage offers a breather between the defense that has been de-livered and the censuring of Peace Democrats that is to come. The sub-sequent paragraph is as powerful as anything in any of Lincoln's public addresses:

> Peace does not appear so distant as it did. I hope it will come soon, and come to stay; and so come as to be worth the keeping in all future time. It will then have been proved that, among free men, there can be no successful appeal from the ballot to the bullet; and that they who take such appeal are sure to lose their case, and pay the cost. And then, there will be some black men who can remem-ber that, with silent tongue, and clenched teeth, and steady eye, and well-poised bayonet, they have helped mankind on to this great consummation; while, I fear, there will be some white ones, unable to forget that, with malignant heart, and deceitful speech, they have strove to hinder it.[24]

Lincoln knew he had crafted a potent and persuasive letter, and he took measures to ensure that those who heard it grasped its full meaning. In his instructions to Conkling he wrote, "You are one of the best public readers. I have but one suggestion. Read it very slowly." But Conkling, rather than read it himself, sat on the platform before tens of thousands and enjoyed the limelight as he had it read aloud to him by I. J. Ketchum, a lawyer.[25]

On September 3, the day of the rally, Lincoln was distressed ("mortified," he said) to discover the letter "botched up, in the Eastern papers, telegraphed from Chicago." He demanded an explanation, and Conkling apologized that it was telegraphed from Chicago to New York "contrary to my express directions" and assured the president that an accurate text of the letter would be published.[26] In fact, on September 3, the entire text appeared in dozens of papers, including the *New York Times*, and it would soon appear as a pamphlet. At the rally in Springfield, Conkling estimated a crowd of over 50,000 people (it reminded one reporter of "a hive in swarming time") and informed Lincoln that the letter "was received . . . with the greatest enthusiasm" and that it "will occupy an important position in the history of our country." According to one account, listeners received it with "shouts, cheers, thanksgiving, and tears."[27]

Commentators rejoiced that Lincoln offered a direct and powerful defense of the Emancipation Proclamation and the use of black troops. "In a few plain sentences," wrote the *Chicago Tribune*, "than which none more important were ever uttered in this country, Mr. Lincoln exonerates himself from the crimes urged against him, shows the untenableness of the position that his enemies occupy, and gives the world assurance that that great measure of policy and justice, which, while it strikes a fatal blow at treason and rebellion, guarantees freedom to three million of Slaves, is to remain the law of the Republic."[28]

The New York diarist George Templeton Strong called the public letter "a straightforward, simple, honest, forcible exposition of [Lincoln's] views, and likely to be a conspicuous document in the history of our times." Boston's customs collector, John Zacheus Goodrich, wrote Lincoln, "What a contrast—the black man trying to save, & the white man trying to destroy his Country. I think Copperheads must feel that they are compared to the Negro quite to their disadvantage." Senator Henry Wilson of Massachusetts sent a note to the president: "May Almighty God bless you for your noble, patriotic and Christian letter will be on the lips and in the hearts of hundreds of thousands this day." The letter "will live in history side by side with your Proclamation," predicted John Murray Forbes, railroad magnate and Lincoln elector.[29]

In an editorial titled "The President's Letter," the *New York Times* declared "the message has all his characteristic solidity of sense and aptness of expression . . . The great charm of this free-and-easy familiar letter, is its utter freedom from everything like a partisan spirit." The paper returned to the letter four days later: "Its hard sense, its sharp outlines, its noble temper defy malice. Even the Copperhead gnaws upon it as vainly as the viper upon a file . . . The most consummate rhetorician never used language more apt to the purpose, and still there is not a word in the letter not familiar to the plainest plowman."[30]

In November, at Gettysburg, Lincoln would demonstrate even more impressively his ability to express complex thoughts simply and appeal directly to the common sense of the audience. As it happened, Conkling also invited Edward Everett, former governor and senator from Massachusetts and a renowned orator, to attend the Springfield rally. Everett declined, and he too sent a letter, but it received little attention. Less than three months later, both Lincoln and Everett would accept an invitation to speak at the dedication of the Soldiers' cemetery.

* * *

Lincoln's Gettysburg Address was both a culmination and a commencement. It crystallized in general terms ideas he had developed more specifically in other places, most notably in his letter to Conkling. The speech, with its invocation of the Declaration of Independence and a "new birth of freedom," spoke to how emancipation had transformed the war since the start of the year, although without explicitly mentioning slavery. It did not have to, given the occasion, all that had transpired, and all that Lincoln had already said during the year. The speech also focused the audience's attention on the end of the war: "the great task remaining before us," and "the unfinished work" of reestablishing government by the people and restoring the Union. Toward that end, even as he spoke, Lincoln was preparing to issue a proclamation on the process of Reconstruction.

When Lincoln returned to Washington from Gettysburg, he became ill with varioloid, a mild form of smallpox. His illness alarmed Unionists of all political persuasions. The *New York World*, a rabidly antiadministration Democratic paper, paused to comment, "Men of his habit of body are not usually long-lived, and the small-pox to a man of his age, even when the health is usually good, is a very serious matter. His death at this time would be a real calamity to the country."[31]

The illness had given Lincoln time to work on his Annual Message, due to be read by a clerk on December 8, the day after the 38th Congress opened. At Gettysburg, Lincoln had defined the war as being fought for freedom and equality. Now he turned his attention to the problem of ending the war and restoring the Union without slavery. According to John Hay, Lincoln considered the restoration of the Union "the greatest question ever presented to practical statesmanship." Toward that end, Lincoln issued a Proclamation of Amnesty and Reconstruction.[32]

In the proclamation, Lincoln offered "full pardon" to persons who "have, directly or by implication, participated in the existing rebellion." There were, to be sure, several categories of exceptions: Confederate civil or diplomatic officers or agents; all who left seats in Congress, or judicial stations, to aid the rebellion; officers above the rank of colonel in the army and lieutenant in the navy; and anyone who treated prisoners of war, white or black, unlawfully.

The pardon would be granted "with restoration of all rights of property, except as to slaves and in property cases where the rights of third parties shall have intervened," to persons who took an oath to "faithfully support, protect and defend the Constitution" and "abide by and faithfully support all acts of Congress passed during the existing rebellion with reference to slaves," as well as "all proclamations of the President made during the existing rebellion having reference to slaves," as long as the Supreme Court did not overturn them.

Lincoln relied on double negatives, a passive voice, and the third person to make two important additional points. Any plans with respect to the freed people that "shall recognize and declare their permanent freedom, provide for their education, and which may yet be consistent, as a temporary arrangement, with their present condition as a laboring, landless, and homeless class, will not be objected to by the national Executive." Finally, the proclamation presents a "mode" whereby national authority and loyal state government can be reestablished. "While the mode presented is the best the Executive can suggest, with his present impressions," concluded Lincoln, "it must not be understood that no other possible mode would be acceptable."[33]

Many abolitionists were unhappy with Lincoln's Proclamation of Amnesty and Reconstruction. They felt it did not go far enough and that it equivocated on the freedom of all slaves and the issue of future rights. At least one abolitionist used the Gettysburg Address to critique the president. Writing in the *Liberator*, Wendell Phillips Garrison, the editor's son, asked, "Has the President so soon forgotten his noble speech at Gettysburg? He said there that the war was a trial whether or not a government of the people, by the people, and for the people, could stand." Connecting the awful events of the New York draft riots to the heroic efforts of black soldiers, Garrison wondered, "Shall we admit to a share in the government the brutal Irishmen, fresh from a July carnival of riot, and reject the colored freedman who perhaps at Wagner, Port Hudson, or Milliken's Bend, has eagerly exposed his life that the republic may live?" Garrison argued that black men were entitled to the full rights of citizenship, including the right to vote; in time, Lincoln's statements would harmonize with Garrison's reading of the "noble speech."[34]

In keeping with his avowed dedication to "the great task remaining before us," that of ending the war, preserving the Union, and abolishing slavery, Lincoln proposed a plan of Reconstruction. He was willing to consider other plans. He was willing to show generosity and magnanimity of spirit. But as he promised at Gettysburg, democracy and freedom must triumph.

Notes

1. Portions of this essay appeared previously as "Read It Very Slowly," *New York Times Disunion Blog*, August 21, 2013. Used with permission.

2. *The Collected Works of Abraham Lincoln*, ed. Roy P. Basler, 9 vols. (New Brunswick, NJ: Rutgers University Press, 1953–1955), 6:48 (hereafter cited as *CW*). On the Gettysburg Address, see Martin P. Johnson, *Writing the Gettysburg Address* (Lawrence: University Press of Kansas, 2013); Gabor Boritt, *The Gettysburg Gospel: The Lincoln Speech That Nobody Knows* (New York: Simon and Schuster, 2008); Douglas L. Wilson, *Lincoln's Sword: The Presidency and the Power of Words* (New York: Vintage, 2006), 196–237; and Garry Wills, *Lincoln at Gettysburg: The Words That Remade America* (New York: Simon and Schuster, 1992). On the Emancipation Proclamation see Louis P. Masur, *Lincoln's Hundred Days: The Emancipation Proclamation and the War for the Union* (Cambridge, MA: Harvard University Press, 2012) and Allen C. Guelzo, *Lincoln's Emancipation Proclamation: The End of Slavery in America* (New York: Simon and Schuster, 2004). On Lincoln and slavery generally see Eric Foner, *The Fiery Trial: Abraham Lincoln and American Slavery* (New York: Norton, 2010).

3. Frederick W. Seward, *Seward at Washington, as Senator and Secretary of State: A Memoir of His Life, with Selections from His Letters, 1861–1872* (New York: Derby and Miller, 1891), 151; *CW*, 7:281.

4. *CW*, 5:357; 6:149–150.

5. Frederick Douglass, "The War and How To End It: An Address Delivered in Rochester, New York, on March 25, 1862," in *The Frederick Douglass Papers, Series One: Speeches, Debates, and Interviews*, ed. John W. Blassingame, 5 vols. (New Haven, CT: Yale University Press, 1985), 3:518.

6. George Livermore, *An Historical Research Respecting the Opinions of the Founders of the Republic on Negroes as Slaves, as Citizens, and as Soldiers* (Boston: John Wilson and Son, 1862), 195.

7. *Opinion of Attorney General Bates on Citizenship* (Washington, DC: GPO, 1863), 7, 12.

8. *CW*, 6:358; 365; 428–429.

9. Noah Brooks, *Mr. Lincoln's Washington: Selections from the Writing of Noah Brooks, Civil War Correspondent*, ed. P. J. Staudenraus (South Brunswick, NJ: A.S. Barnes, 1967), 381–383; *CW*, 6:291.

10. *CW*, 6:364–365.

11. *CW*, 7:1–2.

12. *CW*, 7:243.

13. *Liberator*, May 29, 1863.

14. *Official Journal of the Proceedings of the Convention for the Revision and Amendment of the Constitution of the State of Louisiana* (New Orleans: W.H. Fish, 1864), 71; *Debates on the Convention for the Revision and Amendment of the Constitution*

of the State of Louisiana (New Orleans: W.H. Fish, 1864), 226. Also see Michael Hahn to Lincoln, May 11, 1864, and May 14, 1864, Abraham Lincoln Papers, Library of Congress (hereafter ALP).

15. Nathaniel P. Banks to Lincoln, July 25, 1864, ALP.

16. *CW*, 7:486; Nathaniel P. Banks, Sept. 6, 1864, ALP.

17. *CW*, 6:440.

18. Andrew Johnson, *The Papers of Andrew Johnson*, ed. Leroy P. Graf, Ralph W. Haskins, and Paul H. Bergeron, 16 vols. (Knoxville: University of Tennessee Press, 1967–2000), 7:404; *CW*, 8:216.

19. *CW*, 6:64; 88–89.

20. *CW*, 6:85.

21. *CW*, 6:399.

22. *CW*, 6: 406–410.

23. William O. Stoddard, *Inside the White House in War Times* (New York: Charles Webster, 1890), 229.

24. *CW*, 6:410.

25. *CW*, 6:414.

26. *CW*, 6:430.

27. *Chicago Tribune*, Sept. 4, 1863; James C. Conkling to Lincoln, Sept. 4, 1863, ALP.

28. *Chicago Tribune*, Sept. 3, 1863. Also see Allen Guelzo, "Defending Emancipation: Abraham Lincoln and the Conkling Letter, 1863," *Civil War History* 48 (2002): 313–337.

29. George Templeton Strong, *Diary of the Civil War: George Templeton Strong*, ed. Allen Nevins (New York: MacMillan, 1962), 355; John Z. Goodrich to Lincoln, Sept. 3, 1863, ALP; Henry Wilson to Lincoln, Sept. 3, 1863, ALP; John M. Forbes to Lincoln, Sept. 8, 1863, ALP.

30. *New York Times*, Sept. 3 and Sept. 7, 1863.

31. *New York World* quoted in *Chicago Tribune*, Dec. 9, 1863.

32. Stoddard, *Inside Lincoln's White House*, 69.

33. *CW*, 7:53–57.

34. "The President Falters," *Liberator*, Dec. 18, 1863.

"The Great Task Remaining Before Us"

LINCOLN AND RECONSTRUCTION

George Rutherglen

THE ROAD TO Reconstruction from Lincoln's Gettysburg Address crossed the last years of the Civil War, Lee's surrender at Appomattox Court House, and Lincoln's assassination. In between these momentous events, Lincoln delivered his Second Inaugural, with the promise to act "with malice toward none, with charity for all," and he gave what we know as his "final speech" in the days between Lee's surrender and his own death. Only John Wilkes Booth, who was in the audience for this speech, might have suspected it to be Lincoln's last public address. Lincoln asked his audience to "all join in doing the acts necessary to restoring the proper practical relations" between the Confederate states and the Union, but beyond his defense of the efforts to constitute a new government in Louisiana, he went no further into the details of Reconstruction, and the historical record tragically stops there. We cannot know how he would have reacted to the turbulent events of Reconstruction that he did not live to see, but we must instead seek his legacy in the enduring principles that he endorsed while he was alive.

Lincoln gave these principles memorable form at Gettysburg, echoing the preamble to the Constitution in his reference to government of, for, and by "the people," and by quoting the Declaration of Independence for the proposition that "all men are created equal." These sources figured prominently in Republican advocacy during Reconstruction. To take only one among many examples, Senator Lyman Trumbull of Illinois made the case for the Civil Rights Act of 1866, passed to enforce the Thirteenth Amendment, as necessary to protect "the liberty which was intended to be secured by the Declaration of Independence and the Constitution of the United States originally, and more especially by the amendment which has recently been adopted."[1] Members of Congress did not appeal to what Lincoln would have done if he had lived, but to the principles that he embraced before he died. These did not have determinate implications for reconstructing the proper government of any of the Southern states.

Lincoln remained resolutely opposed to any inflexible plan of Reconstruction. His Second Inaugural offered the hope of reconciling sympathetic white Southerners to the Union, on the optimistic assumption that there were enough of them to form loyal governments in the South. His final speech eschewed any discussion of whether the Confederate states had actually seceded from the Union and had to be readmitted to it. He thought "that question is bad, as the basis of a controversy, and good for nothing at all—a merely pernicious abstraction." In the last years of the war, he took a moderate position on Reconstruction, over the opposition of Radical Republicans. They bitterly criticized his "10 Percent Plan," allowing any Confederate state to form a new constitution after 10 percent of its male electorate pledged future support for the Union. The state had to abolish slavery, but it could deal with the newly freed slaves by special, temporary legislation. The Radicals demanded sterner measures in the Wade-Davis Bill, which Lincoln pocket-vetoed, leading to fierce criticism from them and to a nearly complete break.[2] His final speech makes no reference to the 10 Percent Plan, but it does defend the policies he had supported in Louisiana. Whether he would have adhered to similar policies after the war cannot be known, as the contingencies of political decisions and Southern resistance after his death complicate any prediction about what he might have done in those circumstances.

With respect to the Reconstruction amendments to the Constitution, the historical record rapidly moves from the certainties of his eventual conviction that slavery had to be completely abolished, evident in his support for the Thirteenth Amendment, to speculation about what the contents of the Fourteenth and Fifteenth Amendments might have been. We might be fairly certain that some proposals for equal citizenship, like those now embedded in these amendments, would have become federal law in some form, but not necessarily in the Constitution. Assembling the two-thirds majorities in each house of Congress would have tested even Lincoln's political skills, and obtaining ratification by three-quarters of the states would have required the coercion that congressional Republicans actually used against the South, notably in the case of the Fourteenth

Amendment, in the form of withholding representation in Congress until a state voted for ratification.³ What we do know is that, by ensuring passage of the Thirteenth Amendment, Lincoln set the stage for the constitutional questions that came up in Reconstruction and for the first great civil rights acts. We might have had a Thirteenth Amendment without the Fourteenth or Fifteenth, but not the reverse. We could not have had any civil rights legislation without the grant of power to Congress in each of these amendments to enforce its provisions. Equality before the law and in the right to vote was inconceivable without abolition of slavery. So much is obvious on any reading of the historical record. Less obvious, but far more consequential, was that abolition led directly to claims for equal citizenship, which were vindicated in the Constitution and in federal law. These enactments constitute Lincoln's legacy in Reconstruction, the common issues and political commitments that led forward from the Thirteenth Amendment to the Fourteenth and Fifteenth, and that can then be traced back to the principles that Lincoln espoused at Gettysburg and with increasing fervor as the war progressed.

The Thirteenth Amendment: A New Birth of Freedom

An aura of inevitability surrounds the adoption of the Thirteenth Amendment, as does the progression from one Reconstruction amendment to the next. For all that, the vote in the House of Representatives was remarkably close. The supporters of the amendment just barely met the constitutional requirement of a two-thirds majority, with only two votes to spare. Passage in the Senate was easier, because of the greater representation of Republicans among the senators from states that had remained in the Union. Nevertheless, Lincoln and the other supporters of the amendment had to rely both upon the absence of the Southern states from Congress and upon all their available political capital to convert to their side the necessary number of Democrats in the House.

The passage of the Thirteenth Amendment appears in hindsight to be inevitable only because it was so necessary. The Emancipation Proclamation had very limited coverage, strictly speaking only in Confederate territory then under Confederate control.⁴ It did result in legal recognition of the de facto emancipation of slaves as the Union armies advanced ever deeper into Confederate territory, but even so, it had limited temporal duration because it depended upon exercise of the president's war powers,

which would have lapsed at some point after the end of the war. The proclamation made the former slaves "forever free," but its authority depended
upon the exercise of war powers of necessarily temporary duration. In
addition to questions about the extent of the president's war powers, the
Proclamation also appeared to constitute a taking of property without just
compensation. As the Civil War came to a close, the Thirteenth Amendment was needed to put emancipation on a more secure constitutional
footing. Lincoln had to seek, as he put it, "a king's cure" for the evils of
slavery.[5]

Abolition was, in this sense, a constitutional necessity. It was also a
political necessity. Well before Lincoln issued the Emancipation Proclamation, the war had become one to free the slaves, not simply to save the
Union. De facto emancipation, as slaves gained their freedom by reaching
Union lines and, increasingly, serving in the Union Army, had to be recognized by permanent, constitutional change. In a last-ditch effort to avert
the war, a constitutional amendment to preserve slavery had been passed
by Congress just before Lincoln was inaugurated. A politically desperate
effort in 1861 to save the Union by saving slavery could not survive the
battles of the war that, horrible though they were, freed the slaves wher-
ever the Union Army prevailed. The turning point, which coincided with
Lincoln's own deliberations over whether to issue the Emancipation Proclamation, came with the passage of the Second Confiscation Act and Lincoln's reluctant decision to sign it on July 17, 1862. The act emancipated
any slaves owned by rebels who escaped to Union lines, without judicial
proceedings or any showing that they had been used in the Confederate
war effort.[6] By the time that Lincoln spoke at Gettysburg in 1863, slavery
could have survived only with the survival of the Confederacy, and it could
not coexist with the survival of the Union. When Lincoln resolved at Gettysburg that "these dead shall not have died in vain," he meant that slavery
had to die too, so that the Union could be preserved. As Representative
Glenni Scofield, a Republican from Pennsylvania, said in the congressional debates over the Thirteenth Amendment: "Slavery in the end must die.
It has cost the country too much suffering and too much patriotic blood,
and is in theory an institution too monstrous, to be permitted to live."[7]

The Thirteenth Amendment became inevitable only as Union victory
became more certain. At the same time, however, the consequences of the
amendment itself became ever more uncertain. Some supporters of the
amendment would have limited it to freedom alone. Senator John Henderson, a Republican from Missouri, disowned any further consequences

of the amendment. He said, "In passing this amendment we do not confer upon the negro the right to vote. We give him no right except his freedom and leave the rest to the states."[8] The future president, James A. Garfield, took the opposite position in the House, when he supported legislation to enforce the amendment. He asked: "Have we given freedom to the black man? What is freedom? Is it a mere negation, the bare privilege of not being chained, bought and sold, branded and scourged? If this be all, then freedom is a bitter mockery, a cruel delusion, and it may well be questioned whether slavery were not better."[9] As a purely textual matter, Henderson accurately stated the content of Section 1 of the Thirteenth Amendment, which accomplished emancipation in the self-executing declaration that "neither slavery nor involuntary servitude . . . shall exist within the United States." But Garfield made arguments that captured the need for Section 2 of the amendment, which gave Congress "power to enforce this article by appropriate legislation." In the terms that Lincoln used at Gettysburg, it enabled Congress to complete "the great task remaining before us."

Congress acted to exercise this power by passing the Civil Rights Act of 1866 and the Freedmen's Bureau Bill. Both pieces of legislation were vetoed by President Johnson, and both were then passed by Congress over his veto, the Civil Rights Act with no changes at all, but the Freedmen's Bureau Bill with significant amendments. The Bureau had been set up initially in the War Department to provide assistance to the newly freed slaves and was to last for a year after hostilities ended. As these features of the Bureau make clear, it was originally established under the war power, and, on that basis, Lincoln signed the original legislation shortly before he died. The Freedmen's Bureau Bill would have extended the life of the Bureau indefinitely, but as enacted after another veto by President Johnson, the Bureau was extended only for another two years. Given his original support for the Bureau, we can be fairly sure that Lincoln would have signed the Freedmen's Bureau Bill, although he might well have altered the form that the legislation took.

The same can also be said of Lincoln's likely support for the Civil Rights Act of 1866, which has assumed much greater significance than the Freedmen's Bureau legislation as a permanent part of civil rights law. The 1866 act took up Garfield's question of whether freedom could be of any value to the newly freed slaves in the absence of equal citizenship. The act answered that question firmly in the negative. Under the act, emancipation led to equal civil rights. Johnson's reasons for disagreeing and vetoing the act demonstrate how far his position was from any Lincoln would have taken. Johnson took Henderson's comment about the limits of the Thirteenth Amendment to its logical conclusion. For Johnson, the amendment did nothing more than free the slaves and it did not need to do anything more. As he said in his veto message:

> It cannot, however, be justly claimed that, with a view to enforcement of this article of the Constitution, there is at present any necessity for the exercise of all the powers which this bill confers.

> Slavery has been abolished, and at present nowhere exists within the jurisdiction of the United States: nor has there been, nor is it likely there will be, any attempt to revive it by the people of the States.[10]

He made much the same point in his veto of the Freedmen's Bureau Bill: the Thirteenth Amendment, so far from supporting enactment of the legislation, eliminated any need for it.[11] Such a narrow view of Reconstruction could not be further removed from the open-ended commitments that Lincoln made in the Gettysburg Address.

The debates over the 1866 act gave some inkling of how contentious the process of fulfilling that commitment would be. The act granted citizenship to "all persons born in the United States and not subject to any foreign power" and then went on to provide that all citizens would have the same civil rights to hold property, to make contracts, to participate in judicial proceedings, and to receive the protection of the law, all to be the same "as is enjoyed by white citizens."[12] The remainder of the act then provided for enforcement of these rights, which entailed a considerable expansion of the jurisdiction of the federal courts and of the power of federal prosecutors to enforce the act. The specific provisions of the act provoked considerable debate, but none more than the question whether Congress had the power to pass the act at all.[13] Congress's newly obtained authority to enforce the Thirteenth Amendment did not clearly extend to granting citizenship to four million newly freed slaves, let alone to specifying civil rights that previously had been protected only by state law. Antebellum precedents for the naturalization of whole groups of aliens, either foreign settlers in territory annexed from Spain or France or members of Indian tribes, did not approach the scale of granting citizenship to what was then over 10 percent of the nation's population.

The need to take this step was as great as the constitutional questions that it raised. Without citizenship, the newly freed slaves were threatened with being reduced to the status of stateless persons. As Senator Morrill, a Republican from Vermont, framed the question:

Hitherto we have said that he was a nondescript in our statutes; he had no *status*; he was ubiquitous; he was both man and thing; he was three fifths of a person for representation and he was a thing for commerce and for use. In the highest sense, then, in which any definition can ever be held, this bill is important as a definition. It defines him to be a man and only a man in American politics and in American law; it puts him on the plane of manhood; it brings him within the pale of the Constitution. That is all it does as a definition, and there it leaves him.[14]

The need to define the legal status of the newly free slaves was all the more pressing because, with the demise of slavery, they had to seek out their livelihood in the unfamiliar regime of free labor. As W. E. B. Du Bois characterized their lot, they were otherwise "a horde of starving vagabonds, homeless, helpless, and pitiable in their dark distress."[15] They could not rise above their destitution in material terms without secure, legal, and ascertainable civil rights.

Some Southern states had moved to fill the legal vacuum surrounding the newly freed slave by enacting "Black Codes," which nominally recognized basic civil rights for all persons, but then imposed discriminatory burdens upon blacks in owning property and fulfilling contracts of employment. Vagrancy laws also were deployed against them to force them back to plantation work.[16] Under the codes, they received the fewest possible rights consistent with physical liberty and faced the danger that they would be returned essentially to servitude. The Republicans in Congress acted to meet this emergency for the reasons set out by then-Representative Garfield. The sponsor of the 1866 act in the Senate, Lyman Trumbull, framed the issue in these terms: "Has Congress authority to give practical effect to the great declaration that slavery shall not exist in the United States? If it has not, then nothing has been accomplished by the adoption of the constitutional amendment."[17]

This line of argument did not succeed in sweeping away the doubts about the constitutionality of the act, some of which came from within Republican ranks. Representative Bingham of Ohio, who took a leading role in drafting the Fourteenth Amendment, opposed the act because it conferred civil rights that could only be granted by the Constitution:

> The law in every State should be just; it should be no respecter of persons. It is otherwise now, and it has been otherwise for many years in many States of the Union. I should remedy that not by an arbitrary assumption of power, but by amending the Constitution of the United States, expressly prohibiting the States from any such abuse of power in the future.[18]

These doubts coalesced with concerns among the Republicans that even a statute as momentous as the 1866 act could be undone by a hostile Supreme Court or by a Congress in which Republicans no longer numbered in the majority. One step led to another as a consequence of the combined force of legal principles and the circumstances in which they were enacted into law, which then changed the circumstances in which further enactments became necessary. The Emancipation Proclamation led to the Thirteenth Amendment, which resulted in the 1866 act, whose constitutionality could be ensured only by adoption of the Fourteenth Amendment. The pressure of events caused politics to yield to the logic of expanding civil rights.

The Fourteenth Amendment: Dedicated to the Proposition That All Men Are Created Equal

The first section of the Fourteenth Amendment protects both due process and equal protection in clauses familiar to all lawyers and to many citizens: "nor shall any State deprive any person of life, liberty, or property, without due process of law; nor deny to any person within its jurisdiction the equal protection of the laws." Less familiar are the other clauses in Section 1, granting state and national citizenship and protecting the privileges and immunities of national citizens. So, too, is Section 5, the last section of the amendment, granting Congress the power to enforce its provisions "by appropriate legislation." The middle sections of the amendment, however, have remained obscure, familiar only to specialists in the varied subjects they cover. Sections 2 through 4 concern a miscellaneous collection of issues, whose provisions have lost significance as they have been superseded by subsequent events and as the immediate consequences of the Civil War have receded into the past. They are related to one another only in expressing congressional hostility to President Johnson and to his lenient Reconstruction policies. They have an even more tenuous relationship to Section 1, which has the strongest claim among the amendment's provisions to be inspired by the principles that Lincoln articulated at Gettysburg.

The omnibus character of the Fourteenth Amendment follows partly from the way in which it was drafted, in a process of repeated compromise, rewriting, and rearrangement in the Joint Committee on Reconstruction and then in debates on the floor of the House and the Senate.[19] Part of the length and complexity of the amendment—which runs to nearly twice the length of the Gettysburg Address itself—also follows from its role as the platform on which congressional Republicans ran in the election of 1866, over the determined but ineffectual opposition of President Johnson. Although he was not up for election in 1866, he succeeded in giving the Republican majority an unusual victory in a midterm election, in which they succeeded in preserving their overwhelming victory in 1864.[20] The middle sections of the amendment reflect the Republican election strategy of running against Johnson, who had opposed the amendment. That strategy, we can safely assume, would have been very different if Lincoln had remained in office. Lincoln signed the Thirteenth Amendment after it passed Congress. Johnson took the unprecedented step of denouncing the Fourteenth Amendment, just days after it had secured congressional approval.[21] We can assume that Lincoln would have had greater influence over the content of the amendment than Johnson, but we cannot know what that would have produced.

The middle sections of the amendment illustrate the difficulty of making any such prediction. Sections 2, 3, and 4 deal, respectively, with decreasing the representation of states in the House to the extent that they disenfranchise male citizens; with denying public office to Confederate supporters who had held office before the war and sworn to uphold the Constitution; and with validating Union debt, invalidating Confederate debt, and preventing payment of compensation to former slaveholders. Section 2 on disenfranchisement raised the most urgent concerns, both of principle and politics, which later led to adoption of the Fifteenth Amendment. In the absence of either constitutional provision, Republicans faced the dire prospect of increased representation of Southern states in the House with decreased support in those states for their own party. Abolition made the notorious "three-fifths clause" in the original Constitution obsolete, while disenfranchisement of the newly freed slaves undermined the party's most likely base of support in the South. As a matter of principle, we now take it as axiomatic that full citizenship requires full voting rights. The country, however, was not ready for this proposition in 1866, and so the Republicans proposed Section 2 as a halfway measure, but one with the undesirable implication that the vote could be denied on the basis of race. Radical Republicans expressed great dissatisfaction with the amendment for exactly this reason.[22] Feminists, too, were outraged by the reference in Section 2 to the "male inhabitants" of a state as the only eligible voters, seemingly approving the traditional exclusion of women from the franchise.[23]

Sections 3 and 4 of the amendment were also solicitous of public opinion, but by taking sterner measures toward the South than Section 2. Section 3 responded to Johnson's free exercise of the pardon power, which relieved Confederate supporters of the personal consequences of betraying the Union. This provision made supporters of the Confederacy who had held state and federal office before the war ineligible for these offices until their disability was lifted by a two-thirds vote of each house of Congress, effectively taking the pardon power in this respect away from the president and conferring it upon Congress. Section 4 prevented any attempt at the state or federal level to compensate former slaveholders or to pay off the holders of Confederate debt, while guaranteeing the validity of Union debt. All these provisions appealed to voters in the North, who were anxious to punish former federal and state officials who had violated their oath of office and were concerned about payment of their own pensions and other debts owed by the federal government. These provisions predictably antagonized voters in the South, but their votes did not matter so long as their representatives and senators could not take seats in Congress. If Lincoln had lived, he might have resisted antagonizing the South in this way, but he might well have been swayed by the need to ensure support in the North. As events played out, both Sections 3 and 4 took effect without protest but with few lasting consequences as the subjects they addressed faded from the national agenda. Section 2, as we will see, was never effectively enforced.

Section 1 stands as the amendment's enduring contribution to constitutional law and to principles of equality. The due process and equal protection clauses extended those principles beyond "citizens," which was the limit of coverage in the 1866 act, to "any person," including aliens, and, as it subsequently turned out, corporations. The breadth of coverage of these clauses was matched only by the abstract terms in which they were cast. The generality of "due process" and "equal protection" present a striking contrast to the specificity of the rights protected by the 1866 act. These provisions, as well as those granting citizenship and protecting the privileges and immunities of citizens, have the same grandeur and simplicity as Lincoln's words at Gettysburg, which, in turn, echoed the opening words of the Declaration of Independence, that "all men are created equal."

In an enactment with legal consequences, however, such abstract language inevitably created ambiguity and invited disputes, which have been attached to these clauses since they took effect and down to the present day.[24] While the amendment was under consideration, however, the uncertain meaning of Section 1 broadened its appeal. Different factions within the Republican Party, and outside it as well, could see in these provisions whatever they wanted. Most of the debate over the amendment focused elsewhere than on Section 1, which gained such wide support because it could receive such different interpretations. No one knew precisely what "due process," "equal protection," or, for that matter, the "privileges and immunities" of citizenship meant.

In structure, Section 1 roughly follows Section 1 of the 1866 act, even as it proceeds at a much higher level of generality. Both provisions first grant citizenship, then identify the rights of citizenship, and conclude by offering due process and equal protection for those rights. This parallel confirms the purpose of the amendment in preserving the constitutionality of the act, and, indeed, the act was soon reenacted under the congressional power to enforce the Fourteenth Amendment. Another parallel, to the proposal by Radical Republicans for the language of the Thirteenth Amendment, brings out their ambition to enact a general constitutional guarantee of "equality before the law." Senator Charles Sumner, Republican of Massachusetts, proposed that the Thirteenth Amendment read as follows: "All persons are equal before the law, so that no person can hold another as a slave."[25] That language, which anticipated the equal protection clause, proved to be too radical for moderate Republicans in 1864, and, in some respects, too moderate for the Radicals in 1866.

Section 1 of the amendment did not save its other provisions, particularly Sections 2 and 3, from withering criticism that they conceded too much. Thaddeus Stevens, leader of the Radical Republicans in the House (as Sumner was their leader in the Senate), lamented "the omission of many better things" that the amendment might have accomplished:

"I find that we shall be obliged to be content with patching up the worst portions of the ancient edifice, and leaving it, in many of its parts, to be swept through by the tempests, the frosts, and the storms of despotism."[26] Although he strongly supported Section 1, and focused his criticism on Sections 2 and 3, he could not foresee the storms that would also sweep through its provisions. It would not be effectively enforced for more than a century. Its sweeping terms meant different things to different people, and not, initially, what they meant to him. Confirmation that its great clauses could be narrowly construed came quickly, when the Supreme Court narrowed the privileges and immunities of national citizenship to a short and puzzling list of rights, concerned mainly with travel of one kind or another: to the national capital, to seaports, on the high seas, and in foreign countries.[27]

The effect of this decision, which remains good law to this day, was to transfer to the due process and equal protection clauses almost all the weight of protecting individual rights. Yet these clauses also received interpretations that turned in a narrow direction soon after the end of Reconstruction. The Supreme Court first drastically limited the power of Congress to prohibit private discrimination under the enforcement sections of the Thirteenth and Fourteenth Amendments.[28] Under the former, Congress was limited essentially to eliminating the "badges and incidents" of slavery, basically amounting to what it had already done under the 1866 act. Under the latter, it could address only "state action" that resulted in discrimination on the basis of race, relieving private individuals and firms of any independent obligation not to discriminate. *Plessy v. Ferguson* inaugurated the regime of "separate but equal."[29] Meanwhile, instead of promoting racial equality, the Fourteenth Amendment became an obstacle to progressive legislation through the doctrine of "substantive due process."[30] The long and intricate history of how this came to pass and how it was eventually overcome in *Brown v. Board of Education* need not be recounted here.[31]

As Justice Jackson observed just before *Brown* was decided, "controversies have raged over the cryptic and abstract words" of the amendment.[32] If not foreseeable in all their detail, the likelihood of the controversies themselves was entirely predictable. The sobering explanation given by Thaddeus Steven for why he accepted "so imperfect a proposition" as the Fourteenth Amendment still has currency today: "I answer, because I live among men and not among angels; among men as intelligent, as determined, and as independent as myself, who, not agreeing with me, do not choose to yield their opinions to mine. Mutual concession, therefore, is our only resort, or mutual hostilities."[33] The context of this speech makes clear that he referred to the hostility within Congress, but he might equally have referred to the hostilities of the Civil War. The Battle of Gettysburg marked the turning point in that war, yet the war did not end for almost two more years. The adoption of the Fourteenth Amendment made equality a fundamental principle of constitutional law, but it has become a reality only fitfully and with delays that have stretched over a century and half. Eventual vindication of the amendment's promise in *Brown* has been followed by decades of further litigation over its implementation. In light of this history, "mutual concession" might well understate the obstacles in the way of progress toward a common understanding of "equality before the law." Great principles might be born out of great conflicts, but they do not necessarily bring those conflicts to an end, either as soon or as favorably as their supporters might have expected.

This returns us to the contrast between Section 1 and the middle sections of the amendment. The former has had a long history of contested interpretation and enduring significance. The latter have rarely been tested, either by political action or judicial decisions. With the benefit of hindsight, we can say that Stevens rightly placed his faith in the long-term principles of Section 1, while accepting the short-term compromises, especially in Sections 2 and 3, which both failed to give voting rights to former slaves and to deny them to Confederate supporters. A similar rationale has been offered to reconcile the existence of segregated schools in the District of Columbia with Congress's original understanding of racial equality in the Fourteenth Amendment: that Congress at the time might not have understood that the amendment prohibited racial segregation, but that the principles espoused by Stevens eventually required this interpretation of the amendment.[34] Yet even an enduring commitment to abstract principles must admit of varying interpretations. The meaning of these terms has crystallized, to the extent it has, only after a long and tortuous course of judicial interpretation.

It did not meet immediately with universal acceptance. Hostilities did not cease with the amendment's approval by Congress. Ratification of the amendment was forced upon the Southern states as a condition of regaining their seats in Congress. They remained, to this extent, in the "grasp of war," as Republicans characterized the constitutional basis for Reconstruction. Literal warfare also persisted, in the terrorist attacks by groups, such as the Ku Klux Klan, upon the former slaves and their supporters in the South. These attacks were met with force by the occupying Union Army and by legislation that expanded federal prohibitions against Southern defiance. But when the Union Army left the South, it also left the newly freed slaves and their supporters unprotected. The revolution wrought by the Civil War and Reconstruction did not progress easily to constitutional recognition of equal rights. The battle for political control of the South was another, violent and unwonted, reminder of Gettysburg.

The Fifteenth Amendment: Government by the People

Voting we take to be the hallmark of citizenship. The course of Reconstruction made this the last right to be recognized in the Constitution, and in the era of Jim Crow, it was among the first to be taken away from black citizens. The repeal of federal protection for voting rights solidified white domination of governments throughout the South.[35] All sides eventually recognized the importance of the franchise, either in solidifying the gains from Reconstruction by extending the vote to blacks or by eroding those gains by confining it to whites. Yet that understanding came late for lack of support among the almost universally white electorate. Even that electorate was limited by sex and by property qualifications. It was only after the Fifteenth Amendment that universal male suffrage became the standard measure of political equality, and through subsequent constitutional amendments was then extended to women, and then further still.[36] For Lincoln himself, black suffrage became an issue that he addressed publicly only late in his life, and he gave it only very tentative and limited support.[37] Abolitionists were split over the issue, and it was left to black leaders, such as Frederick Douglass, to recognize that "emancipation led inexorably to demands for civic equality."[38]

As Reconstruction actually unfolded, the Fifteenth Amendment developed out of issues left unresolved by the Fourteenth, just as the Fourteenth developed out of attempts to enforce the Thirteenth Amendment. Exactly the same political dilemma that led to Section 2 of the Fourteenth Amendment also led to Section 1 of the Fifteenth: Southern whites would gain power in Congress if they could take advantage of increased representation in the House and, at the same time, disenfranchise black voters. The Republicans first tried to resolve the dilemma by changing the rules on representation, and when that didn't work, they turned directly to the right to vote. Because of the way that Section 2 of the Fourteenth Amendment was framed, it might have diminished representation of Northern states that disqualified male voters on grounds other than race. Moreover, it could be enforced only through the complicated and time-consuming process of reapportionment, which typically occurred only once each decade after the census. And, in fact, it has never been enforced by reducing the congressional representation of any state, even after an abortive attempt to do so following the census of 1870, and later, the census of 1900.[39] As Republicans faced up to the urgency of their political dilemma, especially as resistance to Reconstruction persisted in the South, they overcame their reluctance to sponsor the amendment. In a change of attitude that was as swift as it was definitive, the issue moved from one that could not make it onto the Republican platform at the national convention in 1868 to an amendment approved by Congress in 1869 and ratified in 1870.[40]

The change in legal doctrine could not have been more dramatic. Within a decade, black males had gone from being the object of property rights to gaining the legal status of equal citizens, a change that could be inferred from the Gettysburg Address but was never fully endorsed by Lincoln before his death. Yet it remained an open question just what this transformation accomplished. All the Reconstruction amendments could be evaded by one means or another. Abolition under the Thirteenth Amendment did not apply to "punishment for crime whereof the party shall have been duly convicted." Southern states took advantage of this exception to reimpose slavery through convict labor as punishment for a wide range of crimes, from vagrancy to "criminal suretyship" laws punishing allegedly fraudulent breaches of employment contracts. The Fourteenth Amendment, as we have just seen, framed fundamental rights in the most abstract, and therefore contestable, terms. Equal protection could be interpreted either to allow racial segregation, because it was "separate but equal," or to prohibit it as inherently discriminatory. The Fifteenth Amendment, for its part, did not affirmatively grant any voting rights but simply prohibited any denial of such rights "on account of race, color, or previous condition of servitude." Voting rights litigation has, ever since then, been preoccupied with identifying and prohibiting one subterfuge after another for racial discrimination, from the "grandfather clause" that made it easier for whites than for blacks to register to vote to the "white primary" that excluded blacks from participating in elections that effectively determined who would hold office in states dominated by the Democratic Party.[41] In our day, voter identification laws have been attacked on the same grounds.

This is not to say that the Fifteenth Amendment had no effect whatsoever. The more closely such effects were confined to purely legal consequences, the more innovative the decisions under the amendment appeared to be. Decisions during Reconstruction upheld federal legislation to prohibit private interference with the right to vote, passed under Section 2 of the Fifteenth Amendment and the general power of Congress over federal elections.[42] Superficially neutral attempts to disenfranchise blacks, as in the "grandfather clause" and the "white primary" cases, were struck down as intentionally discriminatory.[43] But it was not until the Voting Rights Act of 1965 that black registration to vote rose above minimal levels in the South. That development involved an irony all its own. Apart from the few cases just mentioned, the Fifteenth Amendment suffered for nearly a century from crippling underenforcement. When voting rights were finally effectively recognized by the Warren Court, it turned to the Fourteenth Amendment rather than the Fifteenth to hand down most of its landmark decisions on reapportionment, the poll tax, and the enforcement power of Congress.[44] Equal protection became the dominant source of law protecting the right to vote. It cured the negative focus of the Fifteenth Amendment solely on racial discrimination and looked to other ways in which the right to vote might be denied. Reapportionment, for instance, benefited white voters just as much, and, in numerical terms, far more than black voters. Under Jim Crow and in the civil rights movement, the Fifteenth Amendment suffered from neglect. When voting rights were largely ignored as too political for the Supreme Court, the amendment predictably received little attention. Yet when the Court finally overcame its reluctance to intervene, the amendment was largely eclipsed by broader principles of constitutional equality found in the Fourteenth Amendment.

To appreciate the genuine influence of the Fifteenth Amendment, it is necessary to step back from the ascertainable consequences that can be attributed to its presence and look at the likely consequences of its absence. In the terms used during Reconstruction, the amendment accomplished a momentous transition: from "civil rights" that primarily protected individuals in their dealings with one another to "political rights" that prohibited discrimination in the processes of government. Supporters of the earlier enactments in Reconstruction emphasized that they did not reach political rights to participate in self-government.[45] The Fifteenth

Amendment crossed this divide—from government "for the people" to government "by the people"—as a matter of constitutional text and legal doctrine, and, over the long term, in the perspective of scores of years, it has to be viewed as a success. It established principles essential to American democracy firmly grounded in the Constitution.

* * *

We can now see that the further constitutional amendments extending the right to vote on the basis of sex and age began from the premises of political equality established by the Fifteenth Amendment, as did the judicial decisions expanding the equal protection clause from the sphere of purely civil rights to political rights. To accept this conclusion is not to take a blinkered, triumphalist view of civil rights but to vindicate what Frederick Douglass saw as the inexorable transition from abolition of slavery to full citizenship regardless of race. Making that transition a reality, rather than simply a formality of legal doctrine, has proved to be anything but inevitable. Events might well have taken a different course, and the course they did take has cost more and lasted longer than anyone expected. On balance, the history of civil rights since Reconstruction inspires something of the same sense of a great victory, narrowly achieved at tragic expense, as Lincoln evoked at Gettysburg.

Conclusion

The Reconstruction amendments also evoke the same commitment to principles of equality as Lincoln did at Gettysburg. What remains imponderable is how those principles would have been implemented under his leadership. All the amendments authorize Congress to enforce their provisions "by appropriate legislation," and Congress acted swiftly, but not without intense debate, to exercise that authority. No policy on Reconstruction would have avoided similar controversy, even if it had been guided by a president who had saved the Union and ended slavery during the Civil War. The policies that Lincoln's commanders established in occupied Confederate territory varied from the precursor of "forty acres and a mule" adopted by General Sherman in South Carolina to the harsh regime of contractual labor imposed by General Butler in Louisiana.[46] Those alternatives reflected choices along only one of the many dimensions in which policy had to be made, and made to work, during

Reconstruction: the terms on which the former Confederate states would be readmitted to "normal relations" with the Union; the role of the Union Army and the Freedmen's Bureau in enforcing federal law and protecting civil rights in the South; and whether the Republican Party could obtain any significant level of political support there, while maintaining its base in the North.

We know such issues of implementation to be crucial to any program of civil rights. We have little idea of how Lincoln would have addressed them, even if he demonstrated a remarkable capacity for growth, acknowledged even by his critics among the Radical Republicans. He signed the Emancipation Proclamation and then the Thirteenth Amendment, even though the constitutional basis for the first was open to question and the Constitution gave him no official role in the second. We can speculate that his support would have extended to the principles of equal citizenship found in the Fourteenth and Fifteenth Amendments, without believing that it was inevitable. Any view of the seemingly inexorable logic of expanding conceptions of equality must be refracted through the fractious politics of assembling a coalition willing to share its power with those who are powerless. Seen in this light, the halting progress of civil rights in Reconstruction and thereafter should come as no surprise. We should, instead, take heart from another phrase of Lincoln's, that we have been touched "by the better angels of our nature."

Lincoln reminded his audience at Gettysburg "to be here dedicated to the great task remaining before us." The Reconstruction amendments accomplished part of that task, as did the civil rights acts of that era and of the twentieth century. Instead of seeing progress toward equality to be inexorable, we might do better to see it as inevitably incomplete. It was Andrew Johnson, after all, who prematurely declared an end to the need for civil rights legislation with the ratification of the Thirteenth Amendment. The Lincoln we know from Gettysburg would not have done so.

Notes

1. 39th Cong., 1st Sess. 474 (remarks of Sen. Trumbull). For a comprehensive account of the many references to the Declaration of Independence during Reconstruction, see Alexander Tsesis, *For Liberty and Equality: The Life and Times of the Declaration of Independence* 179–201 (2012).

2. Eric Foner, *Reconstruction: America's Unfinished Revolution* 35–37, 60–62 (1988).

3. William Gillette, *Retreat from Reconstruction 1869–1879* 5–6 (1979).

4. Proclamation No. 17, 12 Stat. 1268, 1269 (Jan. 1, 1863).

5. Michael Vorenberg, *Final Freedom: The Civil War, the Abolition of Slavery, and the Thirteenth Amendment* 176–210 (2001).

6. Foner, supra note 2, at 215–217.

7. Cong. Globe, 38th Cong., 2d Sess. 144 (1865).

8. Cong. Globe, 38th Cong., 1st Sess. 1465 (1864).

9. Cong. Globe, 39th Cong., 1st Sess. App. 66 (1866).

10. Cong. Globe, 39th Cong., 1st Sess. 1681 (1866).

11. Ibid. at 915–917 (1866).

12. Act of April 19, 1866, § 1, 14 Stat. 27.

13. George Rutherglen, *Civil Rights in the Shadow of Slavery: The Constitution, Common Law, and the Civil Rights Act of 1866*, 49–69 (2013).

14. Cong. Globe 39th Cong., 1st Sess. 570 (1866) (remarks of Sen. Morrill).

15. W. E. B. Du Bois, The Freedmen's Bureau, in *Du Bois on Education* 95 (Eugene F. Provenzo, Jr. ed., 2002).

16. Rutherglen, supra note 13, at 46–49.

17. Cong. Globe, 39th Cong., 1st Sess. at 1758 (remarks of Sen. Trumbull).

18. Ibid. at 1291 (remarks of Rep. Bingham).

19. William E. Nelson, *The Fourteenth Amendment: From Political Principle to Judicial Doctrine* 40–63 (1988).

20. Foner, supra note 2, at 265–267.

21. 39th Cong., 1st Sess. 3349 (1866).

22. Foner, supra note 2, at 254–255.

23. Ibid. at 255–256.

24. Nelson, supra note 19, at 61.

25. Cong. Globe, 38th Cong., 1st Sess. 1482 (1864).

26. Cong. Globe, 39th Cong., 1st Sess. 3148 (1866) (remarks of Rep. Stevens). He later conceded the need for compromise, for instance, on the deletion of specific protections for black voting rights. Nelson, supra note 19, at 52–54.

27. Slaughter-House Cases, 83 U.S. 36 (1873).

28. Civil Rights Cases, 109 U.S. 3 (1883).

29. 163 U.S. 537 (1896).

30. Lochner v. New York, 198 U.S. 45 (1905).

31. 347 U.S. 483 (1954).

32. Mullane v. Central Hanover Bank & Trust Co., 339 U.S. 306 (1950).

33. Cong. Globe, 39th Cong., 1st Sess. 3148 (1866) (remarks of Rep. Stevens).

34. Alexander M. Bickel, *The Original Understanding and the Segregation Decision*, 69 Harv. L. Rev. 1, 63–64 (1955).

35. Michael J. Klarman, *From Jim Crow to Civil Rights: The Supreme Court and the Struggle for Racial Equality* 30–39 (2004).

36. U.S. Const. amends. XIX (sex), XXIV (18 years of age), XXVI (no poll tax).

37. Eric Foner, *The Fiery Trial: Abraham Lincoln and American Slavery* 330–332 (2010).

38. Foner, supra note 2, at 75.

39. George Zuckerman, *Consideration of the History and the Present Status of Section 2 of the Fourteenth Amendment*, 30 Fordham L. Rev. 93, 107–24 (1961) ("No state has ever suffered a reduction in congressional representation through its disfranchisement of adult male citizens.").

40. Foner, supra note 2, at 446, 448.

41. Klarman, supra note 35, at 69–71, 135–141.

42. Rutherglen, supra note 13, at 86.

43. Samuel Issacharoff, Pamela S. Karlan, and Richard Pildes, *The Law of Democracy: Legal Structure of the Political Process* 96–119, 217–248 (4th ed. 2012).

44. Ibid. at 42–48, 126–176, 516–526.

45. Rutherglen, supra note 13, at 52.

46. Foner, supra note 2, at 50–60.

II

Immigration and the Gettysburg Address

NATIONALISM AND EQUALITY AT THE GATES

Alison Clark Efford

THE BODIES OF hundreds of immigrant soldiers would rest in the cemetery Abraham Lincoln dedicated that clear autumn day in 1863. Back in July, some of these men had charged into battle behind emerald-green regimental flags, blessed by Roman Catholic priests; some took their orders in German.[1] One of the German-speaking officers at Gettysburg, General Carl Schurz, corresponded regularly with the president, reminding him that the Union Army relied on the service of hundreds of thousands of immigrant troops.[2] Schurz would go on to become the era's most successful immigrant politician, while another foreign-born general, the Hungarian American Julius Stahel, had a more somber distinction: he was one of the two commanders leading the military procession before Lincoln's famous speech on November 19, 1863.[3]

Represented by men such as Schurz and Stahel, European-born Union soldiers knew that Lincoln meant to include them when he said that the United States had been founded "dedicated to the proposition that all men are created equal." That the president considered them equals went without saying—it was literally unremarked at the time. As immigrants, the soldiers faced a hard enough struggle for economic security and respect to remain vigilant in defense of their rights, but as w̶ acquire a robust form of citizenship. "Free white p̶ naturalize, and some states did not even require th̶ process before they cast ballots.[4] The opportunitie̶ particular immigrants seemed to confirm the fulso̶ founding ideals of the United States that appeared in the Gettysburg Address. Indeed, the men who immigrated from Europe to North America before the Civil War influenced Lincoln, with the president refining his ideas of equality while courting their votes and rebuffing their critics.

Immigrants arriving in the United States since 1863 have, in their turn, sometimes invoked the potent vision that crystallized at Gettysburg. In fighting unjust treatment, they have followed Lincoln in foregrounding equality. Like the wartime president, marginalized newcomers have placed the sweeping ideals of the Declaration of Independence at the heart of their understanding of the Constitution. And immigrants, too, have urged the United States to perform the sleight of hand of transforming itself by dedicating itself to principles unchanged since 1776. These sentiments—although usually not Lincoln's exact words—have had a special appeal to the men of color and women who together have made up the majority of post–Civil War immigrants. Like other nonwhite men, and women of all races, they have recognized the power of the Gettysburg Address precisely because their full inclusion in American life has not been self-evident. The Address itself was ambiguous about what equality meant for people whom the American government had traditionally relegated to an inferior status. Lincoln's wording was broad enough that Americans could easily interpret his "new birth of freedom" to mean the survival of a nation that had always accepted racial and gender discrimination.

Even as the foreign-born shared with many other Americans the experience of grasping at the equality Lincoln heralded, they faced unique obstacles in his military nationalism. Although Lincoln was never militaristic or jingoistic, he asserted the imperative of defending the nation. He firmly believed that the Civil War was necessary in order that an exceptional country might "endure." As a result, he commemorated North America's bloodiest battle by calling for yet more sacrifice in the name of the nation. The whole thrust of the speech was, of course, that national preservation would serve the cause of equality, but as historian David Potter warned, Americans should not assume that Lincoln was right. Writing in the late 1960s, Potter understood that the Gettysburg Address epitomized Lincoln's great fusing of nationalism and equality. Still, the historian worried that this fusion "gave to nationalism a sanction which, frequently since then, it has failed to deserve."[5] The rhetoric of the Civil War president obscured the fact that nationalism could also exclude and marginalize.

The history of immigrant rights since the Civil War makes Potter's case for approaching the nationalism of the Gettysburg Address with caution. Some of the speech's admirers have taken its intense commitment to national defense to be a justification for classifying immigrants as an external threat. If immigrants are outsiders to the state, questions of their equality can be deemed irrelevant. Such thinking was behind the perpetuation of racist naturalization laws and the erection of new restrictions and exclusions, all of which encoded racial injustice anew after the Civil War. Certainly, Lincoln had not contemplated that the United States might become what historian Erika Lee calls a "gatekeeping nation."[6] In 1863, he had intended to bind nationalism to equality, but because he had also been deliberately vague about who was included and what equality entailed, those two strands of the Gettysburg Address could always come apart.

* * *

Before the Civil War, although only white immigrants could naturalize and become American citizens, people of color also entered the United States. The importation of people enslaved was outlawed in 1808, the year before Abraham Lincoln was born in a small Kentucky cabin, but forced migration from Africa and Central America continued clandestinely for decades. Newcomers from other sources increased markedly during the late 1840s. In 1848, with the conclusion of the Mexican-American War, tens of thousands of Spanish-speakers found themselves living in the United States. The inhabitants of conquered Mexican territory were technically eligible for American citizenship, setting a precedent for future immigrants from Mexico, but there were still numerous examples of Hispanic men being stripped of property or prevented from testifying in court.[7] While the US government was solidifying its control of western North America in the late 1840s, Chinese laborers first began to arrive to work the California goldfields. Although not enslaved, they were often subjected to violence and always denied citizenship. In the experience of many immigrants from Africa, Mexico, and China, the words of the Declaration of Independence stood as empty platitudes.

It was a surge of Europeans, however, that was attracting attention to the issue of immigration while Lincoln was representing his Illinois district in the House of Representatives from 1847 to 1849. Irish migration had begun in earnest with the onset of the Great Famine, and it would leave the Irish-born the country's largest immigrant group, over 1.6 million strong, on the eve of the Civil War.[8] Because the Irish were mostly impoverished Catholics, they faced discrimination and even, in isolated cases, exclusion. Massachusetts and New York turned away the occasional pauper, usually Irish, before gatekeeping became a national concern.[9] Anglo-Americans also sometimes expressed their contempt for the Irish in cartoons that depicted them with dark, ape-like features. For all this spite, Irish immigrants were always white enough to naturalize and vote. In Northern cities, they entered politics in force as Democrats who especially valued white supremacy, despised Protestant reforms such as temperance, and thought that tariffs and other federal economic initiatives usually benefited the wealthy and well-connected.[10]

Sizable groups of Britons and Scandinavians also arrived before the Civil War, and they were much more likely than the Irish to agree with Lincoln's Whig and later Republican politics, but a greater number of immigrants came from German Europe. After the war, Germans would overtake the Irish as the largest immigrant group, and they already totaled nearly 1.3 million in 1860. Like the Irish, they moved largely to the North, but a higher proportion of Germans spilled westward and settled in rural areas.[11] If British and Scandinavian immigrants came to antislavery politics through Protestant Christianity and an economic worldview that included a place for the federal government in empowering men to achieve independence, the dynamic in the German-American community was more interesting.[12]

The unsuccessful Revolutions of 1848 helped Lincoln develop a bond with German Americans that would inform the fusing of nationalism and equality in the Gettysburg Address. As Lincoln sat in Congress, revolutionaries across Europe rose up against their hereditary rulers demanding the formation of nation-states governed by male citizens. He welcomed this sign that republican principles were on the march, and when he was back in Springfield in 1849, he led a meeting of local citizens who asked the American government to support their "brethren" in Hungary by recognizing the breakaway republic.[13] Julius Stahel, present at the Gettysburg Address, was one of the Hungarians whose dramatic fight against the Austrian monarchy Americans found particularly captivating. But most of the Forty-Eighters who crossed the Atlantic participated in the German revolts, which authorities more quickly suppressed. Lincoln would work with several of these German-American Forty-Eighters, including George Schneider, who had fought in Bavaria's Rhine Province for a German republic. The future president met the exiled revolutionary after Schneider moved to Chicago in the early 1850s and took a position editing the stridently antislavery *Illinois Staatszeitung*. When the dispute over slavery in Kansas and Nebraska drew Lincoln back into politics in 1854, the two men became allies. Schneider was a member of the Illinois delegation that proposed Lincoln's name as a possible vice presidential candidate at the 1856 Republican National Convention. In a brief speech, he extravagantly claimed, "There is no people more strongly in favor of freedom than the German population of the State of Illinois."[14]

The prospect of winning the votes of the German population of Illinois increased Lincoln's interest in Forty-Eighters. Like other Republicans, he believed immigrants might decide elections in the Midwest. Many secular and Protestant German Americans imbibed the ethos of 1848 and followed the antislavery Forty-Eighters into the Republican Party. The fact that, contrary to Schneider's characterization, the political affiliations of German Americans were far from settled only enhanced the importance of Forty-Eighters in the minds of vote-counting Republicans.[15]

During the 1850s, as he campaigned for the Republican Party and ran for senator against Stephen Douglas, Lincoln angled for German-American support and confronted a vigorous but short-lived anti-immigrant party. As the Whig organization was collapsing under the weight of the Kansas-Nebraska controversy, one of the alternatives to emerge was the nativist American Party. The Know-Nothings, as they were commonly known, opposed "the influence of Popish priests" and "the elevation of foreigners to office", in the words of one New Yorker. Their platforms routinely advocated curbing immigration by making naturalization more difficult and restricting the ability of immigrants to vote or hold public office. The Know-Nothings elected eight governors and over one hundred congressmen before the issue of slavery completely overwhelmed the political landscape a few years later.[16] Encountering their nativist politics would reinforce Lincoln's ideas of equality.

In response to the blaze of anti-immigrant vitriol, Lincoln articulated how immigrants fit into the ideology that he later expressed in the Gettysburg Address. In an 1855 letter to his close friend Joshua Speed he wrote:

I am not a Know-Nothing. That is certain. How could I be? How can any one who abhors the oppression of negroes, be in favor of degrading classes of white people? Our progress in degeneracy

appears to me to be pretty rapid. As a nation, we began by declaring that *"all men are created equal."* We now practically read it "all
men are created equal, *except negroes."* When the Know-Nothings
get control, it will read "all men are created equal, except negroes,
and *foreigners, and Catholics."*[17]

By repeating "equal" in a drumbeat, Lincoln indicated how important
equality was to his politics—even if his nationalism frequently took
precedence in practice. He took the word from the Declaration of Independence, which he and other Republicans somewhat credulously
read as evidence that Americans had appreciated equality more deeply
at the founding than they did in the 1850s. Anticipating his remarks
at Gettysburg, Lincoln suggested that the United States could be re-
formed through rededication to its founding ideals. Unlike his best-
remembered speech, the private comment positioned white immigrants
within his broader understanding of American values. He stubbornly
framed immigration as an issue of equality, resisting any impulse to
distinguish between insiders and outsiders. He must have understood
the nativist position that governments could legitimately control "foreigners" in the United States because they were potential Americans
only and therefore external to the nation, but he saw opposition to immigrants as discrimination pure and simple. Nonetheless, throughout
the passage, Lincoln assumed that immigrants were white. He was sensitive to the oppression of African Americans, but he ignored the fact
that naturalization law had explicitly excluded nonwhite immigrants
from citizenship since 1790.

Lincoln's German-American colleagues presented similar arguments
about immigrant equality—with similar blind spots—more forcefully
and publicly. Carl Schurz was a Forty-Eighter who had arrived as a cocky
twenty-three-year-old in 1852 and would become Lincoln's strongest link
to the German-speaking community. (During the campaign of 1860
Schurz reported to his wife that the Republican presidential nominee had,
probably with some exaggeration, named him "foremost of all" among
his stump speakers.[18]) Drawn to the antislavery politics of the Republicans, Schurz tried to prevent Anglo-Americans in the party from flirting
with Know-Nothingism and alienating immigrants. In 1859, he traveled
to Massachusetts to persuade Republicans there not to back a state constitutional amendment that would require that naturalized men wait two
additional years after becoming citizens before they could vote.

Schurz's "True Americanism" speech in Boston was no Gettysburg Address, but it made comparable points about nationalism and equality from an immigrant perspective. Like Lincoln, Schurz began with the founding, speaking emotionally of Boston's Revolutionary-era history. He wished aloud that "every gate-post" be engraved with the words of the Declaration: "That all men are created free and equal, and are endowed with certain inalienable rights." Any abridgement of the rights of naturalized citizens, he said, would undermine these ideals and endanger the whole American experiment: "A violation of equal rights can never serve to maintain institutions which are founded upon equal rights." Schurz condemned slavery but, again like Lincoln, did not count foreign-born people of color as immigrants. He enumerated the contributions of "the German, . . . the Celt, . . . the Frenchman, the Scandinavian, the Scot, the Hollander, the Spaniard, and the Italian," not the African, Mexican, or Asian.[19]

While Schurz celebrated white immigrants in his 1859 speech, he also extolled nation-states, especially the American Republic, as the best guardians of equality. He provided a firsthand account of the European revolutions that Lincoln had carefully followed in the newspapers. The immigrant maintained that if his comrades had succeeded in establishing a united Germany in 1848 and 1849, he never would have had to leave Europe in the first place. In his mind, Germans lacked a regime of equal rights for the very reason that they lacked a nation-state. When the uprisings were "crushed down again," he said in Boston, "I turned my eyes instinctively across the Atlantic Ocean, and America and Americanism, as I fancied them, appeared to me as the last depositories of the hopes of all true friends of humanity."[20] Lincoln did not need Schurz to convince him that national unity and human rights went together or that the United States was "the last best hope of earth," but immigrants served as a direct tie to the liberal nationalism of 1848 and an affirmation of American exceptionalism.[21]

German Americans continued to shape the Republican Party between 1859 and Lincoln's election the following year. When Massachusetts decided to delay voting rights for naturalized men, the Illinoisan and other Midwestern Republicans spoke out against it.[22] Most of them supported rights for white immigrants in principle, and they sought German-American votes. Lincoln himself tried to improve his electoral chances by purchasing a half share in a German-language newspaper in Springfield in 1859.[23] Delegates at the Republican National Convention in May 1860 elected Schurz to the platform committee and unanimously approved a pro-immigrant plank:

> The Republican party is opposed to any change in our naturalization laws, or any state legislation by which the rights of citizens hitherto accorded to immigrants from foreign lands shall be abridged or impaired; and in favor of giving a full and efficient protection to the rights of all classes of citizens, whether native or naturalized, both at home and abroad.[24]

Antebellum immigrant men from Europe had changed Lincoln and his party, confirming the idea that American nationalism and male equality were naturally linked. On the denial of citizenship to immigrants of color, however, the Republican platform had nothing to say.

* * *

The genius of the Gettysburg Address was to encapsulate the transformation of a war for union into a war against slavery. Early in the Civil War, the president had shown himself prepared to prioritize the survival of the nation over the most elemental forms of equality. For over a year of fighting, Lincoln resisted the prompting of Radical Republicans, including Schurz, to move against slavery. With the preliminary Emancipation Proclamation in 1862, Lincoln declared emphatically—and more credibly—that it was no longer necessary to prioritize; saving the nation was in the interests of equality. As Lincoln scholar Harold Holzer has written, the Gettysburg Address was the poetry to the Proclamation's prose.[25] Claiming that the United States was committed to equality was still disingenuous, since it was unclear what the end of slavery would mean for African Americans, but Lincoln did fuse nationalism to the advance of equal rights.

Lincoln did not survive to grapple with the particulars of equality in the reborn nation, but some Republicans continued to extend its reach during Reconstruction. After the Fourteenth Amendment clarified that all persons born or naturalized in the United States were citizens, the Fifteenth Amendment prohibited states from refusing citizens the right to vote based on race. In 1870, Congress had just proposed the suffrage amendment when Charles Sumner, the formidable Radical Republican senator from Massachusetts, asked his colleagues to strike the word "white" from American naturalization requirements. One senator commented that Sumner's measure was opening up the "Chinese question," but Sumner disagreed: "It simply opens the question of the Declaration of Independence and whether we will be true to it. 'All men are created equal,' without distinction of color." Schurz, by then a senator representing Missouri, supported Sumner's plan.[26] In the end, naturalization law was adjusted, but only to allow black immigrants to become citizens. Asians and other nonwhite immigrants still could not. Thanks to the Fourteenth and Fifteenth Amendments, however, a man born in the United States to Chinese parents would be a citizen eligible to vote. For some years following 1865, many of Lincoln's former colleagues pursued the equalitarian strand of the Gettysburg Address.

It was not long, however, before Congress reaffirmed that racism could decouple nationalism and equality with far-reaching consequences. The United States began its career as a gatekeeping nation a little more than a decade after Lincoln's death when intense animus toward Chinese immigrants in California reached Washington, DC. As early as the late 1860s, public figures would offer dueling interpretations of the ideas contained in the Gettysburg Address. Some commentators would argue that the American commitment to equality made race-based exclusion unconscionable, while others would portray exclusion itself as a natural continuation of the fight to preserve an exceptional nation.

To transform racism and the fear of labor competition into exclusionary federal laws, leaders hostile to Chinese immigration appealed to national security. In typical phrasing, E. L. Godkin worried in *The Nation* about an "influx of a horde of barbarians."[27] Godkin, a Protestant immigrant from Ireland, was not a convinced exclusionist. But he saw the Chinese as uncivilized outsiders who might injure the United States as secessionists had, not as individuals deserving of equal membership in the nation. Some Republicans were explicit about the fact that they believed race had always limited the scope of the Declaration of Independence. Senator William M. Stewart of Nevada thought it absurd that the Declaration be understood to mean that "Chinese coolies, that the Bushmen of south African, that the Hottentots, the digger Indians, heathen, pagan, and cannibal shall have equal political rights under this Government with Citizens of the United States."[28] Stewart clearly had racial objections to these groups, but by stressing their foreignness, he could sidestep the m̲
of racial equality and present himself as a defender of the nation.

had not set the foreign-born apart in this way, but he had devoted himself to national defense.

Stewart's mindset predated the Civil War, but his ideas were much easier to implement in its aftermath. The organizational demands of the massive conflict had increased the administrative capacity of the federal government. In contrast to the Know-Nothings of the 1850s, the opponents of Chinese immigration in the 1870s had a state suited to implementing their designs. Having overseen this expansion and buttressed it with soaring nationalist rhetoric, Lincoln was misguided if he thought that the consolidated nation would necessarily stand for equality.

Still, Lincoln's Gettysburg Address had also inspired advocates of continued migration from China. In 1869, the German-born cartoonist Thomas Nast included a Chinese man in his iconic rendering of "Uncle Sam's Thanksgiving Dinner." The diner, wearing his hair in a long queue, is talking to a woman with her head covered, one of the many individuals of different national backgrounds who have gathered around a large table to share a festive meal. A portrait of Lincoln hangs across from the Chinese man, and Nast has penned "free and equal" in the corner of the image.[29] The politically active cartoonist believed that Lincoln would have opposed Chinese exclusion, a position that found agreement among some other Republicans. When the Republican convention narrowly adopted a moderately anti-Chinese plank in 1876, one delegate specifically denounced it as "a departure from the life and memory of Abraham Lincoln."[30]

Some Chinese Americans used terms like Lincoln's in their own defense. Christian convert Chan Pak Kwai told an audience at a missionary school in San Jose, California, "I like the laws of this country because they give equal rights to all men, great and small, rich and poor, white or black. I like these laws if only they were executed according to their true meaning." He echoed Lincoln—and Schurz—in claiming that the *true* meaning of American laws was inclusive. An excerpt from Chan's speech appeared in an 1877 volume that repeatedly stated that if "all men are created free and equal," then all immigrants should be admitted.[31] Propo-nents of _____ migration took Lincoln's sentiments to support their ____ did not quote the Gettysburg Address itself.

of exclusion in 1875, Congress denied entry to Asian suspected prostitutes. In 1882, it excluded Chinese few exceptions, and that year it took the impor-the entry of all immigrants judged to be crimi-s, lunatics, idiots, and people "likely to become a public charge." Many of these clauses could be interpreted according to the racial and gender bias of immigration officials. Inspectors used them, for example, against single women, whose sexual propriety and earning potential were inevitably in doubt.[32] Gatekeeping was racist and sexist, and it became an accepted part of defining the American nation. More legislation was to follow, but Congress had set in motion an exclusionary apparatus that would be augmented by court rulings and bureaucratic decisions. From 1882 on, national preservation justified a restrictive system that reflected and reinforced various inequalities.

In addition to excluding prospective immigrants, gatekeeping laws constructed the "illegal immigrant," a new category that denied some individuals living in the United States of due process and equal protection and subjected whole communities to surveillance and raids. Race-based law legitimized race-based policing, and Chinese immigrants who had arrived in the United States before 1882 were among the victims. It was risky for them to travel abroad because they might not be allowed to return to the United States even when the law was technically on their side. The catalog of injustices included, after 1909, the requirement that all Americans of Chinese descent carry special identification cards.[33]

Lincoln had not considered using such measures to control a group of foreign-born people. One need not overestimate his practical commitment to "the proposition that all men are created equal" to know that he had not imagined Chinese exclusion. The Gettysburg Address reflected Lincoln's preoccupation with slavery and his appreciation of the inclusion evident in the white, male immigrant experience. Lincoln had, of course, resigned himself to all manner of gendered and racial inequities, and his resolve that the "nation might live" could be turned against outsiders. But explicitly excluding a group of immigrants was a new way to disconnect nationalism from equality. It was a precedent that even white immigrants could not afford to take too lightly.

* * *

Regardless of the legislation of 1882, immigration climbed during the late nineteenth century to hold its own in a growing population. The United States was already 13.2 percent foreign-born before the Civil War, and the proportion was exactly the same in 1920.[34] Small numbers of immigrants from China, entering legally and illegally, were joined by people from Japan until 1907, when a "gentlemen's agreement" between leaders of the two countries cut them off. The movement of people back and forth across the southern border of the United States continued, picking up in the 1910s when Mexico experienced internal disruption. Germans and some Irish, Britons, and Scandinavians still came, but immigrants from farther east and south now outnumbered them. Poles, Slovaks, Czechs, Lithuanians, and others left their homes in the German, Austro-Hungarian, and Russian Empires. Jews from Russia saw some of the greatest upward mobility, while Italians distinguished themselves with high rates of return migration.

Opportunities greeted the latest European arrivals, but so too did renewed anti-immigrant sentiment. The willingness of industrial-age immigrants to do tough work in dangerous conditions for scant pay made them indispensable to economic growth, but it also stigmatized them. That these immigrants were overwhelmingly urban also disconcerted a native-born population that was still largely rooted in small-town life. Courts consistently judged Europeans white enough to naturalize, although citizenship was less valuable to white immigrants now than in the Civil War era. Not only did states repeal noncitizen suffrage, but they also began to erect residency and literacy tests that reduced immigrant voting and possibly dissuaded new residents from bothering to naturalize.[35] By the final decade of the nineteenth-century, organizations such as the Immigration Restriction League were claiming that scientific research proved the inherent inferiority of Southern and Eastern Europeans and arguing for further exclusions.[36] From the 1890s to the 1920s, Americans would actively debate further immigration restrictions.

The power of the Gettysburg Address to expand equality was at a low ebb in the early twentieth century as the United States divided over immigration. During this period, Lincoln's nationalism was more likely to be used to steel Americans against perceived threats from abroad than rally them against the menace of inequality at home. As is well known, the great encampment held on the fiftieth anniversary of the Battle of Gettysburg focused on reconciling white Northerners and Southerners. In 1913, the featured speakers avoided much discussion of emancipation, let alone racial equality. At a time when segregation, disfranchisement, and lynching were ravaging the African-American community, the dignitaries quoted the Gettysburg Address—repeatedly—to stress that the nation "must endure," not that it needed "a new birth of freedom." Another glaring absence was any mention of the sacrifice of white immigrants during the war. The same speakers who downplayed equality often gave potted histories that skipped from the founding to the Civil War without the slightest nod to nineteenth-century immigration.[37] At other events, immigrant veterans and their descendants remembered their participation in the conflict, but such commemorations were a minor part of the early twentieth-century culture of Civil War remembrance.

In this context, the Gettysburg Address became more of a message to immigrants than a story about them. The same speech could be a tool for control as well as an instrument of inclusion, and there was a fine line between the two, as the broader educational campaigns of the Grand Army of the Republic revealed. Although the highly influential organization of Union veterans did not exclude immigrants, and its black members kept alive the memory of emancipation, an Anglo-American sensibility pervaded its work. One of its main arguments for increasing the teaching of the Civil War and military-style patriotic rituals was that they would provide an "antidote" to the potentially destabilizing effects of immigration.[38] In 1904, an adviser at the GAR promised that the instruction he advocated would "counteract the dangerous influence of insubordination to law practised [sic] by the misguided sufferers of oppression who have found an asylum in this country, but not yet impressed that any government is justly administered." Grand Army of the Republic leaders believed immigrants would feel loyal to the United States when they understood that it was "just," but they also fretted about the newcomers' "ungovernable temperament."[39]

The veterans would have approved of foreign-born Americans learning Lincoln's oratory for the fiftieth anniversary. On November 19, 1913, two hundred thousand schoolchildren in Chicago alone recited the Address from memory. Outside the public classroom, three hundred foreign-born adults learned the Address as part of their English lessons at the Chicago Hebrew Institute, and dozens of "polyglot" audiences heard it in translation.[40] The original point may have been to forestall dissension, but the exercises also brought immigrants into a community of Americans. Through mass incantation they owned Lincoln's words: "that we here highly resolve that these dead shall not have died in vain—that this nation, under God, shall have a new birth of freedom—and that government of the people, by the people, for the people, shall not perish from the earth." Immigrants could use these uplifting Americanisms to transform a country that often seemed on guard against them.

* * *

Soon World War I would show just how detrimental military nationalism could be to immigrant equality. If emancipation had infused ideas of national defense during the Civil War, the fear of foreign aggression and foreign ideologies characterized preparations for the Great War. When the United States joined the fight against Germany in 1917, Congress quickly gave legal sanction to popular prejudices by criminalizing disloyal speech. In this environment, German Americans found their privileged place among immigrants questioned, especially if they were socialists or anarchists. A mob lynched German-born socialist Robert Prager in a fit of nationalism in southern Illinois, authorities deported Russian-born anarchist Emma Goldman for her opposition to the draft when the war ended, and prosecutors indicted Austrian-born socialist Victor Berger for his protests—although the heavily German-American population of Milwaukee, Wisconsin defiantly reelected him to Congress.[41]

Apprehensions about Bolshevism in Russia and labor unrest at home carried the anti-immigrant nationalism of war into peacetime. In the Red Scare of 1919, the Bureau of Investigation raided the offices of unions and other left-wing organizations. Most of the postwar strikers were native-born, but Attorney General A. Mitchell Palmer targeted recent immigrants because they could be deported and because he judged radicalism to be a foreign threat.[42] The raids ended quickly in 1920, but restrictionist lawmakers exploited the hysteria, warning of a rush of "undesirable" immigrants from Central Europe. Republican Congressman Albert Johnson predicted "ships coming to Ellis Island with immigrants hanging over the edges."[43] He likened immigrants to military invaders, the clearest way that ideas of national defense could unleash the forces of inequality. Johnson had more in common with Lincoln than it might at first seem: he too spoke of saving the United States from an attack that could lead to its disintegration.

In 1924 Johnson was instrumental in finalizing legislation that essentially prohibited Asian immigration and drastically cut the number of people permitted to enter the United States from Southern and Eastern Europe. That year's Immigration Act barred Asians as "aliens ineligible for citizenship" and finalized an elaborate quota system. A formula based on a statistical gloss of the 1890 census allocated plenty of spots to people from Britain, Ireland, Germany, and Scandinavian countries but limited migration from the rest of Europe and gave miserly quotas to African and Asian countries. Immigration from other parts of the Americas was not subject to restriction, mostly because of the demand for seasonal labor from Mexico, but there were other ways under existing law to exclude Latino and Caribbean men—and especially women—with limited means.[44]

With the discriminatory quotas and ban on Asian immigration in place, another war precipitated a startling episode that demands evaluation in light of the Gettysburg Address. After Japan attacked the American naval base at Pearl Harbor, Hawaii, in 1941, fears of an invasion were directed at Americans of Japanese ancestry, including US citizens who had never visited Japan. Since gatekeeping laws already treated people of Asian descent as interlopers, President Franklin D. Roosevelt faced little opposition when he authorized the expulsion of Japanese Americans from the Pacific Coast. The War Relocation Authority transported over 110,000 people to camps in the interior. Forced detention ripped people from their jobs and businesses, compelling some families to sell property at a loss or default on real estate taxes. Japanese Americans felt betrayed; their constitutional rights had been abrogated because of their ancestry or place of birth.[45]

Japanese-American internment distorted rather than completely disregarded the logic of the Gettysburg Address. Lincoln's speech had moved equality closer to the center of American nationalism, while Roosevelt's action moved it further away. But there was little in the Gettysburg Address to prevent the demands of national preservation—urgently felt—from overwhelming the ideal of equality—imprecisely defined. During World War II, the War Relocation Authority naturally presented internment as a defensive move that was "in the interests of military security."[46] Several facts contradict this contention: no Japanese American was ever found guilty of espionage or sabotage, Japanese Americans living in Hawaii escaped persecution because the islands depended on their labor, and Americans of German and Italian ancestry escaped blanket detention.[47] Given the difference in historical context, it is pointless to guess whether Lincoln would have acquiesced to the singling out of a group of Americans because of their background. Since his death, gatekeeping had legitimated the persecution of Asian Americans. Racist laws and procedures had branded members of this broad group permanently foreign, making the shockingly unequal treatment of citizens of Japanese descent in many respects unsurprising.

Although much had changed since the Civil War, one man thought he knew what Lincoln would have said about internment. Kiyoshi Okamoto, one of the majority of internees who had been born in the United States, led a protest of "our pauperization, our evacuation, our deportation, through military force, our concentration, our detention and, denials to us of freedom, liberty, justice, equity." In a statement circulated in the camp at Heart Mountain, Wyoming, Okamoto quoted Lincoln—not the Gettysburg Address, but Lincoln's First Inaugural. On March 4, 1861, the president had said in passing, "If by mere force of numbers a Majority should deprive a Minority of any Constitutional Right, it might in a moral point of view justify a revolution."[48] Lincoln only gestured to minority rights because he considered that principle irrelevant to the issue at hand, secession. He was dismissing the idea that the majority of Americans who had elected him must capitulate to a slaveholding minority. Okamoto ignored the context and misrepresented Lincoln, perhaps because he thought of Lincoln as an emancipator dedicated to freedom, liberty, and equality. For interned Japanese Americans, Lincoln still represented equality—that other strand of the Gettysburg Address.

* * *

In response to World War II, Congress lifted the ban on nonwhite naturalization and began to make special provisions for refugees, but it was not until the 1960s that there was a wholesale resurrection of the equalitarian Lincoln and a significant rewriting of immigration law. That decade, one hundred years on from the Civil War, African Americans seized opportunities that an official centennial commission missed. Most memorably, Martin Luther King, Jr. reclaimed the Gettysburg Address in his speech at the 1963 March on Washington. Determined to transform the United States by revitalizing old ideals, King anchored his dream for America in Lincoln's promise of emancipation.[49]

The way in which the civil rights movement revived Lincoln's legacy helped encourage immigration reform. Even before 1963, leaders such as Harry S. Truman and John F. Kennedy had campaigned for new laws by asserting a link between nationalism and equality that was somehow both obvious and unrealized. Kennedy first published *A Nation of Immigrants* in 1958, and he was revising it in 1963 when he was assassinated. The text that his brother completed in 1964 described how each wave of immigrants dreamed of equality—not equality of condition, it clarified, but the equality of the Declaration of Independence: "That all men are created

equal . . . [and] endowed by their Creator with certain unalienable rights."
To the Kennedys, the principle of equality was reason enough to lift the
exclusions of 1924.[50]

The landmark Immigration and Nationality Act of 1965 replaced national quotas with preferences for certain workers and the family members of US residents. There were still restrictions: borders were carefully
controlled, and entrance was denied people for reasons that included poor
mental or physical health, ideological heterodoxy, or the risk of becoming
a public charge. Moreover, the annual limit on immigration remained
low, a cap of 20,000 applied to each country, and no more than 120,000
people were allowed in from the Americas. But exempting the immediate
family members of citizens from these caps led to unanticipated chain
migration. In fact, unintended consequences have been the story of immigration law since 1965. Although the act's framers were opposed to
race-based law, they incorrectly assumed that Southern and Eastern Europeans, not Africans, Latin Americans, or Asians, would be the prime
beneficiaries.[51]

With explicit references to race removed from immigration and naturalization law, it seemed that the Gettysburg vision of equality had
triumphed in this aspect of American life. Having survived a series of
trials, the United States was born again with equality apparently ascen-
dant. Immigration diversified after 1965, with border control counting
over 7.1 million Asians and 9.5 million people from Latin America and
the Caribbean arriving between 1970 and 2000. The flow from Africa
picked up in the 1990s, reaching over 350,000 that decade.[52] By 2010,
the proportion of the population born abroad was 12.9 percent, on a par
with 1860 or 1920.[53] When all these newcomers attended school or studied for the naturalization test, they learned American history as Lincoln
told it: national reform through rededication to enduring ideals.

In contrast to the official events of 1913 and 1963, the 150th anniversary of Gettysburg Address featured immigrants. The 2013
commemoration in Pennsylvania vibrated with Lincoln's words celebrating founding ideals, brave men, unfinished work, and rebirth.
It included wreath laying, prayers, music, and over a dozen speeches.
Yet the "emotional highpoint" of the program, according to the
Washington Post, was the naturalization of sixteen new American
citizens.[54] The director of Citizenship and Immigration Services, Ale-
jandro Mayorkas, commented that his parents had brought him from
Cuba as a baby. Now he introduced the candidates for naturalization by

country of origin. The son of an immigrant from Italy, Supreme Court Justice Antonin Scalia, then administered the Oath of Allegiance. At its conclusion, a well-bundled crowd offered up the day's longest ovation, leaving the impression that welcoming immigrants had been the point all along.[55] One of the new Americans, a native of Congo, conveyed the power of the moment: "This feeling of having the freedom and ability to accomplish anything we can in our lives, it's very exciting." She did not parse the Address's nuances, but she was "thrilled" to help preserve its memory.[56]

Yet the Congolese American's enthusiasm belied the struggles of the most recent immigrants. American laws may not mention race, but discrimination continues in other forms, including the governmental failure to recognize the distinctive economic, geographic, and historical relationship between the United States and less wealthy countries in Latin America. For many reasons, the United States receives many more immigrants, especially from its southern neighbors, than the law allows. A system that stubbornly ignores reality has created a population of over 11 million unauthorized immigrants with very few rights. A slim majority of the immigrants without legal authorization are from Mexico, and they are joined by many people from El Salvador, Guatemala, and Honduras. The group contains Europeans too, but the category of "illegal immigrant" is unmistakably racialized. Despite the prejudicial designation, immigrants without authorization are embedded in American life. Some came as children and grew up pledging allegiance to the United States. Most are very closely related to citizens and legal residents. They pay various taxes and attend public schools.[57] But their very existence has been defined as a security breach. Members of this significant population have very limited claim on the founding principles that Lincoln promoted at Gettysburg, and their status has become the leading immigration challenge of the twenty-first century.

* * *

The difficulty in using the Gettysburg Address to resolve the tragedy of "illegality" was on display in a cluster of events in July 2014. That month, Americans became aware that over 60,000 unauthorized and unaccompanied minors from Central America had been imprisoned for crossing the southern border during the previous year.[58] Like 1850s Know-Nothings, post–Civil War Chinese exclusionists, and early-twentieth-century restrictionists, opponents of Latino immigration assumed a defensive posture, holding tiny but impassioned demonstrations across the country. At one protest in Murrieta, California, a woman was photographed wearing a T-shirt reading, "If you can't feed them, don't breed them." Such dehumanizing slogans were accompanied by references to a new "invasion."⁵⁹ The history of gatekeeping made it unremarkable to compare immigrants—even children leaving untenable conditions—to armed combatants.

Also in July 2014, on Independence Day, President Barack Obama held his annual ceremony naturalizing members of the US armed forces and their spouses at the White House. Like European-born Union soldiers at Gettysburg, this racially diverse group of military personnel embodied military sacrifice for the nation. At the event two years earlier, Obama had made observations that Lincoln would have appreciated. The twenty-first-century president had spoken of the "extraordinary audacity" of American independence and recounted how immigrants had contributed to every aspect of the country's history, including taking up arms "to preserve our union" during the Civil War.⁶⁰ In 2014, Obama's speech was more subdued, but he alluded to his efforts to offer unauthorized immigrants a path to citizenship and keep "the door open."⁶¹

The naturalization of military personnel from every continent demonstrated how far the Gettysburg gospel of extending inclusion by recasting founding values had carried the United States. Obama's struggle to reform immigration law marked its limits. Although the president had taken some steps on his own, Congress had resisted authorizing extra funding to process the unaccompanied minors or regularizing the status of undocumented immigrants. A year earlier, the country had seemed to be on the brink of another breakthrough in immigration law, but progress stalled in the summer of 2014.

Ultimately, the Gettysburg Address does not supply easy answers to the immigration dilemmas of the twenty-first century. When politicians such as John Kennedy channeled Lincoln, it was to use the spirit of equality to fight exclusionary laws based explicitly on race or nationality. The burden of illegality is trickier. In 1882, 1924, and 1942, gatekeepers effectively tied the exclusion and imprisonment of immigrants to Lincoln's other priority of national defense. Aspiring immigration reformers might do well to reflect on the reception of the Gettysburg Address over 150 years and note that military nationalism must be handled carefully. It can both spur and hobble human rights.

Notes

1. Susannah Ural, *The Harp and the Eagle: Irish-American Volunteers and the Union Army* (New York: New York University Press, 2006), 166, 163.

2. See letters in Carl Schurz, *Speeches, Correspondence and Political Papers of Carl Schurz*, ed. Frederic Bancroft, vol. 1 (New York: G. P. Putnam's Sons, 1913).

3. Gabor Boritt, *The Gettysburg Gospel: The Lincoln Speech That Nobody Knows* (New York: Simon and Schuster, 2006), 95.

4. Alexander Keyssar, *The Right to Vote: The Contested History of Democracy in the United States* (New York: Basic Books, 2000), 33.

5. David M. Potter, "The Civil War in the History of the Modern World: A Comparative View," in *The South and the Sectional Conflict* (Baton Rouge: Louisiana State University Press, 1968), 298.

6. Erika Lee, *At America's Gates: Chinese Immigration During the Exclusion Era* (Chapel Hill: University of North Carolina Press, 2003), 18.

7. David J. Weber, ed., *Foreigners in Their Native Land: Historical Roots of the Mexican Americans* (Albuquerque: University of New Mexico Press, 2003), 140–160.

8. US Bureau of the Census, *Abstract of the Eighth Census* (Washington, DC: GPO, 1865), 620–623.

9. Hidetaka Hirota, "The Moment of Transition: State Officials, the Federal Government, and the Formation of American Immigration Policy," *Journal of American History*, 99(2013): 1095–1096.

10. David R. Roediger, *Wages of Whiteness: Race and the Making of the American Working Class* (London: Verso, 1991), 133–156.

11. Alison Clark Efford, *German Immigrants, Race, and Citizenship in the Civil War Era* (New York: Cambridge University Press, 2013), 9–11.

12. William E. Gienapp, *The Origins of the Republican Party, 1852–1856* (New York: Oxford University Press, 1987), 424.

13. Timothy Mason Roberts, *Distant Revolutions: 1848 and the Challenge to American Exceptionalism* (Charlottesville: University of Virginia Press, 2009), 55.

14. Republican National Convention, *Proceedings of the First Three Republican National Conventions of 1856, 1860 and 1864* (Minneapolis: C.W. Johnson, 1893), 67.

15. Efford, *German Immigrants, Race, and Citizenship*, 53–85.

16. Tyler Anbinder, *Nativism and Slavery: The Northern Know Nothings and the Politics of the 1850's* (New York: Oxford University Press, 1992), 80, ix.

17. Lincoln to Joshua Speed, Aug. 24, 1855, in *Speeches and Writings, 1832–1858: Speeches, Letters, and Miscellaneous Writings* by Abraham Lincoln (New York: Library of America, 1989), 1:363.

18. Carl Schurz to Margarethe Schurz, Oct. 2, 1860, in *Intimate Letters of Carl Schurz, 1841–1869*, ed. and trans. Joseph Schafer (Madison: State Historical Society of Wisconsin, 1928), 226.

19. Schurz, "True Americanism," Apr. 18, 1859, in *Speeches, Correspondence and Political Papers of Carl Schurz*, 1:58, 65, 56.

20. Ibid., 50.

21. Annual Message to Congress, Dec. 1, 1862.

22. *Manitowoc Wisconsin's Demokrat,* May 1, 1860.

23. Harold Holzer, *Lincoln President-Elect: Abraham Lincoln and the Great Secession Winter, 1860–1861* (New York: Simon and Schuster, 2008), 149.

24. Republican National Convention, *Proceedings of the Republican National Convention Held at Chicago, May 16, 17, and 18, 1860* (Albany: Weed Parsons, 1860), 82.

25. Harold Holzer, *Lincoln: Seen and Heard* (Lawrence: University of Kansas Press, 2000), 180–190.

26. Cong. Globe, 41st Cong., 2nd sess., 5122, 5123 (July 2, 1870).

27. *The Nation,* April 13, 1876, 241.

28. Quoted in Andrew Gyory, *Closing the Gate: Race, Politics, and the Chinese Exclusion Act* (Chapel Hill: University of North Carolina Press, 1998), 54.

29. Thomas Nast, "Uncle Sam's Thanksgiving Dinner," *Harper's Weekly,* Nov. 20, 1869, 745.

30. Quoted in Gyory, *Closing the Gate,* 84.

31. Otis Gordon, *The Chinese in America* (Cincinnati: Hitchcock and Walden, 1877), 191, 125.

32. Mae Ngai, *Impossible Subjects: Illegal Aliens and the Making of Modern America* (Princeton, NJ: Princeton University Press, 2004), 78–80.

33. Lee, *At America's Gates,* 226.

34. Roger Daniels, *Coming to America: A History of Immigration and Ethnicity in American Life* (New York: Perennial, 2002), 124–125.

35. Keyssar, *Right to Vote,* 136–159.

36. John Higham, *Strangers in the Land: Patterns of American Nativism, 1860–1925* (New Brunswick, NJ: Rutgers University Press, 1955), 102–103.

37. Lewis E. Beitler, ed., *Fiftieth Anniversary of the Battle of Gettysburg* (Harrisburg, PA: W.S. Ray, 1914), 95–178.

38. Ibid., 247.

39. *Journal of the Thirty-Eighth National Encampment of the Grand Army of the Republic, Boston, Massachusetts, August 17th and 18th, 1904* (Chicago: M. Umbdenstock, 1904), 262.

40. *Los Angeles Times,* Nov. 11, 1913.

41. David M. Kennedy, *Over Here: The First World War and American Society* (Oxford: Oxford University Press, 1980), 68, 289–290.

42. Higham, *Strangers in the Land,* 226–233.

43. *The New York Evening World,* Dec. 11, 1920, 2.

44. Ngai, *Impossible Subjects,* 21–55, 77, 82.

45. Roger Daniels, *Prisoners Without Trial: Japanese Americans in World War II* (New York: Hill and Wang, 1993).

46. War Relocation Authority, "Relocation of Japanese-Americans," pamphlet, May 1943, Manuscripts and University Archives, University of Washington, Seattle, http://www.lib.washington.edu/exhibits/harmony/Documents/wrapam.html.

47. Daniels, *Prisoners Without Trial*, 30, 46–48.

48. Kiyoshi Okamoto, "We Should Know," unpublished essay, Feb. 25, 1944, available online at http://www.resisters.com/images/WeShdKnow1.jpg.

49. See Ray Arsenault's chapter in this volume.

50. John F. Kennedy, *A Nation of Immigrants*, rev. ed. (New York: Harper and Row, 1964), 68.

51. Daniels, *Guarding the Golden Door: American Immigration Policy and Immigrants since 1882* (New York: Hill and Wang, 2004), 134–137.

52. Paul Spickard, *Almost All Aliens: Immigration, Race, and Colonialism in American History and Identity* (New York: Routledge, 2007), 346, 370, 381.

53. Elizabeth M. Grieco et al., "The Foreign-Born Population in the United States: 2010," US Bureau of the Census, May 2012, www.census.gov/prod/2012pubs/acs-19.pdf.

54. Steve Vogel, "Gettysburg Address Remembered at Ceremony," *Washington Post*, Nov. 19, 2013, http://www.washingtonpost.com/politics/gettysburg-address-remembered-at-ceremony/2013/11/19/3e5fd0c4-5150-11e3-9e2c-e1d01116fd98_story.html.

55. "150th Anniversary of the Gettysburg Address," C-SPAN, Nov. 19, 2013, footage online at http://www.c-span.org/video/?316201-1/150th-anniversary-gettysburg-address.

56. Vogel, "Gettysburg Address Remembered."

57. For a snapshot, see Jeffrey S. Passel and D'Vera Cohn, "A Portrait of Unauthorized Immigrants in the United States," Pew Hispanic Center, Washington, DC, Apr. 14, 2009, http://www.pewhispanic.org/files/reports/107.pdf.

58. David Nakamura, "Number of Unaccompanied Children Crossing Texas Border Dropped Sharply in July, Obama Administration Says," *Washington Post*, Aug. 7, 2014, http://www.washingtonpost.com/blogs/post-politics/wp/2014/08/07/number-of-unaccompanied-children-crossing-texas-border-dropped-sharply-in-july-obama-administration-says/.

59. Leo Hohmann, "Hundreds of Cities Fight Back Against 'Invasion,'" WorldNetDaily, July 15, 2014, http://www.wnd.com/2014/07/hundreds-of-cities-fight-back-against-invasion/; and "Tempers Flare at Immigration Protest in Murrieta," NBC News, July 7, 2014, http://www.nbcnews.com/news/us-news/tempers-flare-immigration-protest-murrieta-n150346.

60. Barack Obama, "President Speaks at a Naturalization Ceremony," the White House, July 4, 2012, footage online at http://www.whitehouse.gov/photos-and-video/video/2012/07/04/president-obama-speaks-naturalization-ceremony.

61. Barack Obama, "President Speaks at a Naturalization Ceremony," the White House, July 4, 2014, transcript online at http://www.whitehouse.gov/photos-and-video/video/2014/07/04/president-speaks-naturalization-ceremony#transcript.

12

Engendering the Gettysburg Address

ITS MEANING FOR WOMEN

Jean H. Baker

THERE WERE ONLY a few women in the audience on November 19, 1863—that famous day in American history when residents joined a procession to Gettysburg's new cemetery, there to witness the consecration of a national burial ground for the dead Union soldiers of the Civil War and the delivery of an address that became, though not immediately, an explanation of the nation's highest ideals. For over a week, everyone in town had known that the president was coming to deliver remarks at the occasion. But following tradition that assigned public places to men, women were not part of the large crowd that greeted Lincoln when he arrived by railroad the night before. They did not accompany him as he walked through town, surrounded by a company of the Invalid Corps and a marching band. Such public events were never perfectly segregated, but still were mostly off limits for respectable females. Instead the women of war-weary Gettysburg leaned out the windows of their homes to wave handkerchiefs and catch a glimpse of their president.

That night, before the next day's bittersweet remembrance of the dead, Gettysburg, according to one reporter, "was in chaos over a new invasion." Crowds flooded into town to join the luminaries: some said as many as thirty thousand had come. "Every housekeeper in Gettysburg has opened a temporary hotel," explained the special correspondent of the *New York Times*. Bands serenaded throughout the night, and, in the town square, the assembled fraternity sang James Gibbons's promise "We are coming, Father Abraham, three hundred thousand more." Emily Souder, a nurse at Camp Letterman Hospital, reported that "the tranquility of the little town was completely broken up."[1]

The next day the official program of arrangements specified that women occupy the right-hand section of the stand and be on the grounds by ten o'clock, for they were not expected to march in the procession to the cemetery. Despite the plans, given the crowd, according to one woman, men took these seats and "there was no place allotted to the ladies." Edward Everett's daughter Charlotte had a reserved place and so did Jennie Wills, the wife of David Wills, the principal promoter of a cemetery and organizer of the consecration ceremony. Pregnant with her fourth child, Jennie Wills had ridden in the carriage with Edward Everett to the cemetery and was no doubt exhausted from tending to the thirty-eight visitors, including the president, who had crowded into her home to spend the night. Soon she would be hosting a reception after the ceremony.

A group of nurses from Camp Letterman, emboldened by their service at the large army hospital on the edge of town, had come. One proudly noted that she was close enough to hear the president's three-minute Address. Two young girls sat on the steps that led to the stands. Sarah Bushman pushed her way through the crowd until she stood thirty feet from the president, whom she later recalled as "a tall awkward figure with one of his trouser legs hitched up on his boot." Still, his speech impressed her: "It goes far to compensate for the horrors of battle."[2] Another remembered sorrowfully walking the grounds before the crowd arrived. "Tears filled my eyes . . . So many of them [the wounded soldiers], I had seen depart to the silent land, so many I had learned to respect and my thoughts followed them."[3] Years later, when it was easy to admire what had become a patriotic text, Mrs. William Sheads, a former nurse at Camp Letterman, remembered the Address as "clear in language, sound in thought and fitted for the occasion, but nothing remarkable."[4]

Most local women had chosen not to come; they were too busy, adhering to the age-old prescription: "A man works from sun to sun / A woman's work is never done." Sarah Rogers explained that she "went up the street and saw the procession going out to the cemetery and then came home to work . . . saw the President and a great many distinguished men but had little time to look at them."[5] A photograph of the parade to the cemetery displays three nuns, probably from the Catholic Sisters of Charity, observing the beginning of the parade as they turn away, to return to their obligations as nurses. Lydia Minter did not attend, she explained in a later interview, because she was not attracted to public oratory.[6] In the traditional division of the sexes—males in public life with intentions of dominating events requiring the participation of the whole community; females in domestic roles focusing on the family—women were not expected to appear at such a ceremonial affair. For the most part, even the women of Gettysburg, empowered as they were by their wartime contributions to the cause, followed the prescription.

According to the rules of common law as expounded in William Blackstone's popular *Commentaries on the Laws of England*, after marriage men and women were one person and he was the one. "By marriage the husband and wife are one in law; that is, the very being or legal existence of the woman is suspended during the marriage or at least is incorporated and consolidated into that of the husband under whose wing, protection and care, she performs everything." In the homely metaphor that Blackstone used to enliven the dry regulations covering the relations of husbands and wives, he compared the married state of women to a small river incorporated into England's larger Thames River: "It loses its sway; it possessth nothing." After marriage a woman was legally covered; the French term "couverture" referred to married women's public invisibility.[7] Such exclusions percolated downward and affected those few women who were not married, the so-called feme sole, or women alone, who never married or who were widows.

These arrangements, many inherited from medieval days, had been assimilated into the laws of every American colony and were continued after the Revolution. In the public world that existed beyond their homes, women could not vote, hold office, serve on juries, or control their own earnings. A woman's husband was the automatic guardian of her children. Represented by their husbands and fathers in civic matters, women had only a marginal presence beyond their homes.[8] While a few women challenged the discriminations of common law—Susan B. Anthony called marriage for women "a regime of servitude"—for most women there was neither reason nor motivation to be engaged in public affairs.[9] And this exclusion—by custom, habit, opinion, and law—would ultimately provide the meaning of the Gettysburg Address for women.

After the Marine Band played the "Old Hundred," Edward Everett began his two-hour oration. He included a detailed description of the Battle of Gettysburg, a history that, one woman complained, the residents of Gettysburg already knew.[10] Then Everett paid tribute to the women of Gettysburg and all Northern women: "The women of the Loyal states if never before have entitled themselves to our highest admiration & gratitude . . . often with fingers unused to toil, often bowed beneath their own domestic cares," they had served in hospitals; they had worked for the US Sanitary Commission, finding in such "homely toils and services" rewards more satisfactory than "those pleasures of the ballroom & the opera house."[11] To modern ears Everett's patronizing dismissal overlooked the range of female experiences both before and during the war and was notably class bound. But the president evidently agreed. In a subsequent exchange of letters, Lincoln applauded Everett's "tribute to our noble women for their angel-administering to the suffering soldiers." The president said nothing about the rest of Everett's speech.[12]

Few civilians in the Union knew better than the women of Gettysburg the reality of what Everett called the war-driven sacrifices of American women. During the summer of 1863, they had first feared the invasion of the Confederates and then endured it. Weeks before the battle, Sallie Broadhead acknowledged her anxiety and apprehension.[13] Yet even after the first Confederate units had drifted into town and insultingly played "Dixie" in the town square, some residents had dismissed the idea that any battle would take place in their prosperous community of 2,400. A more likely place, concluded Fanny Buehler, was nearby Hanover, well known for its shoe factory and grist mills, or the state capital in Harrisburg. Then in early July the battle began. Unlike so many other military engagements during the Civil War that typically took place in rural settings, the town of Gettysburg became a battleground, with civilians under fire, homes transformed into hospitals, food appropriated by hungry soldiers, fields trampled, and livestock confiscated.[14]

One widow found her home taken over by General George Meade and his staff as the headquarters of the Army of the Potomac. Others grabbed their children and took cover from the shelling in stifling cellars, sometimes shared with wounded soldiers. Intrepidly, some tried to protect their livestock with plaintive stories of their family's need. One woman rode out with General O. O. Howard to show him the configuration of the eleven roads whose intersection in Gettysburg had dictated the location of the battle. Another lost her life: on the first day of the battle Jennie Wade was killed by a Confederate sharpshooter while engaged in that most domestic of tasks, baking bread.

No group of women was as threatened by the invasion of a Confederate army as Gettysburg's female African Americans. Sally Myers watched them leave before the battle: "I pity the poor creatures . . . I am glad I am neither a man nor a darkie, though girls are not so much better off." For years Tillie Pierce could see them "with bundles across their backs almost bent to the grave and the greatest consternation depicted on their faces as they hurried along to Harrisburg or Philadelphia."[15] One African-American domestic servant who did not leave was protected by her employer when a rebel soldier tried to kidnap her.[16] In an extraordinary event, local residents freed, from an unguarded wagon, forty black women and children who had been rounded up by Confederates for their return to slavery.[17] Kidnapped into slavery, others, most of whom had been laundresses and domestic servants, never returned. Of the 186 African Americans who had lived in Gettysburg before the war, only 74 were there ten years later.

After the battle the civilians of Gettysburg faced the horrifying prospect of burying thousands of dead soldiers and horses as well as caring for the twenty-seven thousand wounded. Carrie Sheads ran a school for girls in her home on the Chambersburg Pike. Within a week after the battle, she had been transformed into the hard-working lady superintendent of an army hospital. Sallie Stewart announced that the "sight of blood never affected me again" after tending to the soldiers in Camp Letterman for only a few days.[18] Sallie Stewart was only one of a number of women who found themselves drawn into public life, ultimately to find their relationship with the government transformed.

The Gettysburg Address

After Everett's address and the singing of a consecration hymn especially written for the occasion by Benjamin French, President Lincoln rose to deliver his remarks. In time these 272 words would become a much-heralded delineation of American values, and, as such, they would provide a vision for women. To the extent that the Gettysburg Address has been hailed as an American classic, it must be so for all the people. Five times in his short address the president referred to the *nation,* drawing attention in his first sentence to "a new nation conceived in liberty" created by "our fathers." Of course the American Revolution had been a struggle to end British colonialism and was not intended by the founders to be a social transformation. It certainly had not changed the legal position of women or slaves; indeed, Lincoln acknowledged as much when he noted that the United States was *conceived* in liberty, a vision never anticipated to be fixed and certainly not complete. Yet the American Revolution had provided women with the new role of Republican Mothers who, in their maternal capacity, were expected to teach their children the proper understanding of what it meant to be an American and live in a republic without a king. As Linda Kerber has written, "To the mother's traditional responsibility for maintaining the household . . . was added the obligation that she be an informed and virtuous citizen. She was to observe the political world with a rational eye and she was to guide her husband and children in making their way through it . . . But she had no outlet to affect a real political decision."[19]

What the Civil War accomplished for women was to provide possibilities for the future, specifically to temporarily subvert the doctrine of separate spheres, the latter so apparent in women's limited participation at the Gettysburg ceremonies, but not in their devotion to the cause as they confronted war in their community. Indeed, the townspeople of this small town in southern Pennsylvania knew well the supreme sacrifice of "those brave men, living and dead, who struggled here." As female patriots, they had dedicated themselves to the "great test remaining before us" by serving the dead and wounded. As potential for the future, the Gettysburg Address established the possibilities of liberty hedged by Lincoln with the language of maternity—*so conceived*—and then after the test of a civil war, to be established in a new *birth* of freedom. As the expression of Lincoln's long-held view that the nation began in 1776 ("Four score and seven years ago") and that its central vision was expressed in the Declaration of Independence ("all men are created equal"), the Address became a possible manifesto for woman's rights.

Throughout the North, in communities beyond Gettysburg, the war encouraged public acts by women, such as the petitioning undertaken by the Women's Loyal League organized a few months before the Battle of Gettysburg. At the opening meeting of this all-female organization in New York City in May 1863, Elizabeth Cady Stanton invoked a new image of women as citizens of the public sphere. Stanton gave a grace note to domesticity: the mothers who placed their sons on the altar of their country, the nurses of the sick and wounded like Gettysburg's Emily Souder, and the women who knit socks and made jellies for soldiers. But she was mostly interested in the future, extending expectations when she explained that "woman is vitally interested and responsible with men for the final settlement of this problem of self-government . . . the hour is fully come when woman shall no longer be the passive recipient of whatever morals and religion the trade and politics of the nation may decree . . . I ask that you forget that you are women. Forget conventionalisms; forget what the world will say whether you are in your place or out of your place."[20] By 1864 the league had organized a petition to Congress calling for the immediate emancipation of all persons of African descent held to involuntary service or labor. By summer, one hundred thousand signatures had been delivered in an enormous bundle to the office of Massachusetts Senator Charles Sumner. Nearly seven thousand Pennsylvania women had signed what Anthony believed was a first installment in a new birth of freedom that would include women—white and black.[21]

In other communities—Gettysburg was one—women had organized Ladies Aid societies that raised money for the cause through elaborate fairs and gathered homemade goods for distribution on the battlefield. They served as well as agents of the Sanitary Commission, and in their most legendary role they became nurses, while in an extension of their customary roles they became deputy husbands running farms and households. In upstate New York one woman and her daughters brought in a hundred acres of wheat, milked twenty-two cows, made butter and cheese, and still had time and energy to shingle an addition to their home. A few even served as soldiers. Throughout the North women sewed flags, organized relief for distressed widows and orphans, and wrote letters to public officials asking for assistance. One Pennsylvania community sought a charter for a community hall, organized its building, and then used it for meetings. As Rachel Seidman has written, "The war turned work many women had done for their families into patriotic service for the nation and in the process these endeavors gave women a new sense of connection with the nation."[22] Nowhere was this more the case than in Gettysburg, where women sought relief from both the State of Pennsylvania and the federal government for damages to their property suffered during the battle.

After the war fourteen Gettysburg women put in claims for reimbursement from the federal government for everything from broken fences to stolen clothes. In her petition, Julia Hopkins, the African-American wife of the janitor of the Lutheran Seminary, sought damages of $393.35 for lost bedding, quilts, tin buckets, one pair of shoes, and sixty–three chickens. Harriet Krauth asked for compensation for four "good" mattresses, towels, and jars of pickles.[23] As most women throughout the North knew—and none better than those who lived in Gettysburg—service during the war had changed their understanding of sexual politics, modulating the boundaries of what was private and what was public. Neither separated spheres nor the diminished legal agency of females had any reality in the horror of the great battle at Gettysburg. Lincoln's words suggested that they too might have "a new birth of freedom" after the war.

If liberty, according to Lincoln, had only been conceived but not completed during the American Revolution, and if the Civil War offered opportunities for its extension primarily for the African-American enslaved but perhaps for women too, such an unmet pledge was also the case for Lincoln's second proposition: the "new nation brought forth" by the founders was "dedicated to the proposition that all men are created equal." Here, as Garry Wills and others have suggested, Lincoln employed the Declaration of Independence with its natural rights philosophy available for women in their capacity as human beings. The crowd, according to Wills, departed from the blood-drenched fields of Gettysburg not knowing that they had been delivered a conception of government with a new agenda based on the Declaration of Independence. "The Declaration of Independence was closer to being *the* founding document of the United States than the Constitution . . . Everyone in the vast throng was having his or her intellectual pocket picked . . . Lincoln had revolutionized the Revolution, giving people a new past to live with one that would change their future indefinitely."[24] Even at the time, there were complaints that the president had overlooked the Constitution in his emphasis on the Declaration of Independence and its mandate that all men are created equal.[25]

Lincoln's future for the nation was predicated on the principle from Jefferson's Declaration of Independence establishing the equality of all men. Though Lincoln had not quoted the rest of Jefferson's sentence, the self-evident truths included "the inalienable rights of life, liberty and the pursuit of happiness and to secure these rights, governments are instituted among men, deriving their just powers from the consent of the governed."

In 1848, fifteen years before the Battle of Gettysburg and Lincoln's Address, a group of women had met in Seneca Falls, New York, to organize a woman's movement. Their Declaration of Rights and Sentiments was modeled on the Declaration of Independence. Its authors understood that there was little in the US Constitution that would serve as a catalyst for feminist principles of equality. Like Lincoln, these women believed that the American Revolution promised but had not delivered liberties to all. Like Lincoln, who had the abolition of slavery on his mind, they believed that the nation had been conceived to install these freedoms. In their belief half the population had been denied them not because of their race, but because of their sex. Lucy Stone, one of the leaders of the early women's movement, had begun her journey to women's rights by arguing against slavery. Soon she made the connection of what Southerners called "the peculiar institution" to her own diminished status as an American woman. And to the irritation of the males who presided over the antislavery movement, she was, she announced defiantly, a woman before she was an abolitionist.

In the second paragraph of their Declaration Elizabeth Cady Stanton revised Jefferson's words to read: "We hold these truths to be self-evident: that all men *and women* are endowed by their Creator with certain inalienable rights and that among these are life, liberty and the pursuit of happiness and to secure these rights governments are instituted, deriving their just powers from the consent of the governed."

Next, in the Declaration of Rights and Sentiments, came the indictment of men, and through these charges a description of the contemporary discriminations against women—among them, the closure of nearly all colleges to women, the legal discrimination that made her civilly dead, the failure to allow women to control their wages, the exclusion of women from the professions, the different code of morals for men and women, the destruction of women's self-respect and self-confidence, and the denial of the suffrage. Women were, in a phrase borrowed from Blackstone, "civilly dead," and so this convention of women and some men, including Frederick Douglass, resolved that "all laws which . . . place her in a position inferior to man are contrary to the great precept of nature and therefore are of no force or authority." As Lincoln proclaimed the need for commitment to the dead and through such devotion to the great task ahead of a "new birth of freedom," so years before the dedicated women of Seneca Falls had entered "upon the great work before us . . . We shall use every instrumentality within our power to effect our object."[26]

For increasing numbers of these female activists, though their numbers then and now would remain small, the principal task was to gain the vote, and hence Lincoln's commitment in the final line of the Gettysburg Address that "a government of the people, by the people, for the people, shall not perish from the earth" reaffirmed one of their primary goals.

After the War

The visions presented by Lincoln in the Gettysburg Address, by the Founding Fathers in the Declaration of Independence, and by the founding mothers in the Declaration of Rights and Sentiments were words, powerful in their eloquent statements of intentions. But as President Barack Obama recently recognized, "self-evident truths are not self-executing." In the period after the Civil War, women tried to seize the opportunity to obtain the vote. In the beginning of their crusade they had examined and excoriated many of the discriminations practiced against them. In some states before the Civil War, they had been successful in lobbying legislatures to pass Married Women Property Acts, whereby women could control their inheritances. But after the war, they singled out the vote as the focus of their attention. It was, they believed, the essential act of American political identity and ever the most precious of liberties in the national political culture.

A necessary transaction in any democracy between the people and those to whom they delegate authority, suffrage emerged in the postwar period as both a powerful symbol of equality with men and a lever to obtain the necessary reforms to achieve equality. If women could vote, went the argument, they could end barriers that prevented women from serving on juries or attending public universities or controlling their wages. If women could vote as the acknowledged guardians of their homes, then they could reform the corrupt practices of American party politics. If women could vote, then they could end the unequal pay that made them work at the same jobs as men but earn less. If women could vote, then their wartime sacrifices would be acknowledged.

Ever a blunt instrument, the vote was nevertheless essential if women were ever to gain equality with men. As Elizabeth Cady Stanton had recognized years before the postwar campaign for women's suffrage, "Man must know the advantage of voting for they all seem very tenacious about the right . . . Had we not a vote to give might not the office holders and seekers propose some change in woman's condition?"[27] Otherwise they were in the same civic category as children, lunatics, and idiots; in fact, the Greek origin of the word "idiots" referred to those who did not participate in public affairs. Even those men who came to the United States as immigrants had more rights than they. "President Lincoln's proclamations are a dead letter unless backed up by the immortal declaration, 'All men are created equal.'"[28]

Women activists had never been admirers of Lincoln and hence paid little specific attention to his Gettysburg Address. Rather it was the shared principles of self-government and equality from the Declaration of Independence on which they based their movement. In the judgment of Stanton and Anthony, Lincoln had been far too dilatory in freeing enslaved Americans, and, even lacking the vote, they had supported his opponent John C. Fremont in the presidential election of 1864. Like Frederick Douglass, who saw in the Declaration of Independence a necessary doctrine for emancipation, they complained of a weak administration that permitted "our most sacred rights to drift away."[29] Yet it was Lincoln who in the Gettysburg Address facilitated the incorporation of the Declaration of Independence into mainstream views. The president had raised the Declaration to an essential national document, far beyond its time-bound vindication of the Revolution.

In 1866, after the ratification of the Thirteenth Amendment abolishing slavery, the US Congress began formal discussions that resulted in the Fourteenth and Fifteenth Amendments. These additions to the Constitution were intended to protect African Americans, an especially important consideration as the white South moved to pass Black Codes returning freed slaves to peonage. Federal protections were also necessary to assure the political power of the Republican Party. A defeated white Confederacy that denied black men the right to vote but benefited from the Constitution's new definition of slaves as five fifths of a person would automatically increase the representation of the former Confederacy in the House of Representatives. The solution for this problem, in a sea change of power resulting from the war, no longer rested with the states but with the federal government.

For the most part, the argument for female inclusion in politics made during Reconstruction was based on the natural rights philosophy delineated by Lincoln in the Gettysburg Address and by the feminist leaders at Seneca Falls in the Declaration of Rights and Sentiments. Their practical connection was based on the similarity of women's civic circumstances to those of freed blacks. Susan B. Anthony argued that "disenfranchisement in a republic is as great an anomaly, if not cruelty, as slavery itself. It is therefore the solemn duty of Congress in guaranteeing a republican form of government to every State of this Union to see that there be no abridgement of suffrage among persons responsible to law on account of color or sex."[30]

Besides their references to the equality promised by the Declaration of Independence, the women of this period found in Section 4 of Article IV of the Constitution a possible additional claim for their inclusion: this section guaranteed to every state a republican government. By denying women their public rights, and especially that of choosing their representatives and thereby delegating to them the sovereign authority of the people, the federal government was acting illegally by violating the constitutional promise of a republican government.

When Congress began to consider amendments to the US Constitution that would protect the civil rights of freed blacks, Elizabeth Cady Stanton and Susan B. Anthony hastened to Washington to begin their lobbying of hostile congressmen. They were the leaders of the only group in the nineteenth century who did not have significant support in Congress and who were forced to work alone and outside the legislative halls in their efforts to get the ballot. Other disenfranchised groups, from propertyless white males in the early nineteenth century to black males after the Civil War, had benefited from the support of those in power. As the war ended, activist women had been dismayed when, during a meeting of the American Equal Rights Association, their male colleagues had called for land, the vote, and guarantees of citizenship for African Americans but had made no mention of women. As Susan B. Anthony wrote a friend, "The hour of adjustment of reconstruction is coming and it is our duty to educate the people to demand justice as the first—the chief cornerstone."[31]

According to Wendell Phillips, whom this first generation of feminists had previously counted as an ally, "One question at a time. This hour belongs to the negro"—to which the acerbic Elizabeth Stanton responded, "Do you believe that the African race is composed entirely of males?"[32] Frederick Douglass, another former ally, now employed graphic rhetoric to sever the connection between black men and all women. Black men were hunted down, dragged from their homes, and hung from lampposts. Only when women were lynched would they have the credibility to demand rights equal to black men, sentiments that entirely overlooked the sexual violence against black women.[33]

Despite such disappointments, the insistent Stanton was convinced that the time had come "to bury the black man and the woman in the citizen." Using their only weapon—what one historian has called "signatures of citizenship," they gathered signatures on a petition for universal suffrage and tried to convince a hostile Congress to support women's suffrage.[34] Soon they would discover that petitions were not sufficient, and they organized a newspaper called *The Revolution*.[35]

The most that can be said of their campaign in 1866 and 1867 is to suggest that advocates of women's suffrage prevented a retrograde effort by Congressman Thomas Jencks of Rhode Island to amend the Constitution by restricting voting for federal offices to literate male citizens. In fact the final version of the Fourteenth Amendment, today's pillar of American liberties, offered possibilities for women in its first section that all persons born or naturalized in the United States "are citizens of the United States and of the State wherein they reside." This first section denied states the right to deprive any person or life, liberty, or property without due process of law; and in its final clause prevented government from denying to any person equal protection of the law. Surely, argued the women, to deny the franchise to a class of adults abrogated the equal protection of the laws.

Here was potent, actionable language that might be used by women to claim their equality with men in so far as elemental rights—and avenues toward equality such as suffrage—were concerned. Later courts would agree; a century after the Civil War, applications of due process and equal protection under the law, as well as interpretations of the privileges and immunities clause, became the means to constitutionalize women's rights and thereby enhance their civil liberties. But this advance took time. Those in power in the latter part of the nineteenth century still held to their federalist principles of state authority over suffrage.

In the second section of the Fourteenth Amendment, for the first time in the history of the Constitution, the exclusionary word "male" appeared. Stanton accurately predicted that once the word "male" was introduced into the Constitution it would take years to remove it. This section, which was never applied, dealt with the need to reduce congressional representation if former Confederate states prevented black males from voting. With black males now counted as full persons by the Thirteenth Amendment, the white Southern Democratic Party stood to increase its representation in Congress by as many as twenty-five seats. Republicans needed to ensure that blacks voted and that white Democrats did not gain these seats in Congress.[36] But for women the second section of the Fourteenth Amendment was a damaging, humiliating reversal. Now the US Constitution had been explicitly masculinized; the potentially gender-neutral language of "persons" and "We the People" had been replaced. "Do you see what the sons of the Pilgrims are doing in Congress?" complained Elizabeth Cady Stanton. "Nothing less than trying to get the irrepressible 'male citizen' into our immortal Constitution."[37]

To be sure, the Fourteenth Amendment proved an insufficient protection for blacks in the South, thus affording women a further opportunity for inclusion. Congress, controlled by a Republican Party whose partisan motives coincided with its egalitarian commitment to expand black male rights, created a new amendment. The Fifteenth Amendment did not affirm the right of blacks to vote; its negative language only barred states from making race a qualification for suffrage. Still, activist women hoped to include sex along with race. "We demand in the reconstruction suffrage for all the citizens of the Republic. I would not talk of negroes or women, but of citizens."[38] Yet despite their hopes, Anthony and Stanton, the leaders of the newly created National Woman's Suffrage Association, failed to persuade Congress to broaden the scope of the Fifteenth Amendment, which was ratified in 1870. They also failed in their efforts to gain congressional support for a Sixteenth Amendment. Even in this time of Republican legislative super-majorities, the resolution for a subsequent amendment—dubbed the Susan B. Anthony amendment—was regularly tabled or defeated in the Judiciary Committees of both the House and Senate until 1887 and was defeated on the floor of the House and Senate until 1917.

Thus the intentions of the Gettysburg Address and its proposals for equality remained unfulfilled for women. The law remained wholly masculine, created and executed by men. Certainly Republican congressmen had expanded the limits of citizenship to include black males and in the process had enlarged the scope of the national government in order to guarantee, at least on paper, new liberties. At the same time, the Civil War had exposed women to the public domain beyond their homes and had raised their expectations. But Congress had fallen short of extending any entitlements to women.

Undeterred, activist women moved in other directions to achieve the practical definition of equality that suffrage represented. On November 2, 1872, Susan B. Anthony led her three sisters and a few other women to the polls located in her ward in a barbershop in Rochester's Eighth Congressional District. There, the women handed their paper ballots to election officials who, after checking their registration rolls, accepted the votes. In this presidential election these Rochester women were not the only females exercising what they considered their right of citizenship, delivered in the Fourteenth Amendment. Along with Anthony, hundreds of American women—in New Jersey, St. Louis, and the territory of Washington—took to the streets to vote. In their gloss on the patriotic theme sung in Gettysburg in November 1863, they sang, "We are Coming Uncle Sam, with 15 million more." Some women succeeded in having their votes counted; others watched as election judges tore up their paper ballots. Only Susan B. Anthony was arrested, arraigned, and indicted for the federal offense of illegal voting.

For the women's movement, the arrest was an opportunity to showcase their quest for civic equality. Anthony hoped to provide the women's movement with a judicial target similar to the infamous *Dred Scott* decision of 1857. "Is it a Crime for a United States Citizen to Vote?" she asked. As Anthony informed the magistrate after her arrest, she had cast her ballot not as a woman but as a citizen. With the first clause of the Fourteenth Amendment as her evidence, Anthony asked: If women were not citizens, then what were they? Surely, responded Anthony, they were not minors nor aliens nor idiots nor felons. And slavery had been outlawed. Faced with this conundrum, some men answered that they were not persons, thus placing all women in a new category of demotion.

The federal judge hearing the case was not impressed with the defendant's arguments; the jury played little role in the trial of the *United States v. Susan B. Anthony*. In fact this dignified, bespectacled, gray-haired matron who hardly seemed a threat to the Republic was only permitted to speak after the directed verdict of guilty and after she had been fined one hundred dollars and court costs. In the struggle for equality, Susan B. Anthony had become a convicted felon subject to six months' imprisonment.

When she could finally speak, with the judge telling her to sit down six times, Anthony referred to the ideas presented in the Declaration of Independence, the Gettysburg Address, and the Declaration of Rights and Sentiments. She noted the denial of her right of consent as one of the governed, the denial of her right of representation as one of the taxed, and the denial of her right to a trial by a jury of her peers. Therefore, in the refrain of American women's quest for equality, the court had denied her "sacred rights to life, liberty, property." Henceforth, when she spoke to audiences, Anthony personified the suffrage crusade: "I stand before you as a convicted criminal," she proclaimed.[39] But what she called "the aristocracy of sex" wanted no publicity from this trial, and on technical grounds she was refused the right to appeal her conviction.

Now the women turned from their new departure of seizing the vote as citizens to the courts. The first case involving women's suffrage to reach the Supreme Court involved Virginia Minor, who had been denied the right to vote in St. Louis. Her suit against a registration official in Missouri was addressed by a unanimous court in the 1875 decision of *Happersett v. Minor*. In refusing her a ballot (unlike the registrars in Anthony's Rochester), the local official simply dismissed her with what he believed a sufficient explanation: she was a woman. She was not a male citizen.

Minor's lawyers—who included her husband—based their case on the Fourteenth Amendment. They argued that the citizenship and privileges and immunities clauses guaranteed her right to vote, which had been violated by the state of Missouri.

They did not argue, as a twentieth-century attorney might have, that the plaintiff had been denied equal protection of the law. Attorneys of this postwar generation, writes historian Leslie Goldstein, "viewed the equal protection and due process clauses as clauses about the way the laws should be applied rather than about the limits upon the content of the laws. Twentieth-century activists believed that the privileges and immunities clause was really the forceful mechanism that shielded the basic civil rights of Americans from potentially oppressive state legislation."[40]

Instead, Minor's attorneys found other constitutional grounds for their suit. They argued that female disenfranchisement constituted a collective bill of attainder applied unfairly to all members of a named group, thereby imposing guilt on the basis of who people were (that is, women) rather than on any act they had committed. Preventing women's suffrage also violated the free speech clause of the First Amendment. They invoked the Lincoln-supported Thirteenth Amendment that prohibited involuntary servitude. To be denied the vote in a representative democracy—a government of the people, by the people, and for the people—was a violation of free speech and tantamount to servitude. Moreover, such violations of civil rights compromised their freedom. No longer could the United States make the claim that it was a republic as promised in Article IV of the Constitution.

A unanimous court disagreed. In its view citizenship carried no voting privileges. Nor did the Fourteenth Amendment add to the privileges and immunities of a citizen. Certainly it created no new voters, according to Chief Justice Morrison Waite. The United States had no voters of its own, and women had not been voters in Missouri. "The Constitution of the United States," continued the Chief Justice, "does not confer the right of suffrage upon anyone." Still, the court spent some time in its fourteen-page decision arguing that the United States was still a republic, even if half its population was voiceless.[41]

There were other judicial defeats as women struggled in the postwar era to achieve the equality promised in the Gettysburg Address. In 1872 an Illinois lawyer, Myra Bradwell, who had fulfilled all legal requirements for the bar, was denied admission to the Illinois Supreme Court. That court ruled that as a married woman under the marital common law of couverture, she had none of the autonomy of person and independence of judgment required of attorneys. Any contract she signed could be challenged given her necessary submission under Blackstonian common law to her husband's legal dominion. According to Justice Bradley in an opinion that has earned a place in American history as a classic statement of the durability of couverture: "Man is and should be women's protector and defender. The natural and proper delicacy that belongs to the female sex evidently unfits it for many occupations of civil life . . . The paramount destiny and mission of woman are to fulfill the noble and benign offices of wife and mother."[42]

Four years later, during a year that saw the federal government's efforts at Reconstruction falter and in subsequent years wither away, the suffrage women of America issued a Woman's Declaration of Independence. The occasion was the celebration in Philadelphia of the nation's centennial in July 1876. Its authors noted, as Lincoln had, the unfinished nature of America's experiment in self-government. Like Lincoln they proclaimed their faith in the nation's historic commitment to "broad principles of human rights" as enunciated in the Declaration of Independence. These were not abstract truths but rather were unfulfilled cornerstones of the Republic.

> While all men of every race, and clime and condition have been invested with the full rights of citizenship . . . all women still suffer the degradation of disenfranchisement . . . We ask of our rulers . . . no special favors, no special privileges, no special legislation. We ask justice, we ask equality, we ask that all the civil and political rights that belong to citizens of the United States be guaranteed to us and our daughters forever.[43]

It would be almost another half-century before women gained the right to vote, and the ballot was no panacea for the equality feminists continued to pursue after the ratification of the Nineteenth Amendment in 1920. Like Lincoln they had found the Declaration of Independence to be a basic primer of democracy. They had followed Lincoln's prescription to dedicate themselves to what would remain in the twenty-first century the unfinished business of political equality for women. And they had "highly resolved" to strive for a new birth of freedom based on the democratic principles of government of, by, and for the people.

Notes

1. Gabor Boritt, *The Gettysburg Gospel: The Lincoln Speech That Nobody Knows* (New York: Simon and Schuster, 2006), 73, 85.

2. Sarah Bushman Recollections, Gettysburg Address folder, Adams County Historical Society, Gettysburg (hereafter ACHS); *New York Times,* Nov. 21, 1863.

3. Sophronia Bucklin, *In Hospital and Camp* (Philadelphia: John E. Potter and Company, 1869), 192–193.

4. Mrs. William Sheads, handwritten notes, Gettysburg Address Notes, ACHS.

5. Sarah Rogers, *The Ties of the Past* (Gettysburg: Thomas, 1996), entry for Thursday, Nov. 19, 1863.

6. Mrs. Minter, Personal Accounts of the Battle of Gettysburg, ACHS.

7. Blackstone quoted in Jean H. Baker, *Women and the US Constitution, 1776–1920* (Washington, DC: American Historical Association, 2009), 6.

8. Ibid., 5.

9. Elizabeth Cady Stanton, Susan B. Anthony, and Mathilda Gage, *History of Woman Suffrage* (Rochester, NY: Charles Mann, 1889), 2:455–456 (hereafter Stanton et al., *History of Woman Suffrage*).

10. Fannie Buehler, "Recollections of the Rebel Invasion," Personal Accounts of the Battle of Gettysburg, ACHS.

11. Boritt, *Gettysburg Gospel,* 223.

12. *Collected Works of Abraham Lincoln,* ed. Roy P. Basler, 9 vols. (New Brunswick, NJ: Rutgers University Press), 7:24–25.

13. Sallie Broadhead, Personal Accounts of the Battle of Gettysburg, ACHS.

14. Robert Bloom, "We Never Expected a Battle: Civilians at Gettysburg," *Pennsylvania History* 55 (Oct. 1988): 161–200.

15. Tillie Pierce, Personal Accounts of the Battle of Gettysburg, ACHS.

16. Unknown file, A Colored Servant Maid's Account of the Battle of Gettysburg, ACHS.

17. Boritt, *Gettysburg Gospel,* 24–25.

18. Salome (Sallie) Myers Stewart, Recollections of the Battle of Gettysburg, ACHS.

19. Linda Kerber, *Women of the Republic* (Chapel Hill: North Carolina Press, 1980), 235.

20. *The Selected Papers of Elizabeth Cady Stanton and Susan B. Anthony,* ed. Ann Gordon (New Brunswick, NJ: Rutgers University Press, 1997), 1:492 (hereafter cited as *Selected Papers*).

21. *New York Times,* May 14, 1863.

22. Rachel Seidman, "Beyond Sacrifice: Women and Politics on the Pennsylvania Homefront During the Civil War" (PhD diss., Yale University, 1995), 6.

23. Timothy Smith, Border Damage Claims Filed by Residents of Adams County, ACHS.

24. Garry Wills, *Lincoln at Gettysburg: The Words That Remade America* (New York: Simon and Schuster, 1992), 130, 38.

25. See for example the *Chicago Times*, Nov. 23, 1863.

26. Quotes from 1848 Declaration of Rights and Sentiments.

27. *Selected Papers*, 1:106.

28. Ibid., 1:520.

29. Ibid., 1:524.

30. Stanton et al., *History of Woman Suffrage*, 2: 154.

31. *Selected Papers*, 1:501.

32. Ibid., 1:549.

33. Ibid., 1:549; Stanton et al., *History of Woman Suffrage*, 2:382, 383.

34. Susan Zaeske, *Signatures of Citizenship: Petitioning, Antislavery and Women's Political Identity* (Chapel Hill: University of North Carolina Press, 2003).

35. *Selected Papers*, 2:153, 174.

36. Baker, *Women and the US Constitution*, 30.

37. *Selected Papers*, 1:568.

38. *Elizabeth Cady Stanton As Revealed in Her Letters,* Theodore Stanton and Harriot Stanton Blatch (New York: Arno, 1969), 120.

39. Jean H. Baker, *Sisters: The Lives of the American Suffragists* (New York: Hill and Wang, 2005), 81–87.

40. Leslie Friedman Goldstein, *The Constitutional Rights of Women* (Madison: University of Wisconsin Press, 1988), 67.

41. Quote and commentary from Baker, *Women and the US Constitution*, 34–35.

42. Quoted in Goldstein, *Constitutional Rights of Women*, 70–1.

43. *Selected Papers*, 3:234, 239.

13

The Gettysburg Address
and Civil Rights

Raymond Arsenault

THE CONCEPT OF civil rights has deep historical and rhetorical roots. When civil rights leaders seek to inspire their followers, they often rely on historically coded phrases, words laced with meaning because they have been borrowed from the past. The Reverend Martin Luther King, Jr., for example, reached back to the 1863 Gettysburg Address in the opening paragraph of his famous "I Have a Dream" speech, delivered at the Lincoln Memorial on August 28, 1963. In referencing the Emancipation Proclamation of January 1863, he could have used the normative phrase "one hundred years ago." But instead he declared: "Five score years ago, a great American, in whose symbolic shadow we stand today, signed the Emancipation Proclamation." Many of those in the audience immediately sensed what he was doing; they knew that Abraham Lincoln himself had begun his most famous speech, the Gettysburg Address, with the immortal words "Four score and seven years ago." With a simple turn of phrase, King had connected his speech to the rhetoric and ideals of the Great Emancipator.

The lesson here is clear: words, phrases, and the ideas they convey matter—especially when the author or speaker is able to combine wisdom and rhetoric with human striving and a timely delivery. This simple proposition lies at the heart of Garry Wills's eloquent Pulitzer Prize-winning study, *Lincoln at Gettysburg: The Words That Remade America*. As Wills would have it, when Lincoln memorialized the battlefield at Gettysburg in November 1863, he effected no less than a "revolution in style" and a "revolution in thought," transforming the "United States" from a plural to a singular noun.

Advancing the concept "of a single people" dedicated to equality by repurposing the words of the Declaration of Independence, Lincoln's Gettysburg Address created a vision of democratic nationalism that eclipsed all other interpretations of the nation's founding documents. That it did so with an extreme economy of words—272 in all—is, of course, a marvel. Indeed, the length of the address is out of all proportion to its impact. Because President Lincoln uttered the words that he did, Wills writes persuasively, "we live in a different America."[1]

That America is, among other things, a land where traditions of racial discrimination and inequality are embattled—where succeeding waves of activism crash against the beachheads of oppression and bigotry. During the century and a half since Lincoln's oration at Gettysburg, the political institutions and social and economic mores of a nation once shrouded in chattel slavery have been exposed to a vital and indomitable force generally known as the American civil rights movement.

While there is general agreement about the significance and importance of the American civil rights movement, exploring its origins and evolution has grown increasingly complicated and contentious in recent decades. Problems of definition and emphasis abound. Many scholars now classify the civil rights movement as a subset of a larger African-American freedom struggle; others distinguish between the neo-abolitionist activism of the late nineteenth century and the "modern civil rights movement" of the twentieth century; and still others reserve the "civil rights movement" designation for the "classical" phase of activism from 1954 to 1968, which in turn is often seen as the catalyst for a broader "rights revolution" that came to maturity in the 1970s and beyond. Indeed, since the emergence of movements focusing on the liberation of oppressed groups other than African Americans—Hispanics, Asian Americans, Native Americans, women, the LGBT community, and the physically disabled—it has become fashionable to argue about the length, width, and depth of "the movement."[2]

How any of this relates to the ideological revolution initiated by the Gettysburg Address remains a puzzle, largely because civil rights scholars have been hesitant to enter the dense thicket of intellectual history. One of the few intellectual historians to root around in the dark recesses of the civil rights movement as it relates to the history of ideas is Richard King, the author of *Civil Rights and the Idea of Freedom*. King is both a talented historian and an accomplished student of philosophy and political theory. But unfortunately, his book makes no mention of the Gettysburg Address, and it includes only two brief references to Lincoln, plus one slight reference to the Lincoln Memorial.[3]

The Gettysburg Address itself, like King's book, is striking for what is absent from the text. As Wills has written, "for all its artistry and eloquence," Lincoln's most famous speech "does not directly address the prickliest issues of the historic moment." There is no mention of "slavery" or "emancipation" or even the "Union" that Lincoln held so dear. Most important, for our purposes, the term "civil rights" is nowhere in sight, and very few of the terms closely associated with civil rights are in evidence. Driven as much by ideas as by material circumstances, the American civil rights movement produced a rich lexicon of meaningful words and phrases: racial equality, social justice, voting rights, nonviolent direct action, movement culture, freedom songs, and Black Power, just to name a few. If any of this lexicon was known to Lincoln in 1863, there is no evidence of such knowledge or awareness in the Gettysburg Address.[4]

Yet this linguistic, and perhaps even thematic, disjunction does not rob the Address of its foundational meaning for the civil rights movement. What the Address lacks in specifics is more than made up by a bold declaration of equality. The proposition first enunciated in the Declaration of Independence, "that all men are created equal"—a proposition as frequently forgotten as it was violated during the first eighty-seven years of the Republic—has become, in Lincoln's closing words, "the great task remaining before us . . . that this nation, under God, shall have a new birth of freedom—and that government of the people, by the people, for the people, shall not perish from the earth." Here there are no caveats, no limiting qualifications, just an uncomplicated and glorious assertion of democratic promise.

Can there be any doubt that this redefinition of citizenship, wrapped as it was in the mystique of blood sacrifice and a just war, helped inspire the later struggle for civil rights? I don't think so. And yet, we are still left with the problem of explaining how this inspiration was transmitted and received. Reiterations and reminders of the Address appeared in countless schoolbooks and Independence Day orations from the Reconstruction era on, but there was also something else, something more solid and enduring, linking Lincoln's immortal words to the civil rights movement.[5]

The key link, it seems to me, is the Lincoln Memorial referenced in Richard King's *Civil Rights and the Idea of Freedom*. King's reference to the Memorial appears on the last page of the book in the context of a comparison of public perceptions of the Reverend Martin Luther King, Jr.'s "I Have a Dream" speech during the 1963 March on Washington with two other famous "civil rights" episodes—the 1989 confrontation at Beijing's Tiananmen Square and the Solidarity protest rallies at Warsaw's Wenceslas Square later the same year. Richard King's interest in linking these three events is limited to their shared distortion by the media—a process that seems to dilute their value as legitimate sources of purposeful mass activism. But by bringing up the Lincoln Memorial, he pointed us in the right direction.[6]

In the inner sanctum of the Memorial, Lincoln's most famous speech is enshrined in marble, and it is there that the most direct connection between the Gettysburg Address and civil rights can be found. The words cut into stone in 1922 extended and deepened the sacralization of Lincoln's words. Ten years earlier, the great sculptor Daniel Chester French had used an engraved tablet of the Address to frame his massive bronze sculpture of Lincoln on the grounds of the Nebraska state capitol. After being commissioned to sculpt another statue of Lincoln for the long-awaited Lincoln Memorial in Washington, French collaborated with the architect Henry Bacon to create a complex of memorial halls inside a white marble Hellenic temple framed with Doric columns. On the opposite sides of the central hall that features French's seated figure of Lincoln, two smaller halls display the murals of Jules Guérin and the engraved texts of Lincoln's Second Inaugural Address and the Gettysburg Address. Partially screened by a colonnade of Doric columns, the two small halls use literary and philosophical grandeur to compensate for what they lack in size.[7]

The inclusion of the Gettysburg Address in the new Lincoln Memorial was fitting and fortuitous, but by no means inevitable. Every detail of the Memorial was subject to debate and deliberation by the Lincoln Memorial Commission. Chaired by the former president and then-current Chief Justice of the United States Supreme Court William Howard Taft, the commission had been created by an act of Congress in 1911, and there were few moments of clear consensus during the eleven years of the Memorial's gestation. The site, the design, and the purpose were all subjects of controversy at one time or another. The rancor and disagreements involved aesthetics as well as ideology, often paralleling longstanding battles over the contested legacy of Lincoln. Should the Memorial present him as the Great Emancipator, the savior of the Union, or some combination of the two? Should the iconography of the Memorial portray him, as the historian Merrill Petersen once described the choices, as either "the plain western politician or the grave and dignified statesman"? Which Lincoln would the Memorial enshrine?[8]

In 1926, four years after the Lincoln Memorial's dedication, the AME Zion Church's national convention convened the first large gathering at the site. Speaking to a mass religious service for two thousand followers, Bishop E. D. W. Jones paid homage to Lincoln, insisting, "The immortality of the great emancipator lay not in his preservation of the Union, but in his giving freedom to the Negroes of America." As evidenced by their applause, many members of the all-black crowd were receptive to this view. But Bishop Jones's view was not representative of Americans at large during the racially and ethnically troubled "tribal Twenties." Nor had it been so during the six decades since Lincoln's assassination.[9]

When the Lincoln Memorial Commission began its work in 1911, two years after the Lincoln Centennial celebration, a solid majority of government officials, historians, and ordinary citizens, black and white, viewed Lincoln primarily as a symbol of national unity. In some parts of the South, he was still the "Black Republican" who had forced the issues of secession and the defense of slavery. But many white Southerners, like most white Northerners, had come to see him as a moderate alternative to the Radical Republicans who had foisted the carpetbagger regimes upon the South during Reconstruction. This characterization was compatible with both Wilsonian progressivism and Taft's brand of Republicanism, and as chairman of the commission Taft did everything in his power to embed this image in the Memorial. Even the final choice for the location of the Memorial symbolized intersectional harmony, lying just across the Potomac River from the Arlington home of General Robert E. Lee, another icon of reunion.[10]

At the dedication of the Memorial in early June 1922, the engraved texts of the Gettysburg Address and the Second Inaugural Address were there for all to see, providing testament to an internecine war that had led to emancipation. Yet the virtual absence of any other mention of slavery or abolition or freedom communicated a clear message of "national consensus, linking North and South, on holy, national ground," as the historian Scott Sandage once observed. In his dedication address, President Warren G. Harding assured the crowd—seated in racially segregated sections—that Lincoln was not an abolitionist but rather a unionist who favored emancipation only as "a means to the great end" of "union and nationality."

The other principal speakers, including Taft, followed the president's lead, studiously avoiding the historic issues of slavery and freedom. The only exception was Robert Russa Moton, the black president of the Tuskegee Institute, who gently reminded the platform party and the audience that it was Lincoln who "spoke the word that gave freedom to a race, and vindicated the honor of a nation conceived in liberty and dedicated to the proposition that all men are created equal."[11]

In the days and weeks following the dedication ceremony, the black press registered strong disapproval of the Jim Crow atmosphere at the Memorial. In the *Crisis,* the official organ of the NAACP, W. E. B. Du Bois mocked the ceremony in an article titled "Lincoln, Harding, James Crow, and Taft." No one had expected the Memorial to represent Lincoln as a heroic favorite son of black America, but the assembled dignitaries' utter disregard for the historical importance of emancipation was deeply troubling.[12]

Over the next fifteen years, a number of black intellectuals and liberal white historians attempted, with some success, to restore Lincoln's image as the Great Emancipator. But for most Americans, including many in the black community, he remained a national hero with only a tangential connection to African Americans. By the late 1930s, the increasingly conservative, big-business-oriented Republican Party was no longer the "party of Lincoln," and the Democratic Party, with its strong ties to the white South, had yet to embrace him as a symbol of racial justice. Some of the hundreds of thousands of black voters who shifted from the Republican to the Democratic Party in the mid-1930s may have had pictures of Lincoln in their homes, but far more seem to have put up pictures of FDR, the man who had given them a measure of hope during hard times.[13]

For most blacks as for most whites, a deep and abiding connection between Lincoln and matters of civil rights and racial equality would not take hold until much later. In the post-*Brown* era of the late 1950s and 1960s, as a national civil rights movement became a fixture of American life, Lincoln's image and legacy underwent a profound transformation. Prompted by an enhanced regard for social activism and racial equality, as well as by a search for heroic antecedents, a new generation of biographers and historians explored the linkages between current and past freedom struggles. In the process, the history of everything from slavery and emancipation to the politics of Reconstruction and the Progressive Era was revised to fit a maturing set of democratic sensibilities. The result was a new American history that included, among other revelations, a sharply revised understanding of the texts and contexts of Lincoln's life.

Fortunately, acknowledgment of Lincoln's contributions to the evolution of racial democracy has seldom led to simplistic hagiography. By and large, post-1960 interpretations of Lincoln (at least those outside the confines of children's literature) have proved to be less mythic and more historic than the interpretations that dominated earlier eras. Multidimensional and sensitive to change over time, the works of David Herbert Donald, Eric Foner, and scores of other modern Lincoln scholars stress the complexities, and, in some cases, the contradictions that characterized his life and his politics. If not an enigma, the civil-rights-era Lincoln is, at the very least, a flesh-and-blood human being susceptible to indecision, paradoxical beliefs, and even misplaced priorities. He was, in this view, a man, not a god.[14]

We have also learned that Lincoln—despite his lack of formal schooling—was a sophisticated thinker and writer capable of deliberate and purposeful indirection and ambiguity. This is perhaps the primary revelation in Garry Wills's 1992 masterwork *Lincoln at Gettysburg: The Words That Remade America.* Wills's painstaking explication of the Gettysburg Address brilliantly and persuasively lays out the hidden logic of Lincoln's words and phrases, connecting them to a creative reinvention of democratic nationalism. He does not, however, provide us with any clues about the dissemination or public reception of Lincoln's ideas. The question of how Americans—then, now, and in between—found out about and ultimately came to cherish the stated ideals of the Gettysburg Address is neither asked nor answered.

Trying to get a better fix on this question—and relating it specifically to the struggle for civil rights—brings us back to the Lincoln Memorial. Despite the obvious disappointment felt by black Americans, who were all but excluded by the Washington establishment, and the chorus of aesthetic dissent mustered by architectural critics, the Memorial was an immediate success. Affection and reverence for French's majestic statue of Lincoln was a big part of the popular reaction; indeed, as Merrill Petersen once observed, "The statue quickly became the nation's foremost sculptured icon." Yet it is important to remember that the entire structure, from its reflecting pool and exterior columns to its interior murals and inscriptions, contributed to the Memorial's singular status. "As Lincoln was consecrated in the hearts of the people," Petersen continued, "so was his memorial. Before long a million people a year were coming to visit it.

Some came out of no more than curiosity. Some came in search of peace and strength. Some came with questions."[15]

Whatever their motivations, one suspects that almost all of the Memorial's visitors spent at least a few moments in the interior halls, either gazing up at French's Lincoln or perhaps straining through the filtered light to read at least a few words of the speeches etched in marble. Indeed, no visit to the Memorial is complete without exposure to the moving rhetoric of the Gettysburg Address, from the opening sentence recalling the creation of "a new nation, conceived in Liberty, and dedicated to the proposition that all men are created equal" to the closing declaration "that this nation, under God, shall have a new birth of freedom—and that government of the people, by the people, and for the people, shall not perish from the earth."[16]

The close connection between the Memorial's hallowed words and the civil rights struggle seems obvious today, in an age that both celebrates Lincoln as the Great Emancipator and associates the Memorial dedicated to him as a major civil rights site. For example, all Americans, plus countless millions around the world, immediately recognize the Lincoln Memorial as the backdrop for the 1963 March on Washington and Dr. Martin Luther King, Jr.'s iconic "I Have a Dream" speech. Indeed, it is almost impossible to think of one without thinking of the other—the Memorial and the speech, together and indivisible.[17]

This dual enshrinement of Lincoln and the cause of civil rights, symbolized by the Memorial, is a testament to the federal government's belated commitment to civic equality. But it is important to remember how late this testament emerged. The association of the Memorial—and to some extent the Gettysburg Address—with civil rights did not register with most Americans until 1939, when a dramatic episode first demonstrated what would later become obvious.

The telling episode was the Easter 1939 concert performed by the great black contralto Marian Anderson. Recognized as one of the world's foremost classical singers, Anderson was nonetheless turned away from all of Washington's large concert venues because of her race. The public school board, fearing a precedent that might encourage school desegregation, refused a request to hold the concert in the auditorium of all-white Central High School, and the Daughters of the American Revolution (DAR), the nation's most prominent patriotic organization and the owner of Constitutional Hall, Washington's largest concert venue, invoked the Hall's color bar against black performers.

The DAR's action provoked a storm of controversy, including the February 27 resignation of its most famous member, First Lady Eleanor Roosevelt. The First Lady's resignation helped make Marian Anderson's plight a national and international cause célèbre, energizing the Marian Anderson Citizens' Committee (MACC), a broad-based coalition of organizations and outraged citizens, both black and white, that had formed a week earlier. Over the next month, the MACC—led by NAACP leaders Charles Hamilton Houston and Walter White, and working in close cooperation with Mrs. Roosevelt, the black educator Mary McLeod Bethune, Secretary of the Interior Harold Ickes, and Anderson's promoter Sol Hurok— negotiated unsuccessfully with the DAR while searching for an alternative venue.

Along the way, the stark reality of effectively denying Anderson the right to sing in the nation's capital became an embarrassing failure of American democracy at a time when US officials were asserting the superiority of American institutions and traditions over those of the Nazis and other totalitarian regimes. As Walter White put it, "Such childish discrimination makes ridiculous and hypocritical American protestations against outrages suffered by minorities in Nazi Germany and other parts of the world." To counteract this image of hypocrisy, the United States needed a dramatic and public show of democracy that would confirm Anderson's rights as an American citizen and the nation's claim to virtue.[18]

In desperation, the MACC and concert organizers eventually turned to the option of an outdoor concert, an idea first suggested by Howard University music professor Lulu Childers in January. One possibility considered but abandoned because of inadequate space was Lafayette Park adjacent to the White House. At one point, Sol Hurok suggested that the concert should be held in a park next to Constitution Hall, a gesture that would surely embarrass the DAR's implacable leaders. But this and other makeshift venues didn't receive much support, primarily due to the emergence of a powerful idea that eventually drew everyone involved into its orbit: the idea that the concert should be held at the Lincoln Memorial.

No one knows for sure who first proposed the idea, but the possibility of using the Lincoln Memorial was already being discussed by a Howard University concert sponsoring committee in early March. On March 13, when the NAACP's Board of Directors met in New York, the organization's executive secretary, Walter White, pushed through a resolution designating the Lincoln Memorial as the only proper site for Anderson's recital. A week later Hurok told a *New York Times* reporter that Anderson would indeed sing at the Memorial on Easter Sunday "as a rebuke to all who have snubbed the Negro singer." Though taken aback by Hurok's impulsive statement, White wasted no time in mobilizing the Anderson coalition.[19]

In his 1948 autobiography, White characterized the Lincoln Memorial as "the most logical place" for the Anderson concert. But the logic of holding a major gathering at the seventeen-year-old Memorial was not as obvious in 1939 as it would become later. Over the coming decades, the Memorial would host literally hundreds of mass meetings, including the August 1963 March on Washington for Jobs and Freedom, which drew a quarter of a million people to the west end of the National Mall. Holding a civil rights rally, a concert, or any other mass assemblage at the Memorial was definitely novel, however, in the spring of 1939. The federal agencies responsible for managing the site—the National Park Service and the Department of the Interior—had never granted a permit for a large gathering at the Memorial, and the only black organization of any size to have used the site was the AME Zion Church.[20]

In this context, the choice of the Lincoln Memorial as the backdrop for the Anderson recital was a calculated gamble. The organizers could not be certain how the American public would respond to the juxtaposition of a black concert singer and a white Republican president from Illinois. Physically and aesthetically, the Memorial and the adjacent rectangular reflecting pool stretching eastward toward the Washington Monument represented a stunning site. But the political and cultural implications of staging a controversial concert on sacred ground were complex and potentially dangerous. The situation called for careful planning and just the right touches to ensure that the event communicated the right messages to the right people.

Prior to the planning, however, the organizers faced the task of gaining permission to use the Memorial for such an unprecedented purpose. Here Walter White proved to be the indispensable link to the Department of the Interior. As a longtime friend of both Secretary Harold Ickes and Assistant Secretary Oscar L. Chapman, he was in a good position to lobby for a permit. He did not have to lobby very hard, however. As racial liberals and admirers of both Anderson and the First Lady, Ickes and Chapman needed little or no persuading. Indeed, some accounts credit Chapman as being the first person to urge White to consider using the Memorial for the Anderson concert. "Oh, my God," White supposedly responded, "if we could have her sit at the feet of Lincoln!"[21]

While this particular story may be apocryphal, the Virginia-born assistant secretary certainly smoothed the way for White and his colleagues.
He wasted no time in securing Ickes's approval for White's proposed
"demonstration of democracy." Ickes immediately embraced the idea, but
he did not want to create any political problems for the president. Such
an audacious departure from convention, he reasoned, required presidential approval, especially in a situation indirectly involving the First Lady.
Realizing that the president was within minutes of leaving for a two-week
vacation in Warm Springs, Georgia, Ickes rushed to the White House
to secure presidential blessing. Breathless, but confident that Roosevelt
would see the political value as well as the ethical imperative of holding
the Anderson concert at the Lincoln Memorial, Ickes pressed the depart-
ing president for an immediate answer. Roosevelt was more than oblig-
ing. Having heard enough about Anderson from his wife to last a lifetime,
he was as anxious as anyone to bring the concert-hall controversy to a
close. "She can sing from the top of the Washington Monument if she
wants to," he declared before heading for Georgia.[22]

With the president's approval in hand, Ickes moved quickly. On
March 30, he announced to the world that Marian Anderson would sing
at the Lincoln Memorial on Easter Sunday, April 9. The next step was to
assemble a sponsoring committee that would lend an air of gravitas to the
upcoming concert. Not everyone who was solicited agreed to serve on the
committee, but in a week's time the list of sponsors included 132 names.
Part of the list represented MACC activists, but there was also an array
of political luminaries and celebrities that represented broad-based support from the nation's leaders. In addition to the First Lady and Secretary
Ickes, the sponsors included Chief Justice of the Supreme Court Charles
Evans Hughes; Associate Justices Hugo Black and Stanley Reed; Secretary of the Treasury Henry Morgenthau; Secretary of Commerce Harry
Hopkins; Attorney General Frank Murphy; Secretary of the Navy Claude
Swanson; five members of the House of Representatives; fourteen senators; the Hollywood stars Katharine Hepburn, Fredric March, and Tallu-
lah Bankhead; and the great conductor Leopold Stokowski.

As the day of the concert approached, the organizers, especially White,
pored over every detail, weighing the probable reactions to everything
from the choice of music to the design and distribution of the printed
program. The goal, as White kept reminding his colleagues, was to project an air of dignity that would underscore the importance of the occasion. The front cover of the program, for example, featured the simple

announcement "Howard University and Associated Sponsors Present Marian Anderson at the Lincoln Memorial in Washington, Sunday, April 9, 1939, Five O'clock" on the top half of the page and the opening lines of Lincoln's Gettysburg Address on the bottom half. While waiting for Anderson to sing, members of the audience would have the opportunity to ponder the Address's immortal words: "Fourscore and seven years ago our fathers brought forth on this continent a new nation, conceived in liberty and dedicated to the proposition that all men are created equal." In case anyone missed the point, White also arranged to have the programs distributed throughout the crowd by a mix of black and white Boy Scouts.

By Sunday morning, April 9, everything was ready at the Memorial. The only potential problem was the likelihood of inclement weather. On Saturday afternoon, Washington was hit by a snowstorm, the last cruel touch of a lingering winter. Driving down from New York, White was crestfallen as "sleet began to fall." He later recalled, "With it fell our hopes. We went to bed low in spirits because of the snow piling up on the streets outside. Weeks of thought and all our hard work seemed about to be thwarted by nature. I was almost afraid to look out of the window when I awoke early the next morning. I shouted with happiness to see the sun." As the day progressed, the sun darted in and out, with more drizzle and cold wind than anything else. But the streets were now clear of snow and ready for the final preparations for an expected onslaught of concertgoers.[23]

The probable size of the crowd was still anybody's guess, but the relatively small turnout at the traditional Arlington cemetery sunrise service early that morning suggested that Secretary Ickes's prediction that fifty thousand would show up at the Lincoln Memorial was overly optimistic. By noon, there was a scattering of people near the base of the Memorial steps, early comers who wanted to secure a seat as close to the stage as possible. A few minutes later, Anderson herself, accompanied by the Finnish pianist Kosti Vehanen, arrived at the Memorial for a sound check. After testing the microphones and examining her sheet music, Anderson took a moment to look out over the reflecting pool, a site she had not visited in years. At that moment, it was quiet and beautiful with little hint of what was about to unfold.

When Anderson returned three hours later, it was an altogether different scene. As she stepped out of the limousine at the back of the Memorial, she caught a glimpse of the multitude gathered on the other side. At that moment, she had no way of estimating the size of the crowd. Only later would she learn that as many as seventy-five thousand people had braved the cold to hear her sing. Neither she nor anyone else had ever seen anything quite like it—a gathering of black and white, young and old, rich and poor, that stretched for hundreds of yards around and beyond the reflecting pool. In later years she often encountered individuals who explained why they had come and what the experience meant to them. But at the time she could only imagine the stories lost in the multitude.

It is little wonder that the scene nearly took Anderson's breath away. "I had sensations unlike any I had experienced before," she later declared in her autobiography. "My heart leaped wildly, and I could not talk," she confessed. "I even wondered if I would be able to sing." As Oscar Chapman and Representative Caroline O'Day of New York escorted her to the stage, she emerged from the shadows of the Memorial and encountered the platform party for the first time. The stage, which had been empty earlier in the afternoon, was now filled with Supreme Court justices, Cabinet secretaries, senators, representatives, and other dignitaries, more than two hundred in all. A bit overcome, she was relieved to see that her mother and sisters were also there along with several other blacks, most notably Walter White and Mary McLeod Bethune.

Secretary Ickes, who had the honor of introducing Anderson, opened the program with an eloquent discourse on democratic piety. "In this great auditorium under the sky all of us are free," he began.

> When God gave us this wonderful outdoors and the sun, the moon and the stars, He made no distinction of race or creed or color. And 130 years ago He sent to us one of His truly great in order that he might restore freedom to those who we had disregardfully taken it. In carrying out this task, Abraham Lincoln laid down his life, and so it is appropriate as it is fortunate that today we stand reverently and humbly at the base of this memorial to the great emancipator while glorious tribute is rendered to his memory by a daughter of the race from which he struck the chains of slavery.

In closing, Ickes reinforced the sacred bond between a gloriously talented and beloved black singer and the Great Emancipator. "Genius draws no color line," he declared.[24]

Ickes's remarks drew thunderous applause, but now all eyes were on Anderson. Wrapped in a fur coat to shield her from the wind, with her hair tied back, she walked slowly to the bank of microphones before looking out over the crowd. "She looked slender and beautiful when she emerged between the high marble columns, directly in front of the great Lincoln Memorial which was filled with shadow in the late afternoon light," Kosti Vehanen later wrote. "No one who saw her walking that day down the marble steps will ever forget this unusual and wonderful sight, and few can recall it without tears springing to their eyes." Turning to Kosti, Anderson gave a nod that she was ready to sing. But for a moment or two there was no sound but the whir of newsreel cameras. "My head and heart were in such turmoil that I looked and hardly saw, I listened and hardly heard," she recalled years later, with a poignant sense of wonder.

> All I knew then as I stepped forward was the overwhelming impact of the vast multitude. There seemed to be people as far as the eye could see . . . I had a feeling that a great wave of good will poured out from these people, almost engulfing me. And when I stood up to sing . . . I felt for a moment as though I were choking. For a desperate second I thought that the words, well as I know them, would not come. I sang, I don't know how.

With her eyes closed and her head tilted upward, Anderson began with the opening line of "America": "My country, 'tis of thee / sweet land of liberty." But as she completed the line, some in the crowd realized that she had substituted *we* for *I* at the end. Either from stage fright or premeditation—she never divulged which—she had sung "Of thee *we* sing." Most of the crowd, it seems, did not catch the change of words. All they heard was the most haunting rendition of "America" imaginable, sung against a backdrop dripping with symbolism. Years later, those who were there would try to tell their children and grandchildren what it was like to hear the lyrical words of democracy from such a beautiful voice while looking up at Lincoln's statue. But the emotional intensity of the experience was difficult, if not impossible, to convey. By the time she had finished the last line of "America"—"Our starry flag unfurled / The hope of all the world / In peace and light impearled / God hold secure!"—Anderson had the assembled multitude firmly in her grasp. And she never let go for the rest of the afternoon.

The program progressed through five more selections—an operatic aria by Donizetti, Schubert's "Ave Maria," the Negro spiritual "Gospel Train," the work song "Trampin'," and "My Soul Is Anchored in the Lord," a traditional spiritual adapted by Florence Price, the first African-American woman to gain wide acclaim as a composer. When Anderson came to the end of "My Soul Is Anchored in the Lord," the crowd erupted with applause. She was close enough to the front rows to see tears in the eyes of some of those who could hardly believe what they had just witnessed. Some held up their children, and others bent down to lift their sons or daughters onto their shoulders, all in an effort to help them see the woman responsible for the joyous commotion.

Not knowing quite how to respond, and with tears in her own eyes, Anderson regained her composure by singing the spiritual "Nobody Knows the Trouble I've Seen" as an encore. Once again, as her voice trailed off, the crowd broke out in thunderous applause. Moments passed, and the crowd was still clapping and cheering. But somehow she managed to say a few words before leaving the stage. "I am so overwhelmed, I just can't talk," she exclaimed into the bank of microphones. "I can't tell you what you have done for me today. I thank you from the bottom of my heart."[25]

By then those in the crowd nearest to the stage had surged forward, with others filling in behind, all trying to get into position to thank Anderson personally. Walter White, who was on the stage throughout the ensuing melee, later offered a vivid description of the scene: "As the last notes of 'Nobody Knows the Trouble I've Seen' faded away the spell was broken by the rush of the audience toward Miss Anderson, which almost threatened tragedy." Anderson's recollection echoed White's observation. "There were many in the gathering who were stirred by their own emotions," she recalled, with a measure of understatement. "Perhaps I did not grasp all that was happening, but at the end great numbers of people bore down on me." She added that "they were friendly; all they wished to do was to offer their congratulations and good wishes."

Even so, the crush of the surging crowd endangered both her and the platform guests, many of whom scrambled to get away. Fortunately, a coterie of policemen blocked the crowd long enough to allow her to escape into the recesses of the Memorial, where she found a chair and sat in the shadow of French's towering sculpture of Lincoln only a few feet removed from the marble wall bearing the words of the Gettysburg Address. She remained there for several minutes posing for photographs and mingling with a few stalwart fans that had sneaked through the cordon of security guards. By six o'clock she was gone, having joined her mother and sisters in a rented limousine that whisked them away to a private dinner at a Pennsylvania Avenue mansion.[26]

The entire event, including the postconcert activities, lasted less than an hour. But in that brief time Anderson gained a new life and identity. By merging her image with Lincoln's in such a dramatic way, the thirty-minute recital placed her on a path that few public figures ever followed. Already renowned as a singer, she was forever after an iconic symbol of racial pride and democratic promise. "No one present at that moving performance ever forgot it," the historian Constance McLaughlin Green wrote in 1966.

The meaning of the experience was difficult to articulate, but Mary McLeod Bethune came as close as anyone to capturing the essence of what had happened. In a letter to Charles Houston written the morning after the concert, she confessed that she was having difficulty expressing "what we felt and saw yesterday afternoon." She insisted:

> It cannot be described in words. There is no way. History may and will record it, but it will never be able to tell what happened in the hearts of the thousands who stood and listened yesterday afternoon. Something happened in all of our hearts. I came away almost walking on air. We are on the right track—we must go forward. The reverence and concentration of the throngs . . . told a story of hope for tomorrow—a story of triumph—a story of pulling together—a story of splendor and real democracy. Through the Marian Anderson protest concert we made our triumphant entry into the democratic spirit of American life.

Bethune spoke for the thousands who were actually at the memorial, but Anderson's performance was probably only slightly less moving for those who listened to the live broadcast on NBC radio. The distinguished historian John Hope Franklin, for one, could hardly rein in his emotions nearly seventy years later when reflecting upon the impact of the broadcast, which he listened to in a Goldsboro, North Carolina, parlor. "I couldn't believe my ears," he told an interviewer in 2007, "The thought of Marian Anderson singing at the Lincoln Memorial, with all those dignitaries seated at her feet, stretched my imagination and touched my heart."[27]

In the days and weeks following the concert, millions more read about it in newspapers or magazines or watched the newsreel footage in movie houses. Panoramic shots of the crowd and close-ups of Anderson singing into the microphones with Lincoln in the background appeared in the black press and many of the major dailies, giving visual aid to Americans trying to comprehend an unprecedented event. Readers looking closely at the photographs could see that the crowd was unsegregated and more or less evenly divided between blacks and whites. One of the most influential accounts appeared in Howard Vincent O'Brien's "All Things Considered" column in the *Chicago Daily News*. "Easter Sunday in Washington was a day to be remembered," he wrote, "for on that day was enacted one of the most moving dramas in American history." In closing, he gave the last word to Assistant Secretary Oscar Chapman. "Surely we have nothing to fear," Chapman told O'Brien moments after the concert, "as long as such things are possible in the United States."

O'Brien and Chapman were hardly alone in their enthusiasm, as glowing articles and editorials filled many of the nation's newspapers. But on the political left and in the black press the reaction was often more measured and even negative in a few instances. For example, in the *New Negro Alliance*, the journal of a militant protest organization that often challenged discriminatory hiring practices in the District of Columbia, the editor acknowledged "the golden voice of Marian Anderson." But he went on to point out that there was no reason to believe that the concert had changed anything. "Leaving the majestic natural setting," he observed, "the multitude returned to gross discrimination and vicious segregation . . . Negroes were still unable to attend theaters, use Central High School or Constitution Hall, or exercise their rights as American citizens. The pent-up emotions of thousands of Negroes were discharged quietly over the Reflecting Pool and then the straight-jacket of social policy and racial prejudice was quickly made secure and operative again."[28]

The *New Negro Alliance* editor was correct in pointing out that the short-term impact of the concert was largely symbolic. Nevertheless, that symbolism quickly became one of the roots of a powerful national civil rights movement. By pitting a lone black woman against America's most celebrated patriotic organization—and by doing so in the nation's capital—the Anderson controversy confirmed that racism was more than a regional peculiarity. It was, instead, a stain on the nation's honor. Indeed, as the rising force of fascism promoted rank bigotry and racial oppression, Anderson's unprecedented conquest of the classical music world stood as a testament to the illegitimacy of racial prejudice. The triumph at the Lincoln Memorial was only the first major milestone of a half-century-long career that ultimately broke all barriers large and small, from the color bar at Constitution Hall to the all-white casting tradition at the famed Metropolitan Opera.

Part of Anderson's mystique was a magical voice, a three-octave assortment of sounds so haunting and ethereal that more than one maestro judged her to be the greatest singer of the twentieth century. But Anderson was more than a superbly gifted artist. She was also a symbol of resolute courage and human dignity. Year after year, from the 1940s to the 1960s, polls revealed that she was one of the most admired women in the world, and invariably the only African American near the top of the list. Respected and beloved, she had no rival among black women as an icon of racial pride and accomplishment.[29]

Through it all, of course, she stayed close to Lincoln—and to the words and spirit of the Gettysburg Address. In 1942, the great American composer Aaron Copland wrote a three-movement piece entitled *A Lincoln Portrait*. With two instrumental movements and a third movement spliced with long quotations from Lincoln's speeches, the thirteen-minute-long piece offered a musical representation of the Great Emancipator's life. By the 1960s, *A Lincoln Portrait* had become a stock element of patriotic concerts, but by then Anderson's singing voice had begun to weaken. One solution was to talk more and sing less, and in July 1965, the same month that saw the passage of the long-awaited Voting Rights Act, she served as the Lincoln narrator in the Copland piece for the first time. Accompanied by the Metropolitan Opera Orchestra under the baton of Arthur Fiedler, she immediately made the piece her own, bringing an intensity of emotion that no other artist could match.

Over the next decade, Anderson repeated the moving narration more than thirty times in a variety of settings, from New York's Lincoln Center to the Hollywood Bowl. On one occasion, in Philadelphia, she even performed the narration with Copland himself conducting. She sometimes served as a narrator using other texts, but nothing stirred audiences as much as hearing her intone the final lines of the Gettysburg Address. Aware of her historical connection to the Lincoln Memorial, they responded to Anderson's deep-voiced pronouncement "that the government of the people, by the people, and for the people, shall not perish from the earth" as if Lincoln himself had returned from the grave. Fittingly, during the American bicentennial celebration of 1976, she performed *A Lincoln Portrait* for the last time.[30]

Twenty-three years later, in 2009, the nation celebrated another bicentennial, that of Lincoln's birth on February 12, 1809. The Lincoln Bicentennial Commission spent several years planning the celebration and came up with an array of commemorative events, including three major events.

One of them was a re-creation of the Anderson concert held on the seventieth anniversary of the actual event. This time the festivities included performances by the a cappella group Sweet Honey in the Rock, the Chicago Children's Choir, the US Air Force Band, and the gifted black soprano Denise Graves, who sang a reprise of Anderson's recital. Wearing a stunningly beautiful Parisian gown that Anderson had given her a few months prior to the great contralto's death in April 1993, Graves delivered a masterful performance in front of the approximately fifteen thousand fans that had gathered at the Memorial on a cold Easter Sunday afternoon.

Prior to the singing, the nation's first black secretary of state, Colin Powell, presided over a mass swearing-in ceremony for more than a hundred naturalized citizens. Minutes later, he recited the Gettysburg Address, his normally powerful voice cracking with emotion at several points. Among the crowd there were a number of small children who probably wondered why their parents were tearing up and clutching their little hands so tightly. But at some level just about everyone else understood why Powell was momentarily overcome by the historical significance of the occasion. Lincoln, Anderson, and the Gettysburg Address: the combination was almost too much civic virtue to handle. On the other hand, no one could have been surprised by Powell's choice of text. For nearly fifty years, since the 1960s-era cross-fertilization of the civil rights struggle and the Civil War Centennial, the relevance of the Gettysburg Address to civil rights had been an accepted fact of American life.

Once the commemorative concert was over, all the performers and members of the platform party retired to what some may have considered the unlikeliest of places. The Daughters of the American Revolution, the same group that had barred Marian Anderson from Constitution Hall seventy years earlier, had invited one and all, black and white, to a reception at the organization's headquarters. The invitation was a surprise to many, but the biggest surprise came when the performers and others reached the grand entryway of the DAR building. There standing in the doorway with outstretched hands were two black members of the organization. What this gesture meant—tokenism or a sincere commitment to diversity and inclusiveness—was unclear. But, as the reception unfolded, the sight of so many African Americans wandering through the inner sanctum of a building constructed as a bastion of white privilege conveyed an uplifting image of democratic promise. Here, as elsewhere, Abraham Lincoln's legacy—and Marian Anderson's—had clearly left a deep and visible footprint on the long road to freedom.[31]

Notes

1. William P. Jones, *The March on Washington: Jobs, Freedom, and the Forgotten History of Civil Rights* (New York: Norton, 2014); Garry Wills, *Lincoln at Gettysburg: The Words That Remade America* (New York: Simon and Schuster, 1992), 20, 145–148, 191–203, 263.

2. See Jacquelyn Dowd Hall, "The Long Civil Rights Movement and the Political Uses of the Past," *Journal of American History* 91 (Mar. 2005): 1233–1263.

3. Richard H. King, *Civil Rights and the Idea of Freedom* (New York: Oxford University Press, 1992), 95, 185, 211.

4. Wills, *Lincoln at Gettysburg*, 90–91.

5. Ibid., 263. See Jared Peatman, *The Long Shadow of Lincoln's Gettysburg Address* (Carbondale: Southern Illinois University Press, 2013); and Merrill D. Peterson, *Lincoln and American Memory* (New York: Oxford University Press, 1994), 24, 31–32, 49, 109, 113–116, 148, 191, 198–199, 203, 208, 214, 225, 252, 346–347, 326, 350, 360–361, 365, 371, 376, 379, 383, 385–386, 390, 396–397.

6. King, *Civil Rights and the Idea of Freedom*, 211.

7. Peterson, *Lincoln and American Memory*, 206–217.

8. Ibid., 211.

9. Raymond Arsenault, *The Sound of Freedom: Marian Anderson, the Lincoln Memorial, and the Concert That Awakened America* (New York: Bloomsbury, 2009), 147; Scott A. Sandage, "A Marble House Divided: The Lincoln Memorial, the Civil Rights Movement, and the Politics of Memory, 1939–1963," *Journal of American History* 80 (June 1993): 136–143.

10. Arsenault, *The Sound of Freedom*, 147; Peterson, *Lincoln in American Memory*, 195–255; Sandage, "Marble House Divided," 135–167. See also Roy P. Basler, *The Lincoln Legend: A Study in Changing Conceptions* (Boston: Houghton Mifflin, 1935).

11. Sandage, "Marble House Divided," 141; Peterson, *Lincoln in American Memory*, 214–217; *Chicago Defender*, June 10, 1922; Arsenault, *The Sound of Freedom*, 148.

12. "Lincoln, Harding, James Crow, and Taft," *Crisis* 24 (July 1922): 122; *Chicago Defender*, June 10, 1922; Sandage, "Marble House Divided," 141–142; Arsenault, *The Sound of Freedom*, 148.

13. Peterson, *Lincoln in American Memory*, 255–310; Arsenault, *The Sound of Freedom*, 148. On the dramatic upsurge in Franklin Roosevelt's black electoral support in 1936, see Nancy J. Weiss, *Farewell to the Party of Lincoln: Black Politics in the Age of FDR* (Princeton, NJ: Princeton University Press, 1983), 180–235.

14. See Barry Schwartz, *Abraham Lincoln in the Post-heroic Era: History and Memory in Late-Twentieth Century America* (Chicago: University of Chicago Press, 2008); Richard N. Current, *Speaking of Abraham Lincoln: The Man and His Meaning for Our Times* (Urbana: University of Illinois Press, 1983); Richard N. Current, *The Lincoln Nobody Knows* (New York: McGraw-Hill, 1958); Peterson, *Lincoln in*

American Memory, 311–397; Benjamin P. Thomas, *Abraham Lincoln: A Biography* (New York: Alfred A. Knopf, 195); David Herbert Donald, *Lincoln* (New York: Simon and Schuster, 1995); Doris Kearns Goodwin, *Team of Rivals: The Political Genius of Abraham Lincoln* (New York: Simon and Schuster, 2005); and Eric Foner, *The Fiery Trial: Abraham Lincoln and American Slavery* (New York: Norton, 2011).

15. Peterson, *Lincoln in American Memory*, 216–217. See also Sandage, "Marble House Divided," 135–167.

16. Wills, *Lincoln at Gettysburg*, 263.

17. See Jones, *The March on Washington*.

18. Arsenault, *The Sound of Freedom*, 89–144, 124 (quotation); NAACP press release, typescript, Feb. 17, 1939, folder 44, box 1–2, Marian Anderson—Daughters of the American Revolution Controversy Collection, Moorland-Spingarn Research Center, Howard University, Washington, DC (hereafter cited as MADARCC).

19. Arsenault, *The Sound of Freedom*, 145–146; *New York Times*, Mar. 21, 1939.

20. Walter White, *A Man Called White: The Autobiography of Walter White* (New York: Viking, 1948), 181; Arsenault, *The Sound of Freedom*, 147.

21. Arsenault, *The Sound of Freedom*, 148–149; T. H. Watkins, *Righteous Pilgrim: The Life and Times of Harold L. Ickes, 1874–1952* (New York: Henry Holt, 1990), 651.

22. White, *A Man Called White*, 182; Sandage, "Marble House Divided," 144; Watkins, *Righteous Pilgrim*, 651; Arsenault, *The Sound of Freedom*, 149–150.

23. Lincoln Memorial concert program, Apr. 9, 1939, folder 47, box 1–2, MADARCC; the program is also available in box 412, Marian Anderson Papers, University of Pennsylvania, Philadelphia (hereafter cited as MAP). *New York Times*, Apr. 5, 1939; Sandage, "Marble House Divided," 144–145; Arsenault, *The Sound of Freedom*, 150–157; White, *A Man Called White*, 183.

24. Marian Anderson, *My Lord, What a Morning: An Autobiography* (New York: Viking Press, 1956), 190–191; Harold Ickes's Speech, Apr. 9, 1939, typescript, box 412, MAP; Arsenault, *The Sound of Freedom*, 157–160.

25. Kosti Vehanen, *Marian Anderson: A Portrait* (New York: McGraw-Hill, 1941), 244–245; Anderson, *My Lord*, 190–192; Sandage, "Marble House Divided," 135–136; Allan Keiler, *Marian Anderson: A Singer's Journey* (New York: Simon and Schuster, 2000), 212–213; Arsenault, *The Sound of Freedom*, 160–161.

26. White, *A Man Called White*, 184–185; Anderson, *My Lord*, 191–192; Keiler, *Marian Anderson*, 213; *New York Times*, Apr. 10, 1939; Arsenault, *The Sound of Freedom*, 162. The Pennsylvania Avenue mansion was the home of Dr. Milton and Beatrice Francis. Beatrice Francis to Marian Anderson, Apr. 16, 1939, box 412, MAP.

27. Constance McLaughlin Green, *The Secret City: A History of Race Relations in the Nation's Capital* (Princeton, NJ: Princeton University Press, 1967), 249; Mary McLeod Bethune to Charles Houston, Apr. 10, 1939, folder 4, box 1–1,

MA-DARCC; John Hope Franklin, interview by author, Mar. 1, 2007; Arsenault, *The Sound of Freedom*, 163–164.

28. *Chicago Daily News*, Apr. 18, 1939, box 412, MAP; David Brinkley, *Washington Goes to War* (New York: Alfred A. Knopf, 1988), 19; see also the voluminous newspaper clippings collected by V. D. Johnston in roll D, box 1–3, MA-DARCC; Arsenault, *The Sound of Freedom*, 164–167.

29. Anderson, *My Lord*, 192–309; Keiler, *Marian Anderson*, 218–319; Arsenault, *The Sound of Freedom*, 189–214.

30. Peterson, *Lincoln in American Memory*, 325, 347; Elizabeth B. Crist, *Music for the Common Man: Aaron Copland During Depression and War* (New York: Oxford University Press, 2005), 148–165; *New York Times*, Apr. 19, 1965, Feb. 2, 1966, Aug. 15, 1976; Keiler, *Marian Anderson*, 319–323, 425 n. 108; Arsenault, *The Sound of Freedom*, 211.

31. *Washington Post*, Apr. 9–10, 2009; Peatman, *The Long Shadow of Lincoln's Gettysburg Address*, chapter 5; Program, "Marian Anderson Tribute Concert and Naturalization Ceremony Reception," Apr. 12, 2009, held at the Daughters of the American Revolution National Headquarters, Washington, DC, in author's possession.

14

Widely Noted and Long Remembered

THE GETTYSBURG ADDRESS AROUND THE WORLD

Don H. Doyle

LINCOLN'S BRIEF ORATION at Gettysburg reached far beyond the audience assembled before him at the cemetery that day in November 1863 and, over time, his words would echo around the world. The text of the speech eventually found its way into dozens of languages, and certain phrases would in time be cited by a panoply of foreign heads of state, rebel separatist leaders, radical revolutionaries, and statist conservatives. Foreigners who admired America as an example to the world, and those seeking to mock its pretentions, both made use of Lincoln's Gettysburg Address. For more than a century and a half, parties of all description around the world have made Lincoln speak for them.

The central idea of Lincoln's speech resonated with an ongoing debate about the democratic experiment that had been going on since the American and French Revolutions shook the Atlantic world toward the end of the previous century. Many European liberals, who believed fervently in individual liberty, freedom of speech and religion, and free trade, nonetheless continued to believe that dynastic monarchies, properly checked by constitutional restraints and parliamentary powers, had proven the most stable, workable system of government. Democracies, they feared, were inclined toward what Alexis de Tocqueville called the tyranny of the majority and mob rule, which imperiled individual liberty. Critics also argued that self-governing republics were inherently fragile and given to internal fracture, and that they were especially unsuited to the vast territory and diversity of population found in the United States. All republics, sooner or later, so the argument went, were doomed to descend into either anarchy or despotism.[1]

They had a point. Throughout the Atlantic world, by the 1860s, the experiment in government by the people seemed to have failed. In Europe the revolutionary upheavals that had erupted periodically since the French Revolution in 1789 had produced very little to credit the experiment in self-rule. After Napoleon's defeat at Waterloo, the old regime was challenged by episodic revolutionary upheavals, but following the Revolution of 1848, hailed as the "springtime of nations," most of Europe remained firmly ruled by dynastic monarchies.

The young republics of Latin America offered little consolation. Since winning independence in the 1810s and 1820s, most had succumbed to a tumultuous cycle of pronunciamentos, civil wars, and military dictatorships. Mexico, the former jewel of Spain's American empire, experienced no less than fifty changes of government during four decades of independence. The French invaded Mexico beginning in 1862 with an idea of restoring it to monarchical order and demonstrating to all Latin America the folly of republicanism. For many conservatives, the Empire of Brazil ruled by Dom Pedro II served as an object lesson in the inherent stability of monarchy and further proof that the Latin temperament was ill suited to government by the people.

Lincoln was not bragging when, in his December 1862 address to Congress, he referred to America as the "last best hope of earth." Almost alone among the self-governing nations of the world, the United States provided living proof that government by the people could actually work—and perhaps endure. A diverse and fast-growing population, spread over a vast and expanding territory, the United States had demonstrated that a freely elected government could rule and that power could be passed from one party to another without revolutions and assassinations—that is, until the 1860s.

No wonder that many critics of democracy welcomed the ruin of America's so-called Great Republic. One British Tory gleefully told his fellow members of Parliament that they were witnessing "the bursting of that great Republican bubble which had been so often held up to us as the model." Another predicted that all the American republics would return to monarchy before the century was out. Monarchists across Europe were eager to teach a lesson on the ills of democracy from the demise of the once United States. One Spanish journal mocked the "model republic of what *were* the United States . . . populated by the dregs of all the nations in the world," now doomed to "die in a flood of blood and mire" as a rebuke to "the flaming theories of democracy."[2] Walt Whitman, the American poet, hardly exaggerated when he wrote, "There is certainly not one government in Europe but is now watching the war in this country, with the ardent prayer that the United States may be effectually split, crippled, and dismembered by it. There is not one but would help toward that dismemberment, if it dared."[3]

* * *

Lincoln understood that the aristocratic governing classes of Europe were against him, and he was reaching out for popular support at home and abroad. What gave Lincoln's speech at Gettysburg such sweeping power among the foreign public was his framing of the war within a much greater historic contest over the fate of democracy. The opening of the speech referred to "this nation" brought forth on "this continent," but then he elevated America's trial into a contest that would decide whether "this nation, *or any nation so conceived* and so dedicated, can long endure." When he modestly noted that "the world will little note, nor long remember what we say here," he was again addressing his global audience. The "rebirth of freedom" anticipated in Lincoln's magnificent finish is always interpreted as a veiled reference to the emancipation of American slaves, but for many foreigners the anticipation that "government of the people, by the people, for the people shall not perish from the earth" meant hope for a new birth of political freedom for them.[4]

These phrases were quintessential Lincoln, but they resonated with such force around the world over time because they drew on a familiar vocabulary of international republicanism. *Tout pour le peuple*, one French republican pamphlet proclaimed in 1833; our goal is to realize the dream *par le peuple et pour le peuple* (by the people and for the people).[5] The cadence Lincoln employed—of, by, for the people, nation, republic—had become familiar in European and American oratory and writing by the 1860s. Giuseppe Mazzini, the famed leader of the Italian Risorgimento, in 1833 had called on Young Italy to make revolution "in the name of the people, for the people, and by the people." Again in 1851, Mazzini, trying to explain Italy's historic mission, asked: "What does it mean if not a living Equality, in other words, Republic of the People, by the people, and for the people?"[6]

Even in the pages of the London *Times*, an arch opponent of the republican experiment, variations of the phrase "government by the people" appeared more than two dozen times before 1863 and hundreds of times after that, typically with no specific reference to Lincoln's speech.[7] Lincoln's earlier speeches and writing reveal a familiarity with this international republican language. Such European republican leaders as Mazzini, Garibaldi, Karl Blind, and many others were in correspondence with Lincoln during the war. One of them even sent Lincoln a complete set of Mazzini's work, which Lincoln acknowledged in June 1863.[8] The point is not that Lincoln borrowed from Mazzini, or anyone else, but that he was conversant with the ideas, and the phrasing of ideas, that permeated the international republican discourse.

More than just his wording, Lincoln dramatically framed the war as an epic clash between the defenders of liberty, equality, and self-rule against the advocates of aristocracy, slavery, and hereditary rule. It was pitch perfect to foreign ears. "The first grand war of contemporaneous history is the American war," Karl Marx had written for the *New York Tribune* earlier. The "highest form of popular self-government till now realized is giving battle to the meanest and most shameless form of man's enslaving recorded in the annals of history."[9] Agénor Gasparin, a French advocate of the Union and another correspondent of Lincoln, was the first European to summon Europeans to support the Union in its struggle against the slave power. "One of the gravest conflicts of the age is opening in America," he wrote. "It is time for us to take sides."[10]

Among the diplomatic corps present at Lincoln's speech in Gettysburg, Henri Mercier, the French ambassador to the United States, thought the American war was senseless bloodshed, and neither the battle nor the speech at Gettysburg changed his thinking.[11] Antonio Gallenga, an Italian writer and special correspondent for the London *Times*, reported that the "imposing ceremony" was "rendered ludicrous by some of the luckless sallies of that poor President Lincoln." Gallenga was referring not to the president's speech, which he seemed willing to ignore completely, but to some offhand comments the president had made in response to a serenade the evening before. Gallenga's report described Edward Everett's oration as "dull and commonplace," and though he was fully in sympathy with Italian revolutionary aspirations, he gave no notice to Lincoln's invocation of the new birth of freedom.[12]

The *Times* and other British newspapers printed full transcripts of Lincoln's Gettysburg speech, but few found it worthy of remark.[13] Britain's governing classes generally loathed the idea of government by the people and thought of Lincoln and Seward as charlatans playing to the democratic mob. The British government remained officially neutral, but inside Prime Minister Palmerston's Cabinet most viewed the conflict as an utterly senseless, wasteful war that would end only when the North gave up on the foolish idea of reconstructing the Union. "I think," Earl Russell, the foreign secretary, had written to Palmerston, "we must allow the President to spend his second batch of 600,000 men before we can hope that he and his democracy will listen to reason." Russell, Gladstone, and Palmerston all wanted the war to end with the North recognizing Southern independence and, even more, they wanted cotton to resume its flow to British mills.[14] Now, it seemed, Lincoln was dressing up his war as a high-minded crusade to save government by the people and, God forbid, encourage others in the world to see America's democracy as the "last best hope of earth."

Europeans began reassessing Lincoln even before his tragic death. Goldwin Smith, an Oxford University professor and a supporter of the Union in England, had interviewed the president shortly after his reelection one year following the Gettysburg Address, and he wrote a piece in *MacMillan's* magazine in February 1865 that evaluated the Gettysburg oration with a mix of professorial disdain and gushing admiration. "There are one or two phrases here, such as 'dedicated to the proposition,' which betray a hand untrained in line writing," but to Professor Smith this only proved the prose was Lincoln's own: "Looking to the substance, it may be doubted whether any king in Europe would have expressed himself more royally than the peasant's son." He later wrote of Lincoln's speech: "Not a sovereign in Europe, however trained from the cradle for state pomps, and however prompted by statesmen and courtiers, could have uttered himself more regally than did Lincoln at Gettysburg."[15]

* * *

The news of Lincoln's death sent a wave of grief and outrage through Europe and Latin America. Crowds gathered in the streets of all the major cities. American diplomats abroad reported large public demonstrations and meetings, some of which were carried out at great risk in the face of government censorship on the continent. Government officials issued formal obsequies, but more impressive were the nearly one thousand letters and resolutions sent to US delegations by common citizens: reform organizations; women's groups; students; workers; Masonic lodges; and towns and villages across Europe, Latin America, even a few from Africa and Asia.[16]

It was natural that Lincoln's Gettysburg call for a "new birth of freedom" and his exaltation of government of, by, and for the people would become the intellectual property of the political Left as it battled the privileged aristocracy over control of European and Latin American governments in the decades following 1865. The Union's victory was widely interpreted as a vindicating blow in favor of democratic self-rule. Conservative skeptics who had confidently predicted the democratic experiment was on its way to final ruin in America now witnessed an impressive lesson in democracy's resilience. As one English Radical put it in 1865, "Under a strain such as no aristocracy, no monarchy, no empire could have supported, Republican institutions have stood firm." It was the common people who now "call upon the privileged classes to mark the result."[17]

Mark it they did. Led by John Bright, one of Lincoln's ardent friends and supporters in England, reformers discovered in Lincoln a posthumous supporter of British democracy. The Union's triumph seemed to vindicate them by demonstrating the remarkable strength of popular government during four years of civil war and an assassination. Lincoln was especially popular among British workers. Following the assassination hundreds of workers' societies across Britain and its possessions overseas sent letters of condolence to register their sympathy with Lincoln's ideals.

The Liberal Party government, under the leadership of Prime Minister Earl Russell and William Gladstone, felt growing pressure after 1865 to broaden the franchise, which had been narrowly confined to a small sliver of property-owning males. In 1867 massive public demonstrations took place in Trafalgar Square and Hyde Park in London, and in meeting halls across the British Isles. Repeatedly, Lincoln was invoked as a common man of the people whose example validated the democratic idea. Following a spectacular oratorical duel between Gladstone and Disraeli, the Conservative Party leader, Parliament wound up with a bill that would vastly expand the electorate. When the government tried to ban further public rallies in favor of the bill, Radicals defiantly broke down barricades and staged massive demonstrations in Hyde Park. In May Parliament passed the Reform Act of 1867, and Britain seemed on its way to an American-style government by the people.[18]

Lincoln's voice in British politics was only beginning to gain force. In 1881 Radical Henry Meyer again enlisted Lincoln in the crusade for democracy in Britain: "That government of the people by the people of which noble Abraham Lincoln spoke on the battle-field of Gettysburg as the cause for which men fell there, is the cause which we have yet to fight out peacefully here."[19] By 1885 one of Britain's oldest Radical journals, *Reynold's* newspaper, emblazoned its masthead with Lincoln's dictum, "government of the people, by the people, for the people." Then the Liberal Party, trying to catch up with the democratic tide, appropriated the same phrase as its unofficial motto. As one party stalwart explained it in 1886, Lincoln's address "has not been surpassed in eloquence and power by any orator, ancient or modern," and when that "great principle" of government of, by, and for the people becomes universally acknowledged, then "one of the objects for which Liberalism exists will have been finally achieved."[20]

Soon even the Tories were chanting that "government by the people" lay at the heart of their own Conservative Party goals. Across the political spectrum, it seemed, factions in one of Europe's oldest monarchies were employing Lincoln as the unimpeachable champion of popular government. The words he spoke at Gettysburg a generation earlier had become commonplace in British political discourse by the late 1880s.[21]

While British politicians were busy channeling Lincoln's defense of democracy, woman's rights advocates took the opportunity to throw those same words from Gettysburg back in the faces of the male leadership. One woman reformer in Birmingham mocked the Liberal Party's pretenses in 1885 by charging that what it really wanted was "government of the whole people, for half the people, by the male people."[22] Millicent Fawcett, an ardent suffragist, also chided party leaders by admonishing, "Surely they were not to take away half of their creed by saying that only one half of the people were to enjoy the privilege of self-government."[23] This was only the beginning for the versatile roles Lincoln and his Gettysburg Address were to play among dissident groups claiming a voice in government by the people.

Precisely as the Liberal Party embraced the slogan "Government by the People," the Irish Home Rule movement challenged the British government to make good on such promise by granting Ireland its own government. The Irish Home Rule party won stunning victories in parliamentary elections in 1886, and this exerted enormous pressure on the Liberal Party to live up to the motto it borrowed from Lincoln. The Irish question stirred numerous comparisons to America's recent debacle, and Lincoln as champion of government by the people was often set against Lincoln the defender of the Union against rebel separatists. One Home Rule advocate, speaking before a huge Liberal Party rally in London, remarked that when Lincoln uttered those immortal words, "Government of the people, by the people, for the people . . . he was desirous of having this principle extended and enjoyed by other countries who were still struggling for their political and just rights." The same speaker also extolled the Irish patriots who fought for the American Union and compared them to those who continued the struggle for government by the people.[24] Éamon de Valera, the leader of the Irish Republic, declared, "I believe fundamentally in government of the people by the people and, if I may add the other part, for the people. This is my fundamental creed."[25]

Liberal Unionists broke with their party over the Home Rule question and denounced all such efforts to enlist Lincoln in the cause of Irish independence. "I say to Ireland what the Liberals or Republicans of the North said to the Southern States of America," Joseph Chamberlain thundered in one speech, "'The Union must be preserved.'"[26] Irish nationalists answered by insisting that America's federal Union was created by consent of the member states, while England had subjugated Ireland as part of its colonial empire. Éamon de Valera insisted that "there never can be in the case of Ireland a question of secession because there never has been a union."[27] Whether as champion of government by the people or of preservation of the Union, Lincoln was conscripted by both sides in the Irish question.[28]

* * *

Lincoln's Gettysburg speech also found its way into political discourse on the European Continent after 1865, though never as frequently as in the Anglo-American conversation. John Bigelow, US minister to France, was astonished by the response to Lincoln's death and to the Union's victory: "Familiar as I supposed I was with the currents of public opinion here towards the U.S., I had no idea of the interest with which the progress of our war has been watched by the masses. I am quite sure the death of no other foreign sovereign or subject, by whatever means, would have produced so much emotion." John Bigelow wrote to an American friend, "The death of Lincoln, I think, is destined to work a radical change in the Constitution of France." He was especially impressed by the public address of Comte de Montalembert, one of France's leading liberal Catholic intellectuals, who in May 1865 eulogized Lincoln and hailed the Union's victory as a sign of democracy triumphant. "Every thing which has occurred in America, from all which is to follow in the future, grave teachings will result for us," he predicted, "for, in spite of ourselves, we belong to a society irrevocably democratic."[29]

During the spring and summer of 1865 French liberals took the occasion of public bereavement to register a surreptitious political protest against Napoleon III. They wore black armbands, draped buildings in black, fired salvos from canons, and issued hundreds of resolutions expressing at once grief over America's fallen leader and admiration of Lincoln as a common man who saved the Republic. When French republicans in Nantes took up a popular subscription to raise money for a medal for Mrs. Lincoln, police confiscated the list of subscribers and the money. Some of the leading republicans of the day, including the novelist Victor Hugo, stepped forward to carry on the "two sous subscription" as a defiant gesture of opposition. The result was a large gold medal with a profile of Lincoln on one side, and on the other his tomb flanked by a weeping angel and two African Americans, one an armed male and the other a boy. Inscribed on the tomb were the words: "Lincoln, an honest man, abolished slavery, reestablished the union, saved the Republic without veiling the statue of liberty." The latter phrase echoed an expression from the French Revolution, and it anticipated a project that was begun by French republicans in 1866 to raise a monument in New York Harbor featuring Liberty Enlightening the World.[30]

French-language publications on Lincoln between 1860 and 1920 show a total of 135 books and articles, more than half appearing before 1870. Lincoln's Gettysburg speech received special attention, mostly from French republicans and liberals frustrated by Napoleon III's regime. César Pascal, a French Protestant liberal, in his 1865 tribute biography to the late president, celebrated the *renaissance de liberté* (rebirth of liberty) Lincoln had proclaimed in his *belles paroles* (beautiful words). "In a short speech, both simple and majestic as classic beauty, it rose, without pretension, without doubt, to the highest eloquence."[31] Édouard Laboulaye, a professor at the College de France (and the principal instigator of the Statue of Liberty project), applauded the "simple words" of *le bon Lincoln* that summarized the entire political philosophy of America: "This nation, conceived in liberty, dedicated to equality" wants to maintain on earth *le gouvernement du peuple, par le peuple, et pour le peuple.*[32]

In 1870, in the midst of a disastrous war with Prussia, Napoleon III was captured on the field of battle and imprisoned. Back in Paris the opposition deposed him and, after a period of revolutionary violence under the Paris Commune, France declared the Third Republic. Interest in Lincoln and the American Republic continued to be fed by a stream of biographies and articles, and the campaign to raise money for what came to be known as the Statue of Liberty finally came to fruition in 1886.

* * *

Several nations in the Spanish-speaking world were also in turmoil due to the resurgence of republicanism that followed the Union's victory in 1865. Benito Juárez, the elected president of the Mexican republic, led the movement to defeat the monarchists and Catholic clergy who supported Maximilian's regime. In the face of veiled threats from the United States, Napoleon III decided to withdraw French forces beginning in 1866. The experiment in American monarchism came to an end as Maximilian faced a Mexican firing squad in June 1867. Juárez, hailed as the Abraham Lincoln of Mexico, restored Mexico's republican government.[33]

Cuba, the remaining jewel in Spain's American empire, tried with less success to throw off its European monarchy. Robert Schufeldt, US consul general in Havana, reported to William Seward in January 1862 that news of the war circulated among the slaves and that they "mingle within their songs the significant refrain *Avanza Lincoln, Avanza! Tu eres nuestra esperanza!*" (Onward Lincoln, Onward! You are our hope!).[34] In 1868 Cuban republicans led a war for independence in which they enlisted the slaves by granting them freedom. Known as the Ten Years' War, this rebellion failed to win independence for Cuba, but it put slavery on the road to extinction in Cuba by forcing Spain to enact a "free womb" law for the gradual emancipation of Cuban slaves. The independence of Cuba and the emancipation of its slaves became intertwined; the image of Lincoln could be found in the shanties and in the mansions of progressive-minded Cubans.

Latin Americans had been introduced to Lincoln and his words thanks to a popular biography by the well-known Argentine writer Domingo Faustino Sarmiento, an ardent republican whose earlier book, *Facundo*, had established his reputation as a writer. He had been sent to Washington as Argentina's ambassador and arrived soon after the assassination. Moved by the occasion, he quickly compiled *La Vida de Abran Lincoln*. It was a tribute book, hastily assembled from passages lifted from two existing works in English, and laced with Sarmiento's own interpretation. It was published in New York in 1866 and quickly went to a second and third edition, apparently due to brisk demand in Cuba, where interest in Lincoln ran high.[35]

In Lincoln, Sarmiento wrote in the introduction, "one encounters those affinities that exist between the two Americas" to suggest "useful lessons and warnings for our own government." Sarmiento admired Lincoln less for his exaltation of freedom than for his iron-fisted exertion of central government control. He returned home after his diplomatic tour in America to pursue a political career and was elected president in 1868, during which he deliberately cultivated a reputation as the Argentine Abraham Lincoln, but it was Lincoln the nationalist rather than the Great Emancipator. We see this in his interpretation of the Gettysburg Address. He began with a literal translation of the first four sentences, and then launched into his own novel interpretation of the remainder: "The nation was proclaiming at the top of its voice that the fallen of that battle had not sacrificed their lives in vain, because, with God's guidance, the liberty bathed in their blood would be reborn, and that the government of the people, by the people and for the people is not destined to perish from the face of the earth."[36]

José Martí, a Cuban writer and revolutionary, spent years in exile in the United States, and though he distrusted many things about America, he greatly admired Lincoln as a model of inspired leadership tempered by a strong sense of social justice. Martí defended Lincoln as an opponent of US imperialist ambitions in Latin America, pointing to his refusal to invade Mexico despite great clamor in Congress to do so. As for Gettysburg, Martí seemed impressed by both the battle and Lincoln's concise funeral oration for what they conveyed about national sacrifice and martyrdom for the nation. Martí would return to Cuba to join its second war for independence, and in 1895 meet death in a suicidal charge that left him as a martyr to the nation.[37]

In October 1868, coinciding with the rebellion in Cuba, Spain also experienced a revolutionary upheaval, known as the Glorious Revolution, which abruptly ended the reign of Queen Isabella II. For the first time Spain stood before the world without a monarch. The revolution was led by Juan Prim, a Spanish general and leader of the Progresista Party. Prim had led Spanish forces in the invasion of Mexico in 1862, but he broke with the French commanders once it became clear they wanted to impose a European monarchy over Mexico. He withdrew Spanish forces just before the disastrous French encounter with Mexican republicans at the Battle of Puebla. On his way back to Spain, Prim visited the United

States, met with Abraham Lincoln, and came away with an enduring admiration for the president.

Lincoln became an iconic figure during Spain's liberal revolution, thanks to the writings of Emilio Castelar, a republican president of the First Spanish Republic in 1873, and Rafael María de Labra, an abolitionist and academic who wrote extensively on Lincoln and his role in ending slavery. Castelar hailed Lincoln, along with Benito Juárez, Giuseppe Garibaldi, George Washington, Símon Bolívar, and others, as heroes of the day whose homely virtues and ideals of self-government were worthy of emulation by Spanish republicans. Labra's biographical sketches of antislavery heroes extolled Lincoln for vindicating the revolution begun by Haiti's revolutionary leader Toussaint L'Overture.[38]

One boisterous editorial hailed Spain's revolution by invoking a rendition of Lincoln's message from Gettysburg: "The great truth to be learned in this world of progress is 'government by the people, the whole people through the people and for the people.'"[39] Indeed, Lincoln took on an iconic presence among Spanish progressives during their revolutionary upheaval and long after. Poet Carolina Coronado, whose husband was an American diplomat in Madrid, in her poem "The Redeeming Eagle," hailed Lincoln as an inspiration to Spain's aspirations for democracy and emancipation:

> *In you was born the new dynasty*
> *That will reign in the ageless world, . . .*
> *Humble woodcutter, monarchs go*
> *To place flowers on your tomb*[40]

Spanish enthusiasm for Lincoln faded after 1898, when the American war against Spain led to the loss of Cuba and the Philippines. The arrival of Spain's Second Republic in 1931 was not accompanied by a parallel revival of interest in Lincoln nor his words from Gettysburg. The international Abraham Lincoln Brigade that fought for the republicans during the Spanish Civil War in the 1930s probably tainted Lincoln's reputation among supporters of fascist dictator Francisco Franco.[41]

German immigrants to America had played an important role in the Civil War. More than 10 percent of the Union Army consisted of German-born soldiers, and among the leading military and political figures were men such as Carl Schurz; Franz Sigel; Gustave Koerner; Francis Lieber; Theodor Canisius; and the Salomon brothers of Wisconsin, Karl,

Frederick, and Edward, the latter serving as wartime governor. John G. Nicolay, President Lincoln's private secretary, was one of several Germans who surrounded Lincoln. Letters from soldiers to their relatives, and German-language publications from America, helped keep German citizens informed about events in America.[42]

Karl Marx, the German revolutionary in exile in London, wrote extensively on the American conflict for the Vienna *Presse*. Marx saw the struggle as nothing less than a death struggle of a feudalistic slaveholding aristocracy against the proponents of bourgeois capitalism—Marx took the side of the capitalists. Workers in Europe, Marx believed, stood by Lincoln and the Union because of the "natural sympathy the popular classes all over the world ought to feel for the only popular government in the world." He credited Lincoln for his unostentatious way of enacting revolutionary social change in the guise of mere policy decisions: "It fell to the lot of Abraham Lincoln, the single-minded son of the working class, to lead his country through the matchless struggle for the rescue of an enchained race and the reconstruction of a social world."[43]

Wilhelm Liebknecht, a founder of the German Social Democracy Party and close friend of Marx, became an enthusiastic admirer of Lincoln and America republicanism as a model for Germany. In 1886 he went on a speaking tour of America with Marx's daughter and later wrote a travel account in which he lauded Abraham Lincoln as an inspiration to German democracy.[44]

* * *

During the twentieth century, Lincoln's Gettysburg Address found employment in service of a variety of causes. If "government by the people" had been the most commonly evoked theme during the first half-century of the Address's afterlife, those passages emphasizing the sacrifice of those who "gave their lives that that nation might live" and the need to persevere in the "unfinished work" would become more salient in a century marked by two horrific world wars.

An American film, *Lincoln's Gettysburg Address*, produced by a New York company attracted international attention in 1912. A reviewer in Gloucester, Scotland, described the "very weird scenes": one showing hundreds of dead soldiers, and "suddenly a band of men and maidens dressed in white pass over them, and a man gliding over the bodies blows a trumpet," and ghostly images of the men rise while their corpses remain on the field of battle. The *Rhodesia Herald* applauded it as a "star film" featuring "thrilling scenes on the battlefield" from those "stirring and epoch-making times."[45]

During World War I, European allies fighting the Kaiser's Germany found ample opportunity to invoke Lincoln's speech, partly to appeal for American aid but also to summon citizens to sacrifice, to thank those who gave "the last full measure of devotion," and to justify the war as a defense of common principles of freedom, if not democracy. At Gettysburg, the London *Times* averred in 1915, Lincoln reminded his audience that "in the war still raging they were testing whether a nation conceived in liberty could long endure . . . We are firmly convinced that we ourselves are fighting for this same cause today."[46] British Prime Minister Herbert Asquith, in a dramatic speech before Parliament, resolved not to waiver until victory was theirs, and "almost in Lincoln's own words" repeated "that pledge to the heroic dead which rings through time from the Gettysburg oration."[47]

By the time of Lincoln's centenary in 1909, British newspapers had been reminding readers of Lincoln's birthday and reviewing new Lincoln biographies for years. Political leaders were so accustomed to reciting passages from Lincoln's Gettysburg speech, it hardly seemed necessary to cite their source.[48] As World War I loomed, many British leaders sought to cultivate the idea of a special Anglo-American commitment to free government. More than a century of warfare, commercial rivalry, and simmering resentment on both sides contradicted such efforts. In 1861 Britain had been the first to extend belligerent rights to the Confederacy, and throughout the war Lincoln and his secretary of state, William Seward, were constantly on guard against British intervention in favor of the South. After the war the United States successfully sued Britain for $15 million in damages at the hands of Confederate raiders that had been built in British shipyards in violation of its own neutrality laws.[49]

Just before the fiftieth anniversary of the speech in November 1913, Earl Curzon, the chancellor of Oxford University, gave a widely publicized address at Cambridge in which he lauded Lincoln's Gettysburg Address, along with his Second Inaugural speech, as among the finest examples of the "intellectual patrimony of the English-speaking race."[50]

During World War I, British poet and playwright John Drinkwater enjoyed great success with his play *Abraham Lincoln* in 1918, which went through sixteen printings by 1924, when it was made into a two-reel talking film. The film included a novel rendition of the Gettysburg Address woven into the president's Second Inaugural: "With malice toward none, with charity for all, it is for us to resolve that this nation, under God, shall have a new birth of freedom; and that government of the people, by the people, for the people, shall not perish from the earth."[51]

Another popular book, *Ruggles of Red Gap* (1915) by Henry Leon Wilson, celebrated the international impact of Lincoln's Gettysburg Address. It was immediately made into a Broadway play, later a silent movie, and in 1935 a popular Hollywood movie. It is the amusing story of a British servant named Marmaduke Ruggles, who finds himself in a rough-and-tumble town in the American West after a rich American couple win him in a game of poker. The climactic scene takes place in a Western saloon where Ruggles announces he wants to "leave service" and make something of himself. This, his American friends declare, is exactly what Abraham Lincoln advocated at Gettysburg, but none of them are able to recall just what it was that Lincoln said. Ruggles, played magnificently in the film by the British actor Charles Laughton, while the hushed crowd in the saloon looks on, recites from memory the entire Gettysburg Address as testament to his new-found belief in the American creed of freedom and equality.[52]

During the 1930s Lincoln's allusions in the Gettysburg speech to the ordeal of nations founded on liberty resonated deeply with Western Europeans witnessing the rise of fascism. In 1940, after France and most of northern Europe fell to Hitler's ruthless conquest, Britain was suddenly the last bastion of resistance. Lincoln's words from Gettysburg were put to good use by British leaders summoning America to come to its aid. With London besieged by Hitler's bombing attacks in March 1941, John Jacob Astor, an American-born British MP from the eminent New York Astor family, broadcast a response to President Franklin Roosevelt's promise of American aid to Britain: "Given the tools of war, we are confident we shall not fail," Astor assured the Americans, who then employed Lincoln's words by promising "freedom shall not perish from the earth."[53]

During World War II, Winston Churchill came to rival Lincoln as an orator of world renown. He, too, learned to make effective use of Lincoln in his appeals to America and its "special relationship" with Britain. For years Churchill had been raising the alarm against the rise of Nazi Germany, and in May 1940 he became prime minister following the resignation of Neville Chamberlin, whose ignominious efforts to appease Hitler had failed. Churchill immediately called on America to aid Britain in its lonely struggle to survive and restore freedom to Europe. "We shall never surrender," Churchill promised in a stirring speech in June 1940, soon after taking office. "And even if, which I do not for a moment believe, this Island or a large part of it were subjugated and starving, then our Empire beyond the seas, armed and guarded by the British Fleet, would carry on the struggle, until, in God's good time, the New World, with all its power and might, steps forth to the rescue and the liberation of the old."[54] It helped that Churchill's mother was American, for, despite his aristocratic pedigree, he could present himself as the embodiment of the "special re-lationship" between Britain and America. The Anglo-American bond was based not only on a common language, culture, and shared history, the British were eager to explain, but also on a common commitment to gov-ernment by the people. Churchill could think of no better way to assure Americans of these shared democratic values than to declare his admira-tion for Lincoln's Gettysburg Address. Soon after the Japanese attacked Pearl Harbor and America entered the war, Churchill gave a memorable speech before the US Congress in which he reminded his audience of his "American forebears" and assured them that "I have been in full harmony all my life with the tides which have flowed on both side of the Atlantic against privilege and monopoly, and I have steered confidently towards the Gettysburg ideal of 'government of the people by the people for the people.'"[55]

Lincoln also played a small but very poignant role in a propaganda film produced by the British Ministry of Information in 1940. *Words for Battle* was directed by Humphrey Jennings, who masterfully enveloped Lincoln and the Gettysburg Address within a carefully crafted version of Britain as the last bulwark of democratic Europe, faithful ally of America, and bastion of hope against the evils of fascism. The film opens with actor Laurence Olivier reading from England's iconic poets—Milton, Brown-ing, Blake, and Kipling—as the camera soars above the white cliffs of Dover and then takes viewers into England's grand cathedrals and quaint villages. Next come images of Winston Churchill rallying the British soldiers, while his voice resounds with the words of one of his greatest speeches beckoning Britain to battle: "We shall fight on the beaches, we shall fight on the landing grounds, we shall fight in the fields and in the streets, we shall fight in the hills; we shall never surrender" and promis-ing that Britain will "carry on the struggle" until America comes to rescue the old world.

The camera then shifts to a statue of Lincoln, which had been placed in Parliament Square in 1920. It is a replica of the twelve-foot bronze statue created by Augustus Saint-Gaudens, an Irish-born immigrant to America. Known as "Abraham Lincoln, the Man" or "Standing Lincoln," Saint-Gaudens depicted a pensive president who, it appears, has just risen from his chair and is about to speak. As the camera closes in on Lincoln, Olivier reads from the Gettysburg Address and finishes with a slight but telling modification to the last phrase. Instead of specifying "*this* nation" the British version has Olivier saying "that *the* nation under God shall have a new birth of freedom, and that government of the people, by the people, for the people shall not perish from the earth." Lincoln had become British, and so had his speech at Gettysburg.[56]

* * *

That Lincoln's words from Gettysburg resounded across the Atlantic may not surprise anyone, but they also played an unexpected role in what became the People's Republic of China. Sun Yat-sen, the founding father of the Republic of China, had received a Western education in Hawaii as a boy, and he spent considerable time in the United States during his period of exile in the 1890s and 1900s. As he explained it, the "Three Principles of the People" he devised in the 1890s were inspired by Lincoln's idea of government of, by, and for the people. For China he envisioned a nation *minzu*, the people's national consciousness; *minzhu*, the people's rights to govern themselves; and *minsheng*, the people's livelihood and welfare. In a 1919 public lecture, he praised the United States for achieving a democratic government and praised Lincoln for defending it. During World War II, while China was occupied by the Japanese, the US Post Office in 1942 issued a stamp with images of Lincoln and Sun. Below Lincoln were the words "of the people, by the people, for the people" and, in Chinese characters, Sun's complementary doctrine of the three principles.[57]

As China plunged into its own protracted civil war between 1945 and 1949, communist revolutionaries also went out of their way to align their cause with Lincoln. Thus Mao Zedong told a reporter in 1945 that the new China would be a "free, democratic" nation whose aim was to realize Abraham Lincoln's concept of government by the people and Franklin Roosevelt's Four Freedoms. When those opposing the communists in China created a new constitution for the Republic of China in 1947, it enshrined Sun Yat-sen's three principles of government and promised that theirs would be a "democratic republic of the people, to be governed by the people and for the people."[58]

Lincoln continued to maintain a historical presence in the communist People's Republic of China during the twentieth century, but less often as a champion of democracy than as a defender of national unity against dissident separatist movements in Taiwan, Tibet, and other parts of China. Former president Jiang Zemin, who had attended an American missionary school, took pride in reciting the Gettysburg Address from memory in English. When US President Clinton visited China in 1999, Premier Zhu Rongji made a point of telling him he considered Abraham Lincoln to be a model when it came to maintaining Chinese unity. In 2001 an editorial in the *People's Daily* denounced Washington's support of "two Chinas" and hailed Lincoln who "waged a resolute struggle politically, militarily, and diplomatically against conspirators who tried to create 'two Americas.'"[59]

Elsewhere in Asia, the rise of anticolonial nationalism after World War II found inspiration in Lincoln's words and example. Mohandas Gandhi, as early as 1905, while involved in the civil rights movement in South Africa, wrote a laudatory, if not always accurate, biographical sketch of Lincoln for the newspaper he published. For Gandhi, Lincoln was the symbol of a self-made man who by honest toil and self-education transcended his humble origins. But it was not Lincoln's material success or social ascendance as much as his moral convictions and sense of duty, especially his determination to end slavery, that won Gandhi's admiration. For Gandhi, too, Lincoln was the selfless martyr to the nation, a man who gave his life that others might be free: "It may safely be said that Lincoln sacrificed his life in order to put an end to the sufferings of others." Lincoln "can be said to be still alive," Gandhi thought; he "has become immortal, for his greatness consisted not in his talent or his wealth, but in his innate goodness. A nation that has such good qualities as Lincoln's is bound to rise."[60]

By invoking Lincoln, Gandhi and a wide array of other anticolonial leaders in Asia, Africa, and elsewhere sought to establish their legitimacy among the nations of the world and disarm critics by wrapping themselves in the mantle of Abraham Lincoln. During the Cold War, the US government turned the tables by taking the lead in exporting Lincoln's Gettysburg Address in the service of pro-American, anticommunist appeals abroad. President Dwight Eisenhower, soon after taking office in 1953, launched the United States Information Agency (USIA) to disseminate information aimed at "Telling America's Story to the World." The USIA included radio broadcasts in multiple languages over the Voice of America, libraries with publications on American history and literature, the Fulbright student and faculty exchange program, and a program for publication of books and pamphlets and for the dissemination of American films.[61]

The USIA was in full operation when the 150th anniversary of Lincoln's birth approached in 1959. President Eisenhower appointed a Lincoln Sesquicentennial Commission, which was about to play an important role in bringing Lincoln and the Gettysburg Address before the world at the height of the Cold War. Eisenhower was a great admirer of Lincoln, and, perhaps significantly, he had made a home on a farm in Gettysburg. To commemorate Lincoln's birthday, the Sesquicentennial Commission staged an enormous banquet in Springfield, Illinois, on February 9, 1959. It was attended by some 1,500 people, including a dazzling array of foreign dignitaries from twenty-one nations. To further underscore the international appeal of Lincoln, Eisenhower spoke briefly about him as a world figure.[62]

The keynote speaker for the event was the mayor of West Berlin, Willie Brandt, a former victim of Nazi persecution and another great admirer of Abraham Lincoln. It was natural that Brandt would pick as his theme Lincoln's "House Divided" speech. Berlin had been partitioned into sectors controlled by the United States, Britain, France, and the Soviet Union, and when the Soviets tried to cut off supply routes from the West to Berlin, the United States organized the Berlin airlift. Berlin had become a symbolic island of Western freedom surrounded by the communist bloc. In 1950 General Eisenhower, in his role as head of the US government's Crusade for Freedom, presented a replica of Philadelphia's Liberty Bell to the citizens of West Berlin, and Brandt referred to the bell in his Springfield speech: "The Freedom Bell also reminds us of the immortal work of Abraham Lincoln . . . Engraved on our Freedom Bell are these noble words from the Gettysburg Address: 'That this world,' Lincoln said 'nation,' but today he, too, would include the whole world, 'under God shall have a new birth of freedom.'" The USIA saw to it that a film of Brandt's Springfield address was shown across Germany. It also indirectly sponsored essay contests on Lincoln for German students. Throughout his career, in which he later served as chancellor of West Germany, Brandt continued to refer to Lincoln as an inspiration for Germany and, of course, a symbol of opposition to communism. "This man does not belong to you alone, my friends," Brandt told his audience in Springfield.[63]

During the Cold War, the USIA distributed millions of publications in a multitude of languages as part of its effort in "Telling America's Story to the World." Lincoln, his life story, and his speech at Gettysburg were often featured as the embodiment of American principles of freedom and democracy. The USIA's comic book biography of Abraham Lincoln, issued in 1958 and 1959, and widely distributed around the world, devoted a full page to the Address because it "so classically expresses the democratic ideal."[64]

As the Cold War became entangled with the American civil rights movement, Lincoln's words often became ammunition for criticism and even mockery. During most of its international career, the Gettysburg Address had been celebrated by an array of international figures for its defense of government by the people. During the Cold War, it was often the first line of Lincoln's oration, claiming America to be a nation "conceived in liberty and dedicated to the proposition that all men are created equal," that drew critical attention to the country's racial injustice.

The centennial of the Gettysburg Address took place in November 1963 during a maelstrom of controversy over the civil rights struggle at home and an unpopular war in Vietnam, and three days before the assassination of President John F. Kennedy. It seemed fitting that the ceremony addressed the international influence of the speech. Dean Rusk, then secretary of state, spoke on "International Aspects of Lincoln's Address" and observed that the "central commitments of the American experiment are probably known to more people in other lands through the words of the Gettysburg Address than through those of the Declaration of Independence." Lincoln's speech "has become the most widely read speech ever made by an American and perhaps by anyone in the English tongue. It has been translated into every written language and is cherished around the world."[65]

British ambassador John Chadwick, continuing the tradition of Anglicizing Abraham Lincoln, told the audience that Lincoln's speech had come "to be adopted and established as one of the noblest expressions of British ideals." For Britain, as for its ally America, he continued, "the standard which we must proclaim to all the world, is the moral and spiritual standard defined by Lincoln in the Gettysburg address." Sergio Fenoaltea, the Italian ambassador, remarked that his country was undergoing unification at the same time America was struggling to maintain its Union and that its leaders, Giuseppe Garibaldi and Giuseppe Mazzini, looked to America to lead the world struggle for freedom. It was the French ambassador, Hevré Alphand, who reminded Americans that Lincoln's speech at Gettysburg echoed the ideals of liberty, equality, and fraternity first proclaimed in France. He also broke with the tone of reverent homily to note that America was "still struggling against the dark forces of discrimination which Lincoln opposed."[66]

Historian Richard Current, reflecting on his USIA-sponsored lecture tour of India, noted that "in the present 'cold war,' we have one very valuable asset that the Russians do not: we have an Abraham Lincoln."[67] In the post–Cold War world, Lincoln and his Gettysburg speech would find new roles assigned to them. Seeking to counter the rising anti-American sentiment around the world following the invasion of Iraq in 2003, the Bush administration turned to Abraham Lincoln for help. Karen Hughes, the undersecretary of state, launched a public diplomacy program by installing "Lincoln Corners" in existing public libraries abroad. They were meant to provide collections of Lincoln's speeches and other works and serve as a site for public lectures and films. In a strained effort to align Lincoln to what he proclaimed as a "War on Terror," George W. Bush in his second inaugural address warned that the "rulers of outlaw regimes can know that we still believe as Abraham Lincoln did" that "those who deny freedom to others deserve it not for themselves; and, under the rule of a just God, cannot long retain it."[68]

While the Bush administration was recruiting Lincoln as the embodiment of American values of freedom and equality, others at home and abroad seemed eager to remind the world of another side of Lincoln—the iron-fisted ruler willing to suspend civil liberties and to do whatever it took to protect the nation. Frank J. Williams, a Rhode Island supreme court judge and member of the Abraham Lincoln Bicentennial Commission, told the conservative Heritage Foundation, in effect, that Abraham Lincoln would likely have approved of the treatment of "enemy combatants" at Guantanamo and would have understood the necessity of other infractions of civil liberties in order to protect the homeland in a time of war.[69] Government leaders abroad also invoked Lincoln to justify the curtailment of civic freedoms in the face of terrorism. In 2007 Pakistan's president, Perez Musharraf, criticized for his suspension of constitutional rights, quoted one of Lincoln's aphorisms: "Often a limb must be amputated in order to save a life, but a life is never wisely given to save a limb."[70] This was yet another reminder of what Willie Brandt remarked in 1959, that Lincoln no longer belonged to America, and his words could be enlisted in any number of causes. The Gettysburg Address, however, endured as the most revered statement of the ideals of equality, freedom, and self-government that in our time remain as embattled as they were a century and a half earlier.

Notes

1. Don H. Doyle, *The Cause of All Nations: An International History of the American Civil War* (New York: Basic Books, 2014), 85–105.

2. Donaldson Jordan and Edwin J. Pratt, *Europe and the American Civil War* (Boston: Houghton Mifflin, 1931), 251–252; Edwin Pratt, "Spanish Opinion of the North American Civil War," *Hispanic American Historical Review* 10, no. 1 (1930): 20, quoting El Pensamiento Español, Sept. 6, 1862.

3. Walt Whitman, *Specimen Days and Collect* (Philadelphia: D. McKay, 1883), 64.

4. Doyle, *Cause of All Nations*, 282–283.

5. *Tout pour le peuple, par un homme du peuple* (Paris: chez les marchands de nouveautés, 1833); *Liberté, égalité, fraternité. Honneur et patrie. Tout pour le peuple français* (Paris: chez l'auteur, 1848).

6. Joseph Rossi, *The Image of America in Mazzini's Writings* (Madison: University of Wisconsin Press, 1954), 134–136; Denis Mack Smith, *Mazzini* (New Haven, CT: Yale University Press, 1996), 84; John L. Haney, "Of the People, by the People, for the People," *Proceedings of the American Philosophical Society* 88, no. 5 (Nov. 7, 1944): 359–367; Eugenio F. Biagini, "'The Principle of Humanity': Lincoln in Germany and Italy, 1859," in *The Global Lincoln*, ed. Richard Carwardine and Jay Sexton (New York: Oxford University Press, 2011), 76–94. "Anticipating Lincoln," *Birmingham Gazette*, Aug. 17, 1916, notes an 1830 Swiss antecedent to "government by the people."

7. *The Times* Digital Archive 1785–1985.

8. Lincoln to Alessandro Repetti, June 13, 1863, Fondo Bersellini Repetti del Centro Internazionale Insubrico "C. Cattaneo" e "G. Preti" dell'Università degli Studi dell'Insubria, a Varese. Thanks to Professor Fabio Minazzi for making scanned copies of this and other letters available to me.

9. Karl Marx and Frederick Engels, *The Civil War in the United States* (New York: International, 1969), 23–24.

10. Gasparin, *Uprising of a Great People*, ix–x.

11. Daniel B. Carroll, *Henri Mercier and the American Civil War* (Princeton, NJ: Princeton University Press, 1971), 353.

12. "Gallenga, Antonio Carlo Napoleone," *Encyclopedia Britannica* (Cambridge: University Press, 1910). Amanda Foreman, *A World on Fire: Britain's Crucial Role in the American Civil War* (New York: Random House, 2011), 563; Jared Peatman, *The Long Shadow of Lincoln's Gettysburg Address* (Carbondale: Southern Illinois University Press, 2013), Kindle, 905–910; *Times* (London), Dec. 4, 1863.

13. "Latest Intelligence: America," *Times* (London), Dec. 3, 1863; "America," *Morning Post*, Dec. 4, 1863; "The Field of Gettysburg," *Times* (London), Dec. 4, 1863; "America," *London Daily News*, Dec. 4, 1863; "Foreign and Colonial," *Leeds Mercury*, Dec. 4, 1863; "The Commemoration of Gettysburg," *Dublin Evening Mail*,

Dec. 4, 1863; "The Field Of Gettysburg," *Dundee Courier*, Dec. 5, 1863; "Foreign Intelligence: America," *Essex Standard*, Dec. 9, 1863.

14. Ephraim Douglass Adams, *Great Britain and the American Civil War* (1924; New York: Russell and Russell, 1958), 2:37.

15. Goldwin Smith, "President Lincoln," *Macmillan's*, Feb. 1865, 302; Osborn H. Oldroyd, ed., *Words of Lincoln* (Washington, DC: O. H. Oldroyd, 1895), 84.

16. US Department of State, *The Assassination of Abraham Lincoln, Late President of the United States of America: And the Attempted Assassination of William H. Seward, Secretary of State, and Frederick W. Seward, Assistant Secretary, on the Evening of the 14th of April, 1865: Expressions of Condolence and Sympathy Inspired by These Events* (Washington, DC GPO, 1867), http://archive.org/details/ assassination1267unit.

17. H. C. Allen, "Civil War, Reconstruction, and Great Britain," in *Heard Round the World: The Impact Abroad of the Civil War*, ed. Harold Hyman (New York: Alfred A. Knopf, 1969), 73, quoting Edward Beesly; Brent E. Kinser, *The American Civil War in the Shaping of British Democracy* (Farnham, UK: Ashgate, 2011).

18. "The Reform Demonstration in Hyde Park," *Illustrated Times* (London), May 11, 1867; Adam I. P. Smith, "The Stuff Our Dreams Are Made Of: Lincoln in the English Imagination," in *Global Lincoln*, 125–127; Kinser, *The American Civil War*.

19. Henry Mayers Hyndman, *The Text-Book of Democracy: England for All* (E. W. Allen, 1881), 94.

20. Smith, "The Stuff Our Dreams Are Made Of," 126; "The Need for Liberal Action," *London Daily News*, Nov. 17, 1886.

21. "Opening of a Conservative Club at Grays," *Chelmsford Chronicle*, Aug. 13, 1886; "'Tory Democracy' Is 'Tory Democracy,'" *Reynolds's*, Apr. 15, 1888; *Western Times*, Jan. 27, 1893.

22. A Birmingham Woman, "An Appeal to Certain Radical Apostates," *Pall Mall Gazette*, June 8, 1885.

23. "Mrs. Henry Fawcett on Womanhood Suffrage," *Cambridge Independent Press*, Feb. 6, 1886.

24. "The Home Rule Fight in London," *Freeman's Journal* (Dublin), July 2, 1886.

25. Kevin Kenny, "Freedom and Unity," in *Global Lincoln*, 164.

26. Joseph M. Hernon, "The Use of the American Civil War in the Debate over Irish Home Rule," *American Historical Review* 69, no. 4 (1964): 1025.

27. Kenny, "Freedom and Unity," in *Global Lincoln*, 162.

28. Ibid., 157–170.

29. John Bigelow, *Retrospections of an Active Life: 1863–1865* (New York: Baker and Taylor, 1909), 557. Michael Vorenberg, "Liberté, Égalité, and Lincoln: French Readings of an American President," in *Global Lincoln*, 99, quoting Bigelow to William Cullen Bryant, May 16, 1865. Charles Forbes Montalembert, *La victoire*

du Nord aux États-Unis (Paris: E. Dentu, 1865); Count de Montalembert, *The Victory of the North in the United States* (Boston: Littell and Gay, 1866), quote on 22.

30. Bigelow, *Retrospections of an Active Life: 1865–1866* (New York: Baker and Taylor, 1909); Bigelow, *Retrospections: 1863–65*, 597; Jason Emerson, "A Medal for Mrs. Lincoln," *Register of the Kentucky Historical Society* 109, no. 2 (2011): 187–205.

31. César Pascal, *Abraham Lincoln; sa vie, son caractère, son administration* (Paris: Grassart, 1865), 128–130.

32. Édouard Laboulaye, "Les conferences en Angleterre et en Amérique," Revue des cours littéraires de la France et de l'étranger, Dec. 4, 1869, 309; Édouard Laboulaye, *Questions constitutionnelles* (Paris: Charpentier, 1872), 383.

33. Brian R. Hamnett, *Juárez* (New York: Longman, 1994).

34. US Consul to Havana Robert Schufeldt to Seward, Havana, Jan. 14, 1862, quoted in Dale T. Graden, *Disease, Resistance, and Lies: The Demise of the Transatlantic Slave Trade to Brazil and Cuba* (Louisiana State University Press, 2014), 209.

35. Nicola Miller, "'That Great and Gentle Soul': Images of Lincoln in Latin America," in *Global Lincoln*, 207–210.

36. Ibid., quoting Domingo Faustino Sarmiento, *Vide de Abran Lincoln, Décimo Sesto Presidente de Los Estados Unidos* (D. Appleton y ca., 1873), 213–214. Between 1860 and 1920 a Worldcat.org search identifies thirty-seven books in Spanish with Lincoln in the title, and 280 since 1920.

37. Miller, "'That Great and Gentle Soul,'" in *Global Lincoln*, 206–222; Emeterio S. Santovenia, Lincoln in *Martí: A Cuban View of Abraham Lincoln* (Chapel Hill: University of North Carolina Press, 1953), 45–46.

38. Emilio Castelar, *Cuestiones políticas y sociales* (Madrid: San Martin, 1870), 52, 56–57; Caroline Boyd, "A Man for All Seasons: Lincoln in Spain," in *Global Lincoln*, 194–196. Rafael M. de Labra, *Estudios biográfico-políticos* (Madrid: Impr. de La Guirnalda, 1887), 103–162; Boyd, "Man for All Seasons," in *Global Lincoln*, 195–196.

39. "The Revolution in Spain," *Leeds Times*, Oct. 3, 1868.

40. Boyd, "Man for All Seasons," in *Global Lincoln*, 191.

41. Ibid., 200.

42. Eugenio Biagini, "'The Principle of Humanity': Lincoln in Germany and Italy, 1859–1865," in *Global Lincoln*, 83–85.

43. Marx and Engels, *Civil War*, 48–49; Marx, "Address of the International Working Men's Association to Abraham Lincoln, President of the United States of America," Jan. 28, 1861, Marx and Engels Internet Archive, https://www.marxists.org/archive/marx/iwma/documents/1864/lincoln-letter.htm.

44. Jörg Nagler, "National Unity and Liberty Lincoln's Image and Reception in Germany, 1871–1989," in *Global Lincoln*, 249–251; Hartmut Keil, "German Socialist Immigrants and Political Institutions," in *In the Shadow of the Statue of*

Liberty: Immigrants, Workers, and Citizens in the American Republic 1880–1920, ed. Marianne Debouzy (Chicago: University of Illinois Press, 1992), 263; Wilhelm Liebknecht, *Ein Blick in die Neue Welt* (Stuttgart: J. H. W. Dietz, 1887).

45. *Gloucester Herald*, Oct. 1, 1912; *Rhodesia Herald* (Harare, Zimbabwe), Nov. 28, 1912. "Lincoln's Gettysburg Address" (1912), American Vitagraph Co., NY, IMDb, http://www.imdb.com/title/tt0002309/.

46. "A Great Example," *Times* (London), Apr. 16, 1915.

47. "The Prime Minister and Peace," *Derby Daily Telegraph*, Oct. 12, 1916.

48. "Remembrance Day," *Surrey Mirror*, Aug. 9, 1918; "Lanarkshire Insurance Committee," *Hamilton Advertiser*, Dec. 7, 1918; "South-East Essex," *Essex Newsman*, Dec. 7, 1918.

49. Howard Jones, *Blue and Gray Diplomacy: A History of Union and Confederate Foreign Relations* (Chapel Hill: University of North Carolina Press, 2010).

50. "Parliamentary Speeches," *Cambridge Independent Press*, Nov. 14, 1913; Jared Peatman, *The Long Shadow of Lincoln's Gettysburg Address* (Carbondale: Southern Illinois University Press, 2013), 88–89.

51. John Drinkwater, *Abraham Lincoln: A Play* (London: Sidgwick and Jackson, 1918), 71; J. Searle Dawley, *Abraham Lincoln* (Lee De Forest Films, 1924).

52. Harry Leon Wilson, *Ruggles of Red Gap* (New York: Washington Square Press, 1915); "Ruggles of Red Gap Goes on the Stage," *New York Times*, Dec. 25, 1915; "The Screen," *New York Times*, Sept, 10, 1923; Leo McCarey, director, *Ruggles of Red Gap*, 1935.

53. "We Shall Not Fail," *Gloucester Citizen*, Mar. 17, 1941.

54. "We Shall Fight on the Beaches," June 4, 1940, Churchill Centre, http://www.winstonchurchill.org/learn/speeches/speeches-of-winston-churchill/128-we-shall-fight-on-the-beaches.

55. Peatman, *Long Shadow*, kindle, 1881.

56. Humphrey Jennings, director, *Words for Battle*, 1941, YouTube, https://www.youtube.com/watch?v=nnZ5ExcXMxo; Smith, "The Stuff Our Dreams Are Made Of," 123.

57. Lyon Sharman, *Sun Yat-Sen; His Life and Its Meaning: A Critical Biography* (Stanford: Stanford University Press, 1968), 234, 271, 280, 286; Peatman, *Long Shadow*, Kindle, 1899–1905.

58. Sharman, *Sun Yat-sen*, 271; Alan M. Wachman, "Did Abraham Lincoln Oppose Taiwan's Secession from China?," in *Secession as an International Phenonmenon: From America's Civil War to Contemporary Separatist Movements*, ed. Don H. Doyle (Athens: University of Georgia Press, 2010), 365; De-min Tao, "'A Standard of Our Thought and Action': Lincoln's Reception in East Asia," in *Global Lincoln*, 231–234.

59. Wachman, "Did Abraham Lincoln Oppose Taiwan's Secession," 367.

60. Vinay Lal, "Defining a Legacy: Lincoln in the National Imaginary of India," in *Global Lincoln*, 176–177, quoting M. K. Gandhi, "Abraham Lincoln," in

The Collected Works of Mahatma Gandhi, 100 vols. (New Delhi: Ministry of Information and Broadcasting, Government of India, 1969–), 4:393–495, GandhiServe, http://www.gandhiserve.org/cwmg/VOL004.PD.

61. Jay Sexton, "Projecting Lincoln, Projecting America," in *Global Lincoln*, 293.

62. Peatman, *Long Shadow*, 148, 151–152.

63. Jorg Nagler, "National Unity and Liberty: Lincoln's Image and Reception in Germany, 1871–1989," in *Global Lincoln*, 249–252

64. Peatman, *Long Shadow*, Kindle, 2051.

65. Gettysburg Centennial Commission and Louis M. Simon, *Gettysburg—1963: An Account of the Centennial Commemoration: Report of the Commission to the General Assembly* (Harrisburg, PA: Gettysburg Centennial Commission, 1964), 96.

66. Peatman, *Long Shadow*, Kindle, 2313–2317

67. Sexton, "Projecting Lincoln, Projecting America," in *Global Lincoln*, 299.

68. Ibid., 288–289.

69. Frank Williams, "Abraham Lincoln and Civil Liberties in Wartime," *Heritage Lectures*, no. 834, May 5, 2004, accessible online at the Heritage Foundation, http://www.heritage.org/research/lecture/abraham-lincoln-and-civil-liberties-in-wartime.

70. Lal, "Defining a Legacy," in *Global Lincoln*, 183.

15

The Search for Meaning in Lincoln's Great Oration

Thomas A. Desjardin

SINCE THE GUNS of Gettysburg ceased their booming in early July 1863 and Abraham Lincoln stepped away from his three-minute speech on the same ground four months later, the story of the epic three-day conflict has come to mean many things to many people.[1] Perhaps the most well-known and closely examined element of the story of Gettysburg is the great oration given by the commander in chief at the dedication of the cemetery that had been set aside for the bodies of the Union soldiers who fell in battle.

From the conclusion of his oration, Lincoln's words have been re-peated, assessed, and interpreted in a multitude of ways. Their legacy has left ripples that run through literature, rhetoric, politics, and other fields of endeavor and still resonate today across the world. What we now call simply the Gettysburg Address was not always held in such high esteem nor granted the level of reverence that it enjoys today. The speech's rise from a few simple, dedicatory remarks to one of the greatest oratorical achievements in history reveals as much about how Americans see them-selves as it does about President Lincoln and his brief literary contribution.

The earliest impressions of the meaning of the Gettysburg Address formed the basis for a more elaborate cultural exercise through which the person of Lincoln, the importance of the dedication, and the remarkable eloquence and effectiveness of his speech have resonated down through the generations. Through each successive era, Americans have sum-moned the symbolism of the Address and inserted it into the public con-versation whenever solemnity or inspiration is needed.

The reverence that Americans feel toward it today says a lot about the importance of the event and the speech itself, but it also reveals a great deal about how we have used the famous oration to create an elaborate symbolic imagery—one that is interwoven within a uniquely American set of cultural myths and legends that help us understand who we are and where we have come from as a people.

There are many myths that have sprung from the story of the Gettysburg Address. Perhaps the most prolific is the notion that Lincoln drafted the text on the back of an envelope on his way to the event. Setting aside the inherent connection that exists between envelopes and addresses, this is not just some fanciful notion dreamt up by an early chronicler and repeated relentlessly by the generations that followed. There is a deeper construct at work that helps this particular conception resonate in the minds of Americans.

Roughly taken as a moment in time, the Civil War marks an enormous turning point in the growth and maturation of the United States. In the decades prior to the war, the country was a small but growing entity still rooted in a rural and, by the standards of the great nations then dominating the planet, unsophisticated realm. Americans had begun to see themselves as legitimate rivals to their cousins overseas and their nation as having the potential to become a dominant nation in its own right.

In a military sphere, the war had shown that the United States could produce martial leaders and strategists equal to any that Europe had yet offered. In fact, those who wrote of the great battles of the war described them in the same context as the epic struggles from the Napoleonic era back to the ancient Greeks.

In the age of foreign literary giants such as Charles Dickens and Jane Austen, Americans like Nathaniel Hawthorne wrote *The Scarlet Letter* and Louisa May Alcott penned *Little Women*. At the same time, Harriet Beecher Stowe's *Uncle Tom's Cabin* sold more copies than any volume save the Bible. But as the literary giants of Europe stretched across two thousand miles from Dickens's England past Victor Hugo's France to Leo Tolstoy's Russia, here in the United States they might be found in the same house. Hawthorne, who was educated on the same college campus where Stowe wrote her great work, later purchased a home from the Alcott family 140 miles away. The Alcotts, in turn, had bought the house years earlier with the help of their friend, literary great Ralph Waldo Emerson. Hawthorne later entertained his college chum Henry Wadsworth Longfellow in the home as the Alcotts had once received Henry David Thoreau. Thus could be found five masters of nineteenth-century literature without leaving the warmth of a single Massachusetts fireplace.

At the same time, American painters, sculptors, singers, and actors rose to prominence both here and in Europe, while in industry the young nation was quickly becoming the envy of the world. Americans developed a steam-powered rail system and stretched it across a vast continent. They fitted steam engines to boats and revolutionized travel and transportation. Factories brought European technology to the States and used it to accelerate production to levels that far surpassed the standard of their rivals across the Atlantic.

While their country was becoming a world power in virtually every field of endeavor, Americans could also boast that they had risen to these heights within roughly two centuries of settling the landscape and barely one hundred years since officially throwing off their ties to the old country. There may be no single character who solidifies this notion of American exceptionalism more than the Abraham Lincoln that has come down to us through the generations, and his rhetorical brilliance at Gettysburg fits with great neatness into the construct.

The iconic image of Lincoln as the rough frontier "rail-splitter" who emerged from the Kentucky wilderness to become one of the leading statesmen in world history is reflective of the image that many Americans embrace of their nation as a whole. Rough and primitive just decades earlier, the United States also emerged from the wilderness, shook off its simple, unsophisticated origins, and with remarkable speed rose to a level that equaled that of its more ancient rivals. This result could only have come about due to a unique American quality that is both distinctive and exceptional.

This is a powerful metaphor for the American nation as a whole: a rough and rugged collection of states carved out of the wilderness, yet with such natural prowess and intellect that it could, with little effort, summon greatness in words and deeds formerly ascribed exclusively to royalty.

If any American personifies this exceptional idea, it is the Abraham Lincoln we have created in our national memory. To that end, the Gettysburg Address serves as an important symbol, and the myths and legends that have attached to the speech and event are an important part of how we see ourselves. Our story of Lincoln's rise from a simple, wilderness-bred, self-educated rail-splitter to such an important statesman communicates a uniquely American quality. The idea that a person from such humble origins could craft so few words into one of the greatest orations ever conceived reinforces that sense of exceptionalism. That he could do so on the back of an envelope, as if this brilliance was almost an after-thought, elevates and reinforces this concept.

Perhaps just as important to this notion of American exceptionalism are the key phrases and themes contained in Lincoln's speech. While the Address served the purpose of eulogy for the dead, its brevity and elo-quence also provided an anthem for what truly set the young nation apart from its worldly rivals. As much as anything else, people the world over saw the American Civil War as a test of the great experiment of democ-racy. Young though it was by comparison, the United States was founded on a set of principles on which no other nation at that time owed its begin-nings. This, in the minds of many Americans, is what made the nation ex-ceptional and gave it an honor none of its rivals could claim. By centering his speech on the basic principles of freedom, liberty, and equality, Lin-coln literally gave voice to that which set his country apart in no small way. By doing so in so few words, he provided an easily learned creed that all of his future countrymen and women could memorize and take to heart.

At the time the fighting ended at Gettysburg, few people in the nation perceived it as the great crucible of the conflict, the turning point that it has since come to represent. At the same time, President Lincoln was not so universally revered by his contemporaries as one might perceive looking back through the lens of time. In fact, just nine months after the dedication, there was a widespread feeling that the Union was losing the war and that Lincoln was to blame. Things were so bad by August 1864 that even President Lincoln's supporters doubted he could win reelection in the coming fall. In a letter to Lincoln, *New York Tribune* editor Horace Greeley begged the president to give in to the South. "Our bleeding, bank-rupt, almost dying country," he wrote, "longs for peace—shudders at the prospect of fresh conscriptions, of further wholesale devastations, and of new rivers of human blood. I entreat you to submit overtures for pacifica-tion to the Southern insurgents."[2]

A month later, Greeley made his feelings public. In an editorial in the *Tribune*, he declared, "Mr. Lincoln is already beaten. He cannot be elected. And we must have another ticket to save us from utter overthrow."[3] Lin-coln himself was no more optimistic when he confided to a friend, "You think I don't know I am going to be beaten, *but I do* and unless some great change takes place, badly beaten."[4]

As it happened, a great change did take place when Union forces in the field won significant and decisive victories in two different theaters, and the nation gave Lincoln a vote of confidence at the ballot box to continue the struggle. Clearly, however, the nation in 1864 did not see Lincoln as the revered statesman that most perceive today.

As with the Battle of Gettysburg, Lincoln's speech was not considered by everyone to be as profound then as it is to modern audiences. Though there is considerable disagreement among the accounts of eyewitnesses, the immediate reaction of the crowd may have left even Lincoln with the impression that it had been a failure. The partisan newspapers of the day described the speech predictably according to the political ideology of their sponsors, and those in attendance either left no unusual record of the speech and the reaction to it, or offered varying, even opposing, accounts of each.

Among the most useful accounts of the dedication came from Gettysburg's own *Adams Sentinel,* a newspaper whose offices were a leisurely walk from the scene of the events. The paper dedicated nearly an entire page to the events and ceremonies, beginning with the arrival of the dignitaries the day before. The details provide both useful and anecdotal context such as how many soldiers from each state had already been relocated to the cemetery by that point (1,188 in all) and that "Gov. Curtin, straight, tall, clear-faced, was probably the handsomest gentleman of the party." For all its detail about the two-day happenings, however, the *Sentinel* failed to offer any opinion of the dedicatory speech made by the president. Even the text of the speech, rather than providing some insightful local authority, is the copy that had already been published in newspapers across the Northern states three days earlier.[5]

Perhaps the most interesting of these newspaper reactions came in two parts from the state capital of Harrisburg just forty miles away. Here, the *Patriot and Union* published its assessment the day after the dedication. "We pass over the silly remarks of the President," it read, "for the credit of the Nation we are willing that the veil of oblivion shall be dropped over them and that they shall no more be repeated or thought of."[6]

One hundred and fifty years later, the *Patriot-News,* descendent of the *Patriot and Union,* issued a somewhat tongue-in-cheek retraction of its original opinion. "Our predecessors," they admitted, "perhaps under the influence of partisanship, or of strong drink, as was common in the profession at the time, called President Lincoln's words 'silly remarks,' deserving 'a veil of oblivion.'" In the parlance of modern newspapers it then wrote, "In the editorial about President Abraham Lincoln's speech delivered Nov. 19, 1863, in Gettysburg, the *Patriot & Union* failed to recognize its momentous importance, timeless eloquence, and lasting significance. The *Patriot-News* regrets the error."[7]

In the South, news of the dedication moved more slowly, and most of the details of the event, including the text of Lincoln's speech, reached Southern cities by way of copies of papers from New York or Washington. In Richmond, the media and cultural center of the Confederacy, as well as its political capital, newspapers offered the same impressions. Five days after the dedication, the five major newspapers in the city began reporting anecdotes copied—or "clipped" in the vernacular of the day—from Northern papers. Focusing much ink on Edward Everett, they barely mentioned Lincoln until the eight days after the events.

"After the Orator of the day [Everett], President Pericles, or rather Abe, made the dedicatory speech; but had to limit his observations within small compass, lest he should tell some funny story over the graves of the Immortals."[8] This was a common theme in the Southern press, to portray the chief executive as a clownish figure prone more to silly stories than to soaring prose. Across Virginia, only one newspaper is known to have printed any part of Lincoln's Address and that was the Lynchburg *Virginian*, which printed on December 4 only the first line of it. Papers further South later clipped the sparse details from the Richmond papers, spreading few details across the Confederacy.[9]

Any traveler on the way from Washington, DC to Gettysburg by train in 1863 was required by the logistics of rail to make a stop at the junction in Hanover, a town a few miles to the east. When the train carrying the president made just such a stop on November 18, 1863, the chief executive felt obliged to say a few words of greeting to the few hundred people who had assembled.

As today, "correspondents," or reporters, of the period followed the president whenever possible, hungry for a few words to send across the telegraph lines in time for the next edition of their employer's newspaper or magazine. Lincoln's trip to Gettysburg was no different, and those within earshot recorded the unfortunate events that transpired.

"Well," said Lincoln to the crowd, "you have seen me, and, according to general experience, you have seen less than you expected." The crowd laughed in response, but Lincoln felt a bit more conversation was in order. "You had the Rebels here last summer, hadn't you?" he asked. When the reply came back to him in the affirmative, he responded with an uncharacteristically poor attempt at humor: "Well, did you fight them any?"

A Philadelphia reporter filed this description of the moment. "The people looked at each other with a half-amused, half-puzzled expression, while the long, tall form of the President leaned from the car as he waited the reply." Just a few months since a sharp cavalry skirmish had occurred and the overwhelming carnage just to the east had left no family untouched by the horrors of warfare, the attempt at humor seemed to fall flat. Perhaps in confusion or through some nefarious design, papers in Virginia picked up on these reports and one even informed their readers that this "clownish" act had been the Yankee president's much-reported Gettysburg Address.[10]

Soon after the great events occurred, those who lived in and experienced Gettysburg—both the battle and the dedication—paid no homage to the president's speech. David Wills, organizer of the dedication and in whose home Lincoln had stayed the night before, sent an official report to the Pennsylvania state legislature. In it, he quoted Everett's speech but not Lincoln's.[11] Then, in 1865, former congressman and clerk of the US House of Representatives, Edward McPherson, published a widely read political history of the nation during the war years that included an entire chapter of Lincoln's writings, including several of his speeches. McPherson, however, made no mention of the speech at the dedication, though he had been present at the event, which took place just a mile and a half from his home.[12] Horace Greeley, too, wrote a history of the war that gave a full chapter to the battle at Gettysburg but made no mention at all of Lincoln's oration months later.[13]

Even most of the speeches that eulogized the slain president failed to conjure any image of or mention Gettysburg. Notable among the few exceptions was Ralph Waldo Emerson, who gave a funeral oration for Lincoln in which he declared that the dedication speech "will not easily be surpassed by words on any recorded occasion."[14]

By the late 1860s, a reading of Lincoln's oration was becoming a somewhat common element in patriotic celebrations across the Northern states. When local newspapers described such events, however, the "a" in "address" had yet to be capitalized to make the phrase a formal title, rather than just a descriptive term. The idea of the "Gettysburg Address," as it is known today, had not yet formed. In fact, use of the term "Gettysburg address" was as likely to be connected to Edward Everett's speech as Lincoln's. It was not until 1940 that the formal name, with or without quotes, came into regular use in newspapers and 1970 before nearly all references made use of the term as a capitalized title, often listing it among the other documents of Americana such as the Declaration of Independence.

In the late 1870s an artist began a project that might have rescued the oration from obscurity in the way that Emanuel Leutze had popularized "Washington Crossing the Delaware" in 1851. Albion Bicknell, a Massachusetts artist, began work on a huge painting that would include nearly two dozen life-sized portraits of Lincoln, his cabinet, and a handful of Union generals.

Following the marketing method of the day, Bicknell began painting while he sought subscriptions for buyers who would receive a steel plate engraved lithograph of the finished work two years later. The project was a failure. The painting bears no physical resemblance to the setting of the dedication and includes dignitaries who were not present at the speech. Despite a lack of subscriptions, Bicknell finished the painting, which today hangs in the public library in Malden, Massachusetts. Bicknell's effort not only failed to raise the status of Lincoln's oration in the public imagination, but it may also have discouraged other artists from attempting to capture the same subject on canvas.

Even in its obscurity, Lincoln's speech occasionally received praise from one source or another, though sparingly. An 1891 article that circulated in many newspapers, for example, described a conversation between the correspondent and a New England professor of rhetoric. The professor lamented the lack of adequate contemporary oratory for use in his classroom but referred to the eulogy given by James G. Blaine on the death of President Garfield. It read: "The professor said that the [Blaine] extract, which for some years passed almost unnoticed, just as Lincoln's Gettysburg oration did, has now become almost as familiar as was the immortal Gettysburg address, and is sure to be handed down to posterity as a noble example."[15]

Five years later, the greatest orator of his era, William Jennings Bryant, framed what was becoming the prevailing view of Lincoln's great oration by saying, "His Gettysburg Address is not surpassed, if equaled, in simplicity, force, and appropriateness by any speech of the same length of any language. It is the world's model in eloquence, elegance, and condensation. He might safely rest his reputation as orator on that speech alone."[16]

Once Reconstruction came to an end, the Southern states voted as a solid, cohesive block in nine consecutive presidential elections, an electoral phenomenon that lasted four decades. This tremendous unity of political views could not be overlooked by national politicians of all stripes and helped contribute to a national sense of reconciliation that was accelerated in 1898 when the nation went to war with a foreign power. The war with Spain saw generals of both blue and gray fighting together against a common foe, reigniting a common patriotism and helping both regions set aside their cultural differences, for better or worse.

Less than a decade later, *Scribner's* magazine published a short story by Mary Shipman Andrews, titled "The Perfect Tribute." Andrews was born in Alabama, was raised in Kentucky, and, having married a New York attorney, was living in Syracuse, New York. In this fanciful tale, Lincoln anonymously attends to a Confederate officer, dying of his Gettysburg wounds in a Washington hospital. The Southerner, not realizing his visitor is the president, speaks reverently of the Address at Gettysburg, predicts that children of both regions would recite it in years to come, and wonders not that the audience failed to applaud when Lincoln had finished. "One might as well applaud the Lord's Prayer," he said. "It would be sacrilege."[17]

While Bicknell's artwork failed to popularize Lincoln's Address, Andrews's literary work succeeded wildly. The story was published in book form numerous times and became a hugely popular bestseller, selling more than a half-million copies nationwide. Andrews's mixed Alabama-New York loyalties and her heart-tugging story, told from the perspective of a Southern officer who admired the speech, helped increase the awareness and appreciation of Lincoln's words in the South as much as the North. Thus a new generation was exposed to the Address in a positive, if not melodramatic, way, helping ignite its popularity at a time of rekindled sectional unity and patriotism. In time, the story was eventually made into a feature film in 1935 and a television movie in 1991.

Andrews's story was part of a sort of great awakening for the oration as it rose from relative obscurity to capture the imagination of Americans young and old. In a study of newspapers around the turn of the century, Barry Schwartz determined that mentions of Lincoln's speech grew exponentially—by more than ten times between 1880 and 1900 and then fifteen times more by 1930. At the same time, the speech could be found and heard more and more in schools as divined from a study of textbooks by Jared Peatman in his *The Long Shadow of Lincoln's Gettysburg Address*. No doubt the short duration of the speech and a predilection for rote learning aided in its popularity, and before long a printed copy of the text took its place on the classroom wall alongside portraits of Abraham Lincoln and George Washington.[18]

* * *

Seldom in history has the weight of a prominent father fallen as heavily on a son as it did upon Robert Todd Lincoln. The death of the president in 1865 brought tremendous responsibility to his oldest surviving child, who was then but twenty-two years old. Not only did he have to tend to familial duties, including the arrangements for his father's funeral, but he also had to care for his grieving mother and his brother, Tad, who had turned twelve years old less than a week before their father's death. These duties would be well enough a burden on an average citizen in normal times, but when the father is the president of the United States the burden is compounded. Add to this the fact that this was no ordinary president and that he led the country in extraordinary times, and one can begin to understand the role that Robert took on, willingly or otherwise, after the death of his father. With the deepening withdrawal of his mother and the death of his only surviving sibling Tad in 1871, Robert became the arbiter of his father's legacy.

Conscientious in his role, Robert seemed reluctant to extend his work to public events, almost never agreeing to participate in them as his father's surrogate. This reluctance faded only slightly in 1896, when he agreed to offer a few remarks on the thirty-eighth anniversary of the Lincoln–Douglas debates, fourteen years later at the centennial of his father's birth, and again thirteen years afterward at the dedication of the Lincoln Memorial in Washington, DC. At these last two, however, he declined to speak to the assembled audience.

Though not predisposed to shape the image of his father through public spectacle, Robert played a significant role in the memory of the president as portrayed in print. He willingly answered queries from admirers and scholars and worked closely to shape a biography by Lincoln's secretaries John Hay and John Nicolay, trading access to the president's papers in exchange for the right to edit out whatever he found not to his liking.[19]

Through the many interactions he had with the Gettysburg Address, Robert played a key role in determining which version of his father's speech would be used in an official capacity. The legislation that established the Gettysburg battlefield as a national park in 1895, for example, included a requirement that "a suitable bronze tablet, containing on it the address delivered by Abraham Lincoln, President of the United States, at Gettysburg Nov. 19, 1863, on the occasion of the dedication of the cemetery at that place, and such tablet, having on it besides the address a medallion likeness of President Lincoln, to be erected on the most suitable site within the limits of said park."[20]

Moving at the speed of government, this project came to fruition seventeen years later. As he worked to carry out the requirement, Chief Quartermaster General James Aleshire wrote to Robert in an effort to determine which version of the speech would be most appropriate. By then, Robert had settled on which copy of the Address he preferred, and to General Aleshire he replied, "As I wrote to you before, the Baltimore Fair version represents my father's last and best thought as to the address, and the corrections in it were legitimate for the author, and I think there is no doubt they improve the version as written out for Col. Hay."[21]

This effort resulted in the monument to Lincoln's oration placed within the grounds of the Soldiers' cemetery. Dedicated in 1912, it stands about two hundred fifty yards from where Lincoln originally delivered the words. It also decided which words would be used on iron plaques at each of the other seventy-five national cemeteries across the country at that time.

Arriving at what he considered the preferred version of the Address could not have been difficult for Robert by that time, as the request followed nearly two decades of discussion about the Address and its place in American culture. Nineteen years earlier the Hay-Nicolay biography—all ten volumes of it—became available to the book-buying public after years of studious research that included Robert's aid. The result was highly agreeable to the younger Lincoln, as he explained to John Hay when the work neared completion:

> Many people speak to me & confirm my own opinion of it as a work in every way excellent—not only sustaining but elevating my father's place in History. I shall never cease to be glad that the places you & Nicolay held near him & in his confidence were filled by you & not by others.[22]

With the biography put to rest, Nicolay set about specifically focusing on the Gettysburg speech, and his work culminated in an article in *Century* magazine in 1894. Aware of the growing legend that Lincoln had drafted the speech on the train en route to Gettysburg, he set about disproving the story. While comparing the known copies of drafts of the speech and relying on what he had gained from his intimate knowledge of Lincoln's time and habits as president, Nicolay laid bare the known details of Lincoln's part in the dedication and the writing of his remarks. In this, Robert Todd Lincoln must have also been quite satisfied with the result. When asked some years later to autograph a photograph of his father for an admirer, he declined, as was his custom, but sent instead a bound copy of the *Century* piece, which he signed.[23]

Another opportunity to dwell on his father's great oration came in 1909 with the centennial celebration of his father's birth. The rekindled attention and activity surrounding this event also intensified public interest in what was increasingly becoming known as the president's greatest oration. It was at this time that Robert informed the Gettysburg Park authorities of his preference for public use of the "Baltimore Fair," or Bliss copy, of the text, a decision he reconfirmed during the process of designing the Lincoln Memorial on the National Mall in Washington, DC, which opened to the public in 1922. In doing so, Robert established this version of the text as that which would pass down through future generations as the closest thing to an official version.

* * *

Like his son, subsequent presidents have understood that Lincoln was a very tough act to follow. With this in mind, post-Lincoln instances of presidential participation at Gettysburg anniversaries have met with mixed success. In 1938, for the seventy-fifth anniversary of the battle, President Franklin Roosevelt gave the keynote speech to a crowd estimated at 200,000, while the intense traffic prevented another 100,000 from reaching the field. Roosevelt used the opportunity to pay tribute to his famous predecessor and his ideas:

> But the fullness of the stature of Lincoln's nature and the fundamental conflict which events forced upon his Presidency invite us ever to turn to him for help. For the issue which he restated on this spot seventy-five years ago will be the continuing issue before this nation so long as we cling to the purposes for which the Nation was founded—to preserve under the changing conditions of each generation a people's government for the people's good.[24]

Roosevelt's appearance had begun to establish something of a precedent for important Gettysburg anniversaries, coming as it did just twenty-five years after President Woodrow Wilson had given the keynote address at the fiftieth anniversary of the battle in 1912. Speaking before thousands of

Civil War veterans, Wilson, however, made no reference to Lincoln what-soever. Perhaps a half-century was still not long enough for a Democrat to heap praise upon a Republican.

The use of Lincoln's words at Gettysburg is not limited solely to the writings or speeches of US political leaders or to the United States geo-graphically. The inspirational effect of the Address has carried across generations and oceans, leaving its mark in significant ways. Like all his-torical documents, it is viewed by each generation through a lens created by the experiences of those who live in that era. As a result, the meaning of Lincoln's words change with the passage of years so that they reflect as much about the time in which they are viewed as they do about 1863.

As the Address became more popular into the twentieth century, it became a part of the national and world events that Americans experi-enced. With the onset of two world wars, phrases from the Address found uses in patriotic songs, recruiting and fundraising pamphlets and post-ers, and other wartime propaganda. The ideas raised by Lincoln about whether "a nation conceived in liberty" could long endure were useful concepts against the forces of the Kaiser, then fascism, and eventually the Soviet Union.

In November 1950 the Chicago Historical Society gathered all five known handwritten copies of the Address for an eleven-day exhibition. This marked the first time all five copies had ever been displayed in the same place, and the resulting publicity helped reintroduce the Address to a new generation of Americans.

Spurred by the growth in the oration's popularity, those with a deep interest in the dedication, and its official presidential remarks, searched to uncover and confirm a myriad of details that might shed new light on the event and its historical importance. In 1952, nine years before the Civil War centennial, Josephine Cobb, chief of the Still Photo section at the National Archives, reexamined a glass plate that served as the nega-tive of a photograph taken during the dedication by two photographers employed by Matthew Brady. After some study, Cobb located the unmis-takable visage of a hatless President Lincoln in the process of sitting down on the dais just before the day's ceremonies began. This was the first time anyone had seen, or even known of, an actual photograph of Lincoln at Gettysburg.[25]

In 1978, no doubt as a result of repeated questioning from tourists, researchers at the Gettysburg National Military Park set about studying photographs taken the day of the ceremonies in order to determine the location of the spot where Lincoln stood during his speech. Sometime after, Civil War photography expert William Frassanito made a deeper investigation and determined that the stage set up for the dedication was not in the Soldiers' cemetery at all, but a few yards away in the adjacent and private Evergreen Cemetery. Decades after the dedication, a large iron fence had been erected to separate the two burying grounds with the result—though probably not the intent—of confusing tourists for decades to come. Even if armed with Frassanito's research, one is unlikely to find the exact spot where Lincoln stood. When they ask the inevitable question, visitors today are met with the reply that he stood "somewhere over in that area, but you can't go there. It's private."[26]

* * *

As the Cold War reached its height in the 1960s, so did interest in the Civil War as the centennial of the great conflict neared. In the years leading up to it, a unique set of circumstances aligned that helped bring Lincoln's words into greater public use. With the civil rights movement growing in activity and public awareness, the ideas conjured in the dedication speech became more relevant. Meanwhile, the president of the United States just happened to be a resident of Gettysburg. Dwight Eisenhower had never really had a permanent home prior to the end of World War II.

Ike was a captain during the First World War, and, at that time, the War Department owned the Gettysburg battlefield. It made sense, then, that when the need for training areas became apparent, military planners chose the land over which the famous Pickett's Charge had passed to site a tank-training school. Captain Eisenhower was assigned to command the school and grew fond of the town and the battlefield. Decades later, after the Second World War came to a close, he bought a farm a short distance away, which became the closest thing to a permanent home that he ever knew. During his presidency, Ike would make the relatively short trip from Washington, DC to his "vacation home" adjacent to the battlefield. His fondness for the story of Gettysburg and Lincoln often made its way into Eisenhower's speeches.

The cultural events of the era combined further as the centennial of the Civil War, and its now most famous battle, approached. All these forces seemed to come together with Martin Luther King, Jr.'s "I Have a Dream" speech in August and Eisenhower's fateful standing in for President Kennedy in November at the centennial of Lincoln's great oratory. All these key people and events borrowed heavily from what was more often referred to as the Gettysburg Address.

Eisenhower's fondness may have rubbed off a bit on his vice president, Richard Nixon, whose ancestor was awarded a Medal of Honor for his bravery at Gettysburg and lies buried in one of the graves over which Lincoln spoke a century earlier. Nixon's relationship with the famous speech, however, may have helped inspire an odd event in May 1970, just five days after the killing of four students by National Guard soldiers at Kent State University. Nixon decided to make the short trip to the Lincoln Memorial to speak to students who were then engaged in a protest of the invasion of Cambodia by American troops.

Nixon was accompanied by his valet, to whom he pointed out the large engraving of the Gettysburg Address in the memorial, and he conversed in rambling, almost nonsensical conversations with some of the protestors. The whole affair left Nixon's chief of staff, H. R. Haldeman, admitting in his diary, "I am concerned about his condition," and he added that Nixon's behavior there was "the weirdest day so far."[27]

What is often considered Nixon's greatest triumph, the warming of relations with China, also had a brief connection to Lincoln's great speech. In 1989, during a visit to China, Nixon met with that nation's future president Jiang Zemin, who suddenly recited the Address from memory and in English (a feat he performed again years later during his first encounter with President Bill Clinton). Nixon is said to have joined in the recitation.[28]

Standing on the steps of the Lincoln Memorial in Washington, DC, a little more than two months before the 100th anniversary of Lincoln's great moment, Martin Luther King, Jr. gave his now-immortal "I Have a Dream" speech. King opened his great oration with the words, "Five score years ago, a great American, in whose symbolic shadow we stand today, signed the Emancipation Proclamation."

Just a few days prior to the speech, King had intimated to Al Duckett, a black journalist who was ghostwriting a book for King, that his Washington speech needed to be a "sort of a Gettysburg Address." King succeeded in that his speech has been the subject of much analysis and acclaim, perhaps eclipsed in American oratory only by Lincoln's work a century prior. In fact, President John F. Kennedy was due to speak at the centennial commemoration on the ground of the Soldiers' cemetery at Gettysburg, but he was called away on a political errand to Dallas, Texas, from which he never returned. In his stead, former President

Dwight Eisenhower, whose home was almost within sight of the cemetery, gave the keynote address. Three days later Kennedy was assassinated.²⁹

In a very real way, Lincoln's Address also helped President Jimmy Carter secure peace in the Middle East in 1978. While sitting at the presidential retreat at Camp David just a few miles southwest of the famous battlefield, Carter was then in the fourth day of intense negotiations designed to bring peace between Egypt and Israel—a conflict so old that it predated Moses. When the talks hit an impasse, Carter decided to make use of the nearby historic site.

"We went to the Civil War battlefield at Gettysburg one day," he later recalled, "and I made them both agree not to talk about the Middle East or about anything that happened since 1865."³⁰ Thanks to the legacy of meaning connected to the Gettysburg story since 1863 (much of it literally carved in stone in more than a thousand monuments and markers) Carter's choice was a fertile place for symbolic demonstration and persuasion. Two powers from the same region, grown from the same land but with distinct cultural histories, had once differed so greatly with each other that they engaged in the bloodiest war the continent had ever known; the worst fighting happened on the ground the leaders were then touring.

When that war was over, the two powers became one again, healed their wounds, set aside many of their differences, and, as a result of their peaceful cooperation, became the most powerful nation the world has ever known. If the North and South could do this, then Egypt and Israel had a chance at least. As he admitted later in his memoirs, Carter also wanted to demonstrate the high cost of war and persuade the two leaders to sign the first-ever peace agreement between Israel and an Arab nation.

The Egyptian took to the field right away. As a military student, Sadat had studied Gettysburg in detail and recognized it as the turning point in the Civil War. The Israeli, however, was slower to the mark as he knew nothing about the battle. When the group passed the monument commemorating Lincoln's Gettysburg Address, however, Begin, in a thick Yiddish accent, recited it from memory, perhaps adding an Israeli emphasis to the line "that this nation . . . shall not perish from the earth." It took many more hours of negotiating, but less than a week later the three leaders took part in a historic signing ceremony for an agreement that brought peace between the two long-warring nations.

Though not to such a tragic extent, the next major anniversary of the Address in 2013 created some discomfort for another president. Participating in a project by documentary film producer Ken Burns, commemorating the 150th anniversary of the Gettysburg Address, President Obama agreed to read the speech aloud for Burns to use in his film. Obama's recitation raised eyebrows when he skipped over two of Lincoln's 272-word masterpiece, omitting the phrase "under God." During his administration Obama had made a point of not offending members of any religion, particularly Islam, and critics assumed the omission was a conscious action on the president's part. Obama's spokesman was left to explain to the media that Burns had provided the Nicolay copy of the Address, named in honor of the Lincoln staffer who preserved it. Since this version of the Address did not include the two words in its original, Obama had simply stuck to the script. [See p. 322 for a complete transcription of the Nicolay text.]

This was not the only time that an Obama omission and the Gettysburg Address raised the ire of his critics. As the sesquicentennial anniversary of the dedication drew near in 2013, Obama had been the obvious choice of those planning the commemoration events at Gettysburg. Just a few days before the event, however, the White House announced that the president would not attend the anniversary event but would instead give a speech at the annual meeting of the *Wall Street Journal's* CEO Council.

A decision by any president to avoid giving a speech that would obviously draw intense scrutiny and comparisons with his more eloquent predecessor was not completely unexplainable, but Obama had made his many connections to Lincoln a matter of regular notice. Setting aside the obvious connection between the Great Emancipator and the first US president of African-American heritage, Obama, like Lincoln, hailed from Illinois. He had announced his candidacy seven years earlier near Lincoln's law office in Springfield, and he twice took the official Oath of Office with his hand on Lincoln's Bible. Making his way to his first inauguration in 2009, he chose to follow the same route from Philadelphia to Washington along which Lincoln had passed for his first inauguration in 1861. Whatever the reason, President Obama let pass the opportunity to make presidential oratorical history, whether good or bad, when he declined to attend the 150th anniversary of the dedication.

During numerous events, American politicians and dignitaries have summoned the story of Gettysburg publically, perhaps most recently in the wake of the tragedies of September 11, 2001. At a memorial service marking the first anniversary of the terrorist attacks on the World Trade Center, organizers asked New York then-Governor George Pataki to offer words of consolation and inspiration. Rather than craft words of his own to help give some meaning to this modern tragedy, he instead stepped to the podium and read from Lincoln's Gettysburg Address. As with Eisenhower, Roosevelt, Wilson, Nixon, and Carter before him, Gettysburg was good context for a politician in difficult yet auspicious circumstances.[31]

Despite its delayed start as a cultural icon, the Gettysburg Address has become as renown and oft-quoted a document as any in human history. Yet it is not always a solemn occasion that drives the urge to recall Lincoln's speech. In 2004, sports columnist Frank Deford penned and then recited "A Fenway Park Address" in honor of the unlikely victory of the Boston Red Sox over their archrival the New York Yankees. It was a not-so-heady moment (unless you happen to be a Red Sox fan) but without much effort, nearly every listener could understand without being told directly that the whimsical essay was a rewriting of the Gettysburg Address.

"Now we are engaged again in a great series," wrote Deford, "testing whether, without victory, this city or any city so dedicated to the national pastime can long endure."[32]

On occasions and memorials, reunions and anniversaries alike, words and phrases from the great oration find voice in a multitude of ways. Another example occurred as recently as May 2014 when soldiers and veterans gathered near the Lincoln Memorial at the Vietnam Wall to read the names of those who had fallen in service during the "Global War on Terror" in Iraq since the attacks of September 2001.

On this occasion former General David Petraeus, disgraced into resigning as director of the CIA just over a year and a half earlier, made an unusual public appearance and in civilian clothes to help recite aloud the names of the fallen who had been under his command in Iraq serving in the 101st Airborne. Shielding himself in the solemnity of the event and familiar words of tribute, Petraeus paid respects to "those who gave that last full measure of devotion."[33]

On January 8, 2011, a gunman opened fire outside a grocery store in Tucson, Arizona, killing six people and wounding thirteen more, including Congresswoman Gabrielle Giffords. A few days later, President Obama spoke to the families of the injured and slain. As he did, he pointed out that Giffords and her staff "were fulfilling a central tenet of the democracy envisioned by our founders—representatives of the people answering to their constituents, so as to carry their concerns to our nation's capital. Gabby called it 'Congress on Your Corner'—just an updated version of government of and by and for the people."[34]

These are but a few of the many thousands of similar events, whether solemn or celebratory, that have prompted Americans the world over to call to mind the many meaningful messages carefully and skillfully woven into the nation's most famous public oration. Largely forgotten for decades after its original debut, the Gettysburg Address found purchase in the public imagination and grew in relevance and meaning through generations of American cultural evolution. Today it is symbolic, not only of the ideas that Lincoln had in mind a century and a half ago, but also in the context of the events and cultural themes prevalent in our time.

Fortunately for those who have found courage, comfort, and solace in its meaning over the passage of seven score and eleven years, there is one phrase of the speech that we all must agree was "a flat failure." Lincoln could not have been more wrong in his reckoning that "the world will little note nor long remember what we say here." In fact, he missed his mark by the widest of margins—a colossal mistake in an otherwise flaw-less collection of words, which somehow enhances it all the more. Few events, if any, have been more intensely studied for what was said there than the dedication of the Soldiers' cemetery at Gettysburg.

Notes

1. Portions of this chapter stem from another work by the same author, *These Honored Dead: How the Story of Gettysburg Shaped American Memory.*

2. Horace Greeley to Lincoln, July 7, 1864. Abraham Lincoln Papers, Washington, DC, Library of Congress.

3. *New York Tribune*, August 5, 1864.

4. William F. Zornow, *Lincoln and the Party Divided* (Norman: University of Oklahoma Press, 1954), 112.

5. *Adams Sentinel* (Gettysburg), Nov. 24, 1863.

6. *Patriot and Union* (Harrisburg), Nov. 20, 1863.

7. *Patriot-News* (Harrisburg), Nov. 15, 2013.

8. *Richmond Enquirer*, Nov. 27, 1863.

9. *Virginian* (Lynchburg), Nov. 4, 1863.

10. "The Gettysburg Celebration," *Inquirer* (Philadelphia), Nov. 21, 1863. A good example can be found in "The Cemetery—Speech and Wit of Lincoln," *Virginian* (Lynchburg), Nov. 27, 1863.

11. "Report of David Wills," in *Revised Report Made to the Legislature of Pennsylvania, Relative to the Soldiers' National Cemetery at Gettysburg* (Harrisburg, 1867).

12. Edward McPherson, *A Political History of the United States of America During the Great Rebellion* (Washington, DC, 1865).

13. Horace Greeley, *The American Conflict: A History of the Great Rebellion in the United States of America, 1860–1865* (Chicago, 1866).

14. Ralph Waldo Emerson, "Remarks at the Funeral Services Held in Concord, April 19, 1865," in *Ralph Waldo Emerson (1803–1882): The Complete Works*, vol. 11 (New York and Boston: Houghton, Mifflin, 1904).

15. "Stood the Textbook Test," *Topeka State Journal*, Oct. 11, 1891, among others.

16. William Jennings Bryan, *Speeches of William Jennings Bryan*, vol. 2 (New York: Funk and Wagnalls, 1911).

17. "The Perfect Tribute," *Scribner's*, July 1906, 17–24.

18. Barry Schwartz, "American Journalism's Conventions and Cultures, 1863 to 2013: Changing Representations of the Gettysburg Address," in *Journalism and Memory*, ed. Barbie Zelizer et al. (New York: Macmillan, 2014). Jared Peatman, *The Long Shadow of Lincoln's Gettysburg Address* (Carbondale: Southern Illinois University Press, 2013).

19. "Lincoln's Gettysburg Address," *Century*, Feb. 1894, 3–16.

20. 53rd Cong., 3d Sess., chap. 80, sect. 8 (1895).

21. Robert Todd Lincoln to General Aleshire, May 5, 1909, in John P. Nicholson, "Scrapbook Containing Correspondence & Related Items Regarding the Movement for Placing Bronze Tablets of the Gettysburg Address, 1909–1920," Abraham Lincoln Presidential Library, Springfield, IL.

22. David C. Mearns, *The Lincoln Papers* (New York: Doubleday, 1948), 1:80.

23. Robert Todd Lincoln to J. L. Van Zelm, Feb. 11, 1909, Louise and Barry Taper Collection, Abraham Lincoln Presidential Library, Springfield, IL.

24. "Speech of the President, Gettysburg," July 3, 1838, Hyde Park, NY, FDR Library and Museum.

25. The photo is cataloged at the National Archives, Washington, DC, in Records of the Chief Signal Officer, 111-B-4975.

26. William Frassanito, *Early Photography at Gettysburg* (Gettysburg: Thomas, 1995), 163–167.

27. National Archives/Nixon Presidential Materials Project (NPM); White House Special Files; Staff Member and Office Files; H.R. Haldeman's longhand journals; Vol. V, April 17 – July 22, 1980; May 9, 1970, p. 45.

28. "Meet Jiang Zemin," *Time*, Oct. 27, 1997.

29. David J. Garrow, "King. The March, the Man, the Dream," *American History*, Aug. 2003.

30. Jimmy Carter in Shibley Telhami, ed., *The Sadat Lectures: Words and Images on Peace, 1997–2008* (Washington, DC: US Institute of Peace, 2010), 25.

31. Timothy Williams, "Names of 2,801 Victims Read Aloud in Somber Ground Zero Ceremony," AP, Sept. 11, 2002.

32. Frank Deford, "Fenway Park Address," recited on Morning Edition, NPR, Oct. 13, 2004.

33. "In Reverence to US Troops Who Died in Iraq and Afghanistan, a Reading of Names at Wall," *Washington Post*, May 24, 2014.

34. "Obama in Tucson: Full Text of Prepared Remarks," *Washington Post*, Jan. 12, 2011.

The Five Copies of the Gettysburg Address

The Nicolay Copy
The Hay Copy
The Everett Copy
The Bancroft Copy
The Bliss Copy

There are five extant copies of Abraham Lincoln's Gettysburg Address. Despite the mysterious provenance of the two early drafts, all now repose safely and deliberately in places of historical and cultural significance: the *Nicolay* and *Hay* copies at the Library of Congress in Washington, D.C., the *Everett* copy at the Abraham Lincoln Presidential Library & Museum in Springfield, IL, the *Bancroft* copy at Cornell University in Ithaca, N.Y., and the *Bliss* copy in the Lincoln Bedroom of the White House in Washington, D.C.

For ten days in November 1950—exactly four score and seven years after the Address was first delivered in Gettysburg—all five copies were exhibited together at the Chicago Historical Society. That was the last time all five copies were together. Otherwise, these days each copy sees semi-regular exhibition—save for the Bliss copy, which, given its inaccessible location in the President's private living quarters in the White House, is the least frequently exhibited among the five.

For the first time in one volume, all copies are faithfully transcribed here from the originals—complete with Lincoln's alterations, hyphenations, exact punctuation, and page breaks (identified here by horizontal lines between the text). The characters appearing in these transcriptions are replicas of Lincoln's original markings, including the small "upside-down v" that he often inserted underneath add-ins and the double hyphens that he preferred for line hyphenations. Second only to the originals themselves, these transcriptions offer a unbridled look at the evolution in Lincoln's thinking and writing process as he, knowingly or otherwise, amended and perfected his greatest speech.

* * *

THE NICOLAY COPY

Four score and seven years ago our fathers brought

forth, upon this continent, a new nation, conceived

in liberty, and dedicated to the proposition that

"all men are created equal"

Now we are engaged in a great civil war, testing

whether that nation, or any nation so conceived,

and so dedicated, can long endure. We are met

on a great battle field of that war. We have

come to dedicate a portion of it, as a final rest=

ing place for those who died here, that the nation

might live. This we may, in all propriety do. But, in a

larger sense, we can not dedicate—we can not

consecrate—we can not hallow, this ground—

The brave men, living and dead, who struggled

here, have hallowed it, far above our poor power

to add or detract. The world will little note, nor long

remember what we say here; while it can never

forget what they <u>did</u> here.

we here be dedica

It is rather for us, the living, ~~to stand here,~~

---

ted to the great task remaining before us—

that, from these honored dead we take in=

creased devotion to that cause for which

they here, gave the last full measure of de=

votion—that we here highly resolve these

dead shall not have died in vain; that

the nation, shall have a new birth of free=

dom, and that government of the people, by

the people, for the people, shall not per=

ish from the earth.

THE HAY COPY

Four score and seven years ago our fathers

brought forth, upon this continent, a new nation, con=

ceived in Liberty, and dedicated to the proposition

that all men are created equal.

Now we are engaged in a great civil war, test=

ing whether that nation, or any nation, so conceived,

and so dedicated, can long endure. We are met
                                have
here on a great battle-field of that war. We ~~are~~
come   a
~~met~~ to dedicate a portion of it as ~~the~~ final rest=
        for
ing place ~~of~~ those who here gave their lives that

that nation might live. It is altogether fitting

and proper that we should do this.

But in a larger sense we can not dedicate—

we can not consecrate—we can not hallow this

ground. The brave men, living and dead, who strug=
                               poor
gled here, have consecrated it far above our˄power

to add or detract. The world will little note,

nor long remember, what we say here, but

can never forget what they did here. It is

for us, the living, rather to be dedicated
work
here to the unfinished which they have,

thus far, so nobly carried on. It is rather

for us to be here dedicated to the great
us—
task remaining before —that from these

honored dead we take increased devotion
that
to the cause for which they here gave gave

the last full measure of devotion—that

we here highly resolve that these dead

shall not have died in vain; that this

nation shall have a new birth of freedom;

and that this government of the people, by

the people, for the people, shall not perish

from the earth.

THE EVERETT COPY

Four score and seven years ago our fathers brou

ght forth upon this continent, a new nation, conceived

in Liberty, and dedicated to the proposition that all

men are created equal.

Now we are engaged in a great civil war, testing

whether that nation, or any nation so conceived, and

so dedicated, can long endure. We are met on a great

battle-field of that war. We have come to dedicate

a portion of that field, as a final resting place for

those who here gave their lives, that that nation

might live. It is altogether fitting and proper that

we should do this.

But, in a larger sense, we can not dedicate—

we can not consecrate—we can not hallow—

this ground. The brave men, living and dead, who

struggled here, have consecrated it, far above our

poor power to add or detract. The world will

little note, nor long remember, what we say here, but

it can never forget what they did here. It is for us,

the living, rather, to be dedicated here to the unfin=

ished work which they who fought here, have, thus

far, so nobly advanced. It is rather for us to be

here dedicated to the great task remaining before

us—that from these honored dead we take increas=

ed devotion to that cause for which they here gave

the last full measure of devotion—that we here

highly resolve that these dead shall not have

died in vain—that this nation, under God,

shall have a new birth of freedom—and that,

government of the people, by the people, for the

people, shall not perish from the earth.

THE BANCROFT COPY

Four score and seven years ago our fathers brought

forth, on this continent, a new nation, conceived in

Liberty, and dedicated to the proposition that all

men are created equal.

Now we are engaged in a great civil war, testing

whether that nation, or any nation so conceived, and

so dedicated , can long endure. We are met on a

great battle-field of that war. We have come to

dedicate a portion of that field, as a final resting-

place for those who here gave their lives, that

that nation might live. It is altogether fitting

and proper that we should do this.

But, in a larger sense, we can not dedicate—

we can not consecrate—we can not hallow—this

ground. The brave men, living and dead, who strug=

gled here, have consecrated it far above our poor

power to add or detract. The world will little

note, nor long remember, what we say here, but

it can never forget what they did here. It is

for us the living, rather, to be dedicated here to the

unfinished work which they who fought here have thus

far so nobly advanced. It is rather for us to be

here dedicated to the great task remaining be=

---

fore us—that from these honored dead we take in=

creased devotion to that cause for which they here gave

the last full measure of devotion—that we here high=

ly resolve that these dead shall not have died in

vain—that this nation, under God, shall have

a new birth of freedom—and that government

of the people, by the people, for the people, shall

not perish from the earth.

THE BLISS COPY

Address delivered at the dedication of the

Cemetery at Gettysburg.

Four score and seven years ago our fathers

brought forth on this continent, a new na=

tion, conceived in Liberty, and dedicated

to the proposition that all men are cre=

ated equal.

Now we are engaged in a great civil war,

testing whether that nation, or any nation

so conceived and so dedicated, can long

endure. We are met on a great battle-field

of that war. We have come to dedicate a

portion of that field, as a final resting

place for those who here gave their lives

that that nation might live. It is alto=

gether fitting and proper that we should

do this.

But, in a larger sense, we can not dedi=

cate—we can not consecrate—we can not

hallow—this ground. The brave men, liv=

ing and dead, who struggled here, have con=

secrated it, far above our poor power to add

or detract. The world will little note, nor

long remember what we say here, but it can

never forget what they did here. It is for us,

the living, rather, to be dedicated here to

the unfinished work which they who fou=

ght here have thus far so nobly advanced.

It is rather for us to be here dedicated to

the great task remaining before us—that

from these honored dead we take increased

devotion to that cause for which they gave

the last full measure of devotion—that

we here highly resolve that these dead shall

not have died in vain—that this nation,

under God, shall have a new birth of free=

dom—and that government of the people,

by the people, for the people, shall not per=

ish from the earth.

Abraham Lincoln.

November 19, 1863.

Contributors

HAROLD HOLZER is Chairman of the Abraham Lincoln Bicentennial Foundation. He is the author, coauthor, or editor of forty-seven books on Lincoln and the Civil War era, including *Lincoln at Cooper Union*, for which he won a second-place Lincoln Prize. In 2008 he was awarded the National Humanities Medal by President Bush. Currently he serves as Senior Vice President for Public Affairs at the Metropolitan Museum of Art, where he has worked for the last twenty-two years following more than two decades in public relations in government, politics, and television. He and his wife, Edith, who live in Rye, New York, have two grown daughters and a grandson.

NICHOLAS P. COLE is a Senior Research Fellow in History at Pembroke College, Oxford. He read Ancient and Modern History at University College, Oxford, where he also completed a master's in Greek and Roman History and his doctorate. He has been a Visiting Fellow of the International Center for Jefferson Studies at Monticello and was a Junior Research Fellow in American History at St Peter's College, Oxford. He writes on the history of American political thought and the history of American political institutions.

ROBERT PIERCE FORBES received a PhD from Yale University and a BA in history from George Washington University. He has taught history at the University of Connecticut, Wesleyan, Rutgers, and Yale; and he served as the associate director of Yale's Gilder Lehrman Center for the Study of Slavery, Resistance, and Abolition. He is the author of *The Missouri Compromise and Its Aftermath: Slavery and the Meaning of America*.

He specializes in the history of the United States from the Revolution to 1850, particularly the impact of slavery on the development of American institutions.

SEAN WILENTZ is the George Henry Davis 1886 Professor of American History at Princeton University. He is the author or editor of numerous books, including *The Rise of American Democracy: Jefferson to Lincoln* (awarded the Bancroft Prize in 2006) and *The Best American History Essays on Lincoln*. He is currently writing a history of the rise of antislavery politics in the United States.

CRAIG L. SYMONDS taught history at the US Naval Academy for thirty years. He is the author or editor of twenty-two books, including *Decision at Sea: Five Naval Battles That Shaped American History*, which won the Theodore and Franklin D. Roosevelt Prize; and *Lincoln and His Admirals: Abraham Lincoln, the U.S. Navy, and the Civil War*, which won the Barondess Prize, the Laney Prize, the Lyman Prize, and the Lincoln Prize for 2009.

DEAN GRODZINS is a Visiting Scholar at the Massachusetts Historical Society and a Research Associate at the Harvard Business School, where he has been studying the history of American democracy. He is author of *American Heretic: Theodore Parker and Transcendentalism* and many book chapters and articles. He has taught American history and literature at Harvard University and at Meadville Lombard Theological School; and for fifteen years, he served as editor of *The Journal of Unitarian Universalist History*. He lives with his wife and daughter in Cambridge, Massachusetts.

MARK S. SCHANTZ is Professor of History at Birmingham-Southern College. He is particularly interested in the social, cultural, and religious history of the nineteenth century. He is the author of *Piety in Providence: Class Dimensions of Religious Experience in Antebellum Rhode Island* and *Awaiting the Heavenly Country: The Civil War and America's Culture of Death*.

CHANDRA MANNING teaches nineteenth-century US history at Georgetown University, where she founded and co-directs the Georgetown Workshop in 19th Century US History. She is the author of *What*

This Cruel War Was Over: Soldiers, Slavery, and the Civil War and is working on a book about contraband camps and changing relations between African Americans and the US government in the Civil War era. She holds a PhD from Harvard University, MPhil from the National University of Ireland Galway, and BA from Mount Holyoke College. Above all, she is a Red Sox fan.

ALLEN C. GUELZO is the Henry R. Luce Professor of the Civil War Era at Gettysburg College and the author of *Gettysburg: The Last Invasion, Fateful Lightning: A New History of the Civil War and Reconstruction, Lincoln and Douglas: The Debates That Defined America,* and *Abraham Lincoln: Redeemer President.* He is a past President of the Abraham Lincoln Institute. He is a three-time winner of the Lincoln Prize, and has been a Fellow of the Charles Warren Center and the W. E. B. Du Bois Center at Harvard University, and the James Madison Program in American Ideals and Institutions at Princeton University.

LOUIS P. MASUR is Distinguished Professor of American Studies and History at Rutgers University. He is the author of numerous books, including *Lincoln's Last Speech: Wartime Reconstruction and the Crisis of Reunion, Lincoln's Hundred Days: The Emancipation Proclamation and the War for the Union,* and *The Civil War: A Concise History.* He serves on the Historians' Council of the Gettysburg Trust.

GEORGE RUTHERGLEN is the John Barbee Minor Distinguished Professor of Law at the University of Virginia School of Law. He joined the law school after clerking for Justices William O. Douglas and John Paul Stevens at the Supreme Court of the United States. He has written widely on civil rights, employment discrimination, and civil litigation. His books include *Civil Rights in the Shadow of Slavery: The Constitution, Common Law, and the Civil Rights Act of 1866* and *Employment Discrimination Law: Visions of Equality in Theory and Doctrine.*

ALISON CLARK EFFORD is an associate professor at Marquette University specializing in the history of immigration to the nineteenth-century United States. She is the author of *German Immigrants, Race, Citizenship, and the Civil War Era* and several articles on German Americans. Currently she is working on a book on suicide and the immigrant experience.

JEAN H. BAKER is the Bennett-Harwood Professor of History at Goucher College, where she teaches courses in Civil War and American women's history. She is the author of eleven books, including biographies of the suffragists and Mary Todd Lincoln. She has also appeared on numerous public television and history programs, including "The Contenders." Her most recent book is *Margaret Sanger: A Life of Passion.*

RAYMOND ARSENAULT is the John Hope Franklin Professor of Southern History and Chairman of the Department of History and Politics at the University of South Florida, St. Petersburg. A graduate of Princeton and Brandeis Universities, he has also taught at the University of Minnesota, Brandeis University, the University of Chicago, the Florida State University Study Abroad Center in London, and the Universite d'Angers in France, where he was a Fulbright Lecturer in 1984–1985. The recipient of numerous civil rights and social justice awards, he served as president of the American Civil Liberties Union of Florida from 1998 to 2000, and he is currently chairman of the Organization of American Historians' Committee on Academic Freedom. He is the author of several prize-winning books, including *Freedom Riders: 1961 and the Struggle for Racial Justice,* and *The Sound of Freedom: Marian Anderson, the Lincoln Memorial, and the Concert That Awakened America.* The 2011 PBS *American Experience* documentary *Freedom Riders,* based on his book, won three Emmys and a George Peabody Award. His most recent book, co-edited with Orville Vernon Burton, is *Dixie Redux: Essays in Honor of Sheldon Hackney.* He is currently writing a biography of the legendary African-American tennis star and public intellectual Arthur Ashe.

DON H. DOYLE teaches at the University of South Carolina, where he is McCausland Professor of History. He has been a Fulbright professor in Rome, Genoa, and Rio de Janeiro and has lived abroad in Leeds, London, and Fiesole. He has written extensively about the American South, nationalism, and separatism in the Atlantic world, and the international dimensions of the American Civil War. Among his several books are *Faulkner's County; Nations Divided: America, Italy, and the Southern Question; Secession as an International Phenomenon* (edited); and *Nationalism in the New World* (edited with Marco Pamplona). His latest book is *The Cause of All Nations: An International History of the American Civil War,* a pathbreaking examination of what America's Civil War meant to the world at large.

THOMAS A. DESJARDIN holds a PhD in US history and has written several books on the Civil War with an emphasis on Gettysburg. During the 1990s, he served as the archivist and historian at Gettysburg National Military Park, during which time he advised actor Jeff Daniels for his role as "Chamberlain" in the film *Gettysburg*. He later taught Civil War history at Bowdoin College and the University of Maine. He and his work have been featured on the History Channel, A&E, Discovery, PBS, and C-SPAN. Today, he serves as senior advisor to Maine Governor Paul LePage.

Index